ASPECTS OF POETRY

Modern Perspectives

MODERN PERSPECTIVES

Aspects of Poetry

MARK LINENTHAL
San Francisco State College

LITTLE, BROWN
AND COMPANY
Boston and Toronto

COPYRIGHT © 1963, BY LITTLE, BROWN AND COMPANY (INC.)

ALL RIGHTS RESERVED. NO PART OF THIS BOOK
MAY BE REPRODUCED IN ANY FORM WITHOUT
PERMISSION IN WRITING FROM THE PUBLISHER.

LIBRARY OF CONGRESS CATALOG CARD NO. 63–14624

FIRST PRINTING

*Published simultaneously in Canada
by Little, Brown & Company (Canada) Limited*

PRINTED IN THE UNITED STATES OF AMERICA

ACKNOWLEDGMENTS

*The author is grateful to the following publishers, agents, and authors
for permission to use the material cited:*

HOWARD BAKER for his poem "Pont Neuf" from *A Letter from the
Country and Other Poems* (New Directions, 1941). Copyright
Howard Baker.

BASIC BOOKS PUBLISHING CO., INC. for "The Relation of the Poet to
Day-Dreaming" from *Collected Papers*, Volume IV, by Sigmund Freud.

BOLLINGEN FOUNDATION for the selection from *The Art of Poetry* by
Paul Valéry. Reprinted by permission of the Bollingen Foundation,
New York, from *The Art of Poetry*, Volume 7 of *The Collected Works
of Paul Valéry*, translated by Denise Folliot, Bollingen Series XLV,
1958.

CURTIS BRADFORD for "Yeats's Byzantium Poems: A Study of Their
Development." This essay is a revision of an essay that appeared in
PMLA, LXXV (March, 1960), pp. 110-125. Copyright © 1960 by
Curtis Bradford and Mrs. W. B. Yeats.

COWARD-MCCANN, INC. for "The Bitter Moon" from *The Proof* by
Yvor Winters, published by Coward-McCann, Inc., © 1930 Coward-
McCann. Reprinted by permission.

FABER AND FABER LTD. for "The Three Voices of Poetry" from *On Poetry and Poets* by T. S. Eliot; and for "Art and the Unconscious" from *Art and Society* by Sir Herbert Read.

FARRAR, STRAUS & CUDAHY, INC. for "The Three Voices of Poetry." Reprinted from *On Poetry and Poets* by T. S. Eliot, by permission of Farrar, Straus & Cudahy, Inc. Copyright © 1957 by T. S. Eliot.

GROVE PRESS, INC. for "Orchard" from *Selected Poems of H. D.*, copyright © 1957 by Norman Holmes Pearson, published by Grove Press, Inc.

HARCOURT, BRACE & WORLD, INC. for "Image, Metaphor, Symbol, Myth" from *Theory of Literature* by René Wellek and Austin Warren, copyright, 1942, 1947, 1949, 1956, by Harcourt, Brace & World, Inc., and reprinted with their permission.

THE HOGARTH PRESS LTD. for the selection from *The Notebooks of Malte Laurids Brigge* by Rainer Maria Rilke (translated by John Linton); and for "The Relation of the Poet to Day-Dreaming" from *Collected Papers*, Volume IV, by Sigmund Freud.

HOLT, RINEHART AND WINSTON, INC. for "Rhythm and Sound," "Meter," and "Song and Sonority" from *The Art of Poetry* by Hugh Kenner; and for the commentary on "They Flee from Me" from *Introduction to Poetry* (1951) by Mark Van Doren.

JOHNS HOPKINS PRESS for "The Reproduction of Reality" from *Reality and the Poet in Spanish Poetry*, Chapter I, pp. 3-6, by Pedro Salinas, 1940.

HORIZON PRESS, INC. for "Art and the Unconscious" from *Art and Society* by Sir Herbert Read. Reprinted by permission of the publisher, Horizon Press, Inc.

HOUGHTON MIFFLIN COMPANY for "Metaphor" from *Poetry and Experience* by Archibald MacLeish. Reprinted by permission of the Publisher.

ALFRED A. KNOPF, INC. for "Two or Three Ideas" reprinted from *Opus Posthumous* by Wallace Stevens, edited by Samuel French Morse, by permission of Alfred A. Knopf, Inc., copyright © 1957 by Elsie Stevens and Holly Stevens; the selection from "The Snow Man" from *The Collected Poems of Wallace Stevens*, copyright, 1923 by Wallace Stevens, renewed 1951; and for "Bells for John Whiteside's Daughter" from *Selected Poems* by John Crowe Ransom, copyright, 1924 by Alfred A. Knopf, Inc., renewed 1952 by John Crowe Ransom.

INDIANA UNIVERSITY PRESS for the selection from *The Burning Fountain* by Philip Wheelwright.

LOUISIANA STATE UNIVERSITY PRESS for the selection from *The Philosophy of Literary* Form by Kenneth Burke.

THE MACMILLAN COMPANY for the prose included in "Poetic Figures and Poetic Meaning" from *Exploring Poetry* by Rosenthal and Smith, copyright 1955 by The Macmillan Company; lines from "A Grave" from *Selected Poems* by Marianne Moore, copyright 1935 by Marianne Moore; and for "The Second Coming" from *Collected Poems* by W. B. Yeats, copyright 1924 by The Macmillan Company, renewed 1952 by Bertha Georgie Yeats. All selections listed in this paragraph are reprinted with the permission of the Publisher, The Macmillan Company, New York.

MACMILLAN AND COMPANY LTD. of London for "Poetry for Poetry's Sake" from *Oxford Lectures on Poetry* by A. C. Bradley.

MACMILLLAN COMPANY OF CANADA for "The Second Coming" and lines from "Byzantium" and "Sailing to Byzantium" from *The Collected Poems of W. B. Yeats.*

NEW DIRECTIONS for "Flowers by the Sea," "To Waken an Old Lady," and "Widow's Lament in Springtime" from *The Collected Earlier Poems of William Carlos Williams,* copyright 1938, 1951 by William Carlos Williams; and for "Concerning the Poet" from *Selected Works of Rainer Maria Rilke,* Volume I, translated by G. Craig Houston, all rights reserved. All selections listed in this paragraph are reprinted by permission of New Directions, Publishers.

OXFORD UNIVERSITY PRESS, INC. for "Author's Preface" from *Poems of Gerard Manley Hopkins,* Third Edition, edited by W. H. Gardner. Copyright 1948 by Oxford University Press, Inc. Reprinted by permission.

OXFORD UNIVERSITY PRESS (London) for "Letter to R. W. Dixon, Oct. 5, 1878" from *The Correspondence of Gerard Manley Hopkins and Richard Watson Dixon,* edited by Claude Abbott.

PARTISAN REVIEW for "The Making of a Poem" by Stephen Spender, from *Partisan Review,* Summer 1946.

G. P. PUTNAM'S SONS for "Literature as Knowledge" from *Reason in Madness* by Allen Tate. © 1935 by Allen Tate. Reprinted by permission of G. P. Putnam's Sons.

RANDOM HOUSE, INC. for "Pure and Impure Poetry" by Robert Penn Warren. Copyright 1953 by Robert Penn Warren. Reprinted from *Selected Essays* by Robert Penn Warren, by permission of Random House, Inc.

CHARLES SCRIBNER'S SONS for "The Subway" from *Poems* by Allen Tate. Reprinted by permission of Charles Scribner's Sons.

ST. MARTIN'S PRESS, INC. for "Poetry for Poetry's Sake" from *Oxford Lectures on Poetry* by A. C. Bradley (Macmillan and Company Ltd., London: 1909).

STEPHEN SPENDER for his essay "The Making of a Poem" (*Partisan Review,* Summer 1946).

ALAN SWALLOW for "The Morality of Poetry," "The Scansion of Free Verse," and "Experimental and Traditional Meters" from *In Defense of*

Reason by Yvor Winters, copyright 1947, 1960, by Yvor Winters; and for "Quod Tegit Omnia" from *Collected Poems*, 1952, by Yvor Winters. Reprinted by permission of Alan Swallow, Publisher.

TULANE DRAMA REVIEW for "On Unrhymed Lyrics and Irregular Rhythms" by Bertolt Brecht. Reprinted by permission of the *Tulane Drama Review* from Vol. II, No. 1, pp. 33-38.

A. P. WATT & SON for "The Second Coming" and lines from "Byzantium" and "Sailing to Byzantium" from *The Collected Poems of W. B. Yeats.*

MRS. W. B. YEATS for "The Second Coming" and lines from "Byzantium" and "Sailing to Byzantium" from *The Collected Poems of W. B. Yeats.*

I should like to express my gratitude to James Schevill who suggested some of the selections which I have included; and to Milton H. Johnson, Donald R. Hammonds, and Ronald Q. Lewton of Little, Brown and Company for their patience and cooperation in the preparation of this volume.

M.L.

CONTENTS

The Sources of Poetry

EXPERIENCE

Rainer Maria Rilke, from *The Notebooks of Malte Laurids Brigge* 3

FANTASY

Sigmund Freud, *The Relation of the Poet to Day-Dreaming* 5

INSPIRATION AND ARCHITECTURE

Herbert Read, *Art and the Unconscious* 16
Paul Valéry, *Poetry and Abstract Thought* 26
Stephen Spender, *The Making of a Poem* 48

A POET AT WORK

Curtis Bradford, *Yeats's Byzantium Poems: A Study of Their Development* 64

The Poem

FORM AND CONTENT

A. C. Bradley, *Poetry for Poetry's Sake* 108

THE LANGUAGE OF POETRY

Philip Wheelwright, *The Logical and the Translogical* . . 127

FIGURES OF SPEECH

M. L. Rosenthal and A. J. M. Smith, *Poetic Figures and
Poetic Meaning* 147
René Wellek and Austin Warren, *Image, Metaphor,
Symbol, Myth* 154

VERSE IN POETRY

Hugh Kenner, from *The Art of Poetry* 188
Mark Van Doren, *They Flee from Me* 196
Yvor Winters, from *In Defense of Reason* 201
Gerard Manley Hopkins, *Letter to R. W. Dixon, October 5,
1878* and *Author's Preface to* Poems, *1876-1889* . . 221
Bertolt Brecht, *On Unrhymed Lyrics in Irregular Rhythms* 228

FORM

T. S. Eliot, *The Three Voices of Poetry* 236
Robert Penn Warren, *Pure and Impure Poetry* 250
Kenneth Burke, from *The Philosophy of Literary Form* . . 274

The Function of Poetry

POETRY AND REALITY

Pedro Salinas, from *Reality and the Poet in Spanish Poetry* 305

POETRY AS KNOWLEDGE

Allen Tate, *Literature as Knowledge* 310
Archibald MacLeish, *Metaphor* 337

POETRY AS MORALITY

Yvor Winters, *The Morality of Poetry* 356

POETRY AS CREATION

Wallace Stevens, *Two or Three Ideas* 369

POETRY AND MAN

Rainer Maria Rilke, *Concerning the Poet* 382

INTRODUCTION

The Act of Poetry

If we lived in a world in which people used their legs only to walk or run, we would not know what to make of someone dancing. We do live in a practical age, an age of prose, of factual information seeking practical results, and people without much experience in the reading of poetry often find themselves bored or irritated by it. The purpose of this book is to help inexperienced readers respond to poems by explaining what sort of thing poetry is.

It seems important to point out at the start that the book aims not so much at critical expertness as at a rich human response. Of course critical judgment is a part of that response and a reflection upon it, but beginning students want to ask themselves too soon whether or not a particular poem is good. Judging means measuring according to a chosen standard of excellence; beginners, unwilling to allow their own standards to develop slowly through extensive acquaintance and discussion, are glad to turn from the poem and all its troubling detail in order to affirm some ready-made standard. But responsibility requires genuine response. To the extent that the reader's response is less than it might be, he cannot responsibly decide whether or not the poem is a good one.

Poetry is presented here as an act which begins at some level deep in the human psyche, which employs certain describable means, and which achieves certain ends. Each phase of the process occupies one of the major parts of the book, the first being largely psychological, the second technical or analytic, the third philosophical. Certainly the way critics discuss poetry affects the way we receive it; their discussion is to poetry what theological explanation is to personal religious experience. A particular psychological approach may arouse expectations of divine madness; a purely technical discussion may alert us to the harmony which warring elements of language can achieve in poetry; a philosophical approach may lead us to demand sound moral judgment, for example, or a special kind of knowledge. Each group of essays, then, offers a perspective, a way of looking at and thinking about poetry. Each group implies a general conception of what poetry is. Upon that conception a whole process of judgment may rest. Although inexperienced readers do well to postpone judgment in the interests of a rich response, it is inevitably a part of that response. While helping the reader to respond, the book attempts, by means of its organization, to suggest some of the ways in which intelligent and sensitive readers of our time have arrived at their critical conclusions.

Which way is the right way to judge? What standards should we employ? The questions ask which is the really important part of the book. For the editor at least, "The Poem" constitutes the core of the book though by no means its whole reason for being. Whatever else it may be, poetry is first of all a kind of verbal discourse and poems are verbal structures; since the second group of essays, "The Poem," provides intimate descriptions of them, it deserves a central place. But in order to understand our interest in poetry we must go beyond detailed descriptions to the human setting in which poetry plays an important part, for apart from that setting it has no importance. To put it another way, we cannot really know what poetry is unless we know what it does since, in a sense, it is what it does. The third group of essays, "The Function of Poetry," explains in several ways what poetry does. Finally, readers should approach poetry with neither ritual awe nor easy self-assurance. It should help them to know what the first group, "The Sources of Poetry," proposes: that although poetry may have its democratic roots in a common human activity, it represents a deliberate cultivation, an uncommon elaboration, of that activity.

How, in view of these prefatory remarks, should the book be used? The editor assumes that it will be read in conjunction with one or more anthologies of poetry. He would like "The Poem" to occupy a dominant position in the reader's mind, the essays there focusing attention in various ways upon various aspects of actual poems. "The Sources of Poetry" could be read first as a kind of preparatory introduction. "The Function of Poetry," then, would provide possible justifications of the whole study, justifications which may illuminate the reader's experience of poetry but which he ought to question in the light of that experience.

Part One

THE SOURCES OF POETRY

Writing poetry, like any human activity, is an act of self-expression. But it is an art too, and any adequate theory of the sources of poetry must somehow combine automatic psychological activity and conscious manipulation. Theorists have often emphasized one or the other. For Plato, the first important critic of poetry in the western world and the founder of the romantic tradition, the poet is the unconscious instrument of a transcendent power working through him; self-awareness and the deliberate manipulation of the products of divine inspiration are, he felt, unfriendly to the poetic spirit. Plato's poet is intellectually and morally suspect, the philosopher's inferior. Modern proponents of the romantic view, D. H. Lawrence for example, or the "beat" poets of our own day, locate divinity in the depths of the unconscious and are resentful of intellectual intrusion. On the other hand, the so-called New Critics, by their emphasis on Metaphysical Poetry and their careful analysis of poetic structures, have seemed to favor the contrary view. Most of the writers represented in "The Sources of Poetry" combine inspiration and harmony, energy and order, but in significantly different ways. And all at least imply a connection between the way in which a poem comes to be and the quality of the result.

Experience

The great German poet, Rainer Maria Rilke, is represented by a suggestive fragment from his fictional autobiograhy, The Notebooks of Malte Laurids Brigge. Writing out of his own experience he excludes both direct expression of emotion and conscious contrivance as the creative source, locating it instead in the rich store of remembered experiences which constitute the poet's very self and from which, in time, poetic language involuntarily arises. The implication seems to be that mere emotion or a mere act of will is too insubstantial, too insignificant a part of the self, to express the self adequately.

RAINER MARIA RILKE

From *The Notebooks of Malte Laurids Brigge*

I think I ought to begin to do some work, now that I am learning to see. I am twenty-eight years old, and almost nothing has happened. Let us recall what I have done. I have written a study on Carpaccio which is bad, a drama entitled "Marriage," which sets out to demonstrate a false thesis by dubious means, and some verses. Ah! but verses amount to so little when one begins to write them young. One ought to wait and gather sense and sweetness a whole life long, and a long life if possible, and then, quite at the end, one might perhaps be able to write ten good lines. For verses are not, as people imagine, simply feelings (we have these soon enough); they are experiences. In order to write a single verse, one must see many cities, and men and

3

things; one must get to know animals and the flight of birds, and
the gestures that the little flowers make when they open out to the
morning. One must be able to return in thought to roads in unknown regions, to unexpected encounters, and to partings that had
been long foreseen; to days of childhood that are still indistinct,
and to parents whom one had to hurt when they sought to give one
some pleasure which one did not understand (it would have been
a pleasure to someone else); to childhood's illnesses that so
strangely begin with such a number of profound and grave trans-
formations, to days spent in rooms withdrawn and quiet, and to
mornings by the sea, to the sea itself, to oceans, to nights of travel
that rushed along loftily and flew with all the stars—and still it is
not enough to be able to think of all this. There must be memories
of many nights of love, each one unlike the others, of the screams
of women in labor, and of women in childbed, light and blanched
and sleeping, shutting themselves in. But one must also have been
beside the dying, must have sat beside the dead in a room with
open windows and with fitful noises. And still it is not yet enough
to have memories. One must be able to forget them when they are
many and one must have the immense patience to wait until they
come again. For it is the memories themselves that matter. Only
when they have turned to blood within us, to glance and gesture,
nameless and no longer to be distinguished from ourselves—only
then can it happen that in a most rare hour the first word of a
poem arises in their midst and goes forth from them.

But all my verses had a different origin; so they are not verses.

Translated by JOHN LINTON

Fantasy

Sigmund Freud, *the explorer of the self, appears in an early essay which relates imaginative writing to daydreaming and daydreaming to the play of children. Underlying Freud's discussion is a fundamental distinction, one worth considering, between "reality" and desire. In this essay Freud sees the writer as a man unhappy in the real world who turns for satisfaction to a realm of fantasy. An obvious deduction is that imaginative writing is nothing but the self-indulgence of the psychologically ill. But as Lionel Trilling has argued (in* The Liberal Imagination, *pp. 176-180), borrowing the phrase from Freud himself, "we are all ill," and it is the artist's genius which allows him to make something valuable of his neurosis.*

Freud distinuishes between a release of tension in our minds, the release which provides our primary literary pleasure, and the merely superficial or "formal" pleasures of literature. In separating the source of literary energy from that of literary form, he leaves unexplained, as Herbert Read points out in the next section, the central mystery, the artistic sensibility which converts private fantasies to public use.

SIGMUND FREUD

The Relation of the Poet to Day-Dreaming

We laymen have always wondered greatly—like the cardinal who put the question to Ariosto—how that strange being, the poet, comes by his material. What makes him able to carry us with him in such a way and to arouse emotions in us of which we thought ourselves perhaps not

even capable? Our interest in the problem is only stimulated by the
circumstance that if we ask poets themselves they give us no explanation of the matter, or at least no satisfactory explanation. The
knowledge that not even the clearest insight into the factors con-
ditioning the choice of imaginative material, or into the nature of
the ability to fashion that material, will ever make writers of us
does not in any way detract from our interest.

If we could only find some activity in ourselves, or in people like
ourselves, which was in any way akin to the writing of imaginative
works! If we could do so, then examination of it would give us a
hope of obtaining some insight into the creative powers of imaginative writers. And indeed, there is some prospect of achieving this—
writers themselves always try to lessen the distance between their
kind and ordinary human beings; they so often assure us that every
man is at heart a poet, and that the last poet will not die until the
last human being does.

We ought surely to look in the child for the first traces of
imaginative activity. The child's best loved and most absorbing
occupation is play. Perhaps we may say that every child at play
behaves like an imaginative writer, in that he creates a world of his
own or, more truly, he rearranges the things of his world and orders
it in a new way that pleases him better. It would be incorrect to
think that he does not take this world seriously; on the contrary, he
takes his play very seriously and expends a great deal of emotion
on it. The opposite of play is not serious occupation but—reality.
Notwithstanding the large affective cathexis of his play-world, the
child distinguishes it perfectly from reality; only he likes to borrow the objects and circumstances that he imagines from the tangible and visible things of the real world. It is only this linking of it
to reality that still distinguishes a child's "play" from "day-dreaming."

Now the writer does the same as the child at play; he creates a
world of phantasy which he takes very seriously; that is, he invests
it with a great deal of affect, while separating it sharply from
reality. Language has preserved this relationship between children's play and poetic creation. It designates certain kinds of imaginative creation, concerned with tangible objects and capable of
representation, as "plays"; the people who present them are called
"players." The unreality of this poetical world of imagination, how-

ever, has very important consequences for literary technique; for many things which if they happened in real life could produce no pleasure can nevertheless give enjoyment in a play—many emotions which are essentially painful may become a source of enjoyment to the spectators and hearers of a poet's work.

There is another consideration relating to the contrast between reality and play on which we will dwell for a moment. Long after a child has grown up and stopped playing, after he has for decades attempted to grasp the realities of life with all seriousness, he may one day come to a state of mind in which the contrast between play and reality is again abrogated. The adult can remember with what intense seriousness he carried on his childish play; then by comparing his would-be serious occupations with his childhood's play, he manages to throw off the heavy burden of life and obtain the great pleasure of humor.

As they grow up, people cease to play, and appear to give up the pleasure they derived from play. But anyone who knows anything of the mental life of human beings is aware that hardly anything is more difficult to them than to give up a pleasure they have once tasted. Really we never can relinquish anything; we only exchange one thing for something else. When we appear to give something up, all we really do is to adopt a substitute. So when the human being grows up and ceases to play he only gives up the connection with real objects; instead of playing he then begins to create phantasy. He builds castles in the air and creates what are called daydreams. I believe that the greater number of human beings create phantasies at times as long as they live. This is a fact which has been overlooked for a long time, and its importance has therefore not been properly appreciated.

The phantasies of human beings are less easy to observe than the play of children. Children do, it is true, play alone, or form with other children a closed world in their minds for the purposes of play; but a child does not conceal his play from adults, even though his playing is quite unconcerned with them. The adult, on the other hand, is ashamed of his day-dreams and conceals them from other people; he cherishes them as his most intimate possessions and as a rule he would rather confess all his misdeeds than tell his day-dreams. For this reason he may believe that he is the only person who makes up such phantasies, without having any idea that everybody else tells themselves stories of the same kind. Day-dreaming is a continuation of play, nevertheless, and the motives which lie behind these two activities contain a very good reason for this different behavior in the child at play and in the day-dreaming adult.

The play of children is determined by their wishes—really by the child's *one* wish, which is to be grown-up, the wish that helps to "bring him up." He always plays at being grown-up; in play he imitates what is known to him of the lives of adults. Now he has no reason to conceal this wish. With the adult it is otherwise; on the one hand, he knows that he is expected not to play any longer or to day-dream, but to be making his way in a real world. On the other hand, some of the wishes from which his phantasies spring are such as have to be entirely hidden; therefore he is ashamed of his phantasies as being childish and as something prohibited.

If they are concealed with so much secretiveness, you will ask, how do we know so much about the human propensity to create phantasies? Now there is a certain class of human beings upon whom not a god, indeed, but a stern goddess—Necessity—has laid the task of giving an account of what they suffer and what they enjoy. These people are the neurotics; among other things they have to confess their phantasies to the physician to whom they go in the hope of recovering through mental treatment. This is our best source of knowledge, and we have later found good reason to suppose that our patients tell us about themselves nothing that we could not also hear from healthy people.

Let us try to learn some of the characteristics of day-dreaming. We can begin by saying that happy people never make phantasies, only unsatisfied ones. Unsatisfied wishes are the driving power behind phantasies; every separate phantasy contains the fulfilment of a wish, and improves on unsatisfactory reality. The impelling wishes vary according to the sex, character and circumstances of the creator; they may be easily divided, however, into two principal groups. Either they are ambitious wishes, serving to exalt the person creating them, or they are erotic. In young women erotic wishes dominate the phantasies almost exclusively, for their ambition is generally comprised in their erotic longings; in young men egoistic and ambitious wishes assert themselves plainly enough alongside their erotic desires. But we will not lay stress on the distinction between these two trends; we prefer to emphasize the fact that they are often united. In many altar-pieces the portrait of the donor is to be found in one corner of the picture; and in the greater number of ambitious day-dreams, too, we can discover a woman in some corner, for whom the dreamer performs all his heroic deeds and at whose feet all his triumphs are to be laid. Here you see we have strong enough motives for concealment; a well-brought-up woman is, indeed, credited with only a mimimum of erotic desire, while a young man has to learn to suppress the overweening self-regard he acquires in the indulgent atmosphere surrounding his childhood, so that he may find his proper place in a society that is full of other persons making similar claims.

We must not imagine that the various products of this impulse towards phantasy, castles in the air or day-dreams, are stereotyped or unchangeable. On the contrary, they fit themselves into the changing impressions of life, alter with the vicissitudes of life; every deep new impression gives them what might be called a "date-stamp." The relation of phantasies to time is altogether of great importance. One may say that a phantasy at one and the same moment hovers between three periods of time—the three periods of our ideation. The activity of phantasy in the mind is linked up with some current impression, occasioned by some event in the present, which had the power to rouse an intense desire. From there it wanders back to the memory of an early experience, generally belonging to infancy, in which this wish was fulfilled. Then it creates for itself a situation which is to emerge in the future, representing the fulfilment of the wish—this is the day-dream or phantasy, which now carries in it traces both of the occasion which engendered it and of some past memory. So past, present and future are threaded, as it were, on the string of the wish that runs through them all.

A very ordinary example may serve to make my statement clearer. Take the case of a poor orphan lad, to whom you have given the address of some employer where he may perhaps get work. On the way there he falls into a day-dream suitable to the situation from which it springs. The content of the phantasy will be somewhat as follows: He is taken on and pleases his new employer, makes himself indispensable in the business, is taken into the family of the employer, and marries the charming daughter of

the house. Then he comes to conduct the business, first as a partner, and then as successor to his father-in-law. In this way the
dreamer regains what he had in his happy childhood, the protecting house, his loving parents and the first objects of his affection.
You will see from such an example how the wish employs some
event in the present to plan a future on the pattern of the past.

Much more could be said about phantasies, but I will only allude
as briefly as possible to certain points. If phantasies become over-
luxuriant and over-powerful, the necessary conditions for an out-
break of neurosis or psychosis are constituted; phantasies are also
the first preliminary stage in the mind of the symptoms of illness
of which our patients complain. A broad by-path here branches off
into pathology.

I cannot pass over the relation of phantasies to dreams. Our nocturnal dreams are nothing but such phantasies, as we can make
clear by interpreting them.[1] Language, in its unrivalled wisdom,
long ago decided the question of the essential nature of dreams by
giving the name of "day-dreams" to the airy creations of phantasy.
If the meaning of our dreams usually remains obscure in spite of
this clue, it is because of the circumstance that at night wishes of
which we are ashamed also become active in us, wishes which we
have to hide from ourselves, which were consequently repressed
and pushed back into the unconscious. Such repressed wishes and
their derivatives can therefore achieve expression only when almost
completely disguised. When scientific work had succeeded in elu-
cidating the distortion in dreams, it was no longer difficult to recognize that nocturnal dreams are fulfilments of desires in exactly the
same way as day-dreams are—those phantasies with which we are
all so familiar.

So much for day-dreaming; now for the poet! Shall we dare
really to compare an imaginative writer with "one who dreams in
broad daylight," and his creations with day-dreams? Here, surely,
a first distinction is forced upon us; we must distinguish between
poets who, like the bygone creators of epics and tragedies, take over
their material ready-made, and those who seem to create their
material spontaneously. Let us keep to the latter, and let us also
not choose for our comparison those writers who are most highly
esteemed by critics. We will choose the less pretentious writers of

[1] Cf. Freud, *Die Traumdeutung*.

romances, novels and stories, who are read all the same by the widest circles of men and women. There is one very marked characteristic in the productions of these writers which must strike us all: they all have a hero who is the centre of interest, for whom the author tries to win our sympathy by every possible means, and whom he places under the protection of a special providence. If at the end of one chapter the hero is left unconscious and bleeding from severe wounds, I am sure to find him at the beginning of the next being carefully tended and on the way to recovery; if the first volume ends in the hero being shipwrecked in a storm at sea, I am certain to hear at the beginning of the next of his hairbreadth escape—otherwise, indeed, the story could not continue. The feeling of security with which I follow the hero through his dangerous adventures is the same as that with which a real hero throws himself into the water to save a drowning man, or exposes himself to the fire of the enemy while storming a battery. It is this very feeling of being a hero which one of our best authors has well expressed in the famous phrase, *"Es kann dir nix g'schehen!"*[2] It seems to me, however, that this significant mark of invulnerability very clearly betrays—His Majesty the Ego, the hero of all day-dreams and all novels.

The same relationship is hinted at in yet other characteristics of these egocentric stories. When all the women in a novel invariably fall in love with the hero, this can hardly be looked upon as a description of reality, but it is easily understood as an essential constituent of a day-dream. The same thing holds good when the other people in the story are sharply divided into good and bad, with complete disregard of the manifold variety in the traits of real human beings; the "good" ones are those who help the ego in its character of hero, while the "bad" are his enemies and rivals.

We do not in any way fail to recognize that many imaginative productions have travelled far from the original naïve day-dream, but I cannot suppress the surmise that even the most extreme variations could be brought into relationship with this model by an uninterrupted series of transitions. It has struck me in many so-called psychological novels, too, that only one person—once again the hero—is described from within; the author dwells in his soul

[2] Anzengruber. [The phrase means "Nothing can happen to me!"—Trans.]

and looks upon the other people from outside. The psychological novel in general probably owes its peculiarities to the tendency of modern writers to split up their ego by self-observation into many component-egos, and in this way to personify the conflicting trends in their own mental life in many heroes. There are certain novels, which might be called "excentric," that seem to stand in marked contradiction to the typical day-dream; in these the person introduced as the hero plays the least active part of anyone, and seems instead to let the actions and sufferings of other people pass him by like a spectator. Many of the later novels of Zola belong to this class. But I must say that the psychological analysis of people who are not writers, and who deviate in many things from the so-called norm, has shown us analogous variations in their day-dreams in which the ego contents itself with the rôle of spectator.

If our comparison of the imaginative writer with the day-dreamer, and of poetic production with the day-dream, is to be of any value, it must show itself fruitful in some way or other. Let us try, for instance, to examine the works of writers in reference to the idea propounded above, the relation of the phantasy to the wish that runs through it and to the three periods of time; and with its help let us study the connection between the life of the writer and his productions. Hitherto it has not been known what preliminary ideas would constitute an approach to this problem; very often this relation has been regarded as much simpler than it is; but the insight gained from phantasies leads us to expect the following state of things. Some actual experience which made a strong impression on the writer had stirred up a memory of an earlier experience, generally belonging to childhood, which then arouses a wish that finds a fulfilment in the work in question, and in which elements of the recent event and the old memory should be discernible.

Do not be alarmed at the complexity of this formula; I myself expect that in reality it will prove itself to be too schematic, but that possibly it may contain a first means of approach to the true state of affairs. From some attempts I have made I think that this way of approaching works of the imagination might not be unfruitful. You will not forget that the stress laid on the writer's memories of his childhood, which perhaps seems so strange, is ultimately derived from the hypothesis that imaginative creation, like day-dreaming, is a continuation of and substitute for the play of childhood.

We will not neglect to refer also to that class of imaginative work which must be recognized not as spontaneous production, but as a re-fashioning of ready-made material. Here, too, the writer retains a certain amount of independence, which can express itself in the choice of material and in changes in the material chosen, which are often considerable. As far as it goes, this material is derived from the racial treasure-house of myths, legends and fairy-tales. The study of these creations of racial psychology is in no way complete, but it seems extremely probable that myths, for example, are distorted vestiges of the wish-phantasies of whole nations—the age-long dreams of young humanity.

You will say that, although writers came first in the title of this paper, I have told you far less about them than about phantasy. I am aware of that, and will try to excuse myself by pointing to the present state of our knowledge. I could only throw out suggestions and bring up interesting points which arise from the study of phantasies, and which pass beyond them to the problem of the choice of literary material. We have not touched on the other problem at all, *i.e.* what are the means which writers use to achieve those emotional reactions in us that are aroused by their productions. But I would at least point out to you the path which leads from our discussion of day-dreams to the problems of the effect produced on us by imaginative works.

You will remember that we said the day-dreamer hid his phantasies carefully from other people because he had reason to be ashamed of them. I may now add that even if he were to communicate them to us, he would give us no pleasure by his disclosures. When we hear such phantasies they repel us, or at least leave us cold. But when a man of literary talent presents his plays, or relates what we take to be his personal day-dreams, we experience great pleasure arising probably from many sources. How the writer accomplishes this is his innermost secret; the essential *ars poetica* lies in the technique by which our feeling of repulsion is overcome, and this has certainly to do with those barriers erected between every individual being and all others. We can guess at two methods used in this technique. The writer softens the egotistical character of the day-dream by changes and disguises, and he bribes us by the offer of a purely formal, that is, aesthetic, pleasure in the presentation of his phantasies. The increment of pleasure which is offered us in order to release yet greater pleasure arising from deeper sources in the mind is called an "incitement premium" or technically, "fore-pleasure." I am of opinion that all the aesthetic pleasure we gain from the works of imaginative writers is of the same type as this "fore-pleasure," and that the true enjoyment of literature proceeds from the release of tensions in our minds. Perhaps much that brings about this result consists in the writer's putting us into a position in which we can enjoy our own day-dreams without reproach or shame. Here we reach a path leading into novel, interesting and complicated researches, but we also, at least for the present, arrive at the end of the present discussion.

Inspiration and Architecture

Herbert Read draws upon Freud's theory of id, ego, and super-ego. He argues that the finished work of art has "correspondences" with each of these regions of the psyche and suggests that artistic inspiration may occur when the normal relations among them are upset. Although he grants a certain role to the ego, Read stands with Freud in the romantic tradition. For him the poet's most important function is the materialization of the "instinctual life of the deepest levels of the mind"; "clarity," "proportion," "harmony"—these are "superficial charms."

With the essay by Paul Valéry, the emphasis shifts from poetry as expressive communication to poetry as an end in itself, as art. The selection presents brilliant insights into the nature and function of poetic discourse; it appears here among discussions of the creative process because of Valéry's overwhelming interest in the process. But unlike the preceding writers, Valéry assigns importance equally to inspiration and to conscious calculation. For him the poem is, frankly, a machine for producing inspiration in the reader. When it succeeds, in our exalted state we are ready to believe that the poet worked in a state of sustained inspiration. But we are wrong. The poet, says Valéry, does have inspired moments, but he cannot control their comings and goings. Besides, they leave only raw materials which require his patient reflection and co-ordination before they become powerful and harmonious wholes.

Valéry offers eloquent testimony to poetry's transporting power; although he insists upon the laboriousness of creation, he treats it in a rather summary way. Stephen Spender's "The Making of a Poem" covers much of Valéry's ground, but in more intimate terms. He thinks of writing as a vocation which requires the adaptation of the poet's personality to its demands, and he explains how he makes that adaptation himself. For Spender the vocation is a lofty one; the candor with which he describes his difficulty is remarkable.

HERBERT READ

Art and the Unconscious

There is little doubt
that, in some sense or other, the artist is always to be regarded as
psychotic. He may not be manifestly psychotic: he may rather be
a psychotic type who has found some way of disguising, or compen-
sating for, his psychosis. This was, in effect, the point of view first
adopted by Freud, and the passage in which he defined the nature
of the artist may be taken as a starting-point for our discussion.
Freud has been describing the symptoms of neuroses in general—
the kind of phantasy-life which the neurotic or psychotic individual is compelled to live by the exigencies of his repressed instincts.
At the conclusion of this particular lecture he refers to the artist in
these words:

> Before you leave to-day I should like to direct your attention for a
> moment to a side of phantasy-life of very general interest. There is,
> in fact, a path from phantasy back again to reality, and that is—art.
> The artist has also an introverted disposition and has not far to go
> to become neurotic. He is one who is urged on by instinctive needs
> which are too clamorous; he longs to attain to honor, power, riches,
> fame, and the love of women; but he lacks the means of achieving
> these gratifications. So, like any other with an unsatisfied longing, he
> turns away from reality and transfers all his interest, and all his
> libido too, onto the creation of his wishes in the life of phantasy,
> from which the way might readily lead to neurosis. There must be
> many factors in combination to prevent this becoming the whole
> outcome of his development; it is well known how often artists in
> particular suffer from partial inhibition of their capacities through
> neurosis. Probably their constitution is endowed with a powerful
> capacity for sublimation and with a certain flexibility in the repres-
> sions determining the conflict. But the way back to reality is found by
> the artist thus: He is not the only one who has a life of phantasy;
> the intermediate world of phantasy is sanctioned by general human
> consent, and every hungry soul looks to it for comfort and consola-
> tion. But to those who are not artists the gratification that can be
> drawn from the springs of phantasy is very limited; their inexorable
> repressions prevent the enjoyment of all but the meager daydreams

which can become conscious. A true artist has more at his disposal. First of all he understands how to elaborate his daydreams, so that they lose that personal note which grates upon strange ears and become enjoyable to others; he knows too how to modify them sufficiently so that their origin in prohibited sources is not easily detected. Further, he possesses the mysterious ability to mold his particular material until it expresses the ideas of his phantasy faithfully; and then he knows how to attach to this reflection of his phantasy-life so strong a stream of pleasure that, for a time at least, the repressions are outbalanced and dispelled by it. When he can do all this, he opens out to others the way back to the comfort and consolation of their own unconscious sources of pleasure, and so reaps their gratitude and admiration; then he has won—through his phantasy—what before he could only win in phantasy: honor, power, and the love of women.[1]

This is a very condensed theory of the psychological nature of the esthetic activity, and must be examined with some care. Freud first makes a general statement—that art is a way back from phantasy to reality. By reality it would seem that Freud here means normality, for reality is a relative term without any definite scientific or philosophical basis. By reality we can only mean the objective world as reflected in the sensations of an individual in a normal or average state of physical and mental vitality. Such an individual, it is assumed, has instinctive needs for honor, power, riches, fame, and the love of women; and normally he can satisfy those needs by virtue of his physical strength or his personal charm. The neurotic, however, lacks these means to accomplish such an end, and therefore tries to find compensation for his weakness and satisfaction for such longings in a life of phantasy. That way lie self-delusion, hallucination, madness—the state of neurosis or psychosis. But certain individuals, Freud suggests, have the power to evade the consequences of such a life of phantasy; they have this unusual capacity for sublimation; they can turn their phantasies to some objective use. The phantasies of the average neurotic or psychotic remain bottled up—a repression of forces which ends eventually in the explosion of madness. But the psychotic who is also an artist can so project his phantasies that they become external to his mind. He elaborates them into a form which not only disguises their

[1] *Introductory Lectures on Psychoanalysis*. Trans. by Joan Rivière (London, 1922), pp. 314-5.

purely personal origin, but more precisely their origin in forbidden
and repressed desires or instincts. The artist, that is to say, possesses
the power of universalizing his mental life. But further, and this
step is the most essential one in the process, he has the ability, which
Freud calls mysterious, of so molding that form in the process of
making it material and objective, that the resulting work of art
gives a positive pleasure which has apparently nothing to do with
the origins of the work of art in the unconscious of the artist, but
which seems to be communicated by the physical proportions, the
texture, the tone, the harmony and all the other specific qualities
in a work of art which we call esthetic. And by the fact that he can
in this manner give pleasure to a great number of people, the artist
finally acquires what his psychosis would otherwise have prevented
him acquiring, namely, honor, power, riches, fame, and the love of
women.

Modifications of Freud's Theory

That was the point reached by Freud in 1917, and since then
he has not greatly modified his theory of the nature of the artist.
In some of his earlier papers there are, however, one or two observations which throw further light on the subject. In common with
other psychoanalysts, Freud is mainly concerned with the *themes*
of art; and a good theme is of more interest to him than a good
work of art. Hence the apparent waste of time on a work like Jen-
sen's *Gradiva*. But Freud is too honest to ignore certain difficulties
that arise in fitting the facts to his theory. In a paper on "Literary
Creation and the Daydream,"[2] first published in 1908, he observes
that there is a distinction to be made between writers like the great
epic and tragic poets who receive their themes ready-made, and
writers who elaborate their personal phantasies. He is disposed to
recognize the existence of *collective* dreams or phantasies, embodied in the folklore of a nation, to which the poet has access
and to which he merely gives a more adequate and pleasing form.[3]

[2] This is Freud's "The Relation of the Poet to Day-Dreaming," reproduced
above. (Ed.)
[3] Cf. also *Group Psychology and the Analysis of the Ego*. Trans. by
James Strachey (London, 1922), pp. 114-5. "The myth, then, is the step by
which the individual emerges from group psychology. The first myth was
certainly the psychological, the hero myth; the explanatory nature-myth

But by what means the poet or the artist gives this formal pleasure
—there, at that time, Freud declared himself defeated. For him
it is a mystery. The pleasure given by a work of art is probably
very complex in its workings, but of one thing Freud is certain: the
technique of the poet or the artist is in some way a means of
breaking down the barriers between individual egos, uniting them
all in some collective ego such as we found typical of the undifferentiated life of primitive people—a life in which the world of
phantasy had not yet become an unreal world. Freud concludes by
suggesting that the purely formal or esthetic elements in a work of
art constitute a sort of pleasure-premium or preliminary seduction
which, once it operates on our sensibilities, permits the liberation
of a secondary and superior kind of enjoyment springing from
much deeper pyschic levels. "I believe," he says, "that the esthetic
pleasure produced in us by the creative artist has a preliminary
character, and that the real enjoyment of a work of art is due to
the ease it gives to certain psychic tensions."

Freud himself has frequently admitted that his observations on
this subject have by no means explained all the difficulties. The
actual nature of the preliminary pleasure evoked by a work of art
—is that merely a motor response of our nerves and cortex to certain physical proportions and qualities in an object? Or is it a
more complete and sympathetic projection of feeling into the whole
shape or form of the object? Or is the shape or form itself related
to instinctive factors in the deeper layers of the mind, and not
merely to the motor sensations of the nervous system? All these
questions will have to be resolved by psychological research before we can feel sure that the nature of the esthetic experience has
been accounted for.

---

must have followed much later. The poet who had taken this step and had
in this way set himself free from the group in his imagination, is nevertheless able (as Rank has further observed) to find his way back to it in reality.
For he goes and relates to the group his hero's deeds which he has invented.
At bottom his hero is no one but himself. Thus he lowers himself to the
level of reality, and raises his hearers to the level of imagination. But his
hearers understand the poet, and, in virtue of their having the same relation
of longing towards the primal father, they can identify themselves with the
hero." In this way Freud explains the origin of the myth, but he does not
give us any clue to the manner in which the poet "raises his hearers to the
level of imagination."

Introducing the Id

More recently Freud has elaborated his anatomy of the mental
personality, and though he does not, in this part of his work, make
any direct references to the esthetic problem, some of his observations are suggestive. As formulated in his *New Introductory Lectures,* we have now to regard the individual as being divided into
three levels or degrees of consciousness, called the ego, the super-
ego, and the id. These divisions can only be schematically represented as definite; actually they shade off into one another. The
super-ego in particular is not to be imagined as something separated from the id by the ego; some of its characteristics are derived
directly from the id. The id is "the obscure inaccessible part of
our personality; the little we know about it we have learnt from
the study of dream-work and the formation of neurotic symptoms,
and most of that is of a negative character, and can only be described as all that the ego is not. We can come nearer to the id
with images, and call it a chaos, a cauldron of seething excitement.
We suppose that it is somewhere in direct contact with somatic
[*i.e.,* physical or bodily] processes, and takes over from them instinctual needs and gives them mental expression, but we cannot
say in what substratum this contact is made. These instincts fill it
with energy, but it has no organization and no unified will, only
an impulse to obtain satisfaction for the instinctual needs, in accordance with the pleasure-principle. The laws of logic—above all,
the law of contradiction—do not hold for processes in the id. . . .
There is nothing in the id which can be compared to negation, and
we are astonished to find in it an exception to the philosopher's
assertion that space and time are necessary forms of our mental
acts. In the id there is nothing corresponding to the idea of time,
no recognition of the passage of time, and (a thing which is very
remarkable and awaits adequate attention in philosophic thought)
no alteration of mental processes by the passage of time. . . . It
is constantly being borne in on me that we have made far too little
use for our theory of the indubitable fact that the repressed remains unaltered by the passage of time. This seems to offer us
the possibility of an approach to some really profound truths. . . .
Naturally the id knows no values, no good and evil, no morality.
The economic, or, if you prefer, the quantitative factor, which is

so closely bound up with the pleasure-principle, dominates all its processes. . . ."[4]

As for the ego, Freud says that we can hardly go wrong if we regard it as "that part of the id which has been modified by its proximity to the external world and the influence that the latter has had on it, and which serves for the purpose of receiving stimuli and protecting the organism from them, like the cortical layer with which a particle of living substance surrounds itself. . . . On behalf of the id, the ego . . . interpolates between desire and action the procrastinating factor of thought, during which it makes use of the residues of experience stored up in the memory. In this way it dethrones the pleasure-principle, which exerts undisputed sway over the processes of the id, and substitutes for it the reality principle, which promises greater security and greater success.

". . . What, however, especially marks the ego out in contradistinction to the id, is a tendency to synthetize its contents, to bring together and unify its mental processes, which is entirely absent from the id. . . . It is this alone that produces that high degree of organization which the ego needs for its highest achievements."[5]

The Super-Ego

The super-ego is perhaps more simply described. To this part of the individual's mental life Freud assigns the activities of self-observation, conscience and the holding-up of ideals. It is "the representative of all moral restrictions, the advocate of the impulse towards perfection, in short, it is as much as we have been able to apprehend psychologically of what people call the 'higher' things in human life."

The concept of the super-ego is surely not difficult to understand; most of us have a clear idea of what we mean by "conscience," and Freud's concept is merely that of a wider conscience: the complete function of self-observation and conscious self-discipline and self-direction, but this function becomes so habitual as to be largely unconscious in its operation. In its origin it is based on what Freud calls two momentous facts, one biological—the

---

[4] *New Introductory Lectures on Psychoanalysis.* Trans. by W. J. H. Sprott (London, 1933), pp. 98-100.
[5] *Ibid.*, p. 100.

lengthy dependence of the human child on its parents; and one psychological—the Oedipus complex. Criticizing Kant's famous declaration, that nothing proved to him the greatness of God more convincingly than the starry heavens above us and the moral conscience within us, Freud remarks that "conscience is no doubt something within us, but it has not been there since the beginning. In this sense it is the opposite of sexuality, which is certainly present from the beginning of life, and is not a thing that only comes in later. But small children are notoriously amoral. They have no internal inhibitions against their pleasure-seeking impulses. The rôle, which the super-ego undertakes later in life, is at first played by an external power, by parental authority. The influence of the parents predominates the child by granting proofs of affection and by threats of punishment, which, to the child, mean loss of love, and which must also be feared on their own account. This objective anxiety is the forerunner of the later moral anxiety; so long as the former is dominant one need not speak of super-ego or of conscience. It is only later that the secondary situation arises, which we are far too ready to regard as the normal state of affairs; the external restrictions are intrajected, so that the super-ego takes the place of the parental function, and thenceforward observes, guides, and threatens the ego in just the same way as the parents acted to the child before."

This exposition of Freud's anatomy of the mental personality has necessarily been condensed, but so far as possible I have deliberately kept to Freud's own words. We have now, perhaps, a sufficiently clear picture of the scheme to see its application to the problems we are concerned with. For obviously the work of art has correspondences with each region of the mind. *It derives its energy, its irrationality and its mysterious power from the id, which is to be regarded as the source of what we usually call inspiration. It is given formal synthesis and unity by the ego; and finally it may be assimilated to those ideologies or spiritual aspirations which are the peculiar creation of the super-ego.*

The light which this hypothesis of Freud's throws upon the whole history and development of art, in the race and in the individual, is so revealing that for me personally it constitutes the strongest evidence for the general validity of the theory of psychoanalysis. It has always been an obvious and experienced fact to any man of sensibility that all art was one: that whether in the presence of a prehistoric cave-drawing, a Negro fetish, a Byzantine mosaic, a Gothic cathedral or a Renaissance portrait, he was, in the fundamental elements which give the work of art its esthetic validity, in the presence of identical phenomena. Yet how reconcile the outward diversity of such objects in any general theory of art? Psychoanalysis has shown the way, if only tentatively. We know now that any particular work of art may have its origins in the relatively impersonal and unchanging experiences which are the content of the id; we know that at the other end of the process of elaboration and sublimation these elementary intuitions which the work of art represents are clothed in the ideologies of the super-ego, which in their turn also "perpetuate the past traditions of the race and the people, and which yield but slowly to the influence of the present and to new developments." The ego intermediates between the primal force and the ultimate ideal; it gives form and physical harmony to what issues forceful but amorphous and perhaps terrifying from the id; and then, in the super-ego, it gives to these forms and harmonies the ideological tendencies and aspirations of religion, morality, and social idealism.

Limitations of Freud's Theory

Freud's theory helps us to understand the nature of the impulse that makes a particular individual become an artist; it guides us to the region from which the impulses come that are the origin of a particular work of art; it shows us why this impulse must be elaborated and disguised and given a synthetic unity quite foreign to its original nature;[6] and finally it explains why the artist is required

---

[6] ART AND SEX.—The puritan has always suspected a relationship between art and sex; and in puritanical periods the artist, in aggressive reaction to this attitude, has often given a deliberate sexual appeal to his works. But such art is usually second-rate, and pornography in general is but an inverse moralism, and not directly related to the original libidinal forces of the id.

We must distinguish between the latent and the manifest sexual factors in art. The latent content, as in dreams, is invariably present; and psychoanalysis by its usual methods can often reveal it. But just as in the process of relating or remembering a dream we tend to disguise its sexual nature from ourselves, so in the genuine process of artistic creation the sexual content of the original inspiration becomes disguised. There is very little overt sexual art. Pornography has always existed in civilized countries, but if we consider the great historical phases of art, above all the Egyptian, the Chinese, the Persian, the Byzantine, and the Gothic, we look in vain for

to accommodate his creations to the ideologies which constitute the
religious, moral and social conscience of the race. It still leaves
unexplained the particular kind of sensibility which enables the
artist to convert his phantasies into a material form, which form
incites us to participate in his mode of creation.

Freud is content to leave that process as an unexplained mystery.
But at the end of his chapter on the anatomy of the mental personality, he makes a casual suggestion which perhaps indicates the
lines on which a solution of this problem will be found. He has
been warning us of the provisional nature of the spheres into which
he has divided the human mind, and of the possibility that their
function may vary from person to person, particularly as a result

---

any considerable amount of undisguised sexuality embodied in important
works of art. India is perhaps the only country to which such a generalization does not apply. Even among primitive races, the natural tendency is to
disguise the sexual origin of art. Compare, for example, the evidence given
by Dr. Seligmann: "Although art, and especially decorative art, plays a
much larger part in the life of the majority of Papuo-Melanesians than it
does among ourselves, certain motifs are unaccountably absent. In the first
place the sexual element is scarcely to be found; not only is there an absence
of pornographic detail in art, but even the female genitalia themselves are
seldom represented. This reticence is the more surprising since Papuasians
betray no such reserve in their speech, while the utmost freedom in sexual
affairs is allowed to the unmarried." *The Melanesians of British New
Guinea*, by C. G. Seligmann, M.D. (Cambridge, 1910), p. 38.

Cf. also Freud:

"We may go on to consider the interesting case in which happiness in life
is sought first and foremost in the enjoyment of beauty, wherever it is to be
found by our senses and our judgment, the beauty of human forms and
movements, of natural objects, of landscapes, of artistic and even scientific
creations. As a goal in life this esthetic attitude offers little protection against
the menace of suffering, but it is able to compensate for a great deal. The
enjoyment of beauty produces a particular, mildly intoxicating kind of
sensation. There is no very evident use in beauty; the necessity of it for
cultural purposes is not apparent, and yet civilization could not do without
it. The science of esthetics investigates the conditions in which things are
regarded as beautiful; it can give no explanation of the nature or origin of
beauty; as usual, its lack of results is concealed under a flood of resounding
and meaningless words. Unfortunately, psychoanalysis, too, has less to say
about beauty than about most things. Its derivation from the realms of
sexual sensation is all that seems certain; the love of beauty is a perfect example of a feeling with an inhibited aim. 'Beauty' and 'attraction' are first
of all the attributes of a sexual object. It is remarkable that the genitals
themselves, the sight of which is always exciting, are hardly ever regarded
as beautiful; [The exception is provided by Attic vase painting.] the quality
of beauty seems, on the other hand, to attach to certain secondary sexual
characters." *Civilisation and Its Discontents* (London, 1930), pp. 38-9.

of mental disease. "It can easily be imagined, too," he goes on to say, "that certain practices of mystics may succeed in upsetting the normal relations between the different regions of the mind, so that, for example, the perceptual system becomes able to grasp relations in the deeper layers of the ego and in the id which would otherwise be inaccessible to it."[7] This casual statement, it seems to me, may contain the clue we are seeking. If we picture the regions of the mind as three superimposed strata (we have already noted how inadequate such a picture must be) then continuing our metaphor we can imagine in certain rare cases a phenomenon comparable to a "fault" in geology, as a result of which in one part of the mind the layers become discontinuous, and exposed to each other at unusual levels. That is to say, the sensational awareness of the ego is brought into direct contact with the id, and from that "seething cauldron" snatches some archetypal form, some instinctive association of words, images, or sounds, which constitute the basis of the work of art. Some such hypothesis is necessary to explain that access, that lyrical intuition, which is known as inspiration and which in all ages has been the rare possession of those few individuals we recognize as artists of genius.

Social Function of the Artist

With such a theory we could then go on to explain the social function of the artist. His primary function, and the only function which gives him his unique faculties, is this capacity to materialize the instinctual life of the deepest levels of the mind. At that level we suppose the mind to be collective in its representations, and it is because the artist can give visible shape to these invisible phantasms that he has power to move us deeply. But in the process of giving these phantasms material shape, the artist must exercise a certain skill lest the bare truth repel us. He therefore invests his creation with superficial charms; wholeness or perfection, a due proportion or harmony, and clarity; and these are the works of his conscious mind, his ego. There, I think, the essential function of art ends; there ends the art of Picasso, of Cézanne, of Poussin, of all typical Oriental artists and of all primitive artists. But in certain ages society has made the artist an exponent of the moral and ideal emanations of the super-ego, and art has thus become the

[7] *New Introductory Lectures*, p. 106.

handmaid of religion or morality or social ideology. In that further process art, as art, has always suffered—simply because in such a case the message will always appear more important, more insistent, than the mode of conveyance, and men will forget that in art it is only the mode which matters. But by the mode we mean more than the externals of beauty; we mean above all the driving energy, the uprush of forces which well up from the unconscious.

Ideas, and all the rational superstructure of the mind, can be conveyed by the instruments of thought or science; but those deeper intuitions of the mind, which are neither rational nor economic, but which nevertheless exercise a changeless and eternal influence on successive generations of men—these are accessible only to the mystic and the artist, and only the artist can give them material representations. But the mystic is also an artist, for no true mystic ever becomes aware of these subliminal truths without at the same time being inspired to give them poetic expression.

PAUL VALÉRY

Poetry and Abstract Thought

The idea of Poetry is often contrasted with that of Thought, and particularly "Abstract Thought." People say "Poetry and Abstract Thought" as they say Good and Evil, Vice and Virtue, Hot and Cold. Most people, without thinking any further, believe that the analytical work of the intellect, the efforts of will and precision in which it implicates the mind, are incompatible with that freshness of inspiration, that flow of expression, that grace and fancy which are the signs of poetry and which reveal it at its very first words. If a poet's work is judged profound, its profundity seems to be of a quite different order from that of a philosopher or a scientist. Some people go so far as to think that even meditation on his art, the kind of exact reasoning applied to the cultivation of roses, can only harm a poet, since the principal and most charming object of his desire must be to communicate the impression of a newly and happily born state of creative emotion which, through surprise and pleasure, has the power to remove the poem once and for all from any further criticism.

This opinion may possibly contain a grain of truth, though its simplicity makes me suspect it to be of scholarly origin. I feel we have learned and adopted this antithesis without reflection, and that we now find it firmly fixed in our mind, as a verbal contrast, as though it represented a clear and real relationship between two well-defined notions. It must be admitted that that character always in a hurry to have done, whom we call *our mind,* has a weakness for this kind of simplification, which freely enables him to form all kinds of combination and judgments, to display his logic, and to develop his rhetorical resources—in short, to carry out as brilliantly as possible his business of being a mind.

At all events, this classic contrast, crystallized, as it were, by language, has always seemed to me too abrupt, and at the same time too facile, not to provoke me to examine the things themselves more closely.

Poetry, Abstract Thought. That is soon said, and we immediately assume that we have said something sufficiently clear and sufficiently precise for us to proceed, without having to go back over our experiences; and to build a theory or begin a discussion using this contrast (so attractive in its simplicity) as pretext, argument, and substance. One could even fashion a whole metaphysics—or at the least a "psychology"—on this basis, and evolve for oneself a system of mental life, of knowledge, and of the invention and production of works of the mind, whose consequence would inevitably be the same terminological dissonance that had served as its starting point. . . .

For my part I have the strange and dangerous habit, in every subject, of wanting to begin at the beginning (that is, at my *own* beginning), which entails beginning again, going back over the whole road, just as though many others had not already mapped and traveled it. . . .

This is the road offered to us, or imposed on us, by *language.*

With every question, before making any deep examination of the content, I take a look at the language; I generally proceed like a surgeon who sterilizes his hands and prepares the area to be operated on. This is what I call *cleaning up the verbal situation.* You must excuse the expression equating the words and forms of speech with the hands and instruments of a surgeon.

I maintain that we must be careful of a problem's first contact with our minds. We should be careful of the first words a question utters in our mind. A new question arising in us is in a state of infancy; it stammers; it finds only strange terms, loaded with adventitious values and associations; it is forced to borrow these. But it thereby insensibly deflects our true need. Without realizing it we desert our original problem, and in the end we shall come to believe that we have chosen an opinion wholly our own, forgetting that our choice was exercised only on a mass of opinions that are the more or less blind work of other men and of chance. This is what happens with the programs of political parties, no one of which is (or can be) the one that would exactly catch our temperament and our interests. If we choose one among them, we gradually become the man suited to that party and to that program.

Philosophical and aesthetic questions are so richly obscured by the quantity, diversity, and antiquity of researches, arguments, and solutions, all produced within the orbit of a very restricted vocabulary, of which each author uses the words according to his own inclinations, that taken as a whole such works give me the impression of a district in the classical Underworld especially reserved for deep thinkers. Here, are the Danaïdes, Ixions, and Sisyphuses, eternally laboring to fill bottomless casks and to push back the falling rock, that is, to redefine the same dozen words whose combinations form the treasure of Speculative Knowledge.

Allow me to add to these preliminary considerations one last remark and one illustration. Here is the remark: you have surely noticed the curious fact that a certain *word,* which is perfectly clear when you hear or use it in *everyday* speech, and which presents no difficulty when caught up in the rapidity of an ordinary sentence, becomes mysteriously cumbersome, offers a strange resistance, defeats all efforts at definition, the moment you withdraw it from circulation for separate study and try to find its meaning after taking away its temporary function. It is almost comic to inquire the exact meaning of a term that one uses constantly with complete satisfaction. For example: I stop the word *Time* in its flight. This word was utterly limpid, precise, honest, and faithful in its service as long as it was part of a remark and was uttered by someone who wished to say something. But here it is, isolated, caught on the wing. It takes its revenge. It makes us believe that it has more meanings than uses. It was only a *means,* and it has become an *end,* the object of a terrible philosophical desire. It turns into an enigma, an abyss, a torment of thought. . . .

It is the same with the word *Life* and all the rest.

This readily observed phenomenon has taken on great critical value for me. Moreover, I have drawn from it an illustration that, for me, nicely conveys this strange property of our verbal material.

Each and every word that enables us to leap so rapidly across the chasm of thought, and to follow the prompting of an idea that constructs its own expression, appears to me like one of those light planks which one throws across a ditch or a mountain crevasse and which will bear a man crossing it rapidly. But he must pass without weighing on it, without stopping—above all, he must not take it into his head to dance on the slender plank to test its resistance! . . . Otherwise the fragile bridge tips or breaks immediately, and all is hurled into the depths. Consult your own experience; and you will find that we understand each other, and ourselves, only thanks to our *rapid passage over words*. We must not lay stress upon them, or we shall see the clearest discourse dissolve into enigmas and more or less learned illusions.

But how are we to think—I should say *rethink*, study deeply whatever seems to merit deep study—if we hold language to be something essentially provisional, as a banknote or a check is provisional, what we call its "value" requiring us to forget its true nature, which is that of a piece of paper, generally dirty? The paper has passed through so many hands. . . . But words have passed through so many mouths, so many phrases, so many uses and abuses, that the most delicate precautions must be taken to avoid too much confusion in our minds between what we think and are trying to think, and what dictionaries, authors, and, for that matter, the whole human race since the beginning of language, want us to think. . . .

I shall therefore take care not to accept what the words *Poetry* and *Abstract Thought* suggest to me the moment they are pronounced. But I shall look into myself. There I shall seek my real difficulties and my actual observations of my real states; there I shall find my own sense of the rational and the irrational; I shall see whether the alleged antithesis exists and how it exists in a living condition. I confess that it is my habit, when dealing with problems of the mind, to distinguish between those which I might have invented and which represent a need truly felt by my mind, and the rest, which are other people's problems. Of the latter, more than one (say forty per cent) seem to me to be nonexistent, to be no more than apparent problems: *I do not feel them.* And as for the rest, more than one seem to me to be badly stated. . . . I do not say I am right. I say that I observe what occurs within myself when I attempt to replace the verbal formulas by values and meanings that are nonverbal, that are independent of the language used. I discover naïve impulses and images, raw products of my needs and of my personal experiences. *It is my life itself that is surprised,* and my life must, if it can, provide my answers, for it is only in the reactions of our life that the full force, and as it were the necessity, of our truth can reside. The thought proceeding from that life never uses for its own account certain words which seem to it fit only for external consumption; nor certain others whose depths are obscure and which may only deceive thought as to its real strength and value.

I have, then, noticed in myself certain states which I may well call *poetic,* since some of them were finally realized in poems. They came about from no apparent cause, arising from some accident or other; they developed according to their own nature, and consequently I found myself for a time jolted out of my habitual state of mind. Then, the cycle completed, I returned to the rule of ordinary exchanges between my life and my thought. But meanwhile *a poem had been made,* and in completing itself the cycle left something behind. This closed cycle is the cycle of an act which has, as it were, aroused and given external form to a poetic power. . . .

On other occasions I have noticed that some no less insignificant incident caused—or seemed to cause—a quite different excursion, a digression of another nature and with another result. For example, a sudden concatenation of ideas, an analogy, would strike me in much the way the sound of a horn in the heart of a forest makes one prick up one's ears, and virtually directs the co-ordinated attention of all one's muscles toward some point in the distance, among the leafy depths. But this time, instead of a poem, it was an analysis of the sudden intellectual sensation that was taking hold of me. It was not verses that were being formed more or less easily during this phase, but some proposition or other that was destined to be incorporated among my habits of thought, some formula that would henceforward serve as an instrument for further researches. . . .

I apologize for thus revealing myself to you; but in my opinion it is more useful to speak of what one has experienced than to pretend to a knowledge that is entirely impersonal, and observation with no observer. In fact there is no theory that is not a fragment, carefully prepared, of some autobiography.

I do not pretend to be teaching you anything at all. I will say nothing you do not already know; but I will, perhaps, say it in a different order. You do not need to be told that a poet is not always incapable of solving a *rule of three;* or that a logician is not always incapable of seeing in words something other than concepts, categories, and mere pretexts for syllogisms.

On this point I would add this paradoxical remark: if the logician could never be other than a logician, he would not, and could not, be a logician; and if the poet were never anything but a poet, without the slightest hope of being able to reason abstractly, he would leave no poetic traces behind him. I believe in all sincerity that if each man were not able to live a number of other lives besides his own, he would not be able to live his own life.

My experience has thus shown me that the same *self* can take very different forms, can become an abstract thinker or a poet, by successive specializations, each of which is a deviation from that entirely unattached state which is superficially in accord with exterior surroundings and which is the average state of our existence, the state of undifferentiated exchanges.

Let us first see in what may consist that initial and *invariably accidental* shock which will construct the poetic instrument within us, and above all, what are its effects. The problem can be put in this way: Poetry is an art of Language; certain combinations of words can produce an emotion that others do not produce, and which we shall call *poetic*. What kind of emotion is this?

I recognize it in myself by this: that all possible objects of the ordinary world, external or internal, beings, events, feelings, and actions, while keeping their usual appearance, are suddenly placed in an indefinable but wonderfully fitting relationship with the modes of our general sensibility. That is to say that these well-known things and beings—or rather the ideas that represent them —somehow change in value. They attract one another, they are

connected in ways quite different from the ordinary; they become
(if you will permit the expression) *musicalized*, resonant, and, as
it were, harmonically related. The poetic universe, thus defined,
offers extensive analogies with what we can postulate of the dream
world.

Since the word *dream* has found its way into this talk, I shall
say in passing that in modern times, beginning with Romanticism,
there has arisen a fairly understandable confusion between the
notion of the dream and that of poetry. Neither the dream nor the
daydream is necessarily poetic; it may be so: but figures formed *by
chance* are only *by chance* harmonious figures.

In any case, our memories of dreams teach us, by frequent and
common experience, that our consciousness can be invaded, filled,
entirely absorbed by the production of an *existence* in which objects and beings seem the same as those in the waking state; but
their meanings, relationships, modes of variation and of substitution are quite different and doubtless represent, like symbols or
allegories, the immediate fluctuations of our *general* sensibility un-
controlled by the sensitivities of our *specialized* senses. In very
much the same way the *poetic state* takes hold of us, develops, and
finally disintegrates.

This is to say that the *state of poetry* is completely irregular, in-
constant, involuntary, and fragile, and that we lose it, as we find
it, *by accident*. But this state is not enough to make a poet, any
more than it is enough to see a treasure in a dream to find it, on
waking, sparkling at the foot of one's bed.

A poet's function—do not be startled by this remark—is not to
experience the poetic state: that is a private affair. His function is
to create it in others. The poet is recognized—or at least everyone
recognizes his own poet—by the simple fact that he causes his
reader to become "inspired." Positively speaking, inspiration is a
graceful attribute with which the reader endows his poet: the
reader sees in us the transcendent merits of virtues and graces that
develop in him. He seeks and finds in us the wondrous cause of
his own wonder.

But poetic feeling and the artificial synthesis of this state in some
work are two quite distinct things, as different as sensation and
action. A sustained action is much more complex than any spontaneous production, particularly when it has to be carried out in

a sphere as conventional as that of language. Here you see emerging through my explanations the famous ABSTRACT THOUGHT which custom opposes to POETRY. We shall come back to that in a moment. Meanwhile I should like to tell you a true story, so that you may feel as I felt, and in a curiously clear way, the whole difference that exists between the poetic state or emotion, even creative and original, and the production of a work. It is a rather remarkable observation of myself that I made about a year ago.

I had left my house to relax from some tedious piece of work by walking and by a consequent change of scene. As I went along the street where I live, I was suddenly *gripped* by a rhythm which took possession of me and soon gave me the impression of some force outside myself. It was as though someone else were making use of my *living-machine*. Then another rhythm overtook and combined with the first, and certain strange *transverse* relations were set up between these two principles (I am explaining myself as best I can). They combined the movement of my walking legs and some kind of song I was murmuring, or rather which was being murmured *through me*. This composition became more and more complicated and soon in its complexity went far beyond anything I could reasonably produce with my ordinary, usable rhythmic faculties. The sense of strangeness that I mentioned became almost painful, almost disquieting. I am no musician; I am completely ignorant of musical technique; yet here I was, prey to a development in several parts more complicated than any poet could dream. I argued that there had been an error of person, that this grace had descended on the wrong head, since I could make no use of a gift which for a musician would doubtless have assumed value, form, and duration, while these parts that mingled and separated offered me in vain a composition whose cunningly organized sequence amazed my ignorance and reduced it to despair.

After about twenty minutes the magic suddenly vanished, leaving me on the bank of the Seine, as perplexed as the duck in the fable, that saw a swan emerge from the egg she had hatched. As the swan flew away, my surprise changed to reflection. I knew that walking often induces in me a quickened flow of ideas and that there is a certain reciprocity between my pace and my thoughts —my thoughts modify my pace; my pace provokes my thoughts— which after all is remarkable enough, but is fairly understandable.

Our various "reaction periods" are doubtless synchronized, and it is interesting to have to admit that a reciprocal modification is possible between a form of action which is purely muscular and a varied production of images, judgments, and reasonings.

But in the case I am speaking of, my movement in walking became in my consciousness a very subtle system of rhythms, instead of instigating those images, interior words, and potential actions which one calls *ideas*. As for ideas, they are things of a species familiar to me; they are things that I can note, provoke, and handle. . . . *But I cannot say the same of my unexpected rhythms.*

What was I to think? I supposed that mental activity while walking must correspond with a general excitement exerting itself in the region of my brain; this excitement satisfied and relieved itself as best it could, and so long as its energy was expended, it mattered little whether this was on ideas, memories, or rhythms unconsciously hummed. On that day, the energy was expended in a rhythmical intuition that developed before the awakening in my consciousness of *the person who knows that he does not know music.* I imagine it is the same as when *the person who knows he cannot fly* has not yet become active in the man who dreams he is flying.

I apologize for this long and true story—as true, that is, as a story of this kind can be. Notice that everything I have said, or tried to say, happened in relation to what we call the *External World,* what we call *Our Body,* and what we call *Our Mind,* and requires a kind of vague collaboration between these three great powers.

Why have I told you this? In order to bring out the profound difference existing between spontaneous production by the mind— or rather by our *sensibility as a whole*—and the fabrication of works. In my story, the substance of a musical composition was freely given to me, but the organization which would have seized, fixed, and reshaped it was lacking. The great painter Degas often repeated to me a very true and simple remark by Mallarmé. Degas occasionally wrote verses, and some of those he left were delightful. But he often found great difficulty in this work accessory to his painting. (He was, by the way, the kind of man who would bring all possible difficulty to any art whatever.) One day he said to Mallarmé: "Yours is a hellish craft. I can't manage to say what I want, and yet I'm full of ideas. . . ." And Mallarmé answered:

"My dear Degas, one does not make poetry with ideas, but with *words*."

Mallarmé was right. But when Degas spoke of ideas, he was, after all, thinking of inner speech or of images, which might have been expressed in *words*. But these words, these secret phrases which he called ideas, all these intentions and perceptions of the mind, do not make verses. There is something else, then, a modification, or a transformation, sudden or not, spontaneous or not, laborious or not, which must necessarily intervene between the thought that produces ideas—that activity and multiplicity of inner questions and solutions—and, on the other hand, that discourse, so different from ordinary speech, which is verse, which is so curiously ordered, which answers no need *unless it be the need it must itself create,* which never speaks but of absent things or of things profoundly and secretly felt: strange discourse, as though made by someone *other* than the speaker and addressed to someone *other* than the listener. In short, it is a *language within a language.*

Let us look into these mysteries.

Poetry is an art of language. But language is a practical creation. It may be observed that in all communication between men, certainty comes only from practical acts and from the verification which practical acts give us. *I ask you for a light. You give me a light:* you have understood me.

But in asking me for a light, you were able to speak those few unimportant words with a certain intonation, a certain tone of voice, a certain inflection, a certain languor or briskness perceptible to me. I have understood your words, since without even thinking I handed you what you asked for—a light. But the matter does not end there. The strange thing: the sound and as it were the features of your little sentence come back to me, echo within me, as though they were pleased to be there; I, too, like to hear myself repeat this little phrase, which has almost lost its meaning, which has stopped being of use, and which can yet go on living, though with quite another life. It has acquired a value; and has acquired it *at the expense of its finite significance.* It has created the need to be heard again. . . . Here we are on the very threshold of the poetic state. This tiny experience will help us to the discovery of more than one truth.

It has shown us that language can produce effects of two quite

different kinds. One of them tends to bring about the complete
negation of language itself. I speak to you, and if you have understood my words, those very words are abolished. If you have understood, it means that the words have vanished from your minds and
are replaced by their counterpart, by images, relationships, impulses; so that you have within you the means to retransmit these
ideas and images in a language that may be very different from the
one you received. *Understanding* consists in the more or less rapid
replacement of a system of sounds, intervals, and signs by something quite different, which is, in short, a modification or interior
reorganization of the person to whom one is speaking. And here is
the counterproof of this proposition: the person who does not understand *repeats* the words, or *has them repeated* to him.

Consequently, the perfection of a discourse whose sole aim is
comprehension obviously consists in the ease with which the words
forming it are transformed into something quite different: the
language is transformed first into *non-language* and then, if we
wish, into a form of language differing from the original form.

In other terms, in practical or abstract uses of language, the form
—that is the physical, the concrete part, the very act of speech—does
not last; it does not outlive understanding; it dissolves in the light;
it has acted; it has done its work; it has brought about understanding; it has lived.

But on the other hand, the moment this concrete form takes on,
by an effect of its own, such importance that it asserts itself and
makes itself, as it were, respected; and not only remarked and respected, but desired and therefore repeated—then something new
happens: we are insensibly transformed and ready to live, breathe,
and think in accordance with a rule and under laws which are no
longer of the practical order—that is, nothing that may occur in this
state will be resolved, finished, or abolished by a specific act. We
are entering the poetic universe.

Permit me to support this notion of a *poetic universe* by referring
to a similar notion that, being much simpler, is easier to explain: the
notion of a *musical universe*. I would ask you to make a small sacrifice: limit yourselves for a moment to your faculty of hearing.
One simple sense, like that of hearing, will offer us all we need
for our definition and will absolve us from entering into all the
difficulties and subtleties to which the conventional structure and

historical complexities of ordinary language would lead us. We live by ear in the world of noises. Taken as a whole, it is generally incoherent and irregularly supplied by all the mechanical incidents which the ear may interpret as it can. But the same ear isolates from this chaos a group of noises particularly remarkable and simple—that is, easily recognizable by our sense of hearing and furnishing it with points of reference. These elements have relations with one another which we sense as we do the elements themselves. The interval between two of these privileged noises is as clear to us as each of them. These are the *sounds,* and these units of sonority tend to form clear combinations, successive or simultaneous implications, series, and intersections which one may term *intelligible:* this is why abstract possibilities exist in music. But I must return to my subject.

I will confine myself to saying that the contrast between noise and sound is the contrast between pure and impure, order and disorder; that this differentiation between pure sensations and others has permitted the constitution of music; that it has been possible to control, unify, and codify this constitution, thanks to the intervention of physical science, which knows how to adjust measure to sensation so as to obtain the important result of teaching us to produce this sonorous sensation consistently, and in a continuous and identical fashion, by instruments that are, in reality, *measuring instruments.*

The musician is thus in possession of a perfect system of well-defined means which exactly match sensations with acts. From this it results that music has formed a domain absolutely its own. The world of the art of music, a world of sounds, is distinct from the world of noises. Whereas a *noise* merely rouses in us some isolated event—a dog, a door, a motor car—*a sound evokes, of itself, the musical universe.* If, in this hall where I am speaking to you and where you hear the noise of my voice, a tuning fork or a well-tempered instrument began to vibrate, you would at once, as soon as you were affected by this pure and exceptional noise that cannot be confused with others, have the feeling of a beginning, the beginning of a world; a quite different atmosphere would immediately be created, a new order would arise, and you yourselves would unconsciously *organize* yourselves to receive it. The musical universe, therefore, was within you, with all its associations and proportions—as in a saturated salt solution a crystalline universe awaits the molecular shock of a minute crystal in order *to declare itself*. I dare not say: the crystalline idea of such a system awaits. . . .

And here is the counter proof of our little experiment: if, in a concert hall dominated by a resounding symphony, a chair happens to fall, someone coughs, or a door shuts, we immediately have the impression of a kind of rupture. Something indefinable, something like a spell or a Venetian glass, has been broken or cracked. . . .

The poetic universe is not created so powerfully or so easily. It exists, but the poet is deprived of the immense advantages possessed by the musician. He does not have before him, ready for the uses of beauty, a body of resources expressly made for his art. He has to borrow *language*—the voice of the public, that collection of traditional and irrational terms and rules, oddly created and transformed, oddly codified, and very variedly understood and pronounced. Here there is no physicist who has determined the relations between these elements; no tuning forks, no metronomes, no inventors of scales or theoreticians of harmony. Rather, on the contrary, the phonetic and semantic fluctuations of vocabulary. Nothing pure; but a mixture of completely incoherent auditive and psychic stimuli. Each word is an instantaneous coupling of a *sound* and a *sense* that have no connection with each other. Each sentence is an act so complex that I doubt whether anyone has yet been able to provide a tolerable definition of it. As for the use of the resources of language and the modes of this action, you know what diversity there is, and what confusion sometimes results. A discourse can be logical, packed with sense, but devoid of rhythm and measure. It can be pleasing to the ear, yet completely absurd or insignificant; it can be clear, yet useless; vague, yet delightful. But to grasp its strange multiplicity, which is no more than the multiplicity of life itself, it suffices to name all the sciences which have been created to deal with this diversity, each to study one of its aspects. One can analyze a text in many different ways, for it falls successively under the jurisdiction of phonetics, semantics, syntax, logic, rhetoric, philology, not to mention metrics, prosody, and etymology. . . .

So the poet is at grips with this verbal matter, obliged to speculate on sound and sense at once, and to satisfy not only harmony and musical timing but all the various intellectual and aesthetic conditions, not to mention the conventional rules. . . .

You can see what an effort the poet's undertaking would require if he had *consciously* to solve all these problems. . . .

It is always interesting to try to reconstruct one of our complex activities, one of those complete actions which demand a specialization at once mental, sensuous, and motor, supposing that in order to accomplish this act we were obliged to understand and organize all the functions that we know play their part in it. Even if this attempt, at once imaginative and analytical, is clumsy, it will always teach us something. As for myself, who am, I admit, much more attentive to the formation or fabrication of works than to the works themselves, I have a habit, or obsession, of appreciating works only as actions. In my eyes a poet is a man who, as a result of a certain incident, undergoes a hidden transformation. He leaves his ordinary condition of general disposability, and I see taking shape in him an agent, a living system for producing verses. As among animals one suddenly sees emerging a capable hunter, a nest maker, a bridge builder, a digger of tunnels and galleries, so in a man one sees a composite organization declare itself, bending its functions to a specific piece of work. Think of a very small child: the child we have all been bore many possibilities within him. After a few months of life he has learned, at the same or almost the same time, to speak and to walk. He has acquired two types of action. That is to say that he now possesses two kinds of potentiality from which the accidental circumstances of each moment will draw what they can, in answer to his varying needs and imaginings.

Having learned to use his legs, he will discover that he can not only walk, but run; and not only walk and run, but dance. This is a great event. He has at that moment both invented and discovered a kind of *secondary use* for his limbs, a generalization of his formula of movement. In fact, whereas walking is after all a rather dull and not easily perfectible action, this new form of action, the Dance, admits of an infinite number of creations and variations or *figures*.

But will he not find an analogous development in speech? He will explore the possibilities of his faculty of speech; he will discover that more can be done with it than to ask for jam and deny his little sins. He will grasp the power of reasoning; he will invent stories to amuse himself when he is alone; he will repeat to himself words that he loves for their strangeness and mystery.

So, parallel with *Walking* and *Dancing,* he will acquire and distinguish the divergent types, *Prose and Poetry.*

This parallel has long struck and attracted me; but someone saw it before I did. According to Racan, Malherbe made use of it. In my opinion it is more than a simple comparison. It see in it an analogy as substantial and pregnant as those found in physics when one observes the identity of formulas that represent the measurement of seemingly very different phenomena. Here is how our comparison develops.

Walking, like prose, has a definite aim. It is an act directed at something we wish to reach. Actual circumstances, such as the need for some object, the impulse of my desire, the state of my body, my sight, the terrain, etc., which order the manner of walking, prescribe its direction and its speed, and give it a *definite end.* All the characteristics of walking derive from these instantaneous conditions, which combine *in a novel way* each time. There are no movements in walking that are not special adaptations, but, each time, they are abolished and, as it were, absorbed by the accomplishment of the act, by the attainment of the goal.

The dance is quite another matter. It is, of course, a system of actions; but of actions whose end is in themselves. It goes nowhere. If it pursues an object, it is only an ideal object, a state, an enchantment, the phantom of a flower, an extreme of life, a smile—which forms at last on the face of the one who summoned it from empty space.

It is therefore not a question of carrying out a limited operation whose end is situated somewhere in our surroundings, but rather of creating, maintaining, and exalting a certain *state,* by a periodic movement that can be executed on the spot; a movement which is almost entirely dissociated from sight, but which is stimulated and regulated by auditive rhythms.

But please note this very simple observation, that however different the dance may be from walking and utilitarian movements, it uses the same organs, the same bones, the same muscles, only differently co-ordinated and aroused.

Here we come again to the contrast between prose and poetry. Prose and poetry use the same words, the same syntax, the same forms, and the same sounds or tones, but differently co-ordinated and differently aroused. Prose and poetry are therefore distinguished by the difference between certain links and associations which form and dissolve in our psychic and nervous organism, whereas the components of these modes of functioning are identical. This is why one should guard against reasoning about poetry as one does about prose. What is true of one very often has no meaning when it is sought in the other. But here is the great and decisive difference. When the man who is walking has reached his goal—as I said—when he has reached the place, book, fruit, the object of his desire (which desire drew him from his repose), this possession at once entirely annuls his whole act; the effect swallows up the cause, the end absorbs the means; and, whatever the act, only the result remains. It is the same with utilitarian language: the language I use to express my design, my desire, my command, my opinion; this language, when it has served its purpose, evaporates almost as it is heard. I have given it forth to perish, to be radically transformed into something else in your mind; and I shall know that I was *understood* by the remarkable fact that my speech no longer exists: it has been completely replaced by its *meaning*— that is, by images, impulses, reactions, or acts that belong to you: in short, by an interior modification in you.

As a result the perfection of this kind of language, whose sole end is to be understood, obviously consists in the ease with which it is transformed into something altogether different.

The poem, on the other hand, does not die for having lived: it is expressly designed to be born again from its ashes and to become endlessly what it has just been. Poetry can be recognized by this property, that it tends to get itself reproduced in its own form: it stimulates us to reconstruct it identically.

That is an admirable and uniquely characteristic property.

I should like to give you a simple illustration. Think of a pendulum oscillating between two symmetrical points. Suppose that one of these extremes represents *form*: the concrete characteristics of the language, sound, rhythm, accent, tone, movement—in a word, the *Voice* in action. Then associate with the other point, the acnode of the first, all significant values, images and ideas, stimuli of feeling and memory, virtual impulses and structures of understanding —in short, everything that makes the *content*, the meaning of a discourse. Now observe the effect of poetry on yourselves. You will find that at each line the meaning produced within you, far from destroying the musical form communicated to you, recalls it. The living pendulum that has swung from *sound* to *sense* swings back to its felt point of departure, as though the very sense which is present to your mind can find no other outlet or expression, no other answer, than the very music which gave it birth.

So between the form and the content, between the sound and the sense, between the poem and the state of poetry, a symmetry is revealed, an equality between importance, value, and power, which does not exist in prose; which is contrary to the law of prose —the law which ordains the inequality of the two constituents of language. The essential principle of the mechanics of poetry—that is, of the conditions for producing the poetic state by words—seems to me to be this harmonious exchange between expression and impression.

I introduce here a slight observation which I shall call "philosophical," meaning simply that we could do without it.

Our poetic pendulum travels from our sensation toward some idea or some sentiment, and returns toward some memory of the sensation and toward the potential act which could reproduce the sensation. Now, whatever is sensation is essentially *present*. There is no other definition of the present except sensation itself, which includes, perhaps, the impulse to action that would modify that sensation. On the other hand, whatever is properly thought, image, sentiment, is always, in some way, *a production of absent things*. Memory is the substance of all thought. Anticipation and its gropings, desire, planning, the projection of our hopes, of our fears, are the main interior activity of our being.

Thought is, in short, the activity which causes what does not exist to come alive in us, lending to it, whether we will or no, our present powers, making us take the part for the whole, the image for reality, and giving us the illusion of seeing, acting, suffering, and possessing independently of our dear old body, which we leave with its cigarette in an armchair until we suddenly retrieve it when the telephone rings or, no less strangely, when our stomach demands provender. . . .

Between Voice and Thought, between Thought and Voice, between Presence and Absence, oscillates the poetic pendulum.

The result of this analysis is to show that the value of a poem resides in the indissolubility of sound and sense. Now this is a condition that seems to demand the impossible. There is no relation between the sound and the meaning of a word. The same thing is called HORSE in English, HIPPOS in Greek, EQUUS in Latin, and CHEVAL in French; but no manipulation of any of these terms will give me an idea of the animal in question; and no manipulation of the idea will yield me any of these words—otherwise, we would easily know all languages, beginning with our own.

Yet it is the poet's business to give us the feeling of an intimate union between the word and the mind.

This must be considered, strictly speaking, a marvelous result. I say *marvelous,* although it is not exceptionally rare. I use *marvelous* in the sense we give that word when we think of the miracles and prodigies of ancient magic. It must not be forgotten that for centuries poetry was used for purposes of enchantment. Those who took part in these strange operations had to believe in the power of the word, and far more in the efficacy of its sound than in its significance. Magic formulas are often without meaning; but it was never thought that their power depended on their intellectual content.

Let us listen to lines like these:

or
       Mère des souvenirs, maîtresse des maîtresses. . .

       Sois sage, ô ma Douleur, et tiens-toi plus tranquille. . . .

These words work on us (or at least on some of us) without telling us very much. They tell us, perhaps, that they have nothing to tell us; that, by the very means which usually tell us something, they are exercising a quite different function. They act on us like a chord of music. The impression produced depends largely on resonance, rhythm, and the number of syllables; but it is also the result of the simple bringing together of meanings. In the second of these lines the accord between the vague ideas of Wisdom and Grief, and the tender solemnity of the tone produce the inestimable value of a spell: the *momentary being* who made that line could not have done so had he been in a state where the form and the content occurred separately to his mind. On the contrary, he was in a special phase in the domain of his psychic existence, a phase in which the sound and the meaning of the word acquire or keep an equal importance—

which is excluded from the habits of practical language, as from the needs of abstract language. The state in which the inseparability of sound and sense, in which the desire, the expectation, the possibility of their intimate and indissoluble fusion are required and sought or given, and sometimes anxiously awaited, is a comparatively rare state. It is rare, firstly because all the exigencies of life are against it; secondly because it is opposed to the crude simplifying and specializing of verbal notations.

But this state of inner modification, in which all the properties of our language are distinctly but harmoniously summoned, is not enough to produce that complete object, that compound of beauties, that collection of happy chances for the mind which a noble poem offers us.

From this state we obtain only fragments. All the precious things that are found in the earth, gold, diamonds, uncut stones, are there scattered, strewn, grudgingly hidden in a quantity of rock or sand, where chance may sometimes uncover them. These riches would be nothing without the human labor that draws them from the massive night where they were sleeping, assembles them, alters and organizes them into ornaments. These fragments of metal embedded in formless matter, these oddly shaped crystals, must owe all their luster to intelligent labor. It is a labor of this kind that the true poet accomplishes. Faced with a beautiful poem, one can indeed feel that it is most unlikely that any man, however gifted, could have improvised without a backward glance, with no other effort than that of writing or dictating, such a simultaneous and complete system of lucky finds. Since the traces of effort, the second thoughts, the changes, the amount of time, the bad days, and the distaste have now vanished, effaced by the supreme return of a mind over its work, some people, seeing only the perfection of the result, will look on it as due to a sort of magic that they call INSPIRATION. They thus make of the poet a kind of temporary *medium*. If one were strictly to develop this doctrine of pure inspiration, one would arrive at some very strange results. For example, one would conclude that the poet, since he merely transmits what he receives, merely delivers to unknown people what he has taken from the unknown, has no need to understand what he writes, which is dictated by a mysterious voice. He could write poems in a language he did not know. . . .

In fact, the poet has indeed a kind of spiritual energy of a special nature: it is manifested in him and reveals him to himself in certain moments of infinite worth. Infinite for him. . . . I say, *infinite for him,* for alas, experience shows us that these moments which seem to us to have a universal value are sometimes without a future, and in the end make us ponder on this maxim: *what is of value for one person only has no value.* This is the iron law of Literature.

But every true poet is necessarily a first-rate critic. If one doubts this, one can have no idea of what the work of the mind is: that struggle with the inequality of moments, with chance associations, lapses of attention, external distractions. The mind is terribly variable, deceptive and self-deceiving, fertile in insoluble problems and illusory solutions. How could a remarkable work emerge from this chaos if this chaos that contains everything did not also contain some serious chances to know oneself and to choose within oneself whatever is worth taking from each moment and using carefully?

That is not all. Every true poet is much more capable than is generally known of right reasoning and abstract thought.

But one must not look for his real philosophy in his more or less philosophical utterances. In my opinion, the most authentic philosophy lies not so much in the objects of our reflection as in the very act of thought and in its handling. Take from metaphysics all its pet or special terms, all its traditional vocabulary, and you may realize that you have not impoverished the thought. Indeed, you may perhaps have eased and freshened it, and you will have got rid of other people's problems, so as to deal only with your own difficulties, your surprises that owe nothing to anyone, and whose intellectual spur you feel actually and directly.

It has often happened, however, as literary history tells us, that poetry has been made to enunciate theses or hypotheses and that the *complete* language which is its own—the language whose *form,* that is to say the action and sensation of the *Voice,* is of the same power as the *content,* that is to say the eventual modification of a *mind*—has been used to communicate "abstract" ideas, which are on the contrary independent of their form, or so we believe. Some very great poets have occasionally attempted this. But whatever may be the talent which exerts itself in this very noble undertaking, it cannot prevent the attention given to following the ideas from competing with the attention that follows the song. The DE RERUM NATURA

is here in conflict with the nature of things. The state of mind of
the reader of poems is not the state of mind of the reader of pure
thought. The state of mind of a man dancing is not that of a man
advancing through difficult country of which he is making a topo-
graphical survey or a geological prospectus.

I have said, nevertheless, that the poet has his abstract thought
and, if you like, his philosophy; and I have said that it is at work in
his very activity as a poet. I said this because I have observed it, in
myself and in several others. Here, as elsewhere, I have no other
reference, no other claim or excuse, than recourse to my own experience or to the most common observation.

Well, every time I have worked as a poet, I have noticed that my
work exacted of me not only that presence of the poetic universe I
have spoken of, but many reflections, decisions, choices, and combinations, without which all possible gifts of the Muses, or of
Chance, would have remained like precious materials in a work-
shop without an architect. Now an architect is not himself necessarily built of precious materials. In so far as he is an architect of
poems, a poet is quite different from what he is as a producer of
those precious elements of which all poetry should be composed,
but whose composition is separate and requires an entirely different
mental effort.

One day someone told me that lyricism is enthusiasm, and that
the odes of the great lyricists were written at a single stroke, at the
speed of the voice of delirium, and with the wind of inspiration
blowing a gale. . . .

I replied that he was quite right; but that this was not a privilege
of poetry alone, and that everyone knew that in building a locomotive it is indispensable for the builder to work at eighty miles an
hour in order to do his job.

A poem is really a kind of machine for producing the poetic state
of mind by means of words. The effect of this machine is uncertain,
for nothing is certain about action on other minds. But whatever
may be the result, in its uncertainty, the construction of the machine demands the solution of many problems. If the term *machine*
shocks you, if my mechanical comparison seems crude, please notice
that while the composition of even a very short poem may absorb
years, the action of the poem on the reader will take only a few
minutes. In a few minutes the reader will receive his shock from

discoveries, connections, glimmers of expression that have been accumulated during months of research, waiting, patience, and impatience. He may attribute much more to inspiration than it can give. He will imagine the kind of person it would take to create, without pause, hesitation, or revision, this powerful and perfect work which transports him into a world where things and people, passions and thoughts, sonorities and meanings proceed from the same energy, are transformed one into another, and correspond according to exceptional laws of harmony, for it can only be an exceptional form of stimulus that simultaneously produces the exaltation of our sensibility, our intellect, our memory, and our powers of verbal action, so rarely granted to us in the ordinary course of life.

Perhaps I should remark here that the execution of a poetic work—if one considers it as the engineer just mentioned would consider the conception and construction of his locomotive, that is, making explicit the problems to be solved—would appear impossible. In no other art is the number of conditions and independent functions to be co-ordinated so large. I will not inflict on you a detailed demonstration of this proposition. It is enough for me to remind you of what I said regarding sound and sense, which are linked only by pure convention, but which must be made to collaborate as effectively as possible. From their double nature words often make me think of those complex quantities which geometricians take such pleasure in manipulating.

Fortunately, some strange virtue resides in certain moments in certain people's lives which simplifies things and reduces the insurmountable difficulties I spoke of to the scale of human energies.

The poet awakes within man at an unexpected event, an outward or inward incident: a tree, a face, a "subject," an emotion, a word. Sometimes it is the will to expression that starts the game, a need to translate what one feels; another time, on the contrary, it is an element of form, the outline of an expression which seeks its origin, seeks a meaning within the space of my mind. . . . Note this possible duality in ways of getting started: either something wants to express itself, or some means of expression wants to be used.

My poem *Le Cimetière marin* began in me by a rhythm, that of a French line . . . of ten syllables, divided into four and six. I had as yet no idea with which to fill out this form. Gradually a few hovering words settled in it, little by little determining the subject,

and my labor (a very long labor) was before me. Another poem,
La Pythie, first appeared as an eight-syllable line whose sound came
of its own accord. But this line implied a sentence, of which it was
part, and this sentence, if it existed, implied many other sentences.
A problem of this kind has an infinite number of solutions. But with
poetry the musical and metrical conditions greatly restrict the in-
definiteness. Here is what happened: my fragment acted like a living fragment, since, plunged in the (no doubt nourishing) surroundings of my desire and waiting thought, it proliferated, and
engendered all that was lacking: several lines before and a great
many lines after.

I apologize for having chosen my examples from my own little
story: but I could hardly have taken them elsewhere.

Perhaps you think my conception of the poet and the poem
rather singular. Try to imagine, however, what the least of our acts
implies. Think of everything that must go on inside a man who
utters the smallest intelligible sentence, and then calculate all that
is needed for a poem by Keats or Baudelaire to be formed on an
empty page in front of the poet.

Think, too, that of all the arts, ours is perhaps that which co-
ordinates the greatest number of independent parts or factors:
sound, sense, the real and the imaginary, logic, syntax, and the
double invention of content and form . . . and all this by means of
a medium essentially practical, perpetually changing, soiled, a maid
of all work, *everyday language,* from which we must draw a pure,
ideal Voice, capable of communicating without weakness, without
apparent effort, without offense to the ear, and without breaking
the ephemeral sphere of the poetic universe, an idea of some *self*
miraculously superior to Myself.

STEPHEN SPENDER

The Making of a Poem

Apology

It would be inexcusable
to discuss my own way of writing poetry unless I were able to relate
this to a wider view of the problems which poets attempt to solve

when they sit down at a desk or table to write, or walk around composing their poems in their heads. There is a danger of my appearing to put across my own experiences as the general rule, when every poet's way of going about his work and his experience of being a poet are different, and when my own poetry may not be good enough to lend my example any authority.

Yet the writing of poetry is an activity which makes certain demands of attention on the poet and which requires that he should have certain qualifications of ear, vision, imagination, memory and so on. He should be able to think in images, he should have as great a mastery of language as a painter has over his palette, even if the range of his language be very limited. All this means that, in ordinary society, a poet has to adapt himself, more or less consciously, to the demands of his vocation, and hence the peculiarities of poets and the condition of inspiration which many people have said is near to madness. One poet's example is only his adaptation of his personality to the demands of poetry, but if it is clearly stated it may help us to understand other poets, and even something of poetry.

Today we lack very much a whole view of poetry, and have instead many one-sided views of certain aspects of poetry which have been advertised as the only aims which poets should attempt. Movements such as free verse, imagism, surrealism, expressionism, personalism and so on, tend to make people think that poetry is simply a matter of not writing in metre or rhyme, or of free association, or of thinking in images, or of a kind of drawing room madness (surrealism) which corresponds to drawing room communism. Here is a string of ideas: Night, dark, stars, immensity, blue, voluptuous, clinging, columns, clouds, moon, sickle, harvest, vast camp fire, hell. Is this poetry? A lot of strings of words almost as simple as this are set down on the backs of envelopes and posted off to editors or to poets by the vast army of amateurs who think that to be illogical is to be poetic, with that fond question. Thus I hope that this discussion of how poets work will imply a wider and completer view of poets.

Concentration

The problem of creative writing is essentially one of concentration, and the supposed eccentricities of poets are usually due to mechanical habits or rituals developed in order to concentrate. Concentration, of course, for the purposes of writing poetry, is different from the kind of concentration required for working out a sum. It is a focussing of the attention in a special way, so that the poet is aware of all the implications and possible developments of his idea, just as one might say that a plant was not concentrating on developing mechanically in one direction, but in many directions, towards the warmth and light with its leaves, and towards the water with its roots, all at the same time.

Schiller liked to have a smell of rotten apples, concealed beneath the lid of his desk, under his nose when he was composing poetry. Walter de la Mare has told me that he must smoke when writing. Auden drinks endless cups of tea. Coffee is my own addiction, besides smoking a great deal, which I hardly ever do except when I am writing. I notice also that as I attain a greater concentration, this tends to make me forget the taste of the cigarette in my mouth, and then I have a desire to smoke two or even three cigarettes at a time, in order that the sensation from the outside may penetrate through the wall of concentration which I have built round myself.

For goodness' sake, though, do not think that rotten apples or cigarettes or tea have anything to do with the quality of the work of a Schiller, a de la Mare, or an Auden. They are a part of a concentration which has already been attained rather than the causes of concentration. De la Mare once said to me that he thought the desire to smoke when writing poetry arose from a need, not of a stimulus, but to canalize a distracting leak of his attention away from his writing towards the distraction which is always present in one's environment. Concentration may be disturbed by someone whistling in the street or the ticking of a clock. There is always a slight tendency of the body to sabotage the attention of the mind by providing some distraction. If this need for distraction can be directed into one channel—such as the odor of rotten apples or the taste of tobacco or tea—then other distractions outside oneself are put out of competition.

Another possible explanation is that the concentrated effort of writing poetry is a spiritual activity which makes one completely forget, for the time being, that one has a body. It is a disturbance of the balance of body and mind and for this reason one needs a kind of anchor of sensation with the physical world. Hence the craving for a scent or taste or even, sometimes, for sexual activity. Poets speak of the necessity of writing poetry rather than of a liking for doing it. It is spiritual compulsion, a straining of the mind to attain heights surrounded by abysses and it cannot be entirely happy, for in the most important sense, the only reward worth having is absolutely denied: for, however confident a poet may be, he is never quite sure that all his energy is not misdirected nor that what he is writing is great poetry. At the moment when art attains its highest attainment it reaches beyond its medium of words or paints or music, and the artist finds himself realizing that these instruments are inadequate to the spirit of what he is trying to say.

Different poets concentrate in different ways. In my own mind I make a sharp distinction between two types of concentration: one is immediate and complete, the other is plodding and only completed by stages. Some poets write immediately works which, when they are written, scarcely need revision. Others write their poems by stages, feeling their way from rough draft to rough draft, until finally, after many revisions, they have produced a result which may seem to have very little connection with their early sketches.

These two opposite processes are vividly illustrated in two examples drawn from music: Mozart and Beethoven. Mozart thought out symphonies, quartets, even scenes from operas, entirely in his head—often on a journey or perhaps while dealing with pressing problems—and then he transcribed them, in their completeness, onto paper. Beethoven wrote fragments of themes in notebooks which he kept beside him, working on and developing them over years. Often his first ideas were of a clumsiness which makes scholars marvel how he could, at the end, have developed from them such miraculous results.

Thus genius works in different ways to achieve its ends. But although the Mozartian type of genius is the more brilliant and dazzling, genius, unlike virtuosity, is judged by greatness of results, not by brilliance of performance. The result must be the fullest development in a created aesthetic form of an original moment of insight, and it does not matter whether genius devotes a lifetime to producing a small result if that result be immortal. The difference between two types of genius is that one type (the Mozartian) is able to plunge the greatest depths of his own experience by the tremendous effort of a moment, the other (the Beethovenian) must dig deeper and deeper into his consciousness, layer by layer. What counts in either case is the vision which sees and pursues and attains the end; the logic of the artistic purpose.

A poet may be divinely gifted with a lucid and intense and purposive intellect; he may be clumsy and slow; that does not matter, what matters is integrity of purpose and the ability to maintain the purpose without losing oneself. Myself, I am scarcely capable of immediate concentration in poetry. My mind is not clear, my will is weak, I suffer from an excess of ideas and a weak sense of form. For every poem that I begin to write, I think of at least ten which I do not write down at all. For every poem which I do write down, there are seven or eight which I never complete.

The method which I adopt therefore is to write down as many ideas as possible, in however rough a form, in notebooks (I have at lease twenty of these, on a shelf beside my desk, going back over fifteen years), I then make use of some of the sketches and discard others.

The best way of explaining how I develop the rough ideas which I use, is to take an example. Here is a Notebook begun in 1944. About a hundred pages of it are covered with writing, and from this have emerged about six poems. Each idea, when it first occurs, is given a number. Sometimes the ideas do not get beyond one line. For example No. 3 (never developed) is the one line:—

A language of flesh and roses.

I shall return to this line in a few pages, when I speak of inspiration. For the moment, I turn to No. 13, because here is an idea which has been developed to its conclusion. The first sketch begins thus:—

a)   There are some days when the sea lies like a harp
            Stretched flat beneath the cliffs. The waves
            Like wires burn with the sun's copper glow
                        [all the murmuring blue
                              every silent]

            Between whose spaces every image
            Of sky [field and] hedge and field and boat
            Dwells like the huge face of the afternoon.
            [Lies]

When the heat grows tired, the afternoon
Out of the land may breathe a sigh
[Across these wires like a hand. They vibrate
With]
Which moves across those wires like a soft hand
[Then the vibration]
Between whose spaces the vibration holds
Every bird-cry, dog's bark, man-shout
And creak of rollock from the land and sky
With all the music of the afternoon.

Obviously these lines are attempts to sketch out an idea which exists clearly enough on some level of the mind where it yet eludes the attempt to state it. At this stage, a poem is like a face which one seems to be able to visualize clearly in the eye of memory, but when one examines it mentally or tries to think it out, feature by feature, it seems to fade.

The idea of this poem is a vision of the sea. The faith of the poet is that if this vision is clearly stated it will be significant. The vision is of the sea stretched under a cliff. On top of the cliff there are fields, hedges, houses. Horses draw carts along lanes, dogs bark far inland, bells ring in the distance. The shore seems laden with hedges, roses, horses and men, all high above the sea, on a very fine summer day when the ocean seems to reflect and absorb the shore. Then the small strung-out glittering waves of the sea lying under the shore are like the strings of a harp which catch the sunlight. Between these strings lies the reflection of the shore. Butterflies are wafted out over the waves, which they mistake for the fields of the chalky landscape, searching them for flowers. On a day such as this, the land, reflected in the sea, appears to enter into the sea, as though it lies under it, like Atlantis. The wires of the harp are like a seen music fusing seascape and landscape.

Looking at this vision in another way, it obviously has symbolic value. The sea represents death and eternity, the land represents the brief life of the summer and of one human generation which passes into the sea of eternity. But let me here say at once that although the poet may be conscious of this aspect of his vision, it is exactly what he wants to avoid stating, or even being too concerned with. His job is to recreate his vision, and let it speak its moral for itself. The poet must distinguish clearly in his own mind between that which most definitely must be said and that which must not be said. The unsaid inner meaning is revealed in the music and the tonality of the poem, and the poet is conscious of it in his knowledge that a certain tone of voice, a certain rhythm, are necessary.

In the next twenty versions of the poem I felt my way towards the clarification of the seen picture, the music and the inner feeling. In the first version quoted above, there is the phrase in the second and third lines

The waves
Like wires burn with the sun's copper glow.

This phrase fuses the image of the sea with the idea of music, and it is therefore a key-phrase, because the theme of the poem is the fusion of the land with the sea. Here, then, are several versions of these one and a quarter lines, in the order in which they were written:—

b)   The waves are wires
         Burning as with the secret song of fires

c)   The day burns in the trembling wires
         With a vast music golden in the eyes

d)   The day glows on its trembling wires
         Singing a golden music in the eyes

e)   The day glows on its burning wires
         Like waves of music golden to the eyes.

f)   Afternoon burns upon its wires
         Lines of music dazzling the eyes

g)   Afternoon gilds its tingling wires
         To a visual silent music of the eyes

In the final version, these two lines appear as in the following stanza:—

h)   There are some days the happy ocean lies
         Like an unfingered harp, below the land.
         Afternoon gilds all the silent wires
         Into a burning music of the eyes.

         On mirroring paths between those fine-strung fires
         The shore, laden with roses, horses, spires,
         Wanders in water, imaged above ribbed sand.

Inspiration

The hard work evinced in these examples which are only a fraction of the work put into the whole poem, may cause the reader to wonder whether there is no such thing as inspiration, or whether it is merely Stephen Spender who is uninspired. The answer is that everything in poetry is work except inspiration, whether this work is achieved at one swift stroke, as Mozart wrote his music, or whether it is a slow process of evolution from stage to stage. Here again, I have to qualify the word "work," as I qualified the word "concentration": the work on a line of poetry may take the form of putting a version aside for a few days, weeks or years, and then taking it up again, when it may be found that the line has, in the interval of time, almost rewritten itself.

Inspiration is the beginning of a poem and it is also its final goal. It is the first idea which drops into the poet's mind and it is the final idea which he at last achieves in words. In between this start and this winning post there is the hard race, the sweat and toil.

Paul Valéry speaks of the *"une ligne donnée"* of a poem. One line is given to the poet by God or by nature, the rest he has to discover for himself. My own experience of inspiration is certainly that of a line or a phrase or a word or sometimes something still vague, a dim cloud of an idea which I feel must be condensed into a shower of words. The peculiarity of the key word or line is that it does not merely attract, as, say, the word "braggadocio" attracts. It occurs in what seems to be an active, male, germinal form as though it were the centre of a statement requiring a beginning and an end, and as though it had an impulse in a certain direction. Here are examples:—

A language of flesh and roses

This phrase (not very satisfactory in itself) brings to my mind a whole series of experiences and the idea of a poem which I shall perhaps write some years hence. I was standing in the corridor of a train passing through the Black Country. I saw a landscape of pits and pitheads, artificial mountains, jagged yellow wounds in the earth, everything transformed as though by the toil of an enormous animal or giant tearing up the earth in search of prey or treasure. Oddly enough, a stranger next to me in the corridor echoed my in-

most thought. He said: "Everything there is man-made." At this
moment the line flashed into my head

A language of flesh and roses.

The sequence of my thought was as follows: the industrial landscape which seems by now a routine and act of God which enslaves
both employers and workers who serve and profit by it, is actually
the expression of man's will. Men willed it to be so, and pitheads,
slag-heaps and the ghastly disregard of anything but the pursuit of
wealth, are a symbol of modern man's mind. In other words, the
world which we create—the world of slums and telegrams and
newspapers—is a kind of language of our inner wishes and
thoughts. Although this is so, it is obviously a language which has
got outside our control. It is a confused language, an irresponsible
senile gibberish. This thought greatly distressed me, and I started
thinking that if the phenomena created by humanity are really like
words in a language, what kind of language do we really aspire to?
All this sequence of thought flashed into my mind with the answer
which came before the question: *A language of flesh and roses.*

I hope this example will give the reader some idea of what I
mean by inspiration. Now the line, which I shall not repeat again,
is a way of thinking imaginatively. If the line embodies some of the
ideas which I have related above, these ideas must be further
made clear in other lines. That is the terrifying challenge of poetry.
Can I think out the logic of images? How easy it is to explain here
the poem that I would have liked to write! How difficult it would
be to write it. For writing it would imply living my way through
the imaged experience of all these ideas, which here are mere abstractions, and such an effort of imaginative experience requires a
life-time of patience and watching.

Here is an example of a cloudy form of thought germinated by
the word *cross,* which is the key word of the poem which exists
formlessly in my mind. Recently my wife had a son. On the first
day that I visited her after the boy's birth, I went by bus to the
hospital. Passing through the streets on the top of the bus, they all
seemed very clean, and the thought occurred to me that everything
was prepared for our child. Past generations have toiled so that any
child born today inherits, with his generation, cities, streets, organization, the most elaborate machinery for living. Everything has

been provided for him by people dead long before he was born. Then, naturally enough, sadder thoughts colored this picture for me, and I reflected how he also inherited vast maladjustments, vast human wrongs. Then I thought of the child as like a pin-point of present existence, the moment incarnate, in whom the whole of the past, and all possible futures *cross*. This word *cross* somehow suggested the whole situation to me of a child born into the world and also of the form of a poem about his situation. When the word *cross* appeared in the poem, the idea of the past should give place to the idea of the future and it should be apparent that the *cross* in which present and future meet is the secret of an individual human existence. And here again, the unspoken secret which lies beyond the poem, the moral significance of other meanings of the word "cross" begins to glow with its virtue that should never be said and yet should shine through every image in the poem.

This account of inspiration is probably weak beside the accounts that other poets might give. I am writing of my own experience, and my own inspiration seems to me like the faintest flash of insight into the nature of reality beside that of other poets whom I can think of. However, it is possible that I describe here a kind of experience which, however slight it may be, is far truer to the real poetic experience than Aldous Huxley's account of how a young poet writes poetry in his novel *Time Must Have a Stop*. It is hard to imagine anything more self-conscious and unpoetic than Mr. Huxley's account.

Memory

If the art of concentrating in a particular way is the discipline necessary for poetry to reveal itself, memory exercised in a particular way is the natural gift of poetic genius. The poet, above all else, is a person who never forgets certain sense-impressions which he has experienced and which he can re-live again and again as though with all their original freshness.

All poets have this highly developed sensitive apparatus of memory, and they are usually aware of experiences which happened to them at the earliest age and which retain their pristine significance throughout life. The meeting of Dante and Beatrice when the poet was only nine years of age is the experience which became a symbol in Dante's mind around which the *Divine Comedy* crystallized. The experience of nature which forms the subject of Wordsworth's poetry was an extension of a childhood vision of "natural presences" which surrounded the boy Wordsworth. And his decision in later life to live in the Lake District was a decision to return to the scene of these childhood memories which were the most important experiences in his poetry. There is evidence for the importance of this kind of memory in all the creative arts, and the argument certainly applies to prose which is creative. Sir Osbert Sitwell has told me that his book *Before the Bombardment,* which contains an extremely civilized and satiric account of the social life of Scarborough before and during the last war, was based on his observations of life in that resort before he had reached the age of twelve.

It therefore is not surprising that although I have no memory for telephone numbers, addresses, faces and where I have put this morning's correspondence, I have a perfect memory for the sensation of certain experiences which are crystallized for me around certain associations. I could demonstrate this from my own life by the overwhelming nature of associations which, suddenly aroused, have carried me back so completely into the past, particularly into my childhood, that I have lost all sense of the present time and place. But the best proofs of this power of memory are found in the odd lines of poems written in notebooks fifteen years ago. A few fragments of unfinished poems enable me to enter immediately into the experiences from which they were derived, the circumstances in which they were written, and the unwritten feelings in the poem that were projected but never put into words.

> . . . Knowledge of a full sun
> That runs up his big sky, above
> The hill, then in those trees and throws
> His smiling on the turf.

That is an incomplete idea of fifteen years ago, and I remember exactly a balcony of a house facing a road, and, on the other side of the road, pine trees, beyond which lay the sea. Every morning the sun sprang up, first of all above the horizon of the sea, then it climbed to the tops of the trees and shone on my window. And this memory connects with the sun that shines through my window in London now in spring and early summer. So that the memory is not exactly a memory. It is more like one prong upon which a whole calendar of similar experiences happening throughout years, collect. A memory once clearly stated ceases to be a memory, it becomes perpetually present, because every time we experience something which recalls it, the clear and lucid original experience imposes its formal beauty on the new experiences. It is thus no longer a memory but an experience lived through again and again.

Turning over these old notebooks, my eye catches some lines, in a projected long poem, which immediately re-shape themselves into the following short portrait of a woman's face:—

> Her eyes are gleaming fish
> Caught in her nervous face, as if in a net.
> Her hair is wild and fair, haloing her cheeks
> Like a fantastic flare of Southern sun.
> There is madness in her cherishing her children.
> Sometimes, perhaps a single time in years,
> Her wandering fingers stoop to arrange some flowers—
> Then in her hands her whole life stops and weeps.

It is perhaps true to say that memory is the faculty of poetry, because the imagination itself is an exercise of memory. There is nothing we imagine which we do not already know. And our ability to imagine is our ability to remember what we have already once experienced and to apply it to some different situation. Thus the greatest poets are those with memories so great that they extend beyond their strongest experiences to their minutest observations of people and things far outside their own self-centredness (the weakness of memory is its self-centredness: hence the narcissistic nature of most poetry).

Here I can detect my own greatest weakness. My memory is defective and self-centred. I lack the confidence in using it to create situations outside myself, although I believe that, in theory, there are very few situations in life which a poet should not be able to imagine, because it is a fact that most poets have experienced almost every situation in life. I do not mean by this that a poet who writes about a Polar Expedition has actually been to the North Pole. I mean, though, that he has been cold, hungry, etc., so that it is possible for him by remembering imaginatively his own felt experiences to know what it is like to explore the North Pole. That is where I fail. I cannot write about going to the North Pole.

Faith

It is evident that a faith in their vocation, mystical in intensity, sustains poets. There are many illustrations from the lives of poets to show this, and Shakespeare's sonnets are full of expressions of his faith in the immortality of his lines.

From my experience I can clarify the nature of this faith. When I was nine, we went to the Lake District, and there my parents read me some of the poems of Wordsworth. My sense of the sacredness of the task of poetry began then, and I have always felt that a poet's was a sacred vocation, like a saint's. Since I was nine, I have wanted to be various things, for example, Prime Minister (when I was twelve). Like some other poets I am attracted by the life of power and the life of action, but I am still more repelled by them. Power involves forcing oneself upon the attention of historians by doing things and occupying offices which are, in themselves, important, so that what is truly powerful is not the soul of a so-called powerful and prominent man but the position which he fills and the things which he does. Similarly, the life of "action" which seems so very positive is, in fact, a selective, even a negative kind of life. A man of action does one thing or several things because he does not do something else. Usually men who do very spectacular things fail completely to do the ordinary things which fill the lives of most normal people, and which would be far more heroic and spectacular perhaps, if they did not happen to be done by many people. Thus in practice the life of action has always seemed to me an act of cutting oneself off from life.

Although it is true that poets are vain and ambitious their vanity and ambition are of the purest kind attainable in this world, for the saint renounces ambition. They are ambitious to be accepted for what they ultimately are as revealed by their inmost experiences, their finest perceptions, their deepest feelings, their uttermost sense of truth, in their poetry. They cannot cheat about these things, because the quality of their own being is revealed not in the noble sentiments which their poetry expresses, but in sensibility, control of language, rhythm and music, things which cannot be attained by a vote of confidence from an electorate, or by the office of Poet Laureate. Of course, work is tremendously important, but, in poetry, even the greatest labor can only serve to reveal the intrinsic qualities of soul of the poet as he really is.

Since there can be no cheating, the poet, like the saint, stands in all his works before the bar of a perpetual day of judgment. His vanity of course is pleased by success, though even success may contribute to his understanding that popularity does not confer on him the favorable judgment of all the ages which he seeks. For what does it mean to be praised by one's own age, which is soaked in crimes and stupidity, except perhaps that future ages, wise where we are foolish, will see him as a typical expression of this age's crimes and stupidity? Nor is lack of success a guarantee of great poetry, though there are some who pretend that it is. Nor can the critics, at any rate beyond a certain limited point of technical judgment, be trusted.

The poet's faith is therefore, firstly, a mystique of vocation, secondly, a faith in his own truth, combined with his own devotion to a task. There can really be no greater faith than the confidence that one is doing one's utmost to fulfil one's high vocation, and it is this that has inspired all the greatest poets. At the same time this faith is coupled with a deep humility because one knows that, ultimately, judgment does not rest with oneself. All one can do is to achieve nakedness, to be what one is with all one's faculties and perceptions, strengthened by all the skill which one can acquire, and then to stand before the judgment of time.

In my Notebooks, I find the following Prose Poem, which expresses these thoughts:

> *Bring me peace bring me power bring me assurance. Let me reach the bright day, the high chair, the plain desk, where my hand at last controls the words, where anxiety no longer undermines me. If I don't reach these I'm thrown to the wolves, I'm a restless animal wandering from place to place, from experience to experience.*
>
> *Give me the humility and the judgment to live alone with the deep and rich satisfaction of my own creating: not to be thrown into doubt by a word of spite or disapproval.*
>
> *In the last analysis don't mind whether your work is good or bad so long as it has the completeness, the enormity of the whole world which you love.*

Song

Inspiration and song are the irreducible final qualities of a poet which make his vocation different from all others. Inspiration is an experience in which a line or an idea is given to one, and perhaps also a state of mind in which one writes one's best poetry. Song is far more difficult to define. It is the music which a poem as yet un-thought of will assume, the empty womb of poetry for ever in the poet's consciousness, waiting for the fertilizing seed.

Sometimes, when I lie in a state of half-waking half-sleeping, I am conscious of a stream of words which seem to pass through my mind, without their having a meaning, but they have a sound, a sound of passion, or a sound recalling poetry that I know. Again sometimes when I am writing, the music of the words I am trying to shape takes me far beyond the words, I am aware of a rhythm, a dance, a fury, which is as yet empty of words.

In these observations, I have said little about headaches, mid-night oil, pints of beer or of claret, love affairs, and so on, which are supposed to be stations on the journeys of poets through life. There is no doubt that writing poetry, when a poem appears to succeed, results in an intense physical excitement, a sense of re-lease and ecstasy. On the other hand, I dread writing poetry, for, I suppose, the following reasons: a poem is a terrible journey, a painful effort of concentrating the imagination; words are an ex-tremely difficult medium to use, and sometimes when one has spent days trying to say a thing clearly one finds that one has only said it dully; above all, the writing of a poem brings one face to face with one's own personality with all its familiar and clumsy limitations. In every other phase of existence, one can exercise the orthodoxy of a conventional routine: one can be polite to one's friends, one can get through the day at the office, one can pose, one can draw attention to one's position in society, one is—in a word—dealing with men. In poetry, one is wrestling with a god.

Usually, when I have completed a poem, I think "this is my best poem," and I wish to publish it at once. This is partly because I only write when I have something new to say, which seems more worth while than what I have said before, partly because optimism about my present and future makes me despise my past. A few days after I have finished a poem, I relegate it to the past of all my other wasted efforts, all the books I do not wish to open.

Perhaps the greatest pleasure I have got from poems that I have written is when I have heard some lines quoted which I have not at once recognized. And I have thought "how good and how interesting," before I have realized that they are my own.

In common with other creative writers I pretend that I am not, and I am, exceedingly affected by unsympathetic criticism, whilst praise usually makes me suspect that the reviewer does not know what he is talking about. Why are writers so sensitive to criticism? Partly, because it is their business to be sensitive, and they are sensitive about this as about other things. Partly, because every serious creative writer is really in his heart concerned with reputation and not with success (the most successful writer I have known, Sir Hugh Walpole, was far and away the most unhappy about his reputation, because the "highbrows" did not like him). Again, I suspect that every writer is secretly writing for *someone,* probably for a parent or teacher who did not believe in him in childhood. The critic who refuses to "understand" immediately becomes identified with this person, and the understanding of many admirers only adds to the writer's secret bitterness if this one refusal persists.

Gradually one realizes that there is always this someone who will not like one's work. Then, perhaps, literature becomes a humble exercise of faith in being all that one can be in one's art, of being more than oneself, expecting little, but with a faith in the mystery of poetry which gradually expands into a faith in the mysterious service of truth.

Yet what failures there are! And how much mud sticks to one; mud not thrown by other people but acquired in the course of earning one's living, answering or not answering the letters which one receives, supporting or not supporting public causes. All one can hope is that this mud is composed of little grains of sand which will produce pearls.

A Poet at Work

*With the final selection in Part One
we abandon the psychology of creation for the details of the poet's craft.
Curtis Bradford reproduces Yeats' worksheets and comments upon the
changes that occurred as two poems moved toward completion. In order
to get the full benefit of Bradford's demonstration, the reader would do
well to familiarize himself beforehand with both "Sailing to Byzantium" and "Byzantium" as they appear in their final form. Such preparation will help him to follow the complicated process of development
through successive drafts, a process involving some sudden inspired
leaps, many false starts, much trial and error, and the adaptation in new
circumstances of materials which had earlier been considered and cast
aside.*

CURTIS BRADFORD

Yeats's Byzantium Poems:
A Study of Their Development

1. Background

Yeats's interest in Byzan-
tine art and civilization began in the Nineties and continued
through his life. The first issue of "Rosa Alchemica" (1896) refers
to the mosaic work at Ravenna ("mosaic not less beautiful than the
mosaic in the Baptistery at Ravenna, but of a less severe beauty"),[1]

"Yeats's Byzantium Poems: A Study of Their Development." This essay is
a revision of an essay which appeared in PMLA, LXXV (March 1960), pp.
110-125. Copyright © 1960 by Curtis B. Bradford and Mrs. W. B. Yeats.

[1] The reference to "Byzantine mosaic" in the final text of "Rosa Alchemica" (*Early Poems and Stories*, New York, 1925, p. 467) is not to be

work which Yeats probably saw when in 1907 he travelled in Italy with Lady Gregory. Unfortunately, Yeats has left us no account of his visit to Ravenna. A revision of "The Holy Places," final section of *Discoveries,* made for the 1912 edition of *The Cutting of an Agate,* shows that between 1906 and 1912 Yeats's knowledge of Byzantine history had increased. In 1906 he wrote of "an unstable equilibrium of the whole European mind that would not have come had Constantinople wall been built of better stone"; in 1912 this became "had John Palaeologus cherished, despite that high and heady look . . . a hearty disposition to fight the Turk." In preparation for the "Dove or Swan" section of *A Vision,* which Yeats wrote at Capri in February 1925, and left virtually unchanged in the revised *A Vision* of 1937, Yeats read several books[2] about Byzantine art and civilization and studied Byzantine mosaics in Rome and Sicily. He did not return to Ravenna, being fearful of its miasmal air. Once Byzantium had found a place in "the System," it shortly appeared in the poetry, first in "Sailing to Byzantium," and "Wisdom" (1926–27); then changed, though not utterly, in "Byzantium" (1930).

2. *The Two Byzantiums*

From his reading and, especially, from his experience of Byzantine art Yeats constructed Byzantium, his golden city of the imagination. The Byzantium to which we travel in "Sailing to Byzantium" is Justinian's city as Yeats described it in "Dove or Swan," an imagined land where unity of being has permeated an entire cul-

---

found in the first edition (*The Secret Rose,* London, 1897, p. 224). Yeats added the reference while revising "Rosa Alchemica" for *Early Poems and Stories.* All manuscript material used is in the collection of Mrs. W. B. Yeats. Quotations are made by permission of Mrs. Yeats, The Macmillan Company, and A. P. Watt & Son.

2 The following books about Byzantium are in Yeats's library: O. M. Dalton, *Byzantine Art and Archaeology;* W. G. Holmes, *The Age of Justinian and Theodora,* Vol. 1; Mrs. Arthur Strong, *Apotheosis and After Life;* Josef Strzygowski, *Origin of Christian Church Art* (trans. by Dalton and Braunholtz). Yeats annotated only the Holmes, and of Holmes only the first chapter "Constantinople in the Sixth Century," an elaborate reconstructive description of Byzantium in Justinian's time. Nearly every page of this chapter was marked. Yeats could not have derived his favorable opinion of Byzantine culture from Holmes, whose attitude toward his subject is both condescending and unfriendly. Yeats also collected reproductions of Byzantine mosaics.

ture. Yeats wrote three comments on this poem in a manuscript book and two radio speeches.

The comment in the manuscript book is part of an account of a séance Yeats had with a London medium, Mrs. Cooper. Since Yeats wrote a longer and already published account of a "book test" which was part of this séance (in a letter to Olivia Shakespeare dated 27 October),[3] I quote only a suggestive comment somewhat different from the comment made in the letter: "I had just finished a poem in which a poet of the Middle Ages besought the saints 'in the holy fire' to send their ecstasy." (Transcribed from the manuscript book begun at Oxford, 7 April 1921.) The remark about "a poet of the Middle Ages" reminds us that the "I-persona" in a poem by Yeats is sometimes a dramatization, Yeats, that is, in a mask assumed for the duration of a poem. A knowledge of Yeats's intention here will help us to understand the successive drafts of the poem. In the early draft Yeats is consciously medievalizing; the "poet of the Middle Ages" gradually disappears until the action of the finished poem is timeless, recurrent, eternal.

The second comment was intended for a reading Yeats made from his poems over the BBC, Belfast, 8 September 1931. Yeats omitted both text and comment from the final script:

> Now I am trying to write about the state of my soul, for it is right for an old man to make his soul, and some of my thoughts upon that subject I have put into a poem called "Sailing to Byzantium." When Irishmen were illuminating the Book of Kells and making the jewelled croziers in the National Museum, Byzantium was the center of European civilization and the source of its spiritual philosophy, so I symbolize the search for the spiritual life by a journey to that city.

The third comment occurred in the broadcast "My Own Poetry," given from London, 3 July 1937. It concerns the golden bird:

[3] *Letters* (London, 1954), pp. 730-731. In dating this letter, Allan Wade supplied the year, 1927. I think the letter was written in 1926. It will fit with the 1926 letters between the letters of 24 September and 7 December (pp. 718-719); the first complete TS of "Sailing to Byzantium," quoted below, is dated in Yeats's hand 26 September 1926. In October 1927, after "Sailing to Byzantium" had been printed in *October Blast*, Yeats would not have written that he had "just finished" it. If I am right about the date of this letter, the poem was then far from being the poem we know; it was in the state found in the revised typescript of "Towards Byzantium."

I speak of a bird made by Grecian goldsmiths. There is a record of a tree of gold with artificial birds which sang. The tree was somewhere in the Royal Palace of Byzantium. I use it as a symbol of the intellectual joy of eternity, as contrasted with the instinctive joy of human life.

The central correlative of "Byzantium" is not Justinian's sixth century city. The prose version of the poem makes this clear. I give that as Yeats first wrote it, with a long cancelled passage.

Subject for a poem

Describe Byzantium as it is in the system towards the end of the first Christian millennium. (The worn ascetics on the walls contrasted with their [?] splendour. A walking mummy. A spiritual refinement and perfection amid a rigid world. A sigh of wind—autumn leaves in the streets. The divine born amidst natural decay.)

April 30 [1930]

In ink of a different color, hence presumably at a later time, Yeats cancelled the passage I have placed in parentheses, and wrote over it:

. . . A walking mummy; flames at the street corners where the soul is purified. Birds of hammered gold singing in the golden trees. In the harbour [dolphins] offering their backs to the wailing dead that they may carry them to paradise. (Both passages transcribed from the MS of the 1930 Diary.)

When we look in *A Vision* for a description of Byzantium near the end of the tenth century, we do not easily find it. Perhaps Yeats had in mind the concluding paragraphs of section IV of "Dove or Swan," perhaps he is there describing both Eastern and Western Europe. The thought of those paragraphs is similar to the thought of the original prose version of "Byzantium," quoted above, especially in this passage:

. . . All that is necessary to salvation is known, but as I conceive the age there is much apathy. Man awaits death and judgment with nothing to occupy the worldly faculties and is helpless before the world's disorder, and this may have dragged up out of the subconscious the conviction that the world was about to end. Hidden, except at rare moments of excitement or revelation, and even then shown but in symbol, the stream of *recurrence,* set in motion by the

Galilean Symbol, has filled its basin, and seems motionless for an instant before it falls over the rim. . . . (*A Vision,* 1924, pp. 195-196)

In this later Byzantium unity of being is threatened, though it is miraculously restored when the symbolic dolphins carry the souls of the dead to a Yeatsean paradise, a paradise of art, art which is at once sensual and spiritual. Yeats makes this interpretation of "Byzantium" in a passage cancelled from the MS of his unpublished lecture "Modern Ireland," written for his final American lecture tour of 1932–33. He has been writing of O'Leary, to whom he has ascribed Aristotle's "magnificence." He then stops to comment on "magnificence."

Aristotle says that if you give a ball to [a] child, and if it was the best ball in the market, though it cost but sixpence, it is an example of magnificence: and style, whether in life or literature, comes, I think, from excess, from that something over and above utility which wrings the heart (In my later poems I have called it Byzantium, that city where the saints showed their wasted forms upon a background of gold mosaic, and an artificial bird sang upon a tree of gold in the presence of the emperor; and in one poem I have pictured the ghosts swimming, mounted upon dolphins, through the sensual seas, that they may dance upon its pavements). (Transcribed from the MS. I have placed the cancelled passage in parentheses.)

This comment, taken together with the fact that Byzantine art works break the flood of images, the bitter furies of complexity at the climax of "Byzantium," indicates that Yeats's later Byzantium, though he distinguishes it from his earlier, remains essentially the same. This sameness in difference is a characteristic stratagem with Yeats. In the development of nearly all his recurring symbols new shades of meaning will be added while the old meanings are retained.

3. *The Drafts of "Sailing to Byzantium"*

Yeats composed the drafts of "Sailing to Byzantium" in a loose-leaf notebook, and he did not number his pages before he removed the sheets for filing. I have arranged the drafts in what seems to me their proper order from internal evidence, working back and forward from a typescript version of the poem corrected in Yeats's hand and dated 26 September 1926. According to his own dating of the printed poem, Yeats finished it in 1927. The MSS which precede the typescript are in pencil; those which follow it are in ink. I have reproduced the MSS as exactly as possible, except that I have normalized the spelling. An "X" in front of a line means that it has been cancelled entire; internal cancellations are lined out; then, following a slanting rule, the revised version is given. Actually Yeats wrote his revisions above, below, or at the side of the cancelled words. Passages cued-in from the margins have been inserted in their proper places. I mark the end of each MS page by three asterisks. All other editorial matter, including added punctuation, has been placed between square brackets. The line numbers used follow the *Variorum Edition.* I place its number before a line when it reaches the form in which it was first printed.

[A1]

[After writing two lines of which I can certainly read only the opening words "Farewell friend," Yeats continues approximately as follows:]

     This is no country for old men—if our Lord
X Smiles
     Is a smiling child upon his mother's knees
     And in the hills ~~the old gods~~/ those—I know now
     What name to call them by—still hunt and love
     There is still a love for those that can still sing
X ~~All~~/ For all the
     Forever sing the song that [two cancelled words undeciphered]
        you have sung[4]

       *   *   *
[A2]

X The young

     Here all is young, and grows young day by day
     Even my Lord smiles as upon your knees.
     Upon his mother's knees—[five words undeciphered]

     Here all is young and grows young day by day
X Even my God
X Ev

[4] When this essay was first printed, I did not know of the existence of drafts A1, 2, and 3. I first saw them in Dublin in the summer of 1960.

X And God himself—comes down from [two words undeciphered]
    and smiles
X God lies upon his mother's
    Even God lies upon his mother's ~~lap/~~knees
    And holds out childish hands in play
X ~~And even,~~/And called the gods and we
X And those my fathers called the gods
X And even those I know
X And there are some—and I know not who they be
X ~~My/~~Called the gods, that

* * *
[A3]

All here—my God upon his mother's knees
Holding out his infant hands in play
X The old gods ~~still~~ at their
X The gods
X Those ~~older/~~other gods

X All here—my God
X Ever~~y~~ thing
    All in this land— ~~even my God~~/my maker at his play
    Or else asleep upon his mother's knees
    Those other gods that still—I have heard say

[WBY cancels this line, experiments with other readings in the two lines printed just below, cancels them and puts stet marks under the line above.]

X And those, to whom [two words undeciphered] the mountain
    people say
X Make love in shadow of the twilit trees
    ~~Keep/~~Are at their hunting and their gallantries
    Under the hills as in our fathers' [?] day
    The changing colour of the hills and seas
    All that mankind think they know, being young
    Cry that my tale is told my story sung

* * *
[A4]

X Now I have shipped among these mariners
X And sail south eastward toward Byzantium
X Where in the

X But now I sail among these mariners

X From things becoming to the thing become
X And sail south eastward towards Byzantium
X That I may anchored by the marble stairs
X O water that
X After a dozen storms to come

X I therefore voyage towards Byzantium
X Among these sun browned friendly mariners
X Another dozen days and we shall come
X Among the waves to where the noise of oars
X Under the shadow of its marble stairs

*   *   *

[A5]

I therefore travel towards Byzantium
Among these sun-browned pleasant mariners
Another dozen days and we shall come
Under the jetty and marble stairs
Already I have learned by spout of foam
X Creak of the sail's tackle, or of the oars
Can wake from slumber where it lies
X That fish the souls ride into paradise
That fish whereon souls ride to Paradise

X I fly from things becoming to the thing become
I fly from nature to Byzantium
Among these sunbrowned pleasant mariners
X To the gold and ivory
X I seek for gold and ivory of Byzantium

*   *   *

[A6]

Or Phidias
~~Therefore I travel~~/ Flying from nature towards Byzantium
Among these dark skinned pleasant mariners
I long for St. Sophia's sacred dome
X That I may look on painted [?] columned dome
X Statues of Phidias
X A statue by Phidias   stairs
Mirrored in water where a glint of foam
X Proves that ~~noise~~/ the splashing
X But demonstrates that splash or creak of oar
X Proves that ~~the sudden splashing of the oar~~/ ~~creaking or~~ the splash
    of oars

But demonstrates that the splash of oars
Can ~~wake~~/startle from the slumber where it lies
That fish that bears the soul to paradise

X That I may look on the great churches dome
X Statues of bronze over a marble stair
   For [word undeciphered] of gold and ivory marble stairs
   Mirror-like water where a glint of foam
   But demonstrates that sudden falling oars

[This whole page cancelled]

*   *   *

[A7]

X This Danish merchant on a relic swears
X That he will
X All that afflicts me, but this merchant swears
X To bear me eastward to Byzantium
   But now this pleasant dark skinned mariner
   Carries me towards that great Byzantium
X Where nothing changes
X And ageless beauty
   Where age is living [word undeciphered] to the oars
   That I may look ~~on St. Sophia's dome~~/ on the great shining dome
X On Phidias' marble, ~~or a~~/ or upon marble stairs
X Or mirroring waters where a glint
X On mirroring water, upon sudden foam
   On gold limbed saints and emperors
   After the mirroring waters and the foam
   Where the dark drowsy fins a moment rise
   Of fish, that ~~bear~~/ carry souls to paradise.

*   *   *

[A8]

X And most of all an ~~old~~/ aged thought harried me
X Standing in gold on church or pedestal

X Angel visible or emperors lost in gold

   O dolphin haunted wave of flooding gold
might
fold
sight
bold

*   *   *

[A9]

    Procession on procession, tier on tier
    Saints and apostles in the gold of a wall
X As though it were God's love await
X Symbolic of God's love await my prayer
X Turn their old withered heads and wait my prayer
X Or into sea like   tier
X Or lost   wall
X As if God's love   were
X As if God's burning heart awaits my prayer
X To fill me with
    As if God's love will refuse my prayer
    When prostrate on the marble step I fall
X And cry amid my tears—
    And cry aloud—"I sicken with desire
    ~~Though~~/ And fastened to a dying animal
    Cannot endure my life—O gather me
24   Into the artifice of eternity."

                       * * *

[A10]

    And if it be the dolphin's back   take
                                spring
                                sake
28   Of hammered gold and gold enamelling
    That the Greek goldsmiths make
    And set in golden leaves to sing
    Of present past and future to come
    For the instruction of Byzantium

                       * * *

[A11]

X If it must be the dolphin I shall take
X And if I stride the dolphin I shall take
    The sensual shears being past I shall not take
    No shifting form of nature's fashioning
X The shears being past but such as goldsmiths make
27   But such a form as Grecian goldsmiths make
28   Of hammered gold and gold enamelling
    At the emperor's order for his Lady's sake
    And set upon a golden bough to sing

31   To lords and ladies of Byzantium
32   Of what is past, or passing or to come

      O saints that stand amid God's sacred fire
18   As in the gold mosaic of a wall
  X   Transfigure me and make me what you were
      Consume this heart and make it what you were
  X   Rigid, abstracted, and fanatical
      Unwavering, indifferent, and fanatical
  X   The body buried away—sick with desire
      It faints upon the road—sick with desire
      ~~Being~~/ But fastened to this dying animal
      Or send the dolphin's back and gather me
24   Into the artifice of eternity.

[WBY indicates by arrows that the order of these two stanzas is to
be reversed.]

                        *   *   *

[The first complete version of the poem, which follows, is from a
typescript.[5]]

                       [B1]

                 Towards Byzantium

      All in this land—my Maker that is play
      Or else asleep upon His Mother's knees
      Others, that as the mountain people say
      Are in their hunting and their gallantries
      Under the hills as in our fathers' day
      The changing colours of the hills and seas
      All that men know, or think they know, being young
      Cry that my tale is told my story sung

  X   I therefore travel towards Byzantium
  X   Among these sun-brown pleasant mariners
  X   Another dozen days and we shall come
  X   Under the jetty and the marble stair

      [5] Norman Jeffares gives an eclectic version of this typescript in *RES*, Jan-
uary 1946. My versions are progressive. I print first the typed words, then,
below, Yeats's revisions. These revisions, including the date, are all in
Yeats's hand. There are two copies of this typescript. WBY worked on the
first pages of both copies, that is on stanzas I and II, but on only one copy of
page 2, that is stanzas III and IV. I transcribe the first page that has the latest
revisions and the revised second page.

But now these pleasant dark-skinned mariners
Carry me towards that great Byzantium
Where all is ancient, singing at the oars
That I may look in the great churches dome
On gold-embedded saints and emperors
After the mirroring waters and the foam
Where the dark drowsy fins a moment rise
Of fish that carry souls to Paradise.

O saints that stand amid God's sacred fire
18 As in the gold mosaic of a wall
Consume this heart and make it what you were
Unwavering, indifferent, fanatical
It faints upon the road sick with desire
But fastened to this dying animal
Or send the dolphin's back, and gather me
24 Into the artifice of eternity

The sensuous dream being past I shall not take
A guttering form of nature's fashioning
But rather that the Grecian smithies make
28 Of hammered gold and gold enamelling
At the Emperor's order for his lady's sake
And set upon a golden bough to sing
31 To lords and ladies of Byzantium
32 Of what is past or passing or to come.

*   *   *

[Below is Yeats's revision of the typescript reproduced above.]

[B2]

Towards Byzantium

Here all is young; the chapel walls display
An infant sleeping on His Mother's knees
Weary with toil Teig sleeps till break of day
That other wearied with night's gallantries
Sleeps the morning and the noon away
I have toiled and loved until I slept like these
A glistening labyrinth of leaves [;] a snail
Scrawls upon the mirror of the soul.

But now I travel to Byzantium
With many a dark skinned pleasant mariner
Another dozen days and I shall come

Under the jetty and the marble stair
And after to unwinking wisdom's home
The marvel of the world and gardens where
Transfigurations of the intellect
Can cure this aging body of defect

Transfigured saints that move amid the fire
18   As in the gold mosaic of a wall
Transform this heart and make it what you were
Unfaltering, indifferent, fanatical
It faints upon the road sick with desire
But fastened to this dying animal
Or send the dolphin's back, and gather me
24   Into the artifice of eternity

The sensuous dream being past I shall not take
A guttering form of nature's fashioning
But rather that the Grecian smithies make
Of hammered gold and gold enamelling
At the Emperor's order for his lady's sake
And set upon a golden bough to sing
31   To lords and ladies of Byzantium
32   Of what is past or passing or to come.

                                        September 26, 1926

                        *   *   *

                        [C1]

1   This/ Here/ That is no country for old men—the young
       Pass by me/ That travel singing of their loves, the trees
       Break/ Clad in such foliage that it seems a song
       The shadow of the birds upon the seas
X   The herring in the seas,
X   The fish in shoals
X   The leaping fish, the fields all summer long
X   Praise [several words undeciphered], but no great monument
X   Praise Plenty's horn, but no great monument
       The leaping fish/ The crowding fish commend all summer long
       Deceiving [?] abundance/ Plenty, but no monument
       Commends the never aging intellect
       The salmon rivers, the fish/ mackerel crowded seas
       Flesh/ All/ Fish flesh and fowl, all spring all summer long
X   What/ Commemorate what is begot and dies.
       But praise what is begotten, born and dies
X   And no man raises up a monument

  X To the unbegotten intellect
  X And man has made no mighty monument
  X To praise the unbegotten intellect

  [This page was entirely cancelled.]

*   *   *

[C2]

  X   the trees.
3 X Those dying generations at their song
  X The salmon leap, the mackerel crowded seas
1   That is no country for old men; the young
2   In one another's arms, birds in the trees
3   Those dying generations at their song,
4   The salmon falls, the mackerel crowded seas
    Fish flesh and fowl, all spring and summer long
    Extoll what is begotten, born and dies
    And man has made no monument to extoll
  X The unbegotten wisdom of the soul
    The unborn, undying, unbegotten soul

*   *   *

[C3]

  X Wherefore being old
9   ~~The~~/ An aged man is but a paltry thing
  X An old man is a paltry
    ~~A Paltry business to be old,~~ unless
11   ~~My~~/ Soul clap ~~hands~~/ its hands and sing, and ~~then sing more~~/
     louder sing

               dress
               oar

  X For
  X For every tatter
  X For every mortal born out of the dress
  X As time wears out

  X It is a paltry business to be old
12   For every tatter in its mortal dress

*   *   *

[C4]

9   An aged man is but a paltry thing
    Nature has cast him like a shoe unless
11   Soul clap its hands and sing, and louder sing

12   For every tatter in its mortal dress
  X   And ~~come upon~~/ except that mood in studying
      And there's no singing school like studying
      The monuments of ~~its old~~/ our magnificence
  X   And for that reason have
      And therefore have I sailed the seas and come
16   To the holy city of Byzantium

* * *

[C5]

  X   O saints amid the gold mosaic of a
  X   O saints and martyrs ~~amid~~/ in God's holy fire
18 X   As in the gold mosaic of a wall
  X   Look down upon me sickened with desire
  X   And fastened to this dying animal
  X   Immovable, or moving in a gyre

17   O sages standing in God's holy fire
18   As in the gold mosaic of a wall
19   Come from the holy fire, perne in a gyre
20   And be the singing masters of my soul
      That knows not what it is, sick with desire
      And fastened to a dying animal
      Or send the dolphin's back and gather me
24   Into the artifice of eternity

* * *

[C6]

      The dolphin's journey done I shall not take
26   My bodily form from any natural thing
27   But such a form as Grecian goldsmiths make
28   Of hammered gold and gold enamelling
      At the emperor's order, for his lady's sake
      And set me on a golden bough to sing
31   To lords [and] ladies of Byzantium
      Of what is past or present or to come

* * *

The particular interest of draft A1 is that it shows Yeats starting to work on a poem. Few of his very early drafts have survived; no doubt Yeats destroyed most of them as he progressed beyond them. In such drafts Yeats assembles his materials, gropes his way toward the metrical form he will use, and begins to explore phrasing and to set rhymes. Here Yeats picks two representatives of that youth to which he must bid farewell: the infant Christ on Mary's knees, and those immortal mountain people who turn up so frequently in Yeats's poetry. These persisted through many drafts, though eventually Yeats abandoned both of them in the C drafts. In draft A1 Yeats makes very little progress toward form or language. He does not begin to establish his rhyme scheme, though two words at the ends of lines (knees, sung) will persist through the B1 draft, indeed persist as rhyme sounds, the sole survivors of this uncertain beginning, in the finished poem (trees, seas, dies; young, song, long). Though Yeats begins to pound out lines with five metrical feet—"There is still a love for those that can still sing"—this draft seems to my ear a curious mixture of prose and verse. The lines "And in the hills those—I know not/ What name to call them by—still hunt and love" seem to me prose. The most interesting thing in the A1 draft is the opening line "This is no country for old men." This beginning entirely disappears for many drafts. Yeats returned to it in the C drafts after wandering in the wilderness for a very long time; and when he did, got the opening of the poem right.

Draft A2 carries over from A1 the infant Christ and the mountain people. All of the trial lines finished are now definitely in iambic pentameter verse, and Yeats is beginning to establish his abab rhyme scheme (day, knees, play). When Yeats rewrote the B1 version of this stanza in B2 he again picked up phrases such as "Here all is young" which he had abandoned in the A3 draft.

In the A3 draft Yeats finishes assembling the materials he will use through the B versions of this stanza by adding to the infant Christ and the mountain people a description of the natural beauty of Ireland ("The changing colour of the hills and seas") and the contrast of all this with the old age of his persona. He establishes the stanza form of the finished poem (eight lines of iambic pentameter rhymed ababababcc), and has the rhyme words he will use in B1 in place. Indeed, except for line 3, A3 and B1 are nearly identical.

In page A4 of the drafts the voyager is en route; he has apparently taken ship in Ireland and is sailing "south eastward towards Byzantium," though the mariners who man his ship seem to come from some Mediterranean country. There is only a hint of the eventual sharp contrast between the country of the young and Byzantium, which is the substance of stanzas I and III of the finished poem, in the draft lines "But now I sail among these mariners / From things becoming to the thing become." Yeats slowly works in detail; "mariners" become "sun browned friendly mariners," and Byzantine detail such as the marble steps and the boat landing is added to contrast with the Irish detail of A3. A5 begins with a revision of the last four lines of A4; then Yeats introduces the symbolic dolphin, that will persist through all the drafts of the poem. He tries but quickly abandons detail describing the voyage—"Creak of the sail's tackle," and becomes more urgent when he writes "I fly from nature to Byzantium." Surely this draft line is the seed from which the first three stanzas of the finished poem will grow slowly. At the end of this page Yeats begins to try out descriptive details that will evoke Byzantium for us, a process which he continues on A6. Eventually Yeats reserved such Byzantine detail as he uses for the third and fourth stanzas of his poem. In "gold and ivory of Byzantium" we are on our way to the golden bird. The dome of Hagia Sophia, introduced in A6, has disappeared from the finished poem, along with the ivory, the marble stairs, and Phidias' statue, but it will magnificently reappear along with the dolphin in "Byzantium." On A7 Yeats achieves the substance of stanza II as that will appear in the earliest version of the complete poem, the typescript with the title "Towards Byzantium." His imagined persona, "a poet of the Middle Ages," is clearly present for the first time when Yeats writes "This Danish merchant on a relic swears." The relic is certain evidence that Yeats is medievalizing, and "Danish merchant" suggests that Yeats recalled the Danish kingdom that had its center in medieval Dublin. Yeats quickly cuts away particularity, goes on to explore and largely abandon detail about Byzantium with which he had already experimented, and then introduces a new detail, a mosaic picture, in the draft line "On gold limbed saints and emperors." This is a shadow of an image used in stanza III of the finished poem.

On A8 Yeats describes his imagined mosaic in greater detail—the saints become an angel momentarily; he then lists a series of rhyme words which he never did use. On A9 stanza III begins to take shape. The figures in the imagined mosaic have become a procession of saints and apostles.

> in the gold of a wall
> As though it were God's love.

They will refuse the protagonist's prayer:

> "I sicken with desire
> And fastened to a dying animal
> Cannot endure my life—O gather me
> Into the artifice of eternity."

The splendid final line of stanza III seems to have sprung full blown; while composing Yeats often invented especially felicitous phrases without false starts. During the process of this remarkable draft Yeats gets five of his eventual rhyme words into place—wall, desire, animal, me, eternity—and nearly completes lines 21–24.

A10 is the first draft of stanza IV; again, this takes shape quickly. Its principal image, the golden bird singing among golden leaves, is in place as is the description of the content of its song. Five rhyme words have been chosen—take, enamelling, sing, come, Byzantium —though the final couplet will be transposed in the next draft. Line 28 is finished. At the top of A11 Yeats continues work on stanza IV and very nearly completes it. At the beginning he carries over the dolphin from the preceding draft and symbolizes the protagonist's journey from time to eternity by a ride on the dolphin's back; then he abandons this for "The sensual shears," presumably the shears of Atropos. In line 30 "And set in golden leaves to sing" becomes "And set upon a golden bough to sing"; placing the golden bird upon the talismanic golden bough is surely a felicitous change. What was a descriptive detail without associations becomes a complex image charged with associations. Seven of the eight rhyme words are in place; line 30 is nearly finished, lines 27, 28, 31, and 32 are finished.

On the lower half of the page Yeats returns to stanza III and makes good progress with it. The first two lines gain intensity when Yeats reverses the elements of his comparison: we are no longer merely contemplating a mosaic picture; the saints "stand amid God's sacred fire / As in the gold mosaic of a wall." The protagonist prays to these saints.

> Consume this heart and make it what you were
> Unwavering, indifferent, and fanatical.

This prayer differs radically from that in the finished poem, where the "sages" are asked to "be the singing-masters of my soul." At the end of the page stanza III is less far along than stanza IV, but six rhyme words are in place and two lines are finished (18, 24).

Drafts B1 and B2 which follow, the type-script of the complete poem and a revision of the typescript, are adopted from the A drafts. At the end of the revision stanzas III and IV are virtually complete; Yeats has still not achieved any lines he will keep in stanzas I and II.

Yeats begins by picking up a phrase from A4 for his title; he then goes on in stanza I to describe the Ireland from which his protagonist will sail to Byzantium. This stanza is still very much in process. There are hints at the country of the young in "Are in their hunting and their gallantries" and "The changing colours of the hills and seas," and the old age theme begins to appear at the close of the draft. Stanza II begins as in A5, then Yeats cancels four lines and writes another version which slightly changes A7. In stanzas III and IV he makes a few important changes: he drops "and" from the fourth line of III and changes the imagery and improves the wording of the first two lines of IV:

> The sensual shears being past I shall not take
> No shifting form of nature's fashioning

becomes

> The sensuous dream being past I shall not take
> A guttering form of nature's fashioning.

In revising this typescript Yeats makes stanza I more precisely Irish than it has been or will be by his reference to Teig, and we see the "poet of the Middle Ages" giving way to WBY in the line "I have toiled and loved until I slept like these"; the revision ends with a portentous metaphor: "a snail / Scrawls upon the mirror of the soul." Yeats has rewritten every line, and yet he has still not achieved anything that he will keep. In revising stanza II Yeats again rewrote every line without achieving any final results. He drops his first references to the dolphin and the mosaic picture; by reserving these for stanza III he enhances the drama of their appearances. Again, as in stanza I, he is on the way to stanza II of the finished poem, especially in the closing couplet "Transfigurations of the intellect / Can cure this aging body of defect." The slight changes made in III and IV require no comment.

Stanzas I and II were still far from finished when Yeats dated his revision 26 September 1926. Apparently he left the poem in this form for some months, for his own dating of the finished poem is 1927. On page C1 Yeats is moving very rapidly toward the final version of stanza 1. He abandons all specifically Irish allusion[6] in favor of a country of the young that is timeless and placeless. This he vividly describes in a series of images of sensuality: lovers, trees, birds, fish which all "praise what is begotten, born and dies," whereas "man has made no mighty monument / To praise the unbegotten intellect." On this page Yeats puts seven rhyme words in place, he nearly finishes lines 2 through 6, he completes his first line. Lines 7 and 8 are still far from finished, though their essential ingredients are present in the words "mighty monument" and "unbegotten intellect." Yeats nearly completed his first stanza on page C2. Though his magnificent seventh and eighth lines still elude him, he completes lines 1–4 and improves lines 5 and 6.

On pages C3 and C4 Yeats accomplished equal wonders with drafts of his new second stanza. There is no hint yet of the scarecrow of line 10, that already many-times-tried figure from Yeats's phantasmagoria, but in this partial draft Yeats does complete lines 9, 11, and 12. At line 11 Yeats greatly enhances the drama of his poem when he recollects Blake's vision of the soul of his dead brother carried up to heaven clapping its hands for joy.[7] On sheet C4 Yeats gets all his rhyme words in place, finishes lines 9, 11, 12, and 16, and nearly finishes the remaining lines. When we recall what a weak thing stanza II was in "Towards Byzantium," these pages show us Yeats's creative power at its height.

Much less required to be done to stanzas III and IV, though the changes Yeats makes are among the most interesting to be found in these drafts. Yeats begins with an improved version of his first five lines which takes off directly from the revised typescript. Yeats breaks this off after introducing the word "gyre." Then he starts again, changes the saints to sages, and completes lines 17–20 in

[6] Yeats had rather frequently to reduce the amount of Irish allusion in his works. In the scenario and early drafts of *The King of the Great Clock Tower*, for instance, the King is O'Rourke of Breifny whose grandfather had married Dervorgilla. The excision of O'Rourke helped to make the myth Yeats was writing universal.

[7] G. B. Saul notes (*Prolegomena*, Philadelphia, 1957, p. 123) that L. A. G. Strong commented on this allusion in *Personal Remarks* (New York, 1953), p. 32.

final form. When Yeats changed the saints to sages he again made
his poem more universal; with this change he seems to abandon entirely his "poet of the Middle Ages." He now prays to the wise of
all ages and cultures who have preceded him into eternity or, as
Yeats would have said, "the other life," that they become "the singing masters of my soul." The introduction of the word "gyre" is
also critically important, for it raises the question of the degree to
which Yeats intended "Sailing to Byrantium" to be read as a "sys-
temic" poem. The word "gyre" does not occur very frequently in
Yeats's poetry. When it does, as in his late poem "The Gyres," it is
usually emblematic of the cyclical process of history.[8] In the cancelled lines where Yeats first introduced "gyre" into the drafts of
"Sailing to Byzantium," it was applied to the protagonist; he was
"immovable, or moving in a gyre." This is Yeats's way of saying
that he was involved in the historic process. Now Yeats has his
protagonist beseech the sages to leave momentarily the holy fire
which symbolizes their eternal ecstasy and enter the gyre again in
order that they may "be the singing masters of my soul," may help
him put off the "dying animal" and enter the "artifice of eternity,"
help him, that is, to become a golden bird singing on a golden
bough. In lines 21–24 Yeats retains most of the wording used in the
revised typescript.

On sheet C6 Yeats makes a slight revision of stanza 4. In line
25 he introduces a second allusion to the dolphin, and he finishes
lines 26–28, replacing "A guttering form" by "My bodily form" and
returning to an earlier reading "Grecian goldsmiths" in preference

[8] In revising "the Two Trees" for *Selected Poems,* 1929, Yeats introduced "gyring" into line 15. I think the change was suggested to him by the
phrase "circle of our life" in the original:

> There, through bewildered branches, go
> Winged Loves borne on in gentle strife,
> Tossing and tossing to and fro
> The flaming circle of our life.
> *Countess Kathleen* through *Poems,* 1929
> There the Loves—a circle—go,
> The flaming circle of our days,
> Gyring, spiring to and fro
> In those great ignorant leafy ways;
> *Selected Poems,* 1929

Yeats identifies the gyre with the winding stair, always, I think, emblematic
of the historical cycle, in his letter to Sturge Moore, 26 Sept. [1930]. (*Correspondence,* p. 163).

to "Grecian smithies." Lines 29–32 are nearly identical in the revised typescript and C6.

A good deal remained to be done to "Sailing to Byzantium" before it could be printed in *October Blast*. To begin, its happy title is nowhere to be found in the drafts. Yeats made changes in every stanza, and greatly improved his poem in the process.

Stanza 1. Yeats improved the diction and, I think, the movement of lines 5 and 6 when he changed

> Fish flesh and fowl, all spring and summer long
> Extoll what is begotten, born and dies

to read

> Fish flesh or fowl, commend all summer long
> Whatever is begotten born and dies.

His new seventh and eighth lines must be discussed along with his revision of line 14. In the C drafts these read

> 7 And man has made no monument to extoll
> 8 The unborn, undying, unbegotten soul
> 14 The monuments of our magnificence

Yeats's new seventh line "Caught in that sensual music all neglect" beautifully summarizes the thought of lines 1-6, a summary needed before Yeats goes on to state his contrast in line 8. In the C drafts Yeats does use "monument" in stanzas I and II, but his repetition is much less effective than in the finished poem. The repetition is not exact ("monument / monuments"), and these essential words, anticipatory of the entire development of the poem, are buried in the lines where they occur. In revising Yeats transferred "monument" to the beginning of line 8, making it plural, and sharpened his contrast of change with permanence: "Monuments of unageing intellect." With the revision of line 14 to read "Monuments of its own magnificence" monuments becomes a key or pivotal word in stanzas I and II. This revision had another result. In the C4 draft of stanza II five of the eight lines are, to my ear, in regular iambic pentameter (9, 12, 13, 14, 15), an incidence unusually high for Yeats's later poetry. The revision breaks up this tick-tock.

Stanza II. In line 10 Yeats replaced the cast shoe image with a scarecrow image, perhaps because "Nature has cast him like a shoe" makes Nature awkwardly horsy. In line 13 Yeats introduced the reading "Nor is there singing school but studying," which is less colloquial and syntactically tighter than "And there's no singing school like studying" found in the C drafts. Again, as with the change in line 14 discussed above, Yeats reduces the number of regular iambic lines. In line 15 he put an inversion into normal order: "have I sailed" becomes "I have sailed."

Stanza III. Yeats's revision of this stanza was radical. In the C5 draft lines 20–24 went

> And be the singing masters of my soul
> That knows not what it is, sick with desire
> And fastened to a dying animal
> Or send the dolphin's back and gather me
> Into the artifice of eternity.

Before printing the poem in *October Blast* Yeats revised these lines to read

> And be the singing masters of my soul.
> Consume my heart away; sick with desire
> And fastened to this dying animal.
> It knows not what it is; and gather me
> Into the artifice of eternity.

Donald Davie has suggested to me that Yeats made this revision because he came to feel a need to start "a new musical (i.e., metrical and syntactical) unit with 'sick with desire.'" What Yeats does is to break down one flowing syntactical unit into four syntactical units, the phrasing of all these units is made more crisp and pungent, and they are separated by heavier syntactical stops. When Yeats does this, he sets up a powerful counterpoint between the metrical unit, the line, and the syntactical unit, the clause. His revision also changed the thought of these lines. In the C version it is the soul "That knows not what it is"; in the finished poem the human heart knows not what it is. To achieve this more audacious statement, Yeats introduces the new thought "Consume my heart away" in line 21 and drops "knows not what it is" two lines. The syntactically weak subordinate clause "That knows not what it is" becomes a main clause "It knows not what it is." The consequence of these changes was momentous for when "knows not what it is" was dropped two lines it displaced the dolphin, present from the first uncertain beginnings of the poem.

Stanza IV. The dolphin once gone, Yeats had to drop his second allusion to it. In line 25 "The dolphin's journey done I shall not take" becomes "Once out of nature I shall never take," a clear and dramatic summary of the action of the poem up to this point and a very tight articulation with line 24. Yeats re-wrote line 29 ("At the emperor's order, for his lady's sake / To keep a drowsy emperor awake") and had, I think, a minor and a major reason for doing so. The minor reason was to avoid the repetition of "lady's" with "ladies" in line 31, made awkward by the different grammatical form of the words. More important, the dropped phrase, since it clearly expresses a chivalric idea, was a final touch of medievalizing that had to go lest it interfere with the timelessness of the finished poem. The change in line 30 shows how important revisions that seem slight can be:

> And set me on a golden bough to sing

becomes

> Or set upon a golden bough to sing.

"Set me" has the unfortunate effect of reminding us that the protagonist is still a mortal man praying for a new incarnation; in the revised line the reincarnation has miraculously occurred. Finally, in the last line of his poem Yeats returns to the reading found in B1 and B2; "Of what is past or present or to come / Of what is past, or passing, or to come."

The most surprising thing about these drafts is the persistence of the dolphin and its final disappearance. I believe that "Byzantium" grew in part from this suppression of the dolphin. The phrasing of the second poem is in several places anticipated in phrases dropped during the drafting of the first (e.g., "Grecian smithies"); its principal action is anticipated in such draft lines as

> Or send the dolphin's back, and gather me
> Into the artifice of eternity.

The explanation of Yeats's return to Byzantium is partly to be found in an exchange of letters with Sturge Moore. On 16 April 1930, Moore wrote, "Your *Sailing to Byzantium,* magnificent as

the first three stanzas are, lets me down in the fourth, as such a
goldsmith's bird is as much nature as a man's body, especially if it
only sings like Homer and Shakespeare of what is past or passing or
to come to Lords and Ladies." Yeats wrote the original prose version
of "Byzantium" on 30 April 1930, almost immediately on receiving
Moore's letter; he had a complete version done by 11 June. On 4
October 1930, Yeats wrote to Moore of "Byzantium": "The poem
originates from a criticism of yours. You objected to the last verse
of *Sailing to Byzantium* because a bird made by a goldsmith was
just as natural as anything else. That showed me that the idea
needed exposition." Yeats completed the poem in September, but
continued to improve it. When Moore was designing a cover for
The Winding Stair, he inquired about the dolphin: "Is your dolphin to be so large that the whole of humanity can ride on its back?"
Yeats replied: "One dolphin, one man. Do you know Raphael's
statue of the Dolphin carrying one of the Holy Innocents to Heav-
en?" We should remember, however, that Yeats wrote at the end
of the prose version of "Byzantium" that the idea of a second Byzantium poem had been in his head for some time.

4. The Drafts of "Byzantium"

The successive drafts of "Byzantium" were composed in a bound
manuscript book, from which I have transcribed them. Even though
the pages on which Yeats wrote were fixed by the binding, the
order of drafts is not always easy to determine. Yeats usually began on the right hand page of a two page opening, reserving the
left hand page for revision and rewriting. Revisions written in pencil occur throughout the drafts. I believe that these are late, and
that they were done at one time, so I note them. When there is no
note to the contrary, the drafts are in ink.

[Page 1 of the MS. At the top of the page Yeats established his
rhyme scheme: AABBCDDC.]

X When all that roaring rout of rascals are a bed
X When every roaring rascal is a bed
X When the last brawler's tumbled into bed
X When the emperor's brawling soldiers are a bed
X When the last brawler tumbles into bed
   When the emperor's brawling soldiers are a bed

X When the last
X The last robber
X The last benighted robber or assassin fled
X When the last
X The last robber or his
X The ~~night thieves latest victim~~/ last benighted traveler dead or fled
X Silence fallen
X When starlit purple [?]
X When deathlike sleep ~~destroys~~/ beats down the harlot's song
X And the great cathedral gong
   And silence falls on the cathedral gong
   And the drunken harlot's song

*   *   *

[The page opposite the first, from which lines 1–4 appear to have been copied clean.]

I

When the emperor's brawling soldiers are a bed
The last benighted victim dead or fled;
When silence falls on the cathedral gong
And the drunken harlot's song
A cloudy silence, or a silence lit
Whether by star or moon
I tread the emperor's town,
All my intricacies grown clear and sweet

[Added in pencil.]

   All the tumultuous floods of day recede
   Soldiers, robbers, victims are in their beds
3   Night resonance recedes—night walker's song
   After cathedral gong
X I tread among the dark intricacies
X But a
   I traverse all the town's intricacies
X A starry glittering
X All the town becomes
   Under the starlight dome;
   And things there become,
X Blood begotten shades and images
X A mystery of shades and images
X Mummies or blood begotten images
   Mummies, ~~or~~/ and shades ~~or stony~~/ and hallowed images

*   *   *

[Page 2 of the MS]

                                                    cloth
                                                    path
                                                    light as a breath

X His breathless snores and seems to beckon me
   His breathless body ~~moves and summons~~/ beckons me;
X I ~~call~~/ name it that harsh mystery
   Death and life, or call it sweet life in death
X Death in life, or that dear life in death

   And I adore that mystery
   Harsh death in life, or that dear life in death

   Before me bends ~~a something, man or shade or man~~/ an image man
       or shade
10   Shade more than man, more image than a shade,
X Treads on the intricate
X And though it is all wound in mummy cloth
X And though it seems all wound in mummy cloth
X It treads on the intricate path
X And being wound in the intricate
X And wound in the intricate mummy cloth
X It knows the winding of the path
   What if the limbs are wound in mummy cloth
   That know the winding of the path
   What if the body's dry the mouths lack breath

[The next five lines have been added at the side of the page, in
pencil.]

   Limbs that have been bound in mummy cloth
   Are more content with a winding path
13   A mouth that has no moisture and no breath
   May better summon me
   To adore

   That summon or beckon me
   I adore that mystery
X Called death in life, or
   And call it death in life, or life in death
   That I call death or li [Added in pencil]

15   I hail the superhuman
X Or death in life
   And call it etc.

                         *   *   *

[Page 3 of the MS]

17   Miracle, bird or golden handiwork
18   More miracle than bird or handiwork
  X   Sings to the starlight
  X   Set hidden [?] by golden leaf
  X   [Partial line, undeciphered]
  X   What mighty hand ~~or~~/ and imagined out of metal

      In scorn   stood   imbued
  X   In mockery of nature's blood and petal
  X   In mockery of nature's mire and blood
  X   In mockery   metal
  X   Mocking blind nature's mire and blood
  X   A great
  X   What great artificer [?]
  X   What mind decreed or hammer shaped the metal,
  X   Of golden

      ~~Sings all~~/ ~~Carols~~/Mutters night long out of a golden bough
      ~~Or sings~~/ What the birds of Hades know
  X   Or roused by star or moonlight mocks
  X   Or wakened by the moonlight ~~sings aloud~~/ scorns
      Or by the star or moonlight wakened mocks aloud
  X   Under a golden or a silver petal
  X   Under a golden
  X   Out of the glory of its changeless metal
  X   In mockery of leaf and petal
  X   Mockery of man
22   ~~A~~/ ~~Liv~~/ In glory of changeless metal
      Living leaf or petal
      And man's intricacy of mire and blood

[The following from the side of the page]

  X   Or else by the stars or moon em
      Mutters upon a starlight golden bough
      What the birds of Hades know
      Or by the moon embittered scorns aloud
22   In glory of changeless metal

                              *   *   *

[Page 4 of the MS]

      And there is a certain square where tall flames wind and unwind

And in the flames dance spirits, by ~~that~~/ their agony made pure
And though they are all folded up in flame
It cannot singe a sleeve

> live
> ~~fla~~
> sleeve

X Flames upon the marble
X A flame on the cathedral pavement flits
   At midnight on the marble pavement flits
X A certain flame
X Flames that no ~~wood~~/ ~~fuel~~/ faggot feeds, no hand has lit
   A flame ~~that~~/ nor faggot feeds, ~~no mortal~~/ nor taper lights
   Nor breath of wind disturbs and to ~~this~~/ that flame
X ~~Can~~/ ~~May the~~/ Do ~~all~~ the unrighteous spirits come
   ~~And~~/ May all unpurged spirits come
   And all their blood begotten passion leave

[Three lines in pencil, cued in from the facing page]

   ~~All~~/ ~~The~~/ May blood besotted spirits come
X And all that blood's imagination leave,
   And all blood's fury in that flame may leave
   ~~And the agony of a dan~~/ agony of trance!
   That is a measured dance
   O agony of the ~~fire~~/ flame that cannot singe a sleeve!

*   *   *

[Page 5 of the MS]

33 X A straddle on the dolphin's mire and blood
    X Come the thin shades
    X The
    X The blood besotted
33   A straddle on the dolphin's mire and blood
    X Where the
    X Come spirits where
       ~~These spirits~~/ The crowds approach; the marble breaks the flood;
    X The lettered marble of the emperor;
    X The enchanted ~~marble~~/ pavement of the emperor;
    X Shadowy feet upon the floor,
    X Innumerable ~~feet,~~/ passion heavy feet
    X Intricacy of the dancing floor

    X The intricate pavement of the emperor,

X Flame upon the dancing floor
X Simplicity

    The bronze and marble of the emperor
    Simplicity of the dancing floor

X A crowd of spirits
X Breaks
X The fin tortured
X The dolphin torn
X The dolphin tortured tide breaks
X That dolphin tortured flood breaks into spray
X That gong tormented current breaks ~~in spray~~/ in foam
X The dolphin torn, the gong tormented sea.

* * *

[Opposite page 5 of the MS]

X Breaks
    Breaks the bleak glittering intricacy
X Breaks

                X breaks into ~~foam~~/ spray
                X Breaks
X Blood blind images yet
X Blood blind images that yet
X Where blind images beget
X Where the blind images beget

X ~~Where blind~~/ Break images ~~can~~/ that yet
X Blinder images beget
X The dolphin torn, the gong tormented sea.

    Where blind images can yet
    Blinder images beget
    The dolphin torn and gong tormented sea.

* * *

[Page 6 of MS, with passages cued in from the facing page inserted]

I

1   ~~All the foul~~/ ~~loud~~/ The unpurged images of day recede
    ~~Soldier, robber and victim are~~/ The emperor's drunken soldiers are
        a bed
    Night's resonance recedes, night walker's song
    After cathedral gong;

5   A starlit or a moonlit dome disdains[9]
6   All that man is,
7   All ~~the intricacies~~/ mere complexities
       All ~~the mire and blood~~/ mere ~~blood and~~/ mire and blood of human
             veins

                                    II

9   Before me ~~treads~~/ floats an image, man or shade
10   Shade more than man, more image than a shade;
     X An image that was ~~wound~~/ bound in mummy cloth
     X ~~Best knows~~/ Recalls or can recall that winding path;
13   X A mouth that has no moisture and no breath
     X Cries out the summons
     X Can stoutly summon   X Man's blood ~~may~~/ can
     X Can merrily summon   X Can all blood summon
15   X I hail the superhuman

       [Cued in from the opposite page]

     X ~~Can best~~/ Unbinds the bobbin of the path
     X All   a breathing mouth can
                                X All breathing clay
                                X Mire and blood can summon
11   ~~A bobbin that is~~/ ~~Hades a bobbin~~/ For Hades' bobbin bound in
             mummy cloth
12   ~~Can unravel~~/ May unwind the winding path
13   A mouth that has no moisture and no breath
       Breathing mouths may summon
15   I hail the superhuman

       [Back to original page]

16   ~~And~~/ I call it death in life and life in death.

                                   III

17   Miracle, bird, or golden handiwork,
18   More miracle than bird or handiwork

       [9] Throughout the drafts, and in the Cuala Press *Words for Music,* the
spelling "distains" is found. Yeats would not have distinguished disdains/
distains in pronunciation, according to Mrs. Yeats, and she regards "distains"
as a misspelling that got into print because the Cuala Press set from Yeats's
MS. Whether Yeats corrected "distains" to "disdains" or changed "distains"
to "disdains," it seems certain that he and no other introduced the present
reading in Macmillan's *The Winding Stair.* The *Variorum Edition* shows
that the texts of poems included in *Words for Music* were very carefully
corrected for the Macmillan book. No one but Yeats could have done this
correcting.

    X Mutters upon a starlit golden bough   Planted on a starlit golden
       bough
20 X All that the birds of Hades know   Can like the cocks of Hades
       crow
21   Or by the moon embittered scorn aloud
22 X In ~~changeless~~/ measured [?] metal
    X Living leaf or petal
    X ~~And~~/ Man's ~~intricacy~~/ ~~Or blind~~/ measureless imagery of mire and
      blood

[Cued in from the facing page]

22   In ~~all simplicity of~~/ ~~All that~~/ glory of changeless metal
    X ~~Common~~/ Bird or leaf or petal
    X Living leaf or petal
    X ~~And~~/ Every complexity of mire and blood
23   Common bird or petal
    And all complexities of mire and blood

[Back to original page]

IV

At midnight on the ~~marble~~/ emperor's pavement flits
A flame nor faggot feeds nor taper lights
Nor breath disturbs, X ~~a self~~/ ~~to that~~/ flame begotten flame
              X and to that flame born flame
                a flame begotten flame
X There images and spirits come
X Images and spirits come
X ~~All~~/ There imaged spirits thither come
X ~~And~~/ There all that blood-begotten fury leave
X O agony of trance
X That is a measured dance
X O agony of flame that cannot singe a sleeve

[Cued in from the facing page]

28   Where blood begotten spirits come
29   And all complexities of fury leave.
30   Dying into a dance
31   An agony of trace
32   An agony of flame that cannot singe a sleeve.

                       *   *   *

[Page 7 of the MS]

V

33   A straddle on the dolphin's mire and blood
      ~~The images~~/ Those crowds approach, the ~~marble~~/ metal breaks the
          flood;
35 X ~~Precious metals~~/ The golden smithies of the emperor;
    X ~~Integrity~~/ ~~Simplicity~~/ Integrity of the dancing floor
    X Breaks the bleak ~~glittering intricacies~~/ aimless flood of imagery
      The precious metal of the emperor;
      Marble of the dancing floor
      Breaks that ~~bitter bleak complexity~~/ bright flood, that bleak com-
          plexity
      ~~Where~~/ Images ~~can~~/ that yet
      Worse images beget
40   That dolphin torn, that gong tormented sea.
                         June 11, [1930]

[The revised version of stanza v given below was written into a
blank space on this page some time after Yeats had completed the
next draft of "Byzantium."]

33   A straddle on the Dolphin's mire and blood
      Those crowds approach; smithies break the flood,
35   The golden smithies of the emperor;
36   Marbles of the dancing floor
      Break ~~bleak~~/ bitter, bleak, aimless complexities,
38   Those images that yet
      More images beget
40   That dolphin torn, that gong tormented sea.
                              *   *   *

[Page 8 of the MS]

Byzantium

I

1   The unpurged images of day recede;
2   The emperor's drunken soldiery are a bed;
      Night's resonance recedes, night-walker's song
4   ~~And after that the~~/ After great cathedral gong,
5   A starlit or a moonlit dome disdains
6   All that man is,
7   All mere complexities,
8   ~~All that stupidity and~~/ ~~All mere mire and blood of human veins~~/
          The fury and the mire of human veins.

II

9   Before me floats an image, man or shade.
10 Shade more than man, more image than a shade;
11 For Hades' bobbin bound in mummy cloth
12 May unwind the winding path;
13 A mouth that has no moisture and no breath
    Breathing mouths may summon.
15 I hail the superhuman;
    I call it death in life or life in death.

III

17 Miracle, bird, or golden handiwork,
18 More miracle than bird or handiwork,
19 Planted on a starlit golden bough,
20 Can like the cocks of Hades crow
21 Or by the moon embittered scorn aloud,
22 In glory of changeless metal,
23 Common bird or petal
24 And all complexities of mire or blood.

IV

    At midnight on the emperor's pavement flits
    A flame nor faggot feeds nor taper lights
    Nor breath disturbs, a flame begotten flame,
28 Where blood begotten spirits come
29 And all complexities of fury leave,
30 Dying into a dance,
31 An agony of trance,
32 An agony of flame that cannot singe a sleeve.

                    *   *   *

[Yeats completed this draft on the facing page transcribed below]

V

33 A straddle on the dolphin's mire and blood
    Those crowds approach; smithies break the flood,
35 The golden smithies of the emperor;
36 Marbles of the dancing floor
  X Break bitter, bleak, ~~aimless~~/ stupid aimless furies of complexity,
38 Those images that yet
    ~~More~~/ ~~Fresh~~/ More images beget,
40 That dolphin torn, that gong tormented sea.
  X Break the bleak fury or blind complexity

X Of images that yet
39 X Fresh images beget
37   Break bleak/ blind/ bitter furies of complexity
38   Those images that yet
39   Fresh images beget
40   [That dolphin torn, that gong tormented sea.]

*   *   *

Inserted loose in the manuscript book from which I have been transcribing is a still later MS of "Byzantium," written on two sheets of paper.

In it Yeats made several changes. Stanza IV was revised as follows:

25   At midnight on the emperor's pavement flit
26   Flames that no faggot feeds nor steel has lit
27   Nor storm disturbs, flames begotten of flame,
28   Where blood begotten spirits come, etc.

Then, in stanza V, Yeats made a change that describes the movement of the blood begotten spirits *towards* the emperor's pavement, that is towards paradise, less clearly than earlier versions.

33   A straddle on the dolphin's mire and blood
34   Spirit after spirit! The smithies break the flood, . . .

In stanza II throughout the drafts the reading

A mouth that has no moisture and no breath
Breathing mouths may summon

has persisted. Though I thought this reading might perhaps have authority, Mrs. Yeats told me it had none, that she had heard Yeats speak the poem so often saying "breathless" that she was certain he intended "breathless."

Yeats's attack in the drafts of "Byzantium" is at once quick and precise. After writing the prose version of the poem Yeats added that the subject had been in his head for some time. A study of the drafts shows that indeed it must have been, for the progression of images even in the first draft is essentially that found in the finished poem. Yeats also decided before beginning work on the poem to use once again the stanza used for "In Memory of Major Robert Gregory," "A Prayer for my Daughter," and for the middle section of "The Tower." This has the rhyme scheme AABBCDDC which Yeats set at the head of the "Byzantium" manuscript. In "Byzantium" Yeats did make one slight change in the stanza by reducing the number of metrical feet in lines 6 and 7 from four to three.[10] No doubt the fact that Yeats had already thoroughly explored this stanza partly accounts for the precision of his attack.

On page 1 and the page opposite to it Yeats drafts his first stanza. At the outset he is troubled by excessive detail, an unusual event in Yeats's drafts; he introduces quite a company of sensualists before settling on the soldiery and night-walker of the finished poem: "roaring rout of rascals / every roaring rascal / last brawler / emperor's brawling soldiers" give place to robbers, assassins, benighted travelers. Then silence falls alike on "the cathedral gong / And the drunken harlot's song." In the drafts on the opposite page Yeats retains the soldiers, the benighted victim, the harlot's song, and the cathedral gong; he then sets the night scene and introduces an "I-persona."

> I tread the emperor's town
> All my intricacies grown clear and sweet.

"Intricacies" is the key word in the first draft of "Byzantium"; in the second draft it is replaced by "complexities," the key word of the finished poem. Eventually Yeats will withhold his I-persona until line 15. In the pencil drafts which follow Yeats makes a start on the magnificent line with which the finished poem opens in "All the tumultuous floods of day recede," he transfers "intricacies" from the protagonist to the town, and first introduces the starlit dome of Hagia Sophia. The last four lines of the draft look forward toward the rest of the poem; indeed the last of them, "Mummies and shades and hallowed images" gives too much away. In spite of excess detail that needs to be cut (robbers, victims, mummies, shades, and hallowed images), this is a remarkable first draft. Four rhyme words are in place (recede, beds, song, gong), and line 3 is done.

Page 2 introduces the walking mummy of the prose version.

[10] Marion Witt discussed this stanza in "The Making of an Elegy," *MP*, XLVIII (November 1950), pp. 115-116. Frank Kermode in *Romantic Image* (London, 1957), pp. 38-40, notes that Yeats borrowed the stanza from Cowley's "Ode on the Death of Mr. William Harvey."

Yeats first establishes the rhyme words he will use in lines 11–13, then he makes two false starts in which the entire stanza, as it were, is compressed into two lines. Then in "Before me bends an image man or shade / Shade more than man, more image than a shade" he gets the essence of lines 9–10. He goes on to drafts of 11–14 and has considerable trouble though he does assemble all the materials finally used save "Hades' bobbin." In the first drafts of line 14 the mummy summons the protagonist, that is the poet, relieved of his accidence but still a living man; this perhaps explains why in all the successive drafts of this line Yeats uses the phrase "breathing mouths." Lines 15–16 are nearly complete. At the end of this draft seven rhyme words are in place; lines 10, 13, and 15 are done.

As Yeats returns to the golden bird of "Sailing to Byzantium" on page 3, his speed and assurance seem almost miraculous. He completes lines 17–18 instantly—no doubt he had composed them in his head and is merely writing them down—then has a little trouble with the lines that follow. Once the golden bird mocks nature's mire and blood, the whole stanza has been telescoped, so to speak. Mire and blood need to be reserved for the end of the stanza. Yeats fills out his stanza with description of the bird and its setting, even for a moment inventing an artificer of the bird, whom he quickly drops. Again, by the end of the draft the third stanza is nearly finished: all the rhyme sounds and seven of the rhyme words are in place, lines 17, 18, and 22 are done.

Page 4 opens with a prose outline of the fourth stanza. In my experience of Yeats's MSS, this is an unique event; writing prose versions of poems was part of Yeats's standard practice, but in no other instance known to me does he begin actual composition of a section of a poem with a prose version. Yeats goes on to list possible rhyme words, then begins his drafts. His materials fall into place quickly. The spirits summoned to the purifying dance are first "unrighteous," then "unpurged," then "blood besotted." In the second draft Yeats transfers "unpurged" to his first line with magnificent effect. Yeats finishes none of his lines in this draft, though he does set seven of his rhyme words—lit, flame, come, leave, trance, dance, sleeve. Yeats will sharpen and tighten his phrasing through several further drafts, but the basic work of composition is done.

In the first draft of his final stanza on page 5 Yeats's procedure is equally sure and direct. He writes down line 33, no doubt composed in his head, and goes on to explore details of the Byzantine art works he will use. At first he is content with the mosaic pavement mentioned in the prose version; its "marble" becomes successively "lettered marble," "enchanted pavement," "intricate pavement." Then when he writes "The bronze and marble of the emperor" he is on his way to his second and indirect allusion to the golden bird. Even more interesting is the series of cancelled draft lines in which Yeats works toward his splendid final line; his experiments lead through "fin tortured," "dolphin torn," "dolphin tortured," and "gong tormented" to the inevitability of "The dolphin torn, the gong tormented sea." Yeats ends the draft by experimenting with lines 37–39. The success of this first draft will at once be apparent when a clean copy of the final stanza is assembled:

> A straddle on the dolphin's mire and blood
> The crowds approach; the marble breaks the flood;
> The bronze and marble of the emperor
> Simplicity of the dancing floor
> Breaks the bleak glittering intricacy
> Where blind images can yet
> Blinder images beget
> The dolphin torn and gong tormented sea.

Yeats's second draft, on pages 6 and 7 of the MS, shows what a great writer at the height of his powers can do. For example, the first line in draft 1 reads "All the tumultuous floods of day recede"; now Yeats tries "foul images," "loud images," and then recalls "unpurged" from the first draft of stanza 4 and completes his splendid first line. In line 2 he first takes over the "Soldier, robber, victim" of the first draft, then happily reduces these to a single instance, the drunken soldiers. Yeats keeps lines 3 and 4, then invents lines 5 and 6 in final form out of a mere mention of the starlit dome in draft 1. In line 7 when Yeats changes "intricacies" to "complexities" he changes the key word in his poem. By the time he finishes this draft Yeats has all his rhyme words in place, lines 1, 5, 6, and 7 are done, and the rest nearly done.

In the second draft of stanza II Yeats finishes line 9 by changing "bends an image" to "treads an image," then to "floats an image." He copies line 10 and then goes on to many drafts of lines 11–12;

the enigmatic phrase "Hades' bobbin" develops slowly, but once it is achieved the next line, "May unwind the winding path," comes quickly. Lines 13–16 take the form they will keep throughout the drafts; only line 14 required much change. "May better summon me" of draft 1 becomes successively "Cries out the summons," "Can stoutly summon," "Can merrily summon," "Man's blood can [summon]," "Can all blood summon," "All breathing clay [can summon]," "Mire and blood can summon," "Breathing mouths may summon." At the end of the draft all lines except line 14 are finished. Stanza III required relatively little work. Yeats follows draft 1 closely, but introduces many improvements in diction. In draft 1 line 19 reads "Mutters upon a starlit golden bough"; Yeats changes this to "Planted on a starlit golden bough." "Mutters" somewhat deflates the golden bird, but "planted" carries the deflation further. In line 24 Yeats changes "intricacy" to "complexities," a change implicit in the changed seventh line. At the end of the draft lines 17, 18, 20–23 are done, lines 19 and 24 nearly done.

In revising stanza IV Yeats changes every line but the 26th. In line 25 "marble pavement" becomes "emperor's pavement"; in draft 1 line 28 reads "May all unpurged spirits come"; since Yeats has now introduced "unpurged" into line 1, he puts line 28 through a series of characteristic changes before settling on the reading found in the finished poem, "Where blood begotten spirits come." Lines 28–32 are finished; lines 25–27 require slight revision still.

Stanza V still required a good deal of work. Yeats makes a substantive change when he introduces a second Byzantine art work by adding an allusion to the golden bird. In line 35 Yeats, no doubt unconsciously, introduces in "smithies" a word which he had rejected in the last stanza of "Sailing to Byzantium." In draft II Yeats completes lines 33, 35, and 40, though he has cancelled line 35 in the form it will have in the finished poem. All the rhyme words are in place. The draft is dated June 11, [1930]. Yeats wrote the first prose version of "Byzantium" on April 30. He revised that, presumably after some lapse of time, before beginning his drafts; yet the poem is essentially complete in the second draft just studied. Yeats completed "Byzantium" far more quickly than was usual when he was working on a major poem.

The third and fourth drafts require little comment. In the third draft Yeats changed "soldiers" to "soldiery" in line 2. He introduced "great" into line 4 to give it four feet; it now conforms with the fourth lines of the other stanzas. The second, third, and fourth stanzas show little change. The fifth stanza did require more revision. Yeats decided to retain a form of line 35 which he had cancelled in draft II; line 37 was still giving trouble, which was resolved on the third try. In line 39 "worse images" became "fresh images." By the end of the fourth draft "Byzantium" had very nearly taken the form in which we know the poem.

The materials presented above can help us to make our own readings of the Byzantium poems, and to value properly the many interpretations that have been published. The main lines of my own readings are: Both poems are deeply concerned with Unity of Being, and with the achievement of Unity of Being through art. In "Sailing to Byzantium" the protagonist achieves the temporal aspect of Unity of Being by leaving the country of the young, dominated by sensuality, and sailing to Byzantium, symbol of the spiritual life. "Byzantium" explores Unity of Being in its eternal aspect. At the outset of the poem unpurged images of sensuality give way to a serene image of spirituality, the moonlit dome of Hagia Sophia. Death the summoner, personified as a walking mummy, calls the souls of the departed to paradise. The golden bird is again examined, but alone it is not a sufficient symbol of Yeats's paradise. A sufficient symbol is found when the ghosts of the dead swim through the sensual seas on the backs of dolphins, warm-blooded mammals, toward the mosaic pavement where they dance in the purifying flames. We have moved from complexity to ultimate simplicity; sense and spirit have become one inextricable beam; Unity of Being is an ideal valid both in Time and Eternity.

Part Two

THE POEM

Form and Content

Readers in an age of prose are often suspicious of the attention given by critics and teachers to questions of form. If poets are to be taken seriously, they must have been interested in what they were saying, not in how they said it. Since it is the content that counts, why bother to analyze figures of speech or details of versification which are, after all, only decorative elements? The closely reasoned answer which A. C. Bradley gives in "Poetry for Poetry's Sake" justifies the technical discussions which follow. He says that a poem is uniquely valuable for the experience it provides and that it is a unity of form and content which provides that experience. When we read well, form and content—Bradley calls them "form and substance" —occur as one. Although our analyzing minds may do well to abstract them for separate consideration, they are experienced as a single thing.

Bradley's answer has some important implications for critical theory. For him the special role of poetry, of this unity of form and content, is the satisfaction of human imagination. He regards this satisfaction as intrinsically valuable, a human good which cannot be judged by reference to other human goods such as moral rightness or knowledge. For him the poem is an object of contemplation occupying an aesthetic realm distinct from the realm of practical human desire. But Bradley is no dry formalist; he closes his discussion suggestively. The poet's meaning which satisfies only imagination reaches toward something boundless which might satisfy the whole man, an ultimate perfection toward which philosophy, religion, and the other arts in their own ways also reach.

A. C. BRADLEY

Poetry for Poetry's Sake

The words "Poetry
for poetry's sake" recall the famous phrase "Art for Art." It is far
from my purpose to examine the possible meanings of that phrase,
or all the questions it involves. I propose to state briefly what I
understand by "Poetry for poetry's sake," and then, after guarding
against one or two misapprehensions of the formula, to consider
more fully a single problem connected with it. And I must premise,
without attempting to justify them, certain explanations. We are
to consider poetry in its essence, and apart from the flaws which in
most poems accompany their poetry. We are to include in the idea
of poetry the metrical form, and not to regard this as a mere accident or a mere vehicle. And, finally, poetry being poems, we are to
think of a poem as it actually exists; and, without aiming here at
accuracy, we may say that an actual poem is the succession of experiences—sounds, images, thoughts, emotions—through which we
pass when we are reading as poetically as we can. Of course this
imaginative experience—if I may use the phrase for brevity—differs
with every reader and every time of reading: a poem exists in innumerable degrees. But that insurmountable fact lies in the nature
of things and does not concern us now.

What then does the formula "Poetry for poetry's sake" tell us
about this experience? It says, as I understand it, these things. First,
this experience is an end in itself, is worth having on its own account, has an intrinsic value. Next, its *poetic* value is this intrinsic
worth alone. Poetry may have also an ulterior value as a means to
culture or religion; because it conveys instruction, or softens the
passions, or furthers a good cause; because it brings the poet fame or
money or a quiet conscience. So much the better: let it be valued
for these reasons too. But its ulterior worth neither is nor can directly determine its poetic worth as a satisfying imaginative experience; and this is to be judged entirely from within. And to these
two positions the formula would add, though not of necessity, a
third. The consideration of ulterior ends, whether by the poet in
the act of composing or by the reader in the act of experiencing,

tends to lower poetic value. It does so because it tends to change the nature of poetry by taking it out of its own atmosphere. For its nature is to be not a part, nor yet a copy, of the real world (as we commonly understand that phrase), but to be a world by itself, independent, complete, autonomous; and to possess it fully you must enter that world, conform to its laws, and ignore for the time the beliefs, aims, and particular conditions which belong to you in the other world of reality.

Of the more serious misapprehensions to which these statements may give rise I will glance only at one or two. The offensive consequences often drawn from the formula "Art for Art" will be found to attach not to the doctrine that Art is an end in itself, but to the doctrine that Art is the whole or supreme end of human life. And as this latter doctrine, which seems to me absurd, is in any case quite different from the former, its consequences fall outside my subject. The formula "Poetry is an end in itself" has nothing to say on the various questions of moral judgment which arise from the fact that poetry has its place in a many-sided life. For anything it says, the intrinsic value of poetry might be so small, and its ulterior effects so mischievous, that it had better not exist. The formula only tells us that we must not place in antithesis poetry and human good, for poetry is one kind of human good; and that we must not determine the intrinsic value of this kind of good by direct reference to another. If we do, we shall find ourselves maintaining what we did not expect. If poetic value lies in the stimulation of religious feelings, *Lead, Kindly Light*[1] is no better a poem than many a tasteless version of a Psalm: if in the excitement of patriotism, why is *Scots, Wha Hae*[2] superior to *We Don't Want to Fight*? if in the mitigation of the passions, the Odes of Sappho will win but little praise: if in instruction, Armstrong's *Art of Preserving Health* should win much.

Again, our formula may be accused of cutting poetry away from its connection with life. And this accusation raises so huge a problem that I must ask leave to be dogmatic as well as brief. There is plenty of connection between life and poetry, but it is, so to say, a connection underground. The two may be called different forms of the same thing: one of them having (in the usual sense) reality, but seldom fully satisfying imagination; while the other offers

[1] Newman.
[2] Burns.

something which satisfies imagination but has not full "reality."
They are parallel developments which nowhere meet, or, if I may
use loosely a word which will be serviceable later, they are analogues. Hence we understand one by help of the other, and even, in
a sense, care for one because of the other; but hence also, poetry
neither is life, nor, strictly speaking, a copy of it. They differ not
only because one has more mass and the other a more perfect shape,
but because they have different *kinds* of existence. The one touches
us as beings occupying a given position in space and time, and having feelings, desires, and purposes due to that position: it appeals
to imagination, but appeals to much besides. What meets us in
poetry has not a position in the same series of time and space, or,
if it has or had such a position, it is taken apart from much that
belonged to it there; and therefore it makes no direct appeal to
those feelings, desires, and purposes, but speaks only to contemplative imagination—imagination the reverse of empty or emotionless,
imagination saturated with the results of "real" experience, but
still contemplative. Thus, no doubt, one main reason why poetry
has poetic value for us is that it presents to us in its own way something which we meet in another form in nature or life; and yet the
test of its poetic value for us lies simply in the question whether it
satisfies our imagination; the rest of us, our knowledge or conscience, for example, judging it only so far as they appear transmuted in our imagination. So also Shakespeare's knowledge or his
moral insight, Milton's greatness of soul, Shelley's "hate of hate"
and "love of love," and that desire to help men or make them happier which may have influenced a poet in hours of meditation—all
these have, as such, no poetical worth: they have that worth only
when, passing through the unity of the poet's being, they reappear
as qualities of imagination, and then are indeed mighty powers in
the world of poetry.

I come to a third misapprehension, and so to my main subject.
This formula, it is said, empties poetry of its meaning: it is really
a doctrine of form for form's sake. "It is of no consequence what a
poet says, so long as he says the thing well. The *what* is poetically
indifferent: it is the *how* that counts. Matter, subject, content, substance, determines nothing; there is no subject with which poetry
may not deal: the form, the treatment, is everything. Nay, more:
not only is the matter indifferent, but it is the secret of Art to

'eradicate the matter by means of the form,' "—phrases and statements like these meet us everywhere in current criticism of literature and the other arts. They are the stock-in-trade of writers
who understand of them little more than the fact that somehow
or other they are not "bourgeois." But we find them also seriously used by writers whom we must respect, whether they are
anonymous or not; something like one or another of them might
be quoted, for example, from Professor Saintsbury, the late
R. A. M. Stevenson, Schiller, Goethe himself; and they are the
watchwords of a school in the one country where ethetics has
flourished. They come, as a rule, from men who either practice one
of the arts, or, from study of it, are interested in its methods. The
general reader—a being so general that I may say what I will of
him—is outraged by them. He feels that he is being robbed of almost all that he cares for in a work of art. "You are asking me," he
says, "to look at the Dresden Madonna as if it were a Persian rug.
You are telling me that the poetic value of *Hamlet* lies solely in its
style and versification, and that my interest in the man and his fate
is only an intellectual or moral interest. You allege that, if I want
to enjoy the poetry of *Crossing the Bar,* I must not mind what
Tennyson says there, but must consider solely his way of saying it.
But in that case I can care no more for a poem than I do for a set
of nonsense verses; and I do not believe that the authors of *Hamlet*
and *Crossing the Bar* regarded their poems thus."

These antitheses of subject, matter, substance on the one side,
form, treatment, handling on the other, are the field through
which I especially want, in this lecture, to indicate a way. It is a
field of battle; and the battle is waged for no trivial cause; but the
cries of the combatants are terribly ambiguous. Those phrases of
the so-called formalist may each mean five or six different things.
Taken in one sense they seem to me chiefly true; taken as the general reader not unnaturally takes them, they seem to me false and
mischievous. It would be absurd to pretend that I can end in a few
minutes a controversy which concerns the ultimate nature of Art,
and leads perhaps to problems not yet soluble; but we can at least
draw some plain distinctions which, in this controversy, are too
often confused.

In the first place, then, let us take "subject" in one particular
sense; let us understand by it that which we have in view when,

looking at the title of an unread poem, we say that the poet has chosen this or that for his subject. The subject, in this sense, so far as I can discover, is generally something, real or imaginary, as it exists in the minds of fairly cultivated people. The subject of *Paradise Lost* would be the story of the Fall as that story exists in the general imagination of a Bible-reading people. The subject of Shelley's stanzas *To a Skylark* would be the ideas which arise in the mind of an educated person when, without knowing the poem, he hears the word "skylark." If the title of a poem conveys little or nothing to us, the "subject" appears to be either what we should gather by investigating the title in a dictionary or other book of the kind, or else such a brief suggestion as might be offered by a person who had read the poem, and who said, for example, that the subject of *The Ancient Mariner* was a sailor who killed an albatross and suffered for his deed.

Now the subject, in this sense (and I intend to use the word in no other), is not, as such, inside the poem, but outside it. The contents of the stanzas *To a Skylark* are not the ideas suggested by the word "skylark" to the average man; they belong to Shelley just as much as the language does. The subject, therefore, is not the matter *of* the poem at all; and its opposite is not the *form* of the poem, but the whole poem. The subject is one thing; the poem, matter and form alike, another thing. This being so, it is surely obvious that the poetic value cannot lie in the subject, but lies entirely in its opposite, the poem. How can the subject determine the value when on one and the same subject poems may be written of all degrees of merit and demerit; or when a perfect poem may be composed on a subject so slight as a pet sparrow,[3] and, if Macaulay[4] may be trusted, a nearly worthless poem on a subject so stupendous as the omnipresence of the Deity? The "formalist" is here perfectly right. Nor is he insisting on something unimportant. He is fighting against our tendency to take the work of art as a mere copy or reminder of something already in our heads, or at the best as a suggestion of some idea as little removed as possible from the familiar. The sightseer who promenades a picture-gallery, remarking that this portrait is so like his cousin, or that landscape the very image of his birthplace, or who, after satisfying himself that one picture

[3] Catullus.
[4] *Robert Montgomery.*

is about Elijah, passes on rejoicing to discover the subject, and nothing but the subject, of the next—what is he but an extreme example of this tendency? Well, but the very same tendency vitiates much of our criticism, much criticism of Shakespeare, for example, which, with all its cleverness and partial truth, still shows that the critic never passed from his own mind into Shakespeare's; and it may be traced even in so fine a critic as Coleridge, as when he dwarfs the sublime struggle of Hamlet into the image of his own unhappy weakness. Hazlitt by no means escaped its influence. Only the third of that great trio, Lamb, appears almost always to have rendered the conception of the composer.

Again, it is surely true that we cannot determine beforehand what subjects are fit for Art, or name any subject on which a good poem might not possibly be written. To divide subjects into two groups, the beautiful or elevating, and the ugly or vicious, and to judge poems according as their subjects belong to one of these groups or the other, is to fall into the same pit, to confuse with our preconceptions the meaning of the poet. What the thing is in the poem he is to be judged by, not by the thing as it was before he touched it; and how can we venture to say beforehand that he cannot make a true poem out of something which to us was merely alluring or dull or revolting? The question whether, having done so, he ought to publish his poem; whether the thing in the poet's work will not be still confused by the incompetent Puritan or the incompetent sensualist with the thing in *his* mind, does not touch this point; it is a further question, one of ethics, not of art. No doubt the upholders of "Art for Art's sake" will generally be in favor of the courageous course, of refusing to sacrifice the better or stronger part of the public to the weaker or worse; but their maxim in no way binds them to this view. Rossetti suppressed one of the best of his sonnets, a sonnet chosen for admiration by Tennyson, himself extremely sensitive about the moral effect of poetry; suppressed it, I believe, because it was called fleshly. One may regret Rossetti's judgment and at the same time respect his scrupulousness; but in any case he judged in his capacity of citizen, not in his capacity of artist.

So far then the "formalist" appears to be right. But he goes too far, I think, if he maintains that the subject is indifferent and that all subjects are the same to poetry. And he does not prove his point

by observing that a good poem might be written on a pin's head,
and a bad one on the Fall of Man. That truth shows that the subject *settles* nothing, but not that it counts for nothing. The Fall of
Man is really a more favorable subject than a pin's head. The Fall
of Man, that is to say, offers opportunities of poetic effects wider in
range and more penetrating in appeal. And the fact is that such a
subject, as it exists in the general imagination, has some esthetic
value before the poet touches it. It is, as you may choose to call it,
an inchoate poem or the débris of a poem. It is not an abstract idea
or a bare isolated fact, but an assemblage of figures, scenes, actions,
and events, which already appeal to emotional imagination; and it
is already in some degree organized and formed. In spite of this a
bad poet would make a bad poem on it; but then we should say he
was unworthy of the subject. And we should not say this if he
wrote a bad poem on a pin's head. Conversely, a good poem on a
pin's head would almost certainly transform its subject far more
than a good poem on the Fall of Man. It might revolutionize its subject so completely that we should say, "The subject may be a pin's
head, but the substance of the poem has very little to do with it."

This brings us to another and a different antithesis. Those figures, scenes, events, that form part of the subject called the Fall of
Man, are not the substance of *Paradise Lost;* but in *Paradise Lost*
there are figures, scenes, and events resembling them in some degree. These, with much more of the same kind, may be described
as its substance, and may then be contrasted with the measured
language of the poem, which will be called its form. Subject is the
opposite not of form but of the whole poem. Substance is within
the poem, and its opposite, form, is also within the poem. I am not
criticizing this antithesis at present, but evidently it is quite different from the other. It is practically the distinction used in the old-
fashioned criticism of epic and drama, and it flows down, not un-
sullied, from Aristotle. Addison,[5] for example, in examining *Paradise Lost* considers in order the fable, the characters, and the sentiments; these will be the substance: then he considers the language,
that is, the style and numbers; this will be the form. In like manner, the substance or meaning of a lyric may be distinguished from
the form.

Now I believe it will be found that a large part of the contro-

[5] *Spectator,* 267, &c.

versy we are dealing with arises from a confusion between these two distinctions of substance and form, and of subject and poem. The extreme formalist lays his whole weight on the form because he thinks its opposite is the mere subject. The general reader is angry, but makes the same mistake, and gives to the subject praises that rightly belong to the substance.[6] I will give an example of what I mean. I can only explain the following words of a good critic[7] by supposing that for the moment he has fallen into this confusion: "That mere matter of all poetry—to wit, the appearances of nature and the thoughts and feelings of men—being unalterable, it follows that the difference between poet and poet will depend upon the manner of each in applying language, meter, rhyme, cadence, and what not, to this invariable material." What has become here of the substance of *Paradise Lost*—the story, scenery, characters, sentiments as they are in the poem? They have vanished clean away. Nothing is left but the form on one side, and on the other not even the subject, but a supposed invariable material, the appearances of nature and the thoughts and feelings of men. Is it surprising that the whole value should then be found in the form?

So far we have assumed that this antithesis of substance and form is valid, and that it always has one meaning. In reality it has several, but we will leave it in its present shape, and pass to the question of its validity. And this question we are compelled to raise, because we have to deal with the two contentions that the poetic value lies wholly or mainly in the substance, and that it lies wholly or mainly in the form. Now these contentions, whether false or true, may seem at least to be clear; but we shall find, I think, that they are both of them false, or both of them nonsense: false if they concern anything outside the poem, nonsense if they apply to something in it. For what do they evidently imply? They imply that there are in a poem two parts, factors, or components, a substance and a form; and that you can conceive them distinctly and separately, so that when you are speaking of the one you are not

[6] What is here called "substance" is what people generally mean when they use the word "subject" and insist on the value of the subject. I am not arguing against this usage, or in favor of the usage which I have adopted for the sake of clearness. It does not matter which we employ, so long as we and others know what we mean. (I use "substance" and "content" indifferently.)

[7] George Saintsbury.

speaking of the other. Otherwise how can you ask the question, In which of them does the value lie? But really in a poem, apart from defects, there are no such factors or components; and therefore it is strictly nonsense to ask in which of them the value lies. And on the other hand, if the substance and the form referred to are not in the poem, then both the contentions are false, for its poetic value lies in itself.

What I mean is neither new nor mysterious; and it will be clear, I believe, to any one who reads poetry poetically and who closely examines his experience. When you are reading a poem, I would ask—not analyzing it, and much less critizing it, but allowing it, as it proceeds, to make its full impression on you through the exertion of your re-creating imagination—do you then apprehend and enjoy as one thing a certain meaning or substance, and as another thing certain articulate sounds, and do you somehow compound these two? Surely you do not, any more than you apprehend apart, when you see some one smile, those lines in the face which express a feeling, and the feeling that the lines express. Just as there the lines and their meaning are to you one thing, not two, so in poetry the meaning and the sounds are one: there is, if I may put it so, a resonant meaning, or a meaning resonance. If you read the line, "The sun is warm, the sky is clear,"[8] you do not experience separately the image of a warm sun and clear sky, on the one side, and certain unintelligible rhythmical sounds on the other; not yet do you experience them together, side by side; but you experience the one *in* the other. And in like manner when you are really reading *Hamlet,* the action and the characters are not something which you conceive apart from the words; you apprehend them from point to point *in* the words, and the words as expressions of them. Afterwards, no doubt, when you are out of the poetic experience but remember it, you may by analysis decompose this unity, and attend to a substance more or less isolated, and a form more or less isolated. But these are things in your analytic head, not in the poem, which is *poetic* experience. And if you want to have the poem again, you cannot find it by adding together these two products of decomposition; you can only find it by passing back into poetic experience. And then what you recover is no aggregate of factors, it is a unity in which you can no more separate a substance and a form than

[8] Shelley, "Lines Written in Dejection Near the Bay of Naples."

you can separate living blood and the life in the blood. This unity has, if you like, various "aspects" or "sides," but they are not factors or parts; if you try to examine one, you find it is also the other. Call them substance and form if you please, but these are not the reciprocally exclusive substance and form to which the two contentions *must* refer. They do not "agree," for they are not apart: they are one thing from different points of view, and in that sense identical. And this identity of content and form, you will say, is no accident; it is of the essence of poetry in so far as it is poetry, and of all art in so far as it is art. Just as there is in music not sound on one side and a meaning on the other, but expressive sound, and if you ask what is the meaning you can only answer by pointing to the sounds; just as in painting there is not a meaning *plus* paint, but a meaning *in* paint, or significant paint, and no man can really express the meaning in any other way than in paint and in *this* paint; so in a poem the true content and the true form neither exist nor can be imagined apart. When then you are asked whether the value of a poem lies in a substance got by decomposing the poem, and present, as such, only in reflective analysis, or whether the value lies in a form arrived at and existing in the same way, you will answer, "It lies neither in one, nor in the other, nor in any addition of them, but in the poem, where they are not."

We have then, first, an antithesis of subject and poem. This is clear and valid; and the question in which of them does the value lie is intelligible; and its answer is, *In the poem.* We have next a distinction of substance and form. If the substance means ideas, images, and the like taken alone, and the form means the measured language taken by itself, this is a possible distinction, but it is a distinction of things not in the poem, and the value lies *in neither of them.* If substance and form mean anything *in* the poem, then each is involved in the other, and the question in which of them the value lies has no sense. No doubt you may say, speaking loosely, that in this poet or poem the aspect of substance is the more noticeable, and in that the aspect of form; and you may pursue interesting discussions on this basis, though no principle or ultimate question of value is touched by them. And apart from that question, of course, I am not denying the usefulness and necessity of the distinction. We cannot dispense with it. To consider separately the action or the characters of a play, and separately its style or versification, is both legitimate and valuable, so long as we remember what we are doing. But the true critic in speaking of these apart does not really think of them apart; the whole, the poetic experience, of which they are but aspects, is always in his mind; and he is always aiming at a richer, truer, more intense repetition of that experience. On the other hand, when the question of principle, of poetic value, is raised, these aspects *must* fall apart into components, separately conceivable; and then there arise two heresies, equally false, that the value lies in one of two things, both of which are outside the poem, and therefore where its value cannot lie.

On the heresy of the separable substance a few additional words will suffice. This heresy is seldom formulated, but perhaps some unconscious holder of it may object: "Surely the action and the characters of *Hamlet* are in the play; and surely I can retain these, though I have forgotten all the words. I admit that I do not possess the whole poem, but I possess a part, and the most important part." And I would answer: "If we are not concerned with any question of principle, I accept all that you say except the last words, which do raise such a question. Speaking loosely, I agree that the action and characters, as you perhaps conceive them, together with a great deal more, are in the poem. Even then, however, you must not claim to possess all of this kind that is in the poem; for in forgetting the words you must have lost innumerable details of the action and the characters. And, when the question of value is raised, I must insist that the action and characters, as you conceive them, are not in *Hamlet* at all. If they are, point them out. You cannot do it. What you find at any moment of that succession of experiences called *Hamlet* is words. In these words, to speak loosely again, the action and characters (more of them than you can conceive apart) are focused; but your experience is not a combination of them, as ideas, on the one side, with certain sounds on the other; it is an experience of something in which the two are indissolubly fused. If you deny this, to be sure I can make no answer, or can only answer that I have reason to believe that you cannot read poetically, or else are misinterpreting your experience. But if you do not deny this, then you will admit that the action and characters of the poem, as you separately imagine them, are no part of it, but a product of it in your reflective imagination, a faint analogue of one aspect of it taken in detachment from the whole. Well, I do not dispute, I would even insist, that, in the case of so long a poem as *Hamlet,* it may be necessary from time to time to interrupt the poetic experience, in order to enrich it by forming such a product and dwelling on it. Nor, in a wide sense of 'poetic,' do I question the poetic value of this product, as you think of it apart from the poem. It resembles our recollections of the heroes of history or legend, who move about in our imaginations, 'forms more real than living man,' and are worth much to us though we do not remember anything they said. Our ideas and images of the 'substance' of a poem have this poetic value, and more, if they are at all adequate. But they cannot determine the poetic value of the poem, for (not to speak of the competing claims of the 'form') nothing that is outside the poem can do that, and they, as such, are outside it."[9]

Let us turn to the so-called form—style and versification. There is no such thing as mere form in poetry. All form is expression. Style may have indeed a certain esthetic worth in partial abstraction from the particular matter it conveys, as in a well-built sentence you may take pleasure in the build almost apart from the meaning. Even so, style is expressive—presents to sense, for example, the order, ease, and rapidity with which ideas move in the writer's mind—but it is not expressive of the meaning of that particular sentence. And it is possible, interrupting poetic experience, to decompose it and abstract for comparatively separate consideration this nearly formal element of style. But the esthetic value of style so taken is not considerable;[10] you could not read with pleasure for an hour a composition which had no other merit. And in poetic experience you never apprehend this value by itself; the style is here expressive also of a particular meaning, or rather is one aspect of that unity whose other aspect is meaning. So that what you apprehend may be called indifferently an expressed meaning or a significant form. Perhaps on this point I may in Oxford appeal to authority, that of Matthew Arnold and Walter Pater, the latter at any rate an authority whom the formalist will not despise. What

[9] These remarks will hold good, *mutatis mutandis,* if by "substance" is understood the "moral" or the 'idea' of a poem, although perhaps in one instance out of five thousand this may be found in so many words in the poem.

[10] On the other hand, the absence, or worse than absence, of style, in this sense, is a serious matter.

is the gist of Pater's teaching about style, if it is not that in the end the one virtue of style is truth or adequacy; that the word, phrase, sentence, should express perfectly the writer's perception, feeling, image, or thought; so that, as we read a descriptive phrase of Keats's, we exclaim, "That is the thing itself"; so that, to quote Arnold, the words are "symbols equivalent with the thing symbolized," or, in our technical language, a form identical with its content? Hence in true poetry it is, in strictness, impossible to express the meaning in any but its own words, or to change the words without changing the meaning. A translation of such poetry is not really the old meaning in a fresh dress; it is a new product, something like the poem, though, if one chooses to say so, more like it in the aspect of meaning than in the aspect of form.

No one who understands poetry, it seems to me, would dispute this, were it not that, falling away from his experience, or misled by theory, he takes the word "meaning" in a sense almost ludicrously inapplicable to poetry. People say, for instance, "steed" and "horse" have the same meaning; and in bad poetry they have, but not in poetry that *is* poetry.

> "Bring forth the horse!" The horse was brought:
> In truth he was a noble steed!

says Byron in *Mazeppa*. If the two words mean the same here, transpose them:

> "Bring forth the steed!" The steed was brought:
> In truth he was a noble horse!

and ask again if they mean the same. Or let me take a line certainly very free from "poetic diction":

> To be or not to be, that is the question.

You may say that this means the same as "What is just now occupying my attention is the comparative disadvantages of continuing to live or putting an end to myself." And for practical purposes—the purpose, for example, of a coroner—it does. But as the second version altogether misrepresents the speaker at that moment of his existence, while the first does represent him, how can they for any but a practical or logical purpose be said to have the same sense?

Hamlet was well able to "unpack his heart with words," but he will not unpack it with our paraphrases.

These considerations apply equally to versification. If I take the famous line which describes how the souls of the dead stood waiting by the river, imploring a passage from Charon:

Tendebantque manus ripae ulterioris amore,[11]

and if I translate it, "and were stretching forth their hands in longing for the further bank," the charm of the original has fled. Why has it fled? Partly (but we have dealt with that) because I have substituted for five words, and those the words of Virgil, twelve words, and those my own. In some measure because I have turned into rhythmless prose a line of verse which, as mere sound, has unusual beauty. But much more because in doing so I have also changed the *meaning* of Virgil's line. What that meaning is *I* cannot say: Virgil has said it. But I can see this much, that the translation conveys a far less vivid picture of the outstretched hands and of their remaining outstretched, and a far less poignant sense of the distance of the shore and the longing of the souls. And it does so partly because this picture and this sense are conveyed not only by the obvious meaning of the words, but through the long-drawn sound of "tendebantque," through the time occupied by the five syllables and therefore by the idea of "ulterioris," and through the identity of the long sound "or" in the penultimate syllables of "ulterioris amore"—all this, and much more, apprehended not in this analytical fashion, nor as *added* to the beauty of mere sound and to the obvious meaning, but in unity with them and so as expressive of the poetic meaning of the whole.

It is always so in fine poetry. The value of versification, when it is indissolubly fused with meaning, can hardly be exaggerated. The gift for feeling it, even more perhaps than the gift for feeling the value of style, is the *specific* gift for poetry, as distinguished from other arts. But versification, taken, as far as possible, all by itself, has a very different worth. Some esthetic worth it has; how much, you may experience by reading poetry in a language of which you do not understand a syllable. The pleasure is quite appreciable, but it is not great; nor in actual poetic experience do

[11] *Aeneid*, VI, 314.

you meet with it, as such, at all. For, I repeat, it is not *added* to the
pleasure of the meaning when you read poetry that you do understand: by some mystery the music is then the music *of* the meaning, and the two are one. However fond of versification you might
be, you would tire very soon of reading verses in Chinese; and
before long of reading Virgil and Dante if you were ignorant of
their languages. But take the music as it is *in* the poem, and there
is a marvelous change. Now

> It gives a very echo to the seat
> Where Love is throned,[12]

or "carries far into your heart," almost like music itself, the sound

> Of old, unhappy, far-off things
> And battles long ago.[13]

What then is to be said of the following sentence of the critic
quoted before:[14] "But when any one who knows what poetry is
reads—

> Our noisy years seem moments in the being
> Of the eternal silence,[15]

he sees that, quite independently of the meaning, . . . there is
one note added to the articulate music of the world—a note that
never will leave off resounding till the eternal silence itself gulfs
it"? I must think that the writer is deceiving himself. For I could
quite understand his enthusiasm, if it were an enthusiasm for the
music of the meaning; but as for the music, "quite independently
of the meaning," so far as I can hear it thus (and I doubt if any one
who knows English can quite do so), I find it gives some pleasure,
but only a trifling pleasure. And indeed I venture to doubt whether,
considered as mere sound, the words are at all exceptionally beautiful, as Virgil's line certainly is. . . .

Pure poetry is not the decoration of a preconceived and clearly
defined matter: it springs from the creative impulse of a vague
imaginative mass pressing for development and definition. If the

[12] *Twelfth Night,* II, iv.
[13] Wordsworth, "The Solitary Reaper."
[14] Saintsbury, *History of English Prosody,* iii, pp. 74-71.
[15] Wordsworth, "Ode on the Intimations of Immortality."

poet already knew exactly what he meant to say, why should he write the poem? The poem would in fact already be written. For only its completion can reveal, even to him, exactly what he wanted. When he began and while he was at work, he did not possess his meaning; it possessed him. It was not a fully formed soul asking for a body: it was an inchoate soul in the inchoate body of perhaps two or three vague ideas and a few scattered phrases. The growing of this body into its full stature and perfect shape was the same thing as the gradual self-definition of the meaning. And this is the reason why such poems strike us as creations, not manufactures, and have the magical effect which mere decoration cannot produce. This is also the reason why, if we insist on asking for the meaning of such a poem, we can only be answered, "It means itself."

And so at last I may explain why I have troubled myself and you with what may seem an arid controversy about mere words. It is not so. These heresies which would make poetry a compound of two factors—a matter common to it with the merest prose, *plus* a poetic form, as the one heresy says: a poetical substance *plus* a negligible form, as the other says—are not only untrue, they are injurious to the dignity of poetry. In an age already inclined to shrink from those higher realms where poetry touches religion and philosophy, the formalist heresy encourages men to taste poetry as they would a fine wine, which has indeed an esthetic value, but a small one. And then the natural man, finding an empty form, hurls into it the matter of cheap pathos, rancid sentiment, vulgar humor, bare lust, ravenous vanity—everything which, in Schiller's phrase,[16] the form should extirpate, but which no mere form can extirpate. And the other heresy—which is indeed rather a practice than a creed—encourages us in the habit so dear to us of putting our own thoughts or fancies into the place of the poet's creation. What he meant by *Hamlet,* or the *Ode to a Nightingale,* or *Abt Vogler,* we say, is this or that which we knew already; and so we lose what he had to tell us. But he meant what he said, and said what he meant.

Poetry in this matter is not, as good critics of painting and music often affirm, different from the other arts; in all of them the content is one thing with the form. What Beethoven meant by his symphony, or Turner by his picture, was not something which you

[16] Not that to Schiller "form" meant mere style and versification.

can name, but the picture and the symphony. Meaning they have, but *what* meaning can be said in no language but their own: and we know this, though some strange delusion makes us think the meaning has less worth because we cannot put it into words. Well, it is just the same with poetry. But because poetry is words, we vainly fancy that some other words than its own will express its meaning. And they will do so no more—or, if you like to speak loosely, only a little more—than words will express the meaning of the Dresden Madonna. Something a little like it they may indeed express. And we may find analogues of the meaning of poetry outside it, which may help us to appropriate it. The other arts, the best ideas of philosophy or religion, much that nature and life offer us or force upon us, are akin to it. But they are only akin. Nor is it the expression of them. Poetry does not present to imagination our highest knowledge or belief, and much less our dreams and opinions; but it, content and form in unity, embodies in its own irreplaceable way something which embodies itself also in other irreplaceable ways, such as philosophy or religion. And just as each of these gives a satisfaction which the other cannot possibly give, so we find in poetry, which cannot satisfy the needs they meet, that which by their natures they cannot afford us. But we shall not find it fully if we look for something else.

And now, when all is said, the question will still recur, though now in quite another sense, What does poetry mean? This unique expression, which cannot be replaced by any other, still seems to be trying to express something beyond itself. And this, we feel, is also what the other arts, and religion, and philosophy are trying to express: and that is what impels us to seek in vain to translate the one into the other. About the best poetry, and not only the best, there floats an atmosphere of infinite suggestion. The poet speaks to us of one thing, but in this one thing there seems to lurk the secret of all. He said what he meant, but his meaning seems to beckon away beyond itself, or rather to expand into something boundless which is only focused in it; something also which, we feel, would satisfy not only the imagination, but the whole of us; that something within us, and without, which everywhere

> makes us seem
> To patch up fragments of a dream,

> Part of which comes true, and part
> Beats and trembles in the heart.[17]

Those who are susceptible to this effect of poetry find it not only, perhaps not most, in the ideals which she has sometimes described, but in a child's song by Christina Rossetti about a mere crown of wind-flowers, and in tragedies like *Lear,* where the sun seems to have set for ever. They hear this spirit murmuring its undertone through the *Aeneid,* and catch its voice in the song of Keats's nightingale, and its light upon the figures on the Urn, and it pierces them no less in Shelley's hopeless lament, *O world, O life, O time,* than in the rapturous ecstasy of his *Life of Life.* This all-embracing perfection cannot be expressed in poetic words or words of any kind, nor yet in music or in color, but the suggestion of it is in much poetry, if not all, and poetry has in this suggestion, this "meaning," a great part of its value. We do it wrong, and we defeat our own purposes when we try to bend it to them:

> We do it wrong, being so majestical,
> To offer it the show of violence;
> For it is as the air invulnerable,
> And our vain blows malicious mockery.[18]

It is a spirit. It comes we know not whence. It will not speak at our bidding, nor answer in our language. It is not our servant; it is our master.

[17] Shelley, "Is it that in some brighter sphere?"
[18] *Hamlet,* 1. i.

The Language of Poetry

In an age of prose readers are likely also to distrust what seems to be the illogicality of the language of poetry. If the poet is serious, why his habitual evasions of clarity, his violations of plain sense, his irresponsible emotion? Proceeding as he does, any value his discourse may have as truth can be only accidental; at best he expresses his feelings. But as Philip Wheelwright points out, such readers have a very narrow notion of what is real and of what may be meaningful statements about reality. In "The Logical and the Translogical" he summarizes the assumptions about language which rest upon an exclusively scientific view of the real. Arguing that these assumptions apply only to certain kinds of experiences, he proposes a contrary set of principles to cover other kinds. The result is a powerful argument for a precision of language radically different from that of scientific statement, a precision which not only allows but actually requires vagueness, paradox, shifting meanings, and mystery.

Although a major theoretical difference separates Wheelwright from Bradley, it is worth nothing how closely they finally approach one another. Whereas Bradley's view is primarily aesthetic and for him the poet is a maker, creator of an object of contemplation, Wheelwright's is epistemological and his poet is a knower. But Wheelwright's knower deals in iconic signs, signs which not only mean but which resemble what they mean and are therefore valued for their own sake. If this resemblance between the sign and what it signifies were carried far enough, knowledge would be indistinguishable from mystical union, union which dissolves the barrier between the knower and the known. It is precisely this tendency which is touched upon when Bradley finds his aesthetic object reaching toward a meaning which is more than aesthetic, an ultimate perfection. For both men the suggestion of something as yet unspoken is the life of art.

PHILIP WHEELWRIGHT

The Logical and the Translogical

Let me try to set down what I take to be the main assumptions which underlie the logician's view, and in general the scientist's view, of what language at its best should be. Of course no man is purely logical all day long, and even a logician will find many human occasions when it is wise to depart from professional usage. But the danger is that he tends to take the properties and laws of logical language as his standard, his point of departure for interpreting and evaluating language in general; and when he does this his view of the humanistic employments of language—in literature, art, religion, and expressive discourse generally—may become gravely distorted.

The method I am employing in this chapter is dialectical, in the sense practiced by Socrates in the earlier Platonic Dialogues and tersely formulated in the Scholastic formula, *Omnis determinatio est negatio.* That is to say, all definition involves exclusion; in determining exactly what a thing is, we thereby implicitly determine what it is not. To define a concept is to declare by one and the same act what it does mean and what it does not mean. Likewise when we define a belief, we therein define by implication what that belief opposes, and hence what contrary belief could be held about the matter without self-contradiction. This last point is of greatest importance for the understanding of dialectical method as employed in this chapter, and more generally for spiking the claims of any dogma that parades itself as the only possible way of looking at a matter. For with respect to any belief that one holds there must be the logical possibility of holding some opposite belief; if not, then one's belief is a mere tautology, which is to say no real belief at all but only a verbal imposture. To believe in God is to recognize the logical possibility of atheism; indeed, to believe in God with any intellectual and moral vitality is to recognize that the position of atheism has grounds, that it offers a challenge, that it is a redoubtable antagonist to the belief which one has elected to hold. Again, in order to believe intelligently in the law of universal physical causation one must be able to understand what a reasonable opponent or doubter of this belief can mean by his heresy. Analogously, then, if we set down the basic assumptions of logical discourse and clearly understand what they affirm, we can thereby discover what they deny and hence what counter-assumptions, non-logical or rather trans-logical in character, it is possible to postulate as a basis for expressive discourse.

The main assumptions of logical discourse have been tradition-ally given as four: the Law of Identity ("A is A"), the Law of Con-tradiction, or more accurately of Non-Contradiction ("A is not at once B and non-B"), the Law of Excluded Middle ("A is either B or not B"), and the Law of Sufficient Reason ("Whatever is true must have a sufficient reason why it is true"). These traditional laws of logic need interpretation, however, if they are to disclose anything about the nature of logical language. To say without qualification "A is A" is to utter a tautology and therefore to say nothing really at all. The Law of Identity in its traditional form silences dissent by its sheer nothingness; it cannot be significantly denied, only because it cannot be significantly affirmed. On the other hand, if we interpret it as saying that a logical term, A, should have a clearly defined meaning and should keep that mean-ing unchanged throughout a given investigation or discourse, then the Law does say something: it sets up a procedure to be followed, hence indicates by implication that there are contrary procedures to be avoided; and so it now becomes possible, from the new form of the Law, as it was not from the old, to deduce certain apriori characteristics of non-logical, non-literal language.

Now there is a most essential difference between the postulates which steno-language requires, and postulates of non-logical or trans-logical language which are dialectically derived from them. The postulates of logic say "must," the postulates of expressivity say "may." This is evident both analytically and experientially. Logic has to operate by fixed laws from which it cannot depart without losing its logical character. Its laws, therefore, involve a "must," or, obversely, a "cannot." It declares, "If you wish to be logical you *must* avoid contradiction"; which is to say, "You *cannot* contradict yourself and still remain logical." Now what is involved in chal-lenging the absolute validity of the Law of Non-Contradiction? Surely not that one must contradict himself at every turn; but that there *may* be elements of radical paradox in expressive discourse, which cannot be reduced to perfect logical consistency without distorting the meaning which they connote. "Must" and "cannot" belong to the world of *Anangkê*, of iron necessity. Their real antitheses, belonging to the world of freedom, are "need not" and "may." In short, the two uses of language are not on a par. Steno-language represents a set of limiting cases, so to speak, in a universe of infinite semantic possibilities.

Of course we should not rest content with the bare apriori possibilities of the case. Language does not automatically become expressive just because it is non-logical. We are interested in non-logical possibilities only because they leave room for the operation of language that is genuinely expressive. Dialectic can vindicate such language; only the awakened sensibility can create it. Accordingly three steps, not two, are called for. It will be necessary, first, to reëxamine the main assumptions of steno-language without blind adherence to the way in which they have been traditionally formulated and understood. There are eight such assumptions which strike me as the most essential, and in any case the ones most relevant to our purpose. Following that, I shall proceed to deduce, by strict dialectic, the eight counter-postulates which are *logically allowed for* by our refusal to accept the laws of steno-discourse as absolutely binding. The third step is a passage from the abstract possibility to the concrete instance. Our eight counter-postulates must be *experientially confirmed* by the way in which depth language is found to actually function; and thus the third and most decisive step consists not in argument but in choice of illustrations.

ASSUMPTIONS OF LITERAL LANGUAGE

1. *Assumption of semantic discreteness:* that a linguistic symbol is always distinct, or at least distinguishable, from its referend. Symbol and referend are, so to speak, non-interchangeable. There is nothing of twoness about the figure "2." And although mathematicians do find it useful to employ iconic symbols in geometry—e.g., a blackboard triangle, which at once means the concept "triangle" and is a particular instance of that universal meaning—yet the character of a geometrical drawing, being governed by considerations of propaedeutic convenience, does not affect the nature of the geometrical entities it refers to. Steno-symbols therefore are dispensable; their usage is by stipulation. Any of Euclid's theorems is

as true, though perhaps not so readily apprehended, when expressed in words or in algebraic equations as when represented by a diagram. Similarly in the more general uses of literal language, every literal meaning is assumed to be translatable without essential loss into another language. Dr. C. K. Ogden, the founder of Basic English, once remarked that he conceived it possible to construct an ideally perfect Basic English into which all authentic meanings could be translated; and that whatever apparent meanings should get unavoidably lost in the translation would thereby reveal themselves to be not real *meanings* at all, but merely embellishments.[1]

2. *Assumption of univocation:* that on a given occasion of its use a symbol has one meaning only; or else a plurality of meanings so distinguishable that they can be stated separately and represented by distinct symbols without semantic loss. Overtones of meaning, secondary implications, innuendo, irony, humorous or tragic suggestiveness and such, are treated as materials for explicit restatement in univocal language.

3. *Assumption of definiteness:* that on a given occasion of its use a symbol has a definite and ideally definable meaning. Vagueness is always a fault, a lapse from the logical ideal. The limiting nature of this requirement becomes evident to anyone capable of honest introspection. For none of us is perfectly clear about every aspect of a matter; and he who says, "I understand perfectly," is either deluding himself or parroting a phrase or (what is often a practical necessity) limiting his attention to certain skeletal and formal properties. Steno-language always presumes such limitation and builds upon it.

4. *Assumption of semantic invariance:* that a given sign must keep the same meaning throughout the course of a given argument or a given science. Hobbes speaks as an honorable logician in declaring that "in all discourses wherein one man pretends to instruct or convince another, he should use the same word constantly in the same sense. If this were done (which nobody can refuse without

[1] Dr. Ogden's remark was made conversationally at a gathering in New York some twenty years ago. While he was willing to admit there might be flaws in the system of Basic English as it then stood, he maintained that such flaws were remediable in principle, and that a language of limited vocabulary might eventually be achieved in which no legitimate meanings would lack symbolism.

great disingenuity), many of the books extant might be spared."[2] The requirement is essential where the aim of the discourse is "to instruct or convince."

5. *Assumption of bidimensional significance:* that the referend of any sign is characterized by either of two kinds of integration, possibly in combination; logical universality, established by definition, and existential particularity, established by space-time continuities. These two familiar types of meaning are what Santayana has called concretions in discourse and concretions in existence;[3] the one is expressed through common names ("horse," "green," "above"), the other through proper names or particularized common names ("this horse," "the position in which I am now sitting").

The five preceding assumptions pertain to the *term,* which some logicians have called (long before 1945) the "atomic" constituent of literal language. The next two assumptions have to do with the *proposition,* the "molecular" constituent.

6. *Assumption of truth-value equivalence:* that any true proposition is equally true with any other true proposition, and hence (from Postulate 7) that any false proposition is equally false with any other. Judgments of probability, far from violating, rather confirm this law: for a probability is a degree of approximation to truth, and there could be degrees of approximation only if the truth approximated were regarded as ideally determinate. When we judge, for instance, that the proposition "Man has evolved from lower animal species" is *more probably* true than the proposition "Mars is inhabited by rational beings," we mean that the evidence for the truth of the first proposition is more adequate than the evidence for the truth of the second; we do *not* mean that the first proposition if actually true is any truer than the second proposition

---

[2] Hobbes' declaration is confirmed by his distinction between univocal and equivocal names. *"Univocal* are those which in the same train of discourse signify always the same thing; but *equivocal* those which mean sometimes one thing and sometimes another. . . . Every *metaphor* is by profession *equivocal.* But this distinction belongs not so much to names, for some use them properly and accurately for the finding out of truth; others draw them from their proper sense, for ornament or deceit." *The English Works of Thomas Hobbes of Malmesbury,* edited by Sir William Molesworth (London, 1839): First Section, "Concerning Bodies," Part I, "Computation or Logic," Chapter II, "Of Names." It is not without significance that Hobbes treats logic as a subdivision of the topic, "Concerning Bodies."

[3] George Santayana, *The Life of Reason:* Vol. I, *Reason and Common Sense* (Scribner, 2nd ed., 1922), Chap. VII.

if actually true. The propositions differ not in degree of truth but in the degree to which the available evidence suffices to establish a valid judgment of truth.

Definition and corollary. A *statement* may be defined as any unit of language such that the predicates "true" and "false" may be asserted of it without complete absence of meaning; and a *proposition* as the type of statement used in literal language—i.e., consisting in an assertible relation between *terms,* as defined above. From these definitions taken in conjunction with Assumption 7 we may derive the theorem (traditionally called the Law of Excluded Middle) that every unitary proposition, when adequately stated, is either entirely true or entirely false, and the theorem (traditionally called the Law of Contradiction) that no such proposition can be both true and false.

7. *Assumption of contradictories:* that for every proposition (p) there is another proposition (non-p) such that the truth of either implies the falsity of the other and the falsity of either implies the truth of the other. The assumption as here formulated contains the germs both of the Law of Contradiction and of the Law of Excluded Middle. The present formulation lays bare the postulational character of these "laws," which in their usual formulation appear axiomatic and tautological. It also distinguishes between their sense as indicated in the corollary to Assumption 6 (as limiting the truth-values of any single proposition) and their sense as indicated in Assumption 7 (as involving the interrelation of two assertible contradictory propositions).

8. *Assumption of ideal explicability:* that every true proposition has an intelligible and assignable place in a system of true propositions, to at least some of which it is related by strict implication. The so-called Law of Sufficient Reason in its strictly formal (non-cosmological) interpretation is identical with this postulate, which refers beyond the atomic and molecular levels of semantic complexity (terms and propositions respectively) to what may be called the organic level (relations among propositions).

The eight foregoing assumptions are operative in all logical discourse, and therefore in all literal discourse so far as it is free from logical imperfection. But that they are implicitly postulational, not axiomatic, is proved by the fact that it is possible to question, doubt, or deny each one of them in turn without necessarily talking non-

sense. The method of dialectic can go only so far: having formulated the hidden postulates on which semantic positivism rests, and
having discerned them to be non-tautologous, it can formulate their
logical antitheses and assign them a postulational role of their own.

Pure dialectic suffers, therefore, from the disability that the
postulates which it thus establishes by logical negation are (i) still
hypothetical, since they are in no way declared to be more than
bare possibilities, and (ii) so broadly and abstractly negative as to
be unoriented with respect to any realm of experience to which
they might apply. Although it can demonstrate the apriori possibility of other types of language than the type defined by the eight
postulates of logical discourse, it offers no experiential clue to their
positive nature. Formal dialectic must therefore be supplemented
by *ontological intuition:* whereby the opposing principles are drawn
not merely out of the thin air of logical possibility but out of actual
semantic procedures with respect to certain realms or qualities or
aspects or functions of experience. By this double method we are
enabled to posit provisionally the following eight principles of expressive discourse as at once dialectically opposed to the eight postulates of literal language and as experientially derived from actual
semantic operations. So far as their derivation is experiential—and
this must be judged by the character of the concrete illustrations—
they are not merely postulates but *principles;* and it is by this name
therefore, although not forgetting their postulative character, that
I shall designate them.

PRINCIPLES OF EXPRESSIVE LANGUAGE

1. *Principle of iconic signification:* that there are symbols which,
although they may point beyond themselves, have a largely self-
intentive reference as well.

Non-symbolic signs may also have something of this double
character; in fact, they normally do so except where the situation
has become exclusively practical. Each thing in nature that stirs us
deeply seems at once valuable in itself and a kind of gateway or
threshold to an unexplored Something More. A fetish or a totemic
animal probably has such a character when it first strikes a won-
dering savage as important. It is charged with otherness—not only
an otherness with respect to the savage himself, which makes the
object inherently fascinating, but a potentiality of otherness that

indefinitely exceeds the mind's objective grasp, and suggests infinite unnamed possibilities. Thus the blue stone or the totemic brown bear becomes a thing of mystery, acquires a numinous quality, and the tribesman confronts it with an ambivalent attitude of confidence and dread. The confidence is helped by sacraments, but the dread remains to keep the total experience ambivalent and vibrantly alive. Later, as the dread is drained away, familiarity and fancy transform the original mythic intuitions into mythologies, and ambition degrades the sacraments into magic.

Fortunately the development is not exclusively desiccating. The symbols which develop are, in every healthy culture, still partly iconic—i.e., they mean by resembling—and this shows itself in the love for the medium. Not only what is said but the way of saying it counts; not only the god who is supplicated but the ritual of supplication itself. This is the aesthetic element in experience and in communication, the valuing of a thing for its own sake, without which as a terminus no utilitarian values would have any eventual justification. At its ultimate stage it becomes mysticism—where not only symbol and referend, but also knower and known, merge into one self-intentive whole. Aesthetic contemplation, however, is and should be but a halfway house to mysticism, keeping the self-identification and the discrimination in fairly even balance. An aesthetic icon thus bears the double characteristic of being more than ordinarily itself and yet the adumbration of a something further that is unspoken. The double aspect produces a tension which, at its best, is a harmony in diversity and the very life of the aesthetic situation.

Unlike logical symbols, therefore, it is impossible to substitute one expressive symbol for another without destroying or radically transfiguring the texture of meaning. Expressive meanings, in short, are not stipulative; they are given not by definition but mainly by contextualization.

2. *Principle of plurisignation:* that an expressive symbol tends, on any given occasion of its realization, to carry more than one legitimate reference, in such a way that its proper meaning is a tension between two or more directions of semantic stress. When we say that poetry uses charged language, we mean that the poetic symbol tends characteristically to be plurisignative in this sense: that its intended meanings are likely to be more or less multiple, yet so fused as sometimes to defy any attempted analysis into mono-

signative components, and always to produce an integral meaning that radically transcends the sum of the ingredient meanings. In these last respects plurisignation differs from simple punning. A brief example is Faustus' agonized cry: "See, see where Christ's *blood* streams in the firmament!"[4] Religion—as distinguished from theology on the one hand and superstition on the other—regards plurisignation as not merely a human technique but as the inevitable articulation of divinity, which can speak to men only through "signatures" that combine sacred with secular modes of significance.

3. *Principle of soft focus:* that there are meanings which do not have definite outlines and cannot be adequately represented by terms that are strictly defined. Strict definition is possible only to those who agree upon a semantic convention, which involves the systematic omission of whatever meanings or elements of meaning cannot be commonly shared. Such a common nucleus of meaning establishes a denotation to which a given steno-symbol (verbal or other) may refer. But over and above its denotation every symbol bears a connotative fringe, which is not likely to be altogether the same for everybody. With some words and in some contexts (e.g., the word "square" in geometry) the connotative increment is unimportant and may easily be dismissed as irrelevant to the science in question. Thus if during a mathematical demonstration a blackboard square strikes one of us as ugly and another of us as a well-balanced arrangement of lines, this obviously has no bearing upon the problem of discovering the square's geometrical properties. To the ancient Pythagoreans, on the other hand, the harmonious character of the square was an intrinsic part of its nature, and hence an intrinsic part of what was meant by the figure (an iconic, participating symbol) and by the word designating it (a conventional, potentially stipulative symbol). Now even though all members of the Pythagorean cult may have agreed that the square was a harmonious and noble figure, it is hardly likely that they all thought of these aesthetic and moral properties in exactly the same way. Exactitude in such matters cannot be verified, for exact designation is not possible to anything like the same degree as with the geometrical properties. The Pythagoreans used the verbal and iconic

[4] Christopher Marlowe, *The Tragical History of Dr. Faustus,* Scene xvi. To be sure, the "blood" image functions archetypally as well.

symbols for "square" in a plurisignative manner: the geometrical meaning was a sharply focused semantic nucleus, while the meta-physical meaning was a softly focused semantic fringe.

The recognition of soft focus as a genuinely semantic character-istic of certain situations throws light upon the problem of obscur-ity in poetry. Ignoring such instances of obscurity as proceed from either incompetence or snobbishness, we can accept certain poetic utterances as obscure for either or both of two valid reasons: (1) because the subject matter itself is too subtle and elusive to allow of exact delineation—as in the portrayal of mature human emotions; or (2) because the poet can produce his effect more fully by pro-ducing an ambivalent impression upon the reader's mind. In great as distinguished from transient poetry the ambivalence is justified because it corresponds to a real ambivalence in the nature of things; and thus the second valid reason for ambivalence tends to reduce to the first.

Poetry and expressive language in general have, to be sure, their own kind of precision, but it is essentially different from the pre-cision of literal language. We cannot ask whether one type of language is *more* precise than the other; we can only try to under-stand and accept their differences. The precision of expressive language is paradoxical, for sometimes it can represent its object most precisely by a sort of controlled vagueness. There have been endless disputes about the character of Hamlet, or, in semantic terms, about what the poetic and dramatic indications of Hamlet's *dramatis persona* "really mean." There are virtually no such dis-putes about Polonius. Would Shakespeare have represented Ham-let more precisely by giving as definite indications as he does of Polonius? Obviously not, for the very nature of Hamlet as a "char-acter" or *dramatis persona* is ambivalent—an aura of highly signifi-cant obscurity around a bright, focused center—and one cannot say of him, as of Polonius, "This, just this and not something else, is what Shakespeare meant."

4. *Principle of contextualism:* that an expressive symbol is a controlled semantic variable, the full meaning of which, although identical throughout all instances *on some level of analysis,* tends to shift about within moderate limits. The reason for this limited non-identity is found partly in the iconic, partly in the plurisigna-tive nature of the expressive symbol. On the one hand, life itself is

in continual flux, and the expressive symbol, being iconic, will tend somewhat to reflect that never-ceasing flow in itself. On the other hand, since the plurisign, unlike the monosignative terms of logical discourse, cannot be semantically controlled by explicit definition, its fused multiple meaning must be determined afresh on each occasion—in part by a relatively persistent core of meaning which unites or relates the various semantic occasions together, in part by the entire relevant context which the particular occasion gathers up and generates. In poetry the relevant context of a symbol is controlled to a large degree by the poet's individual manipulation of his medium; in religion it appears to depend more upon the elusive factors of social and individual sensibility to the signature of divinity in the experienced world.

5. *Principle of paralogical dimensionality:* that there are other dimensions or nodi of meaning than those of logical universality and existential particularity, which latter constitute the coördinates of logical discourse. A nodus of meaning is designated a universal when its specificable references are related by virtue of some *publicly verifiable similarity,* of whatever degree of abstraction; it is designated a particular when its specifiable references are related by virtue of some *publicly verifiable space-time contiguity and continuity.* If we examine these two kinds of connection semantically, as nodi of meaning, we discover that they do not exhaust the possibilities of semantic grouping. They constitute two pragmatically important ways in which possible here-nows of the experienceable world are grouped and represented by a symbol. The general concept "horse" represents one kind of grouping, based mainly upon publicly understood similarities relating one horse to another; "Butch" (the name of a horse I once knew) represents another kind of grouping, based mainly upon the partly observed and partly inferred spatio-temporal continuity of the parts and moments of which the horse named Butch is composed.

But clearly other bases of association are possible. Any aesthetic experience is such an alio-dimensional grouping. An artist's characteristic attempt, in its semantic aspect, is to express and communicate an experience comprising a grouping of experiential moments—that is, of perceived and imagined here-nows—for which there is no publicly accepted word, formula, or other symbol already available. In the words of Ezra Pound: "The error of making a statue *of* Night or *of* Charity lies in tautology. The idea has already found its way into language. The function of the artist is precisely the formulation of what has not found its way into language, i.e., any language verbal, plastic or musical."[5] What Pound says of Night and Charity is true both of horseness and of any individual horse: each finds its adequate expression in a language of word concepts—a common noun in the one case, a proper noun in the other—and an exact undistorted reformulation in terms of painting or sculpture is neither possible nor worth attempting. Horseness shoots through experience in a given direction and "means" a grouping of certain qualities and functions that are conventionally conceived as belonging together; the flesh and blood horse now clanking along the pavement outside my window "means" another grouping—in this case, of physically contiguous qualities; whereas the horses of say Donatello, or of deChirico, or of Kenneth Shopen "mean" a more novel and still unconventionalized grouping of qualities, some of which are shared with the dictionary concept "horse," others with the perceptual qualities of live horses that the artist has seen, while some have closest affinity with subtle forms of emotion otherwise inexpressible.

Thus the platitude that great art is universal, although true in a special sense, is misleading: for the integral meaning of a work of art (whatever its component meanings may be) cuts across ex-

[5] Pound's remark was made in an article, "Epstein, Belgion and Meaning," in *The Criterion*, Vol. IX, Serial No. 36 (April, 1930), p. 470. Some months earlier *The Manchester Guardian* had reviewed Jacob Epstein regarding his sculptures in the London Underground House, and had quoted him as saying: "It was my idea to make 'Day' and 'Night' the subjects of two groups over the entrances to the building. . . . It is difficult to describe a sculptural idea, for any art has to speak its own language. Well, 'Night' is a mother-figure with her child-man exhausted and sleeping under her protection and benediction. The curved horizontal lines of the group are expressive of sleep and rest descending on tired mankind. . ." In the January, 1930, issue of *The Criterion* Montgomery Belgion made these remarks the target of an attack which drew much of its ammunition from H. W. B. Joseph's *Logic*. This was the occasion for Ezra Pound's counter-criticism in the article from which I have quoted. Pound then adds:

"When Mr. Epstein says 'Night' is the subject he means rather more. Everybody knows what 'Night' is, but Mr. Epstein or Mr. Phidias or whoever, is presumably intent on expressing a *particular* and definite complex (ideas, emotions, etc.) generally oriented by a rather vague concept already mapped out. The difference is as great as that between firing a bullet in a generally easterly direction and hitting a particular bird."

perience in a different dimension from that of any logical universal whatever, and establishes its own quality of universality—a more concrete and more alive universality than that represented by any dictionary definition. An analogous distinction may be observed between the concrete universality of the Cross as an integral religious symbol and any theological exposition of what the Cross represents; or between the ideal of justice as it appears to men who are sacrificing their lives to uphold it and the idea of justice as employed in a discussion of theoretical ethics.

6. *Principle of assertorial tone:* that statements—for we here consider the molecular order of meanings—vary with respect to the manner in which they are susceptible to affirmation and denial, ranging all the way from "heavy" assertorial tone—which characterizes the literal statement, the proposition—to "light" association or semi-affirmed tension between two or more symbols. A poetic statement differs from a literal statement not, as Dr. Richards used to maintain, in that the one has a merely subjective, the other an objective reference—at least this is an unnecessary and generally irrelevant difference; but in their manner of asserting. There are differences of what may be called *assertorial weight.* A literal statement asserts heavily. It can do so because its terms are solid. It must do so because we are practical busy creatures who want to know just where we stand. A poetic statement, on the other hand, consisting as it does in a conjunction or association of plurisigns, has no such solid foundation, and affirms with varying degrees of lightness.

A stanza from Carl Rakosi's *A Journey Far Away* offers a syntactical illumination of the principle.

> An ideal
> like a canary
> singing in the dark
> for appleseed and barley

Is the poet making a statement here or is he not? If so, the syntax is not quite adequate: the copula "is" is needed for its completion. But try inserting it, and see how fatally that little word destroys the original quality of affirmation! "An ideal is like a canary singing in the dark for appleseed and barley." Note what has been done. Not only has the reader-response been altered through a lessening of the pleasure with which the utterance is received: more than that, the very nature of the affirmation has been changed. This prose version, we feel, overstates its case, it affirms too heavily: no ideal can be so much like a canary as all that! Rakosi's way of singing the matter did not belabor the point; it suggested only that between an ideal and a canary there might be a slight and lovely connection, too tenuous to be expressed by the harsh little word "is." So delicate an affirmation does not seriously jostle our other beliefs; we can accept it as true without mental inconvenience. But the literal statement, by reason of its assertive heaviness, falsifies.

Assertorial weight should not be confused with the strength or force of a poetic statement. Take, for instance, Christina Rossetti's well-known quatrain:

> My heart is like a singing bird
>   Whose nest is in a water-shoot;
> My heart is like an apple-tree
>   Whose boughs are bent with thick-set fruit . . .

If some literal-minded reader should object to the second comparison on the ground that the differences between hearts and apple-trees are more pronounced than their resemblances, we might justly dismiss him as unduly obtuse. In terms of the present analysis he would be making a statement of full assertorial weight which is nevertheless ridiculously weak, contrasting painfully with the simple eloquent force of Miss Rossetti's assertorially lighter statement.

Suppose, again, that the graceful compliment to a lady expressed implicitly by Herrick—

> Her eyes the glow-worn lend thee,
> The shooting stars attend thee . . .

were made explicit and that the lady's charms were set forth with descriptive literalness. Not only the grace, but more subtly the central poetic meaning of the utterance, would be destroyed. Herrick's own statement is by indirection. It is offered more lightly than its prose counterpart would be, but partly for that reason it is all the more forceful and suggestive. Generally speaking, the combination of poetic delicacy and poetic strength is one of the prime distinguishing marks of authentic poetry.

A poetic statement, then, does not usually assert its claims so heavily as a proposition. Its truth is more fragile, and it asks no guarantee. For a poem can be regarded, from a semantic standpoint, as a complex tension among variously related plurisigns. Some phases of the poetic tension have more of a declarative character than others; and as this declarative character becomes more pronounced a phase of the poetic tension may approximate the character of literal statement, yet without quite totally attaining it. Frequently enough a phase of the poetic tension may contain a literal statement as one of its aspects. When Macbeth cries, "If it were done when 'tis done, then 'twere well/It were done quickly," his words contain an unmistakable literal meaning. This literal scenario meaning could be expressed equally well, from a logical standpoint, in another arrangement of words, such as: "If the effects of the deed could but terminate with the performance, it would be well to finish the matter off as quickly as possible." But the literal meaning is only one aspect of the full poetic meaning, and to restate it in the second phraseology is to wrench it away from the associated poetic meanings of the original. The principal poetic meaning in the passage is expressed in the thematic use of the word "done," repeated three times like the tolling of a dirge. Directly and literally the passage asserts the logical proposition I have just formulated; such is its meaning to the reader's clear-cutting intellect. But if the reader reads with his intellect and sensibilities working in collaboration he will hear in that insistent repetition of the word "done" a tragic reminder of the irrevocability of a deed once performed. The reminder is expressed obliquely, but in some mysterious way it gains in power by its very indirection. Now in much the same manner that Bach so often passes from a theme in a minor to a final chord in the major key, Shakespeare again and again in his plays marks the close of an emotional sequence by passing from an oblique to a correspondingly literal statement. Thus after a number of variations have been played upon the "done" theme, Lady Macbeth concludes the matter by declaring explicitly (III. ii) "What's done is done," and again in the sleep-walking scene (V. i) "What's done cannot be undone." In the word "done" as used suggestively throughout the play we have a plurisign, which in these two quasi-literal remarks of Lady Macbeth approximates but does not quite reach the character of a

monosign. Correspondingly, Lady Macbeth's two statements approximate but do not quite reach the character of propositions.

7. *Principle of paradox:* that two statements which by the canons
of strict logic are mutually contradictory, may sometimes be jointly
acceptable. It is not the maneuvered, expository type of paradox
that is relevant here—such as Chesterton's "Darwin was no Dar-
winian," and Lord Russell's analogy between the paradox of physical ether and the paradox of Homer: "We know who Homer *was*
—he wrote the *Iliad* and the *Odyssey;* only we don't know whether
he *existed.*" The aim of such paradoxes is to startle, amuse, and
suggest a fresh perspective. They can be cleared up easily enough
by anyone who takes the trouble to make the appropriate logical
distinctions—between Darwin's views and those of his self-professed
followers, and between the abstract conception of "authorship of
the *Iliad and Odyssey*" and the historical question of whether they
were or were not written by a single man. The paradoxes of expressive language are something more than this.

Generally speaking I would say there are three main uses of
paradox in poetry: I may call them the paradox of surface, the
paradox of depth, and the paradoxical interplay of statement and
innuendo. The first is exemplified, perhaps even a little crudely, by
the conventional oxymoron of Romeo's opening comment upon the
brawl between the two noble houses:

> Why, then, O brawling love! O loving hate!
> O any thing, of nothing first create!
> O heavy lightness! serious vanity!
> Mis-shapen chaos of well-seeming forms!
> Feather of lead, bright smoke, cold fire, sick health!
> Still-waking sleep, that is not what it is!
> This love feel I, that feel no love in this.

So far as these conceits are anything more than courtly rhetoric—
which is to say, so far as they may be conceived to function expressively and not only decoratively—they are surface representations
of the underlying idea expressed in the fourth quoted line.

A depth paradox, on the other hand, aims more directly at some
transcendent truth which is so mysterious and so many-sided in its
suggestions of meaningful possibilities that either half of the paradox taken alone would be grossly inadequate and partisan. The

great paradoxes of traditional theology are of this kind: God's justice *and* God's mercy; God's foreknowledge of all things to come
and man's free will. Eliot's *Four Quartets* contains a number of expressive paradoxes which function in free variations of the same
manner:

> Only through time time is conquered.

> So the darkness shall be light, and the stillness the dancing.

> In order to arrive at what you do not know
> You must go by a way which is the way of ignorance.

> Our only health is the disease
> If we obey the dying nurse . . .[6]

Some of Eliot's depth paradoxes are aided by a serious playfulness
which bears a rough analogy to the examples cited from Chesterton
and Lord Russell. The line, "To be redeemed from fire by fire," in
Little Gidding could be prosaically explicated by a distinction between the fire of damnation and the fire of purgatorial cleansing.
Yet the paradoxical expression is necessary, not arbitrary here, for
it evokes, as an overtone of allusion, the archetypal idea of the finding of life through voluntary death ("He who will save his life
shall lose it . . ."), and more archetypally still, the idea of the
transcendent Oneness that is approached through even the most
discrepant particulars.

The type of paradox most characteristic of poetry is the third:
which occurs when a direct statement—i.e., some part of a poem's
scenario meaning—is either mocked or playfully opposed by the
suggestions latent in the imagery. The opening lines of Donne's
The Extasie offer an illustration:

> Where, like a pillow on a bed,
>   A pregnant bank swelled up, to rest
> The violet's reclining head,
>   Sat we two, one another's best.

> Our hands were firmly cimented
>   With a fast balm which thence did spring,

[6] Quoted from *Four Quartets*, which have been republished in T. S. Eliot,
The Complete Poems and Plays (Harcourt, 1952). The first of the excerpts is
from Part II of "Burnt Norton," the second and third from Part III of "East
Coker," and the last from Part IV of "East Coker."

> Our eye-beams twisted, and did thread
>   Our eyes, upon one double string;
>
> So to'entergraft our hands, as yet
>   Was all the means to make us one,
> And pictures in our eyes to get
>   Was all our propagation.

The latter stanza asserts plainly that there has been no full carnal union and no propagation of new life as yet—a statement which the wooer's plaint is presently to confirm:

> But O alas, so long, so far
>   Our bodies why do we forbear?

The three opening lines, however, had already imprinted on a responsive and uninhibited reader's mind a set of images suggesting both feminine and (with startling bravado) masculine fulfillment— a sly and delicately ribald qualification of the subsequent chaste avowal. Most of the later paradoxes in the poem, on the other hand, are of the second (the depth) type, such as:

> Might thence a new concoction take,
>   And part far purer than he came.
>
> But as all several souls contain
>   Mixtures of things, they know not what,
> Love, these mixed souls, doth mix again,
>   And make both one, each this and that.

Such paradoxes as these underline the theme of the inextricable union, in love's mysteries, of oneness and manyness, purity and concoction, spirituality and bodily expression.

8. *Principle of significant mystery:* that the truth or falsity of an expressive statement transcends to some degree the evidence of any possible set of propositions which might stand to it in the relation of ground—whether deductive or inductive—to consequent. Truth is more than a function of logically articulable evidence; the meaning of an expressive question (and all deeply important questions are expressive to some degree, or have an expressive aspect)—is never entirely exhausted by its possible answers. This is another way of saying (subjectively) that intuition is always a factor in the apprehension of truth, and (objectively) that any integral

truth—as opposed to either conventional or technical truths—involves irreducible semantic and logical surds.

In the general muddle of slovenly thinking which is so prevalent today there is a tendency to confuse the ideas expressed by the words "mysticism" and "mystery." The foregoing semantic analysis shows their difference. Although both meanings have too much semantic plenitude to allow of adequate definition, their difference is indicated by the difference between Principle 1 and Principle 8. The mystical involves a fusing of this and that, of knower and object known, of symbol and referend. The mysterious—i.e., the radically enigmatic, not the temporarily puzzling—is that character or quality or relationship in things which, however much "explained," always transcends in its essence any totality of explanations given. The two elements are deeply interrelated, but analytically distinguishable.

Thus these eight dialectical escapes from the limiting assumptions of steno-language to the liberating principles of expressive language confirm the conclusions reached in Chapter III. In the present chapter we have found, simply by making those eight assumptions explicit and identifying their exact meaning, that there is a set of meaningful possibilities which they deny, and which therefore a critic is free to explore. In the earlier chapter we had discovered the more general psychological assumption which underlies the eight steno-semantic assumptions—namely, that the semantic function belongs only to the operations of intellect upon the data of outer or inner perception, and that the semantic function of emotional experience as such is zero. Although the steno-semanticist admits that emotions may, and doubtless always do, accompany every actual occasion of semantic reference, he maintains that in themselves they tell us nothing about any reality other than their own bare and transient being. Hence the familiar counsel to disregard the promptings of emotion in the search for truth; and the counsel is both right and valuable in two respects. It is right when the truth in question is a logical, monosignative truth, which calls into play man's abstractive intellect in quest of definite and publicly securable results. It is right, again, when the emotional promptings are crude and immature, or foreign to the matter in hand, and the emotional commentary is an impertinence.

Nevertheless "the heart, too, has its reasons." *All* experience has,

to some degree or other, a semantic role: it points, however un-
certainly and dimly, to a reality other than itself and other than
the subject who enjoys the experience. It is the essence of experience to be vector-like: to transcend in reference what it is in existence, and thereby to enact a more or less cognitive role. Emotional
as well as intellectual aspects of mental activity give a kind of
knowledge—not merely knowledge of the subject, such as a psychologist might derive by empirio-intellectual analysis, but knowledge about that towards which the emotion is felt. Love of a thing
is presumptive evidence of the quality "lovable" in that thing, just
as a sensation of green is presumptive evidence of the quality of
green being actually present. Some degree of judgment is implicit
in all experience, emotive as well as sensory, and this implicit judgment tends to make a claim about the nature of things. Further experience and further activity of judgment may, of course, modify
or reverse the original judgment, but this possibility affects sensory
experience too, not emotive experience only. The important discrimination is between good emotions and bad: the quest for truth
and the larger intelligibility require an abandonment of petty
emotions reflecting primitive impulse and ingrown self-love, in
favor of those integral and expansive intuitions—neither exclusive
of intellect nor identical with it—which enable the knower to transcend his natural limitations and penetrate darkly a little way into
the enveloping mystery.

Figures of Speech

If a century ago noble thoughts nobly expressed were ordinarily taken to be the sign of poetry, today it is figurative language. The usual function of prose is thought to be the communication of information, the telling "what" something is, and poetry is expected to analogize, to tell us what something is "like." Since figures of speech draw attention to the likenesses between unlike things, figurative language is considered to be the heart of poetic technique. Two selections are devoted to the subject. Rosenthal and Smith provide a short introduction which shows that imagery and metaphor are no mere decorative additions but essential means to meaning; Wellek and Warren examine a broader, more complex area which includes symbol and myth.

M. L. ROSENTHAL and A. J. M. SMITH

Poetic Figures and Poetic Meaning

Here, near the beginning of our study of poetry, it will be helpful to try to put out of our minds any *preconceived* opinions about its nature, purposes, or methods. Let us forget any such arbitrary laws as that poetry is or ought to be emotional, that it must be "elevated" and "beautiful," or that it must deal with "poetic" subjects. Where these assertions are not too hopelessly vague, they have some validity; but their main tendency is to limit and dilute our appreciation of the poet's art. The subject-matter of poetry is much wider in scope, more immediate and less selective in its sources, and more intense and less respectable in its responses and expression than many people have been taught. "Fair and foul are near of kin" cries the speaker in one of Yeats's poems;

there may be deep significance and even beauty in what seemed only loathsome.

We do, however, need some test of the genuineness and value of a poem. One such test, though it cannot be applied indiscriminately and will vary in usefulness according to the knowledge and the developed sensibility of the reader, is the intensity with which the poet has entered into an experience and recognized and communicated its implications. *The nature of his original experience, whether it be physical, emotional, or intellectual, does not determine the genuineness or goodness of the poem. What counts is the pressure of the feeling and of the thinking generated by the experience.* There are no "poetic" subjects as such; any subject, no matter how apparently unpromising, can be made poetic when shaped by the poetic imagination. Accuracy of perception and clarity of expression—what might, in its finest manifestation, be called "nakedness of vision"—can make of the humblest and even the vilest object a source of poetry, just as it can, also, bring home to us the purest spiritual truths.

Even in disillusioned and bitter poetry, however, it is delight and love that are at the heart of a poet's vision. The vividness of his writing is a direct result of the delight and love. It comes from a sort of visual thirst that drinks eagerly whatever it lights upon:

> Eye, gazelle, delicate wanderer,
> Drinker of horizon's fluid line—

as Stephen Spender has expressed it. In the finest poetry the pictures presented to our senses and imagination are not contrived merely as ornament or illustration, but they themselves generate the meaning of the poem. Over three hundred years ago the Elizabethan poet Samuel Daniel spoke of the way this creation of a meaning through the senses takes place:

> Glory is most bright and gay
> In a flash, and so away.
> Feed apace then, greedy eyes,
> On the wonder you behold.
> Take it sudden as it flies
> Though you take it not to hold;
> When your eyes have done their part,
> Thought must length it in the heart.

But thought cannot ponder fruitfully what our senses have perceived, unless the perceptions are accurate and sharply defined. Accuracy and clarity are marks both of the poet's sincerity and of his craftsmanship. Consider Browning's

> The wild tulip, at end of its tube, blows out its great red bell
> Like a thin clear bubble of blood

or Whitman's

> Earth of the vitreous pour of the full moon just tinged with blue!
> Earth of shine and dark mottling the tide of the river!

These sense-impressions appeal to the eye. The following lines by Herrick add movement, touch, and sound in their presentation of the rippling glitter and swish of a lady's silks as she walks:

> ROBERT HERRICK *Upon Julia's Clothes*
>
> Whenas in silks my Julia goes,
> Then, then (methinks), how sweetly flows
> The liquefaction of her clothes.
>
> Next, when I cast mine eyes and see
> That brave vibration each way free,
> O how that glittering taketh me!

Marianne Moore gives us a curiously comparable sound-picture as she describes a ship's boat on the water:

> —the blades of the oars
> moving together like the feet of water-spiders. . . .
> The wrinkles progress upon themselves in a phalanx—beautiful
>   under networks of foam,
> and fade breathlessly while the sea rustles in and out of the
>   seaweed. . . .

And Milton, to suggest the beauty of a woman's singing, and the loveliness and virtue of the singer herself, actually presents one sensation in terms of another:

> At last a soft and solemn breathing sound
> Rose like a steam of rich distilled perfumes,
> And stole upon the air. . . .

In these passages we find direct sense-impressions and pictured comparisons. Such impressions and comparisons are called *images*.

It is through images that the threefold nature of poetic experience and expression reveals itself as the accurate and intense perception of objects, the stimulation of feeling, and the operation of the mind. Poetic imagery has a sensuous, an emotional, and an intellectual source, and it communicates on all three of these levels.

Imagery is sometimes the direct concrete expression of vivid sense perceptions, but often—as almost all the foregoing instances reveal —it is figurative rather than literal. Figures of speech are not, of course, confined to poetry; they are a part of all linguistic activity except the most rigorously factual, and are familiar to most of us in slang and other popular, inventive, and indeed poetic adventures with language.

In poetry itself the commonest and most useful figures of speech— *simile, metaphor, personification,* and *conceit*—involve comparison, not a comparison between things that are actually very much alike but a comparison between things which have one often unexpected quality in common. The function of the figure is to direct our attention with special vividness to this particular quality. There is no figure involved in comparing a rose to a carnation, but when a poet compares his girl to a rose (in order to suggest her sweetness, freshness, loveliness, and perhaps also the frailty and impermanence of that loveliness) he is not making a literal factual statement; he is appealing to the imagination. Such poetic statements as Burns's "O my luve is like a red, red rose" or Shakespeare's "My Mistress' eyes are nothing like the sun" or the more concentrated "her diamond eyes" (i.e.—her diamond-like eyes) or Campion's "Her brows like bended bows"—statements in which almost always the comparison is explicitly expressed by the use of some such words as *like, as,* and *similar to*—are called similes.

When a figure is presented not as a directly stated comparison but as an identity, then we have not a simile but a metaphor: "My love is a red, red rose," "Her eyes are diamonds," and Tennyson's "The black bat Night" are metaphors. One of the most frequently encountered types of metaphor is personification, well illustrated in such a characteristic image as this from Shelley's *To Night:*

> Blind with thine hair the eyes of Day;
> Kiss her until she be wearied out. . . .

or in Milton's address to the spirit of Melancholy:

> Come, pensive nun, devout and pure,
> Sober, steadfast, and demure. . . .

Sometimes personification is combined with simile, as in the exciting virtuosity of T. S. Eliot's

> . . . the evening is spread out against the sky
> Like a patient etherised upon a table. . . .

The boldness and originality of this image is characteristic of the conceit—a favorite device of the seventeenth-century Metaphysical poets and their modern followers. The principle behind the conceit is that the greater the gap between the two things compared in a simile or identified in a metaphor—the greater, that is, the imaginative leap the poet's mind achieves—the greater the satisfaction and the sharper the conviction. Many successful images, therefore, are paradoxical; they seem fanciful or out-of-kilter until the reader's own mind makes the leap.

From both the esthetic and the psychological points of view the metaphysical poet's aim is to achieve the *widest* possible gap between the arms of his comparison. If the gap is too narrow, that is, if the things or qualities compared are too much alike, the result is flat and dull. If on the other hand, the comparison is, literally, too far-fetched, the failure is of a different sort, and the result is unconvincing or ridiculous.

Any bold far-fetched figure of comparison, whether successful or not, is called a conceit. (The word is related to *concept,* a mental image.) The description of the evening as an etherised patient is a conceit; so is John Donne's famous comparison of absent lovers to a pair of compasses:

> If they be two, they are two so
>   As stiff twin compasses are two;
> Thy soul, the fix'd foot, makes no show
>   To move, but doth, if th' other do.
>
> And though it in the centre sit,
>   Yet, when the other far doth roam,
> It leans, and hearkens after it,
>   And grows erect, as that comes home.

So, too, though a less adventurous one, is Thomas Campion's elab-

oration of images in *Cherry-ripe*. The poet is telling how the lovely
virtuous maiden guards the cherries of her lips:

> Her eyes like angels watch them still;
> Her brows like bended bows do stand,
> Threat'ning with piercing frowns to kill
> All that attempt with eye or hand
> Those sacred cherries to come nigh,
> Till "Cherry-ripe" themselves do cry.

From these brief illustrations it should be clear that an effective
figure of speech is both a perception of reality and a projection of the
imagination. It is a sudden insight into a meaningful relationship
between things not often thought to be like.

Perhaps it would be well to examine a short modern poem in
order to see the application of some of the principles we have been
discussing. In William Carlos Williams' brief poem *Flowers by the
Sea* there is a new and surprising, but sharply convincing vision of
something we may often have looked at but have never actually
seen with the eye of imagination until the poet showed it to us.

WILLIAM CARLOS WILLIAMS *Flowers by the Sea*

> When over the flowery, sharp pasture's
> edge, unseen, the salt ocean
>
> lifts its form—chickory and daisies
> tied, released, seem hardly flowers alone
>
> but color and the movement—or the shape
> perhaps—of restlessness, whereas
>
> the sea is circled and sways
> peacefully upon its plantlike stem

Brief and clear as it is, this little poem states, or, rather, illustrates, a paradox—the paradox that the sea and the pasture suggest
one another's basic nature rather than their own. But the curious
thing about it is that the unexpected reversal of images which
makes the point of the poem emerges suddenly, only after we
have absorbed the whole dazzling picture of the sunny, wind-swept
seaside pasture and felt the tousled, salt-laden atmosphere of the

summer day. The first unexpected identification is that of the restless amalgam of color and movement in the flowers—"the shape perhaps of restlessness"—with the ebb and flow ("tied, released") of the sea waves; and parallel to it, but much richer and grander, is the sudden awareness of the vast blue round of the ocean itself, swaying like an enormous flower. The poem expresses an experience which culminates for poet and reader alike in the intuitive flash at the close: it is not so much that the flowers and the sea are like one another as that the flowers *are* a sea and the sea *is* a flower. The imagination leaves out all but the common elements shared by the flowers and the waves, all but color and movement, that is, or all but the circular shape and the gently swaying motion. Here is the most intense concentration upon what the imagination has isolated for the sake of emphasis. The result is a form of truth, more limited but more precious too than the truth of science and fact, since this is a truth perceived simultaneously by the heart, the imagination, and the mind.

As to the methods by which the poem achieves its effect, the most striking consists in a metaphorical perception—in a seeing of things in terms of other things which emphasizes a hitherto unsuspected identity. Besides this metaphorical structure, we may notice first the simplicity and unaffected rightness of the diction, and then the easy, natural, exact, and colloquial structure of the clauses—virtues common to good prose and good poetry alike. Then again, if we look and listen we grow aware of the skilful but unobtrusive pattern of repeated sounds that marks the poem's movement. And finally, we notice how the unifying paradox of the poem is matched in the contrast between the short, sharp, variable rhythm of the opening half of the poem and the slow, majestic, peaceful swaying of the close.

But what, the reader may now ask, does the poem *mean?*

We would answer: Two things are involved in the poem's meaning. First, there is the evocation of all the associations of delight gathering around the sunny windswept landscape of flowers by the dancing sea. Second, there is the delight that accompanies the appreciation of a paradox. It is the paradoxical reversal of ordinary experience, when in a flash the flowers are seen as a sea and the sea as a flower, that gives the poem unity and point. The effect of the whole poem—what it does for and to us—*that* is the meaning of the poem. For this reason it is all-important to read the plain sense of the poem correctly. We must submit ourselves to the poem the author wrote, not to a vague approximation that our own intuitions, prejudices, and limitations have substituted for it. And in the poem we have been considering this depends on our recognition of its one tremendous metaphor of the flowers and the sea.

RENÉ WELLEK and AUSTIN WARREN

Image, Metaphor, Symbol, Myth

When we turn from classifying poems by their subject matter or themes to asking what kind of discourse poetry is, and when, instead of prose-paraphrasing, we identify the "meaning" of a poem with its whole complex of structures, we then encounter, as central poetic structure, the sequence represented by the four terms of our title. The two main organizing principles of poetry, one of our contemporaries has said, are meter and metaphor; moreover, "metre and metaphor 'belong together,' and our definition of poetry will have to be general enough to include them both and explain their companionship."[1] The general theory of poetry implied by this statement was brilliantly expounded by Coleridge in *Biographia Literaria*.

Have we, in these four terms, a single referent? Semantically, the terms overlap; they clearly point to the same area of interest. Perhaps our sequence—image, metaphor, symbol, and myth—may be said to represent the convergence of two lines, both important for the theory of poetry. One is sensuous particularity, or the sensuous and aesthetic continuum, which connects poetry with music and painting and disconnects it from philosophy and science; the other is "figuration" or "tropology"— the "oblique" discourse which speaks in metonyms and metaphors, partially comparing worlds, precising its themes by giving them impractical translations into other idioms.[2] These are both characteristics, *differentiae*, of literature, in contrast to scientific discourse. Instead of aiming at a system of abstractions consistently expressed by a system of mono-signs, poetry organizes a unique, unrepeatable pattern of words,

[1] Notes appear at the end of this selection. (Ed.)

each an object as well as a sign and used in a fashion unpredictable by any system outside of the poem.[3]

The semantic difficulties of our topic are troublesome, and no ready relief seems possible beyond constant vigilant attention to how terms are used in their contexts, especially to their polar oppositions.

Imagery is a topic which belongs both to psychology and to literary study. In psychology, the word "image" means a mental reproduction, a memory, of a past sensational or perceptual experience, not necessarily visual. The pioneer investigations of Francis Galton, in 1880, sought to discover how far men could visually reproduce the past, and found that men greatly differed in their degree of visualization. But imagery is not visual only. The classifications of psychologists and aestheticians are numerous. There are not only "gustatory" and "olfactory" images, but there are thermal images and pressure images ("kinaesthetic," "haptic," "empathic"). There is the important distinction between static imagery and kinetic (or "dynamic"). The use of color imagery may or may not be traditionally or privately symbolic. Synaesthetic imagery (whether the result of the poet's abnormal psychological constitution or of literary convention) translates from one sense into another, e.g., sound into color. Finally, there is the distinction, useful for the reader of poetry, between "tied" and "free" imagery: the former, auditory and muscular imagery necessarily aroused even though one reads to himself and approximately the same for all adequate readers; the latter, visual and else, varying much from person to person or type to type.[4]

I. A. Richards' general conclusions, as given in his *Principles* of 1924, still seem sound: that "Too much importance has always been attached to the sensory qualities of images. What gives an image efficacy is less its vividness as an image than its character as a mental event peculiarly connected with sensation." Its efficacy comes from its being "a relict" and a "representation" of sensation.[5]

From images as the vestigial representatives of sensations we move with instructive ease to the second line which runs through our whole area—that of analogy and comparison. Even visual images are not to be looked for exclusively in descriptive poetry; and few who have attempted to write "imagist" or "physical" poetry have succeeded in restricting themselves to pictures of the

external world. Rarely, indeed, have they wished to do so. Ezra
Pound, theorist of several poetic movements, defined the "image"
not as a pictorial representation but as "that which presents an intellectual and emotional complex in an instant of time," a "unification of disparate ideas." The Imagist credo asserted, "we believe
that poetry should render particulars exactly and not deal in vague
generalities, however . . . sonorous." In his praise of Dante and
his attacks on Milton, Eliot seems to hold more dogmatically to the
emphasis on *Bildlichkeit.* Dante's, he says, "is a visual imagination." He is an allegorist, and "for a competent poet, allegory means
'clear visual imagery.'" On the other hand Milton's is, unfortunately, an "auditory imagination." The visual imagery in "L'Alle-
gro" and "Il Penseroso" is "all general . . . it is not a particular
ploughman, milkmaid, and shepherd that Milton sees . . . ; the
sensuous effect of these verses is entirely on the ear, and is joined
to the concepts of ploughman, milkmaid, and shepherd."[6]

In all of these pronouncements, the stress is rather on *particularity* and the union of worlds (analogy, e.g., allegory; "unification
of disparate ideas") than it is on the sensuous. The visual image is
a sensation or a perception, but it also "stands for," refers to, something invisible, something "inner." It can be both presentation and
representation at once ("the black bat night has flown" . . . "Yonder all before us lie Desarts of vast eternity"). The image may exist
as "description" or (as in our examples) as metaphor. But may the
images not offered as metaphor, as seen by the "mind's eye," also
be symbolic? Is not every perception selective?[7]

So Middleton Murry, who thinks of "simile" and "metaphor" as
associated with the "formal classification" of rhetoric, advises the
use of "image" as a term to include both, but warns that we must
"resolutely exclude from our minds the suggestion that the image
is solely or even predominantly visual." The image "may be visual,
may be auditory," or "may be wholly psychological." Analogous is
the practice of Louis MacNeice. Though he distinguishes his
terms, using "properties" (*cf.* "stage properties") for perceptions
and reserving "images" for metaphor, he observes the difficulty of
holding to the distinction: for "the properties themselves may be,
in the ultimate analysis, only symbols." Of Wordsworth, MacNeice
remarks that he "does not require many images because his properties carry their own message."[8] In writers as different as Shake-

speare, Emily Brontë, and Poe, we can see that the setting (a system of "properties") is often a metaphor or symbol: the raging sea,
the storm, the wild moor, the decaying castle by the dank, dark
tarn.

Like "image," "symbol" has given its name to a specific literary
movement.[9] Like "image," again, it continues to appear in widely
different contexts and very different purposes. It appears as a term
in logic, in mathematics, in semantics and semiotics and epistemology; it has also had a long history in the worlds of theology ("symbol" is one synonym for "creed"), of liturgy, of the fine arts, and of
poetry. The shared element in all these current uses is probably
that of something standing for, representing, something else. But
the Greek verb, which means to throw together, to compare, suggests that the idea of analogy between sign and signified was
originally present. It still survives in some of the modern uses of
the term. Algebraic and logical "symbols" are conventional, agreed-
upon signs; but religious symbols are based on some intrinsic relation between "sign" and thing "signified," metonymic or metaphoric: the Cross, the Lamb, the Good Shepherd. In literary
theory, it seems desirable that the word should be used in this
sense: as an object which refers to another object but which demands attention also in its own right, as a presentation.[10]

There is a kind of mind which speaks of "mere symbolism,"
either reducing religion and poetry to sensuous images ritualistically arranged or evacuating the presented "signs" or "images" in
behalf of the transcendental realities, moral or philosophical, which
lie beyond them. Another kind of mind thinks of a symbolism as
something calculated and willed, a deliberate mental translation of
concepts into illustrative, pedagogic, sensuous terms. But, says
Coleridge, while allegory is merely "a translation of abstract notions into a picture language, which is itself nothing but an abstraction from objects of the senses . . . ," a symbol "is characterized by a translucence of the special [the species] in the individual,
or of the general [genus] in the special . . . ; above all, by the
translucence of the eternal through and in the temporal."[11]

Is there any important sense in which "symbol" differs from
"image" and "metaphor"? Primarily, we think, in the recurrence
and persistence of the "symbol." An "image" may be invoked once
as a metaphor, but if it persistently recurs, both as presentation

and representation, it becomes a symbol, may even become part of a symbolic (or mythic) system. Of Blake's early lyrics, the *Songs of Innocence* and *of Experience,* J. H. Wicksteed writes: "There is comparatively little *actual symbolism,* but there is constant and abundant use of *symbolic metaphor."* Yeats has an early essay on the "Ruling Symbols" in Shelley's poetry. "One finds in his poetry, besides innumerable images that have not the definiteness [fixity?] of symbols, many images that are certainly symbols, and as the years went by he began to use these with more and more deliberate symbolic purpose"—such images as caves and towers.[12]

What happens with impressive frequency is the turning of what, in a writer's early work, is "property" into the "symbol" of his later work. Thus in his early novels, Henry James painstakingly visualizes persons and places, while, in the later novels, all the images have become metaphoric or symbolic.

Whenever poetic symbolism is discussed, the distinction is likely to be made between the "private symbolism" of the modern poet and the widely intelligible symbolism of past poets. The phrase was first, at least, an indictment; but our feelings and attitude toward poetic symbolism remain highly ambivalent. The alternative to "private" is difficult to phrase: if "conventional" or "traditional," we clash with our desire that poetry should be new and surprising. "Private symbolism" implies a system, and a careful student can construe a "private symbolism" as a cryptographer can decode an alien message. Many private systems (e.g., those of Blake and Yeats) have large overlap with symbolical traditions, even though not with those most widely or currently accepted.[13]

When we get beyond "private symbolism" and "traditional symbolism," there is, at the other pole, a kind of public "natural" symbolism which offers its own difficulties. Frost's poems, some of the best of them, use natural symbols the reference of which we find it difficult to control: we think of "The Road Not Taken," "Walls," "The Mountain." In "Stopping by Woods," "miles to go before I sleep" is literally true of the traveler, we assume; but in the language of natural symbolism, to "sleep" is to "die"; and, if one couples by contrast the "woods are lovely, dark, and deep" (all three adjectives panegyric) with the moral and social check of "promises to keep," one can't wholly reject the passing, not insisted on, equation of aesthetic contemplation with some kind of ceasing to be as a responsible person. Presumably no constant reader of poetry will go wrong with Frost; but, partly because of his natural symbolism, Frost has drawn a wide audience, some of whom, once grasping the possibility of symbols, will bear down too heavily on both the natural symbols and their companions, giving to his plurisigns a fixity and rigidity alien to the nature of poetic statement, especially contemporary poetic statement.[14]

The fourth of our terms is "myth," which appears in Aristotle's *Poetics* as the word for plot, narrative structure, "fable." Its antonym and counterpoint is *logos*. The "myth" is narrative, story, as against dialectical discourse, exposition; it is also the irrational or intuitive as against the systematically philosophical: it is the tragedy of Aeschylus against the dialectic of Socrates.[15]

"Myth," a favorite term of modern criticism, points to, hovers over, an important area of meaning, shared by religion, folklore, anthropology, sociology, psychoanalysis, and the fine arts. In some of its habitual oppositions, it is contraposed to "history," or to "science," or to "philosophy," or to "allegory" or to "truth."[16]

In the seventeenth and eighteenth centuries, the Age of the Enlightenment, the term had commonly a pejorative connotation: a myth was a fiction—scientifically or historically untrue. But already in the *Scienza Nuova* of Vico, the emphasis has shifted to what, since the German Romanticists, Coleridge, Emerson, and Nietzsche, has become gradually dominant—the conception of "myth" as, like poetry, a kind of truth or equivalent of truth, not a competitor to historic or scientific truth but a supplement.[17]

Historically, myth follows and is correlative to ritual; it is "the spoken part of ritual; the story which the ritual enacts." The ritual is performed for a society by its priestly representative in order to avert or procure; it is an "agendum" which is recurrently, permanently necessary, like harvests and human fertility, like the initiation of the young into their society's culture and a proper provision for the future of the dead. But in a wider sense, myth comes to mean any anonymously composed story telling of origins and destinies, the explanations a society offers its young of why the world is and why we do as we do, its pedagogic images of the nature and destiny of man.[18]

For literary theory, the important motifs are, probably, the image or picture, the social, the supernatural (or non-naturalist or irrational), the narrative or story, the archetypal or universal, the symbolic representation as events in time of our timeless ideals, the programmatic or eschatological, the mystic. In contemporary thought, appeal to the myth may center on any one of these, with a spread to others. Thus Sorel speaks of the "General Strike" of all the world's workers as a "myth," meaning that while such an ideal will never become historic fact it must, in order to motivate and dynamize the workers, be presented as a future historical event; myth is program. Thus Niebuhr speaks of Christian eschatology as mythic: the Second Coming and the Last Judgment image as future history what are present, permanent, moral, and spiritual evaluations.[19] If the mythic has as its contrary either science or philosophy, it opposes the picturable intuitive concrete to the rational abstract. Generally, too, in this, the central opposition for literary theorists and apologists, the myth is social, anonymous, communal. In modern times, we may be able to identify the creators—or some of the creators—of a myth; but it may still have the qualitative status of myth if its authorship is forgotten, not generally known, or at any event unimportant to its validation—if it has been accepted by the community, has received the "consent of the faithful."

The term is not easy to fix: it points today at an "area of meaning." We hear of painters and poets in search of a mythology; we hear of the "myth" of progress or of democracy. We hear of "The Return of the Myth in World Literature." Yet we also hear that one can't create a myth or chose to believe one or will one into being: the book has succeeded the myth, and the cosmopolitan city the homogeneous society of the city state.[20]

Does modern man lack myth—or a mythology, a system of interconnected myths? This would be Nietzsche's view: that Socrates and the Sophists, the "intellectuals," had destroyed the life of Greek "culture." Similarly it would be argued that the Enlightenment destroyed—or began destruction of—the Christian "mythology." But other writers think of modern man as having shallow, inadequate, or perhaps even "false" myths, such as the myth of "progress," or of "equality," or of universal education, or of the hygienic and modish well-being to which the advertisements invite. The common denominator between the two conceptions seems to be the judgment (true, probably) that when old, long-felt, self-coherent ways of life (rituals with their accompanying myths) are disrupted by "modernism," most men (or all) are impoverished: as men can't live by abstractions alone, they have to fill their voids by crude, extemporized, fragmentary myths (pictures of what might be or ought to be). To speak of the need for myth, in the case of the imaginative writer, is a sign of his felt need for communion with his society, for a recognized status as artist functioning within society. The French Symbolists existed in self-recognized isolation, were hermetic specialists, who believed the poet must choose between commercial prostitution of his art and aesthetic purity and coldness. But Yeats, for all his veneration of Mallarmé, felt the need of a union with Ireland; so he compounded traditional Celtic mythology with his own mythicizing version of latter-day Ireland, in which the Augustan Anglo-Irish (Swift, Berkeley, and Burke) are as freely interpreted as the American heroes of Vachel Lindsay's imagination.[21]

For many writers, myth is the common denominator between poetry and religion. There exists a modern view, of course (represented by Matthew Arnold and the early I. A. Richards), that poetry will more and more take the place of the supernatural religion in which modern intellectuals can no longer believe. But a more impressive case can probably be made for the view that poetry cannot for long take the place of religion since it can scarcely long survive it. Religion is the greater mystery; poetry, the lesser. Religious myth is the large-scale authorization of poetic metaphor. Thus Philip Wheelwright, protesting that by positivists "religious truth and poetic truth are dismissed as fictions," asserts that the "needed perspective is . . . a mytho-religious one." An older English representative of this view is John Dennis; a relatively recent one is Arthur Machen.[22]

The whole series (image, metaphor, symbol, myth) we may charge older literary study with treating externally and superficially. Viewed for the most part as decorations, rhetorical ornaments, they were therefore studied as detachable parts of the works in which they appear. Our own view, on the other hand, sees the meaning and function of literature as centrally present in metaphor and myth. There are such activities as metaphoric and mythic thinking, a thinking by means of metaphors, a thinking in poetic narrative or vision. All these terms call our attention to the aspects of a literary work which exactly bridge and bind together old divisive components, "form" and "matter." These terms look in both directions; that is, they indicate the pull of poetry toward "picture" and "world" on the one hand and toward religion or *Weltanschauung* on the other. As we survey modern methods of studying them, we can feel that tension. Since older methods treated them as aesthetic devices (albeit conceiving of such as merely decorative), the reactionary danger today is perhaps a too heavy stress on *Weltanschauung*. The Scotch rhetorician, writing at the end of the Neo-Classical period, rather naturally thought of similes and metaphors as calculated, elected; today's analysts, working after Freud, are disposed to see all images as revelatory of the unconscious. It calls for a nice equilibrium to avoid the rhetorical concern on the one hand and on the other both psychological biography and "message hunting."

In the last twenty-five years of literary study, theory and practice have both been pursued. That is, we have attempted typologies of figuration or, more specifically, of poetic imagery; and we have also devoted monographs and essays to the imagery of specific poets or works (with Shakespeare as a favorite subject). The "practical criticism" having gone on with particular ardor, we begin to have some excellent sharp theoretical and methodological papers scrutinizing the sometimes too easy assumptions of the practitioners.

Many have been the attempts at reducing all the minutely subdivided figures—some two hundred and fifty in ambitious lists—into two or three categories. "Schemes" and "tropes" is itself one of these: a division into "sound figures" and "sense figures." Another attempt separates figures of "speech" or "verbal figures" from "figures of thought." Both dichotomies have the fault, however, of suggesting an outer, or outermost, structure which lacks expressive function. Thus, under any traditional system, rhyme and alliteration are both phonetic "schemes," acoustic ornamentations; yet both initial rhyme and end rhyme can serve, we know, as sense binders, as semantic couplers. The nineteenth century regarded the pun as a "play on words," the "lowest form of wit"; the eighteenth century had, with Addison, already classified it as one of the species of "false wit." But Baroque and modern poets use it seriously as a doubling of ideas, a "homophone" or "homonym," a purposed "ambiguity."[23]

Leaving the schemes aside, we may divide the tropes of poetry most relevantly into figures of contiguity and figures of similarity.

The traditional figures of contiguity are metonymy and synecdoche. The relations they express are logically or quantitatively analyzable: the cause for the effect, or the contrary; the container for the contained; the adjunct for its subject ("the village green," "the briny deep"). In synecdoche, the relations between the figure and its referent are said to be internal. We are offered a sample of something, a part intended to stand for its whole, a species representing a genus, matter betokening the form and use to which it is put.

In the familiar passage from Shirley illustrative of the traditional use of metonymy, conventional accoutrements—instruments or tools—stand for social classes:

> Sceptre and crown must tumble down
> And in the dust be equal made
> With the poor crooked scythe and spade.

More striking is the metonymic "transferred adjective," a stylistic trait of Virgil, Spenser, Milton, Gray, classical art-poets: "Sansfoy's dead dowry," shifts the epithet from possessor to thing possessed. In Gray's "drowsy tinklings" and Milton's "merry bells," the epithets refer to the wearers and the ringers of bells respectively. When Milton's gray-fly is "winding her sultry horn," the epithet calls up the hot summer evening linked by association with the sound of the gray-fly. In all such cases, cited out of their context, another, an animistic, kind of reading seems possible. The distinction lies in whether associational logic is operative, or whether, instead, a persistent personalization.

Devotional poetry, Catholic or Evangelical, would seem, at first thought, unavoidably metaphorical, and so it dominantly is. But Dr. Watts, the Neo-Classical hymn writer, gets an impressive effect, moving as well as stately, from metonymy:

> When I survey the wondrous cross
>   On which the Prince of Glory died,
> My richest gain I count but loss
>   And pour contempt on all my pride.
>
> See, from his head, his hands, his side
>   Sorrow and love flow mingled down;

> Did e'er such love and sorrow meet
> Or thorns compose so rich a crown?

A reader trained upon another time style might hear this hymn without perceiving that "sorrow" and "love" equate "water" and "blood." He died for love: his love is cause; the blood, effect. In seventeenth-century Quarles, "pour contempt" would suggest visualizable metaphor, but then the figure would be pursued—perhaps with the fire of pride put out by a bucket of contempt; but "pour" here is a semantic intensive: I contemn my pride vigorously, superlatively.

These are, after all, narrowly restricted uses of the word. Recently some bolder conceptions of metonymy as a literary mode have been suggested, even the notion that metonymy and metaphor may be the characterizing structures of two poetic types— poetry of association by contiguity, of movement within a single world of discourse, and poetry of association by comparison, joining a plurality of worlds, mixing, in the striking phrase of Bühler, a "cocktail of spheres."[24]

In a brilliant critical discussion of Whitman, D. S. Mirsky says, "The separate fractional images of the 'Song of the Broad-Axe' are endless metonymic images, examples, specimens of the elements comprising democratic constructiveness."[25] One might characterize Whitman's usual poetic method as an analytic spreadout, an itemized unpacking, of certain large, parallel categories. In his parallelistic chants like "Song of Myself" he is dominated by the desire to present details, individuals, parts as parts of a whole. For all his love of lists, he is not really a pluralist or personalist but a pantheistic monist; and the total effect of his catalogues is not complexity but simplicity. First he lays out his categories, and then he copiously illustrates them.

Metaphor, which has had the attention of poetic theorists and rhetoricians since Aristotle, who was both, has won large attention in recent years from linguistic theorists also. Richards has protested vehemently against treating metaphor as deviation from normal linguistic practice instead of its characteristic and indispensable resource. The "leg" of the chair, the "foot" of the mountain, and the "neck" of the bottle all apply, by analogy, parts of the human body to parts of inanimate objects. These extensions, however, have become assimilated into the language, and are commonly no longer felt as metaphorical, even by the literarily and linguistically sensitive. They are "faded" or "worn-out" or "dead" metaphor.[26]

We must distinguish metaphor as the "omnipresent principle of language" (Richards) from the specifically poetic metaphor. George Campbell assigns the former to the "grammarian," the latter to the "rhetorician." The grammarian judges words by etymologies; the rhetorician, by whether they have "the effect of metaphor upon the hearer." Wundt would deny the term "metaphor" to such linguistic "transpositions" as "leg" of the table and "foot" of the mountain, making the criterion of true metaphorism the calculated, willed intention of its user to create an emotive effect. H. Konrad contrasts the "linguistic" with the "aesthetic" metaphor, pointing out that the former (e.g., the "leg" of the table) underlines the dominant trait of the object, while the latter is conceived to give a new impression of the object, to "bathe it in a new atmosphere."[27]

Of cases difficult to classify, probably the most important is that of metaphors common to a literary school or generation, shared poetic metaphors. Instances would be "bone-house," "swan-road" "word-hoard," and the other kennings of Old English poets; Homer's "fixed metaphors" such as "rosy-fingered dawn" (used twenty-seven times in the First Book of the *Iliad*); the Elizabethan's "pearly teeth," "ruby lips," "ivory necks," and "hair of golden wire"; or the Augustan's "watery plain," "silver streams," "enameled meadows."[28] To modern readers some of these (notably those from the Anglo-Saxon) are bold and "poetic," while most of the others are faded and quaint. Ignorance, to be sure, can confer an illegitimate originality upon the first examples of an unfamiliar convention. Indeed, the etymological metaphors of a language, not "realized" by those whose native language it is, are constantly taken, by analytically sensitive foreigners, as individual poetic achievements.[29] One has to know intimately both language and literary convention to be able to feel and measure the metaphoric intention of a specific poet. In Old English poetry, "bone-house" and "word-hoard" are undoubtedly of a kind with Homer's "winged words." They are a part of the poet's craft-education and give pleasure to their hearers by their traditionalism, their belonging to the professional, ritual language of poetry. The metaphoric in them is neither wholly realized nor wholly missed: like much ecclesiastical symbolism, they may be said to be ritual.[30]

In our genetically minded age, much attention has naturally been given to the origins of the metaphor, both as a linguistic principle and as a literary mode of vision and operation. "Ontogeny repeats phylogeny"; and, in reverse, we believe we can reconstruct prehistoric culture history through analytic observation of primitive societies and children. According to Heinz Werner, metaphor becomes active among only such primitive peoples as have taboos, objects the "proper" names of which may not be named.[31] We reflect immediately on the rich Jewish talent for metaphorizing the unnamable Jaweh as a Rock, as a Sun, a Lion, and so on, and then upon the euphemisms in our own society. But, obviously, a fearful necessity is not the only mother of invention. We metaphorize also what we love, what we want to linger over, and contemplate, to see from every angle and under every lighting, mirrored, in specialized focus, by all kinds of like things.

If we pass from the motivation of linguistic and ritual metaphor to the teleology of poetic metaphor, we have to invoke something far more inclusive—the whole function of imaginative literature. The four basic elements in our whole conception of metaphor would appear to be that of analogy; that of double vision; that of the sensuous image, revelatory of the imperceptible; that of animistic projection. The four in equal measure are never present: attitudes vary from nation to nation and aesthetic period to aesthetic period. According to one theorist, Graeco-Roman metaphor is almost restricted to analogy (a quasi-legal parallelism), while *das Bild* (the image symbol) is a distinctively Teutonic figure.[32] Such a culture contrast, however, hardly takes care of Italian and French poetry, especially from Baudelaire and Rimbaud to Valéry. A more plausible case could be made for a contrast between periods and between dominating life-philosophies.

Each period style has its own characteristic figures, expressive of its *Weltanschauung;* in the case of basic figures like metaphor, each period has its characteristic kind of metaphoric method. Neo-Classical poetry, for example, is characterized by the simile, periphrasis, the ornamental epithet, epigram, balance, antithesis. Possible intellectual positions are reduced to twos or threes, not pluralities. Frequently the third position is a central and mediatorial position between named polar heresies:

> Some foreign writers, some our own despise,
> The ancients only, or the moderns, prize.

In the Baroque period, characteristic figures are the paradox, the oxymoron, catachresis. These are Christian mystical, pluralist figures. Truth is complex. There are many modes of knowing, each with its own legitimacy. Some kinds of truths have to be stated by negation or calculated distortion. God can be spoken of anthropomorphically, for He made men in His own image; but He is also the transcendental Other. Hence in Baroque religion, truth about God may be expressed through analogical images (the Lamb, the Bridegroom); it may also be expressed through couplings of contradictories or contraries, as in Vaughan's "deep but dazzling darkness." The Neo-Classical mind likes clear distinctions and rational progressions: metonymic movements from genus to species, or particular to species. But the Baroque mind invokes a universe at once of many worlds and of worlds all, in unpredictable ways, connected.

From the point of view of Neo-Classical poetic theory, the characteristic Baroque figures are, of course, in bad taste, "false wit"—either willful perversions of the natural and rational, or insincere acrobatics, whereas historically they are rhetorico-poetic expressions of a pluralist epistemology and a supernaturalist ontology.

"Catachresis" offers an interesting instance. In 1599 John Hoskyns Englishes the term as "abuse" and deplores that it is "nowe growne in fashion. . . ." He thinks of it as a strained phrase, "more desperate than a metaphor," and cites "a voice beautiful to his ears" from Sidney's *Arcadia* as example of a visual term perversely applied to hearing. Pope (*Art of Sinking*, 1728) cites "mow a beard" and "shave the grass" as catachretic. George Campbell (*Philosophy of Rhetoric*, 1776) cites "beautiful voice" and "melodious to the eye" as a catachretic pair, though he admits that "sweet, originally palatal, can now be applied to a scent, a melody, a prospect." Believing that proper metaphor uses the "objects of sensation" to denote the "objects of pure intellection," Campbell deplores the analogizing of sense objects to other sense objects. On the other hand, a recent Catholic rhetorician (of Baroque-Romantic taste) defines catachresis as the metaphor drawn from similarity between two material objects, urges that the merits of the trope be studied, and illustrates it by such figures from Victor Hugo as *"les perles de la rosée"* and *"il neige des feuilles."*[33]

Another kind of metaphor acceptable to Baroque sensibility, tasteless to Neo-Classical, translates the greater into the humbler; we might call it the diminishing or domesticating metaphor. The "spheres" most characteristically mixed by Baroque poetry are the natural world and man's world of crafts and artifices. But knowing that Art is an imitation of Nature, Neo-Classicism finds morbid and perverse the assimilation of Nature to Art. Thomas Gibbons, for example, in 1767, warns against finical and "fantastical" tropes, and cites as examples "the following descriptions of the several parts of the Creation: the embossings of mountains, the enameling of lesser seas, the open-work of the vast ocean, and the fret-work of the rocks."[34]

To be sure, some nature > art metaphors remain in Neo-Classical verse, but it is under condition that the metaphor appear as otiose epithet. Pope's *Pastorals* and *Forest* offer specimens: "Fresh rising blushes *paint* the watery glass"; "there blushing Flora *paints* th' *enamelled* ground." But the line was generally clear; and Dryden, writing in 1681, was not ashamed to confess that when he was a child he thought as a child: "I remember when . . . I thought inimitable Spenser a mean poet in comparison of Sylvester's Du Bartas and was rapt into an ecstasy when I read these lines:

> Now when the winter's keen breath began
> To chrystallize the Baltic ocean,
> To glaze the lakes, to bridle up the Floods,
> And periwig with snow the baldpate woods."[35]

The youthful Milton, another reader of Du Bartas, ends his *Nativity Ode* with a conceit in the same mode. Eliot resumes the tradition in the celebrated opening of "Prufrock"

> When the evening is spread out against the sky
> Like a patient etherized upon a table . . .

The motives behind the Baroque practice are not as readily reducible to one as the Classical protest, unless we simply appeal to its wider inclusiveness, its taste for richness over purity, polyphony over monophony. More specific motives are the appetite for surprise and shock; Christian incarnationism; pedagogic domestication of the remote by homely analogy.

Thus far we have been considering the nature of figuration, with special stress on metonymy and metaphor; and we have suggested the possible period-stylistic character of these figures. We turn now to studies of metaphoric imagery which are literary-critical rather than literary-historical.

Two general studies of metaphoric imagery, one American and the other German, seem to merit specific presentation.

In 1924, Henry Wells published a study of *Poetic Imagery* which attempts to construct a typology, the types inducted, and chiefly illustrated, from Elizabethan literature. Rich in perceptive insights and suggestive generalizations, the book is less successful at systematic construction. Wells thinks of his scheme as achronistic, applicable to all periods, not just to the Elizabethan; and he believes himself to be descriptive, not evaluative, in his work. The basis of his investigation is said to be the arrangement of groups of figures "as they appear on an ascending scale from the lowest, or more nearly literal, to the most imaginative, or impressionistic"; but the scale, that of the "character and degree of imaginative activity," is asserted to have no direct bearing on the evaluation of them. His seven types of imagery, arranged in his own órder, are: the Decorative, the Sunken, the Violent (or Fustian), the Radical, the Intensive, the Expansive, and the Exuberant. They may advantageously be rearranged according to historical and evaluative hints offered by Wells.

The crudest forms, aesthetically, are the Violent and the Decorative, or the "metaphor of the masses" and the metaphor of artifice. The Decorative image, abundant in Sidney's *Arcadia,* is judged "typically Elizabethan." The Violent image, illustrated out of Kyd and other early Elizabethans, is characteristic of an early period of culture; but, since most men stay at a subliterary level, it belongs, in subliterary forms, to "any period"; sociologically, "Fustian" constitutes "a large and socially important body of metaphor." The evaluative judgment of both types is that they are "deficient in the requisite *subjective* element," that they too often link one physical image to another (as in catachresis) instead of relating the "outer world of nature to the inner world of man." Again, in both Decorative and Violent metaphors, the terms of the relationship remain disjunct, fixed, uninvaded by each other. But in the highest forms of metaphor, Wells believes, each term acts upon, alters, the other, so that a third term, a new apprehension, is created by the relationship.

Next, as we go up the scale, come the Exuberant image and the Intensive, the former a subtler version of the Violent, the latter a subtler version of the Decorative. We have left behind obvious forms of display, whether of energy or ingenuity. In the Exuberant image, we have, historically, reached Marlowe, the first of the greater Elizabethans, and Burns and Smart, the Pre-Romantics; this image is, says Wells, "especially prominent in much early poetry." It juxtaposes "two broad and imaginatively valuable terms," two broad, smooth surfaces in face-to-face contact. Otherwise put, this category covers loose comparisons, relationships based on simple evaluative categories. Burns writes:

> My love is like a red, red rose . . .
>
> . . . . .
>
> My love is like a melody
> That's sweetly played in tune.

The common ground between a beautiful woman, a fresh red rose, and a well-played melody is their beauty and desirability; they are all, in kind, the best. It isn't rosy cheeks which makes the woman like a rose, or her sweet voice which makes her like a melody (analogies which would produce Decorative images); her likeness to a rose is not in color, texture, or structure, but in value.[36]

Wells' Intensive image is a neatly visualizable image of the sort associated with illuminated manuscripts and pageants of the Middle Ages. In poetry, it is the image of Dante and, especially, in English poetry, of Spenser. The image is not only clear but—what perhaps follows—diminutive, diagrammatic: Dante's Hell, not Milton's. "Such metaphors are more often than others referred to as emblems or symbols." The pageant figures in "Lycidas"—Camus with his hairy mantle and sedge bonnet, and St. Peter with his mitre and his two keys—are also Intensive images. They are "guild" images: "pastoral" and "elegy" both had, by Milton's time, a stock of motifs and images. There can be stock imagery as well as stock "poetic diction." Its traditional, institutional character and its close relation to the visual arts and symbolic ceremony make Wells, thinking in terms of culture history, attach the Intensive image to conservative religion, to the medieval, the priestly, the Catholic.

The three highest categories are the Sunken, the Radical, and the Expansive (taken, one would think, in ascending order). Briefly, the Sunken is the image of a classical poetry; the Radical, the image of the Metaphysicals, preeminently of Donne; and the Expansive, the image, predominantly, of Shakespeare as well as of Bacon and Browne and Burke. The common denominations of the three, their marks of shared altitude, are their specifically literary character (their recalcitrance to pictorial visualization), their internality (metaphoric thinking), the interpenetration of the terms (their fruitful, procreative marriage).

The Sunken image, not to be confounded with the faded or trite, keeps "below full visibility," suggests the sensuous concrete without definitely projecting and clearing it. Its lack of overtones suits it to contemplative writing: its Elizabethan exemplar is Samuel Daniel, who wrote, in verses admired by Wordsworth and Thoreau:

> unless himself he can
> Erect himself, how poor a thing is man!

But Shakespeare is a master of it. In *Lear,* Edgar says:

> Men must endure
> Their going hence, even as their coming hither;
> Ripeness is all.

"Ripeness" is a sunken image, presumably out of orchards and fields. There is an analogy suggested between the inevitability of natural cycles of vegetation and the cycles of life. A Neo-Classical generation might cite as "mixed" some of Shakespeare's Sunken images:

> O how can summer's honey breath hold out
> Against the wreckful siege of battering days.

This sentence would require elaborate analytic expansion, for it mounts figure on figure: "days" is metonymic for Time, Age, which is then metaphorized as besieging a city and attempting, by battering-rams, to take it. What is attempting—city-like, or ruler of the city-like—to "hold out" against these assaults? It is youth, metaphorized as summer, or more exactly, as the sweet fragrance of summer: the fragrance of summer flowers is to the earth as sweet breath is to the human body, a part of or adjunct of the whole. If one tries to fit together neatly in one image the battering siege and the breath, he gets jammed up. The figurative movement is rapid and hence elliptical.[37]

The Radical image—so-called perhaps because its terms meet only at their roots, at an invisible logical ground, like final cause, rather than by juxtaposed obvious surfaces—is the image the minor term of which seems "unpoetic," either because too homely and utilitarian or because too technical, scientific, learned. The Radical image, that is, takes as metaphoric vehicle something which has no obvious emotive associations, which belongs to prose discourse, abstract or practical. Thus Donne, in his religious poetry, uses many figures from *"le géomètre enflammé."* Again, in the "First Anniversary," he uses a pseudo-medical figure which, except for the specified overlap of its terms, seems perversely oriented in just the wrong (i.e., a pejorative) direction:

> But as some serpent's poison hurteth not
> Except it be from the live serpent shot,
> So doth her virtue need her here to fit
> That unto us, she working more than it.

This is probably the characteristic kind of Radical image: the more obvious and less perverse example would be the compasses figure in Donne's "Valediction Forbidding Mourning." But, as Wells subtly demarks, Radical images can be derived out of romantically suggestive image-areas such as mountains, rivers, and seas, if one adopts an "analytic manner."[38]

Lastly, there is the Expansive image, its name linking it, by contrariety, to the Intensive. If the Intensive is the medieval and ecclesiastical figure, the Expansive is that of prophetic and progressive thought, of "strong passion and original meditation," culminating in the comprehensive metaphors of philosophy and religion represented in Burke, in Bacon, in Browne, and preeminently in Shakespeare. By definition, the Expansive image is one in which each term opens a wide vista to the imagination and each term strongly modifies the other: the "interaction" and "interpenetration" which, according to modern poetic theory, are central forms of poetic action occur most richly in the Expansive metaphor. We may take examples from *Romeo and Juliet*:

> Yet, wert thou as far
> As that vast shore washt with the farthest sea,
> I should adventure for such merchandise.

and from *Macbeth*:

> Light thickens, and the crow
> Makes wing to the rooky wood:
> Good things of day begin to droop and drowse.

In these last lines, Shakespeare gives us a "metaphorical setting for crime," which turns into an Expansive metaphor paralleling night and daemonic evil, light and goodness, yet not in any such obvious and allegoric fashion, but with suggestive particularity and sensuous concreteness: "light thickens"; things "droop and drowse." The poetically vague and the poetically specific meet in the line, "Good things of day begin to droop and drowse." The subject and the predicate work backward and forward on each other as we attend: starting with the verb, we ask what kinds of things—birds, animals, people, flowers—droop or drowse; then, noticing the abstract naming of the subject, we wonder whether the verbs are metaphorical for "cease to be vigilant," "quail timorously before the might of evil."[39]

Rhetoricians like Quintilian already make much of the distinction between the metaphor which animates the inanimate, and that which inanimates the animate; but they present the distinction as one between rhetorical devices. With Pongs, our second typologist, it becomes a grandiose contrast between polar attitudes —that of the mythic imagination, which projects personality upon the outer world of things, which animizes and animates nature, and the contrary type of imagination, which feels its ways into the alien, which de-animizes or unsubjectivizes itself. All the possibilities of figurative expression are exhausted by these two, the subjective and objective poles.[40]

The first form was called by Ruskin the "pathetic fallacy"; if we think of it as being applied upward to God as well as downward to the tree and the stone, we may call it the anthropomorphic imagination.[41] A student of mystical symbolism notes that there are three general types of earthly union available for the symbolic expression of the highest mystical experience: (1) union between inanimate objects (physical mixtures and chemical unions: the soul in the fire of God as spark, wood, wax, iron; God as Water to the soil of the soul, or as the Ocean into which flows the river of the soul); (2) unions figured according to the ways in which the body appropriates the essential elements of its life: "in the Scriptures God is represented by those particular things from which we cannot completely withdraw ourselves—light and air, which enter at every crack, and water, which in one form or other we all receive daily";[42] so, to mystics all over the world, God is the food and drink of the soul, its Bread, Fish, Water, Milk, Wine; (3) human relationships—that of son to father, wife to husband.

The first two of these would be assigned by Pongs to the second ultimate type of metaphoric intuition, that of *Einfühlung,* itself subdivided into the "mystic" and the "magic." The mystic metaphor we have illustrated from the mystics rather than the poets. Inorganic elements are symbolically treated, not as mere concepts or conceptual analogies but as representations which are also presentations.

Magical metaphor is interpreted after the fashion of the art historian Worringer, as an "abstraction" from the world of nature. Worringer studied the arts of Egypt, Byzantium, Persia, arts which "reduce organic nature, including man, to linear-geometrical forms, and frequently abandon the organic world altogether for one of pure lines, forms, and colors." "Ornament detaches itself now . . . as something which does not follow the stream of life but rigidly faces it. . . . The intention is no longer to pretend but to conjure." "Ornament . . . is something taken away from Time; it is pure extension, settled and stable."[43]

Anthropologists find both animism and magic in primitive cultures. The former seeks to reach, propitiate, persuade, unite with personalized spirits—the dead, gods. The latter, pre-science, studies the laws of power exerted by things: sacred words, amulets, rods and wands, images, relics. There is white magic—that of Christian cabalists like Cornelius Agrippa and Paracelsus; and there is black magic, that of evil men. But fundamental to both is the belief in the power of things. Magic touches the arts through image-making. Western tradition associates the painter and sculptor with the skill of the craftsman, with Haephaistos and Daidalos, with Pygmalion, who can bring the image to life. In folklore aesthetics, the maker of images is a sorcerer or magician, while the poet is the inspired, the possessed, the productively mad.[44] However, the primitive poet can compose charms and incantations, and the modern poet can, like Yeats, adopt the magical use of images, literal images, as a means to the use of magic-symbolic images in his poetry.[45] Mysticism takes the contrary line: the image is a symbol effected by a spiritual state; it is an expressive image not a causative image, and it is not necessary to the state: the same spiritual state can express itself in other symbols.[46]

The mystical metaphor and the magic are both de-animizing: they run counter to man's projection of himself into the non-human world; they summon up the "other"—the impersonal world of things, monumental art, physical law. Blake's "Tiger" is a mystical metaphor; God, or an aspect of God, is a Tiger (less than man, more than man); the Tiger in turn (and through the Tiger its Maker) is read in terms of metal forged in great heat. The Tiger is no animal from the natural world of the zoo, a tiger that Blake might have seen at the Tower of London, but a visionary creature, symbol as well as thing.

The magical metaphor lacks this translucency. It is Medusa's mask which turns the living into stone. Pongs cites Stefan George as a representative of this magical attitude, this desire to petrify the living: "It is not the natural drive of the human psyche to project itself from which George's form-giving spiritualization works, but, in its origin, a powerful destruction of biological life, a willed 'estrangement' ('alienation') as the basis for the preparation of the inner, magic world."[47]

In English poetry, Dickinson and Yeats variously reach for this de-animizing, this anti-mystic metaphor: Emily Dickinson when she wants to render the sense of death as well as the experience of resurrection: she likes to invoke the experience of dying, stiffening, petrifying. "It was not death," but it was

> As if my life were shaven
> And fitted to a frame,
> And could not breathe without a key . . .

> How many times these low feet staggered,
> Only the soldered mouth can tell;
> Try! can you stir the awful rivet?
> Try! can you lift the hasps of steel?[48]

Yeats reaches his ultimate of Poetry as Magic in "Byzantium" (1930). In the 1927 "Sailing to Byzantium," he has already set the opposition between the world of biological life: "The young in one another's arms, . . . the mackerel-crowded seas," and the world of Byzantine art, where all is fixed, rigid, unnatural, the world of "gold mosaic" and "gold enameling." Biologically, man is a "dying animal"; his hope for survival is through being "gathered into the artifice of eternity," not again to take "bodily form from any natural thing," but to be a work of art, a golden bird on a golden bough. "Byzantium," from one point of view a tightly written illustration of Yeats' "system," a doctrinal poem, is from another, specifically literary point of view a structure of closely interrespondent non-natural images, the whole composing something like a prescribed ritual or liturgy.[49]

Pongs' categories, which we have rendered with some freedom, have the special character of relating poetic style to view of life.[50] Though each period-style is seen to have its own differentiated versions of them, they are essentially timeless, alternative ways of looking at and responding to life. All three, however, belong outside of the general lines of what is often characterized as modern thought, i.e., rationalism, naturalism, positivism, science. Such a classification of metaphors thus suggests that poetry remains loyal to prescientific modes of thought. The poet keeps the animistic vision of the child and of primitive man, the child's archetype.[51]

In recent years, there have been many studies of specific poets or even specific poems or plays in terms of their symbolic imagery. In such "practical criticism," the assumptions of the critic become important. What is he looking for? Is he analyzing the poet or the poem?

We must distinguish between a study of the spheres from which the images are drawn (which, as MacNeice says, "belongs still more properly to the study of subject-matter,"[52]) and a study of "the ways in which images can be used," the character of the relationship between the "tenor" and the "vehicle" (the metaphor). Most monographs on the imagery of a specific poet (e.g., Rugoff's

Donne's Imagery) belong to the former class. They chart and
weigh a poet's interests by collecting and distributing his metaphors between nature, art, industry, the physical science, the hu-
manities, the city, and the country. But one can also classify the
themes or objects which impel the poet to metaphor, e.g., women,
religion, death, airplanes. More significant than the classification,
however, is the discovery of large-scale equivalents, psychic cor-
relatives. That two spheres repeatedly summon up each the other
may be supposed to show their real interpenetration in the creative psyche of the poet: thus in Donne's "Songs and Sonnets," his
poems of profane love, the metaphoric gloss is constantly drawn
from the Catholic world of sacred love: to sexual love he applies
the Catholic concepts of ecstasy, canonization, martyrdom, relics,
while in some of his "Holy Sonnets" he addresses God in violent
erotic figures:

> Yet dearly I love you, and would be lovéd fain
> But am betrothed unto your enemy.
> Divorce me, untie, or break that knot again,
> Take me to you, imprison me, for I
> Except you enthrall me, never shall be free,
> Nor ever chaste, except you ravish me.

The interchange between the spheres of sex and religion recognizes that sex is a religion and religion is a love.

One type of study stresses the self-expression, the revelation of
the poet's psyche through his imagery. It assumes that the poet's
images are like images in a dream, i.e., uncensored by discretion
or shame: not his overt statements, but offered by way of illustration, they might be expected to betray his real centers of interest.
But it may be questioned whether a poet has ever been so uncritical of his images.[53]

Another assumption, quite certainly mistaken, is that the poet
must literally have perceived whatever he can imagine (on the
strength of which Miss Wade, in her study of Traherne, recon-
structs his early life.)[54] According to Dr. Johnson, an admirer of
Thompson's poems thought she knew his tastes from his works.

> She could gather from his works three parts of his character: that
> he was a great lover, a great swimmer, and rigorously abstinent; but,
> said [his intimate] Savage, he knows not any love but that of the

sex; he was perhaps never in cold water in his life; and he indulges himself in all the luxury that comes within his reach.

Her conception of the poet's personal characteristics and habits was ludicrously inaccurate. Nor can we argue that absence of metaphoric images is equivalent to absence of interest. In Walton's life of Donne there is not a fishing image among its eleven figures. The poetry of the fourteenth-century composer Machaut uses no tropes drawn from music.[55]

The assumption that a poet's imagery is the central contribution of his unconscious and that in it, therefore, the poet speaks as a man, not as an artist, seems, in turn, referable back to floating, not very consistent, assumptions about how to recognize "sincerity." On the one hand, it is popularly supposed that striking imagery must be contrived, and hence insincere: a man really moved would either speak in simple unfigured language or in banal and faded figures. But there is a rival idea that the trite figure evoking the stock response is a sign of insincerity, of accepting a crude approximation to one's feeling in place of a scrupulous statement of it. Here we confuse men generally with literary men, men talking with men writing, or, rather, men talking with poems. Ordinary personal candor and trite imagery are eminently compatible. As for "sincerity" in a poem: the term seems almost meaningless. A sincere expression of what? Of the supposed emotional state out of which it came? Or of the state in which the poem was written? Or a sincere expression of the poem, i.e., the linguistic construct shaping in the author's mind as he writes? Surely it will have to be the last: the poem is a sincere expression of the poem.

A poet's imagery is revelatory of his self. How is his *self* defined? Mario Praz and Mrs. Hornstein have both been amusing at the expense of Miss Spurgeon's Shakespeare, the universal twentieth-century Englishman. It can be assumed that the great poet shared our "common humanity."[56] We need no imagistic key to the scriptures to learn that. If the value of image study lies in uncovering something recondite, it will presumably make it possible for us to read some private signatures, unlock the secret of Shakespeare's heart.

Instead of discovering in his imagery Shakespeare's universal humanity, we may find a kind of hieroglyphic report on his psychic health as it exists when he is composing a specific play. Thus, Miss

Spurgeon says of *Troilus* and *Hamlet,* "Did we not know it for other reasons, we could be sure from the similarity and continuity of symbolism in the two plays that they were written near together, and at a time when the author was suffering from a disillusionment, revulsion, and perturbation of nature such as we feel nowhere else with the same intensity." Here Miss Spurgeon is assuming not that the specific cause of Shakespeare's disillusionment can be located but that *Hamlet* expresses disillusionment and that this must be Shakespeare's own.[57] He could not have written so great a play had he not been sincere, i.e., writing out of his own mood. Such a doctrine runs counter to the view of Shakespeare urged by E. E. Stoll and others which emphasizes his art, his dramaturgy, his skillful provision of new and better plays within the general pattern of preceding successes: e.g., *Hamlet* as a follower-up of *The Spanish Tragedy; The Winter's Tale* and *The Tempest* as a rival theater's equivalents to Beaumont and Fletcher.

Not all studies of poetic imagery, however, attempt to catch the poet off guard or to pursue his inner biography. They may focus, rather, on an important element in the total meaning of a play—what Eliot calls "the pattern below the level of plot and character."[58] In her 1930 essay, "Leading Motives in the Imagery of Shakespeare's Tragedies," Miss Spurgeon herself is primarily interested in defining the image or cluster of images which, dominating a specific play, acts as tone-giver. Samples of her analysis are the discovery in *Hamlet* of images of disease, e.g., ulcer, cancer; of food and the digestive apparatus in *Troilus;* in *Othello,* of "animals in action, preying upon one another. . . ." Miss Spurgeon makes some effort to show how this substructure of a play affects its total meaning, remarking of *Hamlet* that the disease motif suggests that the Prince is not culpable, that the whole state of Denmark is diseased. The positive value of her work lies in this search for subtler forms of literary meaning than ideological generalization and overt plot structure.

More ambitious studies of imagery, those of Wilson Knight, take off, initially, from Middleton Murry's brilliant pages on Shakespeare's imagery (*The Problem of Style,* 1922). Knight's earlier work (e.g., *Myth and Miracle,* 1929, and *The Wheel of Fire,* 1930) is exclusively concerned with Shakespeare; but in later volumes the method is applied to other poets as well, e.g., Milton, Pope, Byron, Wordsworth.[59] The earlier work, clearly the best, keeps to studies of individual plays, studying each in terms of its symbolic imagery, giving particular attention to imagistic oppositions like "tempests" and "music," but also sensitively observing stylistic differentiations between play and play as well as within a play. In the later books, the extravagances of an "enthusiast" are palpable. Knight's exegesis of Pope's *Essays on Criticism* and *on Man* blithely disregards the question of what the "ideas" in those poems could historically have meant to Pope and his contemporaries. Deficient in historical perspective, Knight suffers also from a desire to "philosophize." The "philosophy" he draws from Shakespeare and others is neither original, clear, nor complex: it amounts to the reconciliation of Eros and Agape, of order with energy, and so on with other pairs of contraries. As all the "real" poets bring essentially the same "message," one is left, after the decoding of each, with a feeling of futility. Poetry is a "revelation," but what does it reveal?

Quite as perceptive as Knight's work and much better balanced is that of Wolfgang Clemen, whose *Shakespeares Bilder*[60] carries out the promise of its subtitle that it will study the development and functioning of the imagery. Contrasting the imagery of lyrics and even epics, he insists on the dramatic nature of Shakespeare's plays: in his mature work, it is not Shakespeare "the man" but Troilus who metaphorically in the play thinks in terms of rancid food. In a play, "Each image is used by a specific person." Clemen has a real sense for the right methodological questions to put. In analyzing *Titus Andronicus,* for example, he asks, "On what occasions in the play does Shakespeare use images? Does there exist a connection between the use of imagery and the occasion? What function have the images"— to which questions for *Titus* he has only negative answers. In *Titus,* the imagery is spasmodic and ornamental, but from that we can trace Shakespeare's development to the use of metaphor as *"stimmungsmässige Untermalung des Geschehens"* and as a *"ganz ursprüngliche Form de Wahrnehmung,"* i.e., to metaphorical thinking. He makes admirable comments on the *"abstrakte Metaphorik"* of Shakespeare's Middle Period (with its *"unbildliche Bildlichkeit"*—corresponding to Wells' Sunken, Radical, and Expansive types of imagery); but, writing a monograph on a specific poet, he introduces his type only when, in Shakespeare's "development," it appears; and, though his monograph studies a development, and the "periods" of Shakespeare's work, Clemen remembers that he is studying the "periods" of the poetry, not those of the author's largely hypothetical life.

Like meter, imagery is one component structure of a poem. In terms of our scheme, it is a part of the syntactical, or stylistic, stratum. It must be studied, finally, not in isolation from the other strata but as an element in the totality, the integrity, of the literary work.

[1] Max Eastman, *The Literary Mind in an Age of Science* (New York, 1931), p. 165.

[2] On "Types of Discourse," *cf.* Charles Morris, *Signs, Languages, and Behavior*, New York, 1946, p. 123 ff. Morris distinguishes twelve kinds of "discourse," of which those relevant to our chapter—and our four terms—are "Fictive" (the World of the Novel), "Mythological," and "Poetic."

[3] *Monosign* and *plurisign* are used by Philip Wheelwright, in "The Semantics of Poetry," *Kenyon Review*, II (1940), pp. 263-83. The plurisign is "semantically reflexive in the sense that it is a part of what it means. That is to say, the plurisign, the poetic symbol, is not merely employed but enjoyed; its value is not entirely instrumental but largely aesthetic, intrinsic."

[4] *Cf.* E. G. Boring, *Sensation and Perception in the History of Experimental Psychology*, New York, 1942; June Downey, *Creative Imagination: Studies in the Psychology of Literature*, New York, 1929; Jean-Paul Sartre, *L'Imagination*, Paris, 1936.

[5] I. A. Richards, *Principles of Literary Criticism*, London, 1924, Chapter XVI, "The Analysis of a Poem."

[6] Ezra Pound, *Pavannes and Divisions*, New York, 1918; T. S. Eliot, "Dante," *Selected Essays*, New York, 1932, p. 204; Eliot, "A Note on the Verse of John Milton," *Essays and Studies by Members of the English Association*, XXI, Oxford, 1936, p. 34.

[7] "Modern psychology has taught us that these two senses of the term 'image' overlap. We may say that every spontaneous mental image is to some extent symbolical." Charles Baudoin, *Psychoanalysis and Aesthetics*, New York, 1924, p. 28.

[8] J. M. Murry, "Metaphor," *Countries of the Mind*, 2nd series, London, 1931, pp. 1-16; L. MacNeice, *Modern Poetry*, New York, 1938, p. 113.

[9] An admirable study of one literary movement and its influence upon another is René Tauin's *L'Influence du symbolisme français sur la poésie américaine* . . . , Paris, 1929.

[10] For the terminology here followed, *cf.* Craig la Drière, *The American Bookman*, I (1944), pp. 103-4.

[11] S. T. Coleridge, *The Statesman's Manual: Complete Works* (ed. Shedd, New York, 1853), Vol. I, pp. 437-8. This distinction between symbol and allegory was first clearly drawn by Goethe. *Cf.* Curt Richard Müller, *Die geschichtlichen Voraussetzungen das Symbolbegriffs in Goethe's Kunstanschauung*, Leipzig, 1937.

[12] J. H. Wicksteed, *Blake's Innocence and Experience* . . . , London, 1928, p. 23; W. B. Yeats, *Essays*, London, 1924, p. 95 ff., on Shelley's "Ruling Symbols."

When do metaphors become symbols? (a) When the "vehicle" of the metaphor is concrete-sensuous, like the lamb. The cross is not a metaphor but a metonymic symbol, representing Him who died upon it, like St. Lawrence's gridiron and St. Catherine's wheel, or representing suffering, in which case the *instrument* signifies that which it does, the effect of its action. (b) When the metaphor is recurrent and central, as in Crashaw and Yeats and Eliot. The normal procedure is the turning of images into metaphors and metaphors into symbols, as in Henry James. In "Domes of Byzantium," *Southern Review*, VII (1941), pp. 639-52, Howard Baker studies in detail how images in Yeats' early poems (fire, birds, hawks, towers) become symbols in the later work.

[13] The "Blakean heterodoxy," says M. O. Percival (*Blake's Circle of Destiny*, New York, 1938, p. 1), "was equally traditional with Dante's orthodoxy." Says Mark Schorer (*Blake*, New York, 1946, p. 23): "Blake, like Yeats, found metaphorical support for his dialectical view in . . . the system of correspondence of Swedenborg and Boehme, in the analogical pursuits of the cabalists, and in the alchemy of Paracelsus and Agrippa."

[14] *Cf.* the comments on Frost of Cleanth Brooks, *Modern Poetry and the Tradition*, Chapel Hill, 1939, p. 110 ff.

[15] *Cf.* Nietzche, *Die Geburt der Tragödie*, Leipzig, 1872.

[16] For a representative group of definitions, *cf.* Lord Raglan's *The Hero . . .*, London, 1937.

[17] *Cf.* Fritz Strich, *Die Mythologie in der deutschen Literatur von Klopstock bis Wagner*, Berlin, 1910. 2 vols.

[18] S. H. Hooke, *Myth and Ritual*, Oxford, 1933; J. A. Stewart, *The Myths of Plato*, London; Ernst Cassirer, *Philosophie der symbolischen Formen*, Vol. II, "Das mythische Denken," Berlin, 1925, p. 271 ff.

[19] George Sorel, *Reflexions on Violence* (tr. T. E. Hulme), New York, 1914; Reinhold Niebuhr, "The Truth Value of Myths," *The Nature of Religious Experience . . .*, New York, 1937.

[20] *Cf.* especially R. M. Guastalla, *Le Myth et le livre: essai sur l'origine de la littérature*, Paris, 1940.

[21] *Cf.* Donald Davidson, "Yeats and the Centaur," *Southern Review*, VII (1941), pp. 510-16.

[22] Arthur Machen's *Hieroglyphics*, London, 1923, ably (if untechnically, and in a highly romantic version) defends the view that religion (i.e., myth and ritual) constitutes the larger climate within which alone poetry (i.e., symbolism, aesthetic contemplation) can breathe and grow.

[23] The standard ancient classification of the schemes and tropes is Quintilian's *Institutes of Oratory*. For the most elaborate Elizabethan treatment, *cf.* Puttenham's *Arte of English Poesie* (ed. Willcock and Walker), Cambridge, 1936.

[24] Karl Bühler, *Sprachtheorie*, Jena, 1934, p. 343; Stephen J. Brown, *The World of Imagery*, p. 149 ff., and Roman Jakobson, "Randbemerkungen zur Prosa des Dichters Pasternak," *Slavische Rundschau*, VII (1935), pp. 357-73.

[25] D. S. Mirsky, "Walt Whitman: Poet of American Democracy," *Critics Group Dialectics*, No. 1, 1937, pp. 11-29.

[26] G. Campbell, *Philosophy of Rhetoric*, London, 1776, pp. 321, 326.

[27] Richards, *Philosophy of Rhetoric*, London, 1936, p. 117, calls Campbell's first type the "verbal metaphor," for he holds that literary metaphor

is not a verbal linkage but a transaction between contexts, an analogy between objects.

28 *Cf.* Milman Parry, "The Traditional Metaphor in Homer," *Classical Philology,* XXVIII (1933), pp. 30-43. Parry makes clear Aristotle's unhistoric identification of Homer's metaphorism with that of later poets; compares Homer's "fixed metaphors" to those of Old English poets and (more restrictedly) to those of eighteenth-century Augustans.

29 *Cf.* C. Bally, *Traité de stylistique française,* Heidelberg, 1909, Vol. I, p. 184 ff.: "Le langage figuré." On pp. 194-5, Bally, speaking not as a literary theorist but as a linguist, classifies metaphors as: "Images concrètes, saisies par l'imagination, images affectives, saisies par une opération intellectuelle. . . ." His three categories I should call (1) poetic metaphor; (2) ritual ("fixed") metaphor; and (3) linguistic (etymological, or buried) metaphor.

30 For a defense of ritual metaphor and guild images in the style of Milton, *cf.* C. S. Lewis, *Preface to Paradise Lost,* London, 1942, pp. 39 ff.

31 *Cf.* Heinz Werner, *Die Ursprünge der Metapher,* Leipzig, 1919.

32 Hermann Pongs, *Das Bild in der Dichtung.* I: *Versuch einer Morphologie der metaphorischen Formen.* Marburg, 1927. II: *Voruntersuchungen zum Symbol.* Marburg, 1939.

33 L. B. Osborn, *The . . . Writings of John Hoskyns,* New Haven, 1937, p. 125; George Campbell, *Philosophy of Rhetoric,* pp. 335-7; A. Pope, *The Art of Sinking;* A. Dion, *L'Art d'écrire,* Quebec, 1911, pp. 111-2.

34 Thomas Gibbons, *Rhetoric . . . ,* London, 1767, pp. 15-16.

35 John Dryden, *Essays* (ed. W. P. Ker), Oxford, 1900, Vol. I, p. 247 ("Dedication of *The Spanish Friar*").

36 *Cf.* I. A. Richards, *Philosophy of Rhetoric,* London, 1936, pp. 117-18: "A very broad division may be made between metaphors which work through some direct resemblance between the two things, the tenor and the vehicle, and those which work through some common attitude which we may . . . take up towards them both."

37 The later Shakespeare abounds in rapidly shifting figures, what older pedagogues would call "mixed metaphors." Shakespeare thinks quicker than he speaks, one could put it, says Wolfgang Clemen, *Shakespeares Bilder . . . ,* Bonn, 1936, p. 144.

38 H. W. Wells, *Poetic Imagery,* New York, 1924, p. 127. As characteristic users of the Radical image, Wells (*op. cit.,* pp. 136-7) cites Donne, Webster, Marston, Chapman, Tourneur, and Shakespeare, and out of the late nineteenth century, George Meredith (whose *Modern Love* he pronounces "an unusually condensed and interesting body of symbolic thought") and Francis Thompson. From Thompson come the lines:

> At evening, when the lank and rigid trees
> To the mere forms of their sweet day-selves drying
> On heaven's blank leaf seem pressed and flattened.

39 The imagery of *Macbeth* is brilliantly considered by Cleanth Brooks in "The Naked Babe and the Cloak of Manliness," *The Well Wrought Urn,* New York, 1947, pp. 21-46.

40 As far back as Quintilian (*Institutes, Bk.* VIII, chap. 6), a basic distinction between kinds of metaphors has been felt to equate the distinction between organic and inorganic. Quintilian's four kinds are: one sort of living

184   WELLEK *and* WARREN

thing for another; one inanimate thing for another; the inanimate put for the animate; and the animate put for the inanimate.

Pongs calls the first of his types the *Beseeltypus* and the second the *Erfühltypus.* The first animizes or anthropomorphizes; the second empathizes.

[41] For Ruskin on the "Pathetic Fallacy," *cf. Modern Painters,* London, 1856, Vol. III, Pt. 4. The examples cited exempt the simile from indictment because it keeps natural fact separate from emotional valuation.

On the polar heresies of Anthropomorphism and Symbolism, *cf.* M. T.-L. Penido's brilliant book, *Le Rôle de l'analogie en théologie dogmatique,* Paris, 1931, p. 197 ff.

[42] M. A. Ewer, *Survey of Mystical Symbolism,* London, 1933, p. 164-6.

[43] Vossler, Spengler, T. E. Hulme (*Speculations,* London, 1924), and Yeats, as well as Pongs, have been stimulated by Wilhelm Worringer's *Abstraktion und Einfühlung,* Berlin, 1908.

Our first quotation comes from Joseph Frank's admirable study of "Spatial Form in Modern Literature," *Sewanee Review,* LIII (1945), p. 645; our second from Spengler, who quotes Worringer in his discussion of the Magian culture, *Decline of the West,* New York, 1926, Vol. I, pp. 183 ff., 192.

[44] *Cf.* Ernest Kris, "Approaches to Art," in *Psychoanalysis Today* (ed. S. Lorand), New York, 1944, pp. 360-2.

[45] W. B. Yeats, *Autobiography,* New York, 1938, pp. 161, 219-25.

[46] K. Vossler, *Spirit of Language in Civilization* (tr., London, 1932), p. 4. Karl Vossler well remarks that mages and mystics are permanent and opposed types. "There is constant strife between magic, which uses language as a tool and thereby seeks to bring as much as possible, even God, under its control, and mysticism, which breaks, makes valueless, and rejects, all forms."

[47] H. Pongs, *Das Bild,* Vol. I, p. 296.

[48] Emily Dickinson, *Collected Poems,* Boston, 1937, pp. 192, 161; *cf.* also p. 38 ("I laughed a *wooden* laugh") and p. 215 ("A clock stopped—not the mantel's").

[49] For the significance of Byzantium, *cf.* Yeats' *A Vision,* London, 1938, pp. 279-81.

[50] Hermann Nohl, *Stil und Weltanschauung,* Jena, 1920.

[51] *Cf.* Emile Cailliet, *Symbolisme et âmes primitives,* Paris, 1936, for a remarkably unblushing, uncritical acceptance of equivalence between the prelogical mind of primitive peoples and the aims of *Symboliste* poets. To the abstracting, conceptual operations of the modern post-Cartesian intellect, Cailliet contrasts the "participation mystique" of primitive man and the poet, the inability to distinguish between sign and thing signified.

[52] MacNeice, *op. cit.,* p. 111.

[53] *Cf.* Harold Rosenberg, "Myth and Poem," *Symposium,* II (1931), pp. 179 ff.

[54] Gladys Wade, *Thomas Traherne,* Princeton, 1944, pp. 26-37. *Cf.* the critical review of the book by E. N. S. Thompson, *Philological Quarterly,* XXIII (1944), pp. 383-4.

[55] Dr. Johnson, *Lives of the Poets,* "Thomson."

On the argument from imagistic silence, including the examples we cite, *cf.* L. H. Hornstein's penetrating "Analysis of Imagery." *PMLA,* LVII (1942), pp. 638-53.

[56] Mario Praz, *English Studies,* XVIII (1936), pp. 177-81, wittily re-

views Miss Spurgeon's *Shakespeare's Imagery and What It Tells Us,* (Cambridge, 1935), especially its first part, "The Revelation of the Man," with its "fallacy of trying to read . . . into Shakespeare's images his senses, tastes, and interests," and rightly praises Clemen (whose book appeared in 1936) for thinking that "Shakespeare's use and choice of images is not so much conditioned by his own personal tastes as by what are in each case his artistic intentions. . . ."

[57] Miss Spurgeon's essay is reprinted in Anne Bradby's *Shakespeare Criticism, 1919-35,* London, 1936, pp. 18-61.

On autobiography and *Hamlet,* cf. C. J. Sisson, *The Mythical Sorrows of Shakespeare,* London, 1936.

[58] T. S. Eliot, "Hamlet," *Selected Essays,* London, 1932, pp. 141-6.

[59] G. Wilson Knight: *Myth and Miracle: An Essay on the Mystic Symbolism of Shakespeare,* London, 1929; *The Wheel of Fire,* London, 1930; *The Imperial Theme,* London, 1931; *The Christian Renaissance,* Toronto, 1933; *The Burning Oracle,* London, 1939; *The Starlit Dome,* London, 1941.

[60] Wolfgang Clemen, *Shakespeares Bilder,* Bonn, 1936.

Verse in Poetry

Metaphorical elements enjoy the lion's share of critical attention perhaps because these indirections of language lend themselves to prose analysis and explanation. The sounds of poetry, which are more difficult to translate into other terms, remain a mystery. For an inexperienced reader the difficulty becomes acute when verse is treated as a thing apart from the poem's total meaning. The five selections on verse are designed to clarify the matter in two ways: the first two by helping the reader to hear the sound as a part of the poem, those which follow by suggesting possible interpretations of the organization of sound. That these theories of versification differ should not be alarming. Theories of poetry differ, and, as A. C. Bradley puts it, "the gift for feeling it [versification] . . . is the specific gift for poetry as distinguished from other arts."

Directing attention to the sounds which language makes, Hugh Kenner establishes certain guiding principles: that a knowledge of metrical elements is helpful, but helpful only in listening to underlying rhythmic patterns; that rhythm is unavoidable in using language; that it need not be mechanically regular in verse; that meter, which is the intelligent control of rhythm, implies a cooperation of sound and sense. Mark Van Doren demonstrates this cooperation in a famous sixteenth-century poem. He offers two versions of "They Flee From Me," Wyatt's expressive original and another which suffers from Tottel's regularizing mutilations. The juxtaposition makes clear that what the insensitive editor sacrificed to mechanical regularity was an actual measure of meaning achieved through masterly organization of sound.

It is difficult to summarize the differences which separate competing theories of versification, but with little risk of oversimplification we can say that theorists differ primarily on the proper unit of measure. What we seem to require in life and expect in the arts, what endows both with meaning, is some combination of repetition and variation. When repetition rules, we have Tottel's deadening regularity; when *variation, a chaos without meaning. (In some wished-for world there may be meaning without order; but in the world we inhabit, if "anything goes," nothing means anything. It is also true that in our world a ruthlessly imposed order threatens life itself.) If the perpetual problem, then, in life as well as art, is a proper combination of repetition and variation, some unit of measure is essential. Sufficiently suggested, it provides a norm of feeling, a convention, from which expressive departures are possible and by which those departures can be measured.*

If we are to take poetry seriously, its metrical convention, the unit of measure it employs, must be useable: it must somehow express the normal range of our experience. What seems normal has certainly changed over the centuries. This is not to say that the poetry of four hundred years ago is so remote from our experience that it can have no meaning for us; it means only that the pastness of the past must be recognized and accepted before we can recover the poetry of the past. To declare Wyatt's poem hopelessly archaic because its metrical norm is the traditional iambic foot is as absurd as reading it as though it were written this morning.

Yvor Winters, the first of the theorists, is a vigorous conservative. The poetry which he favors—we shall understand his preference more fully in Part Three where his general theory of poetry appears—is a poetry of rational statement in which metrical variations have precise moral implications. His views on meter are best summarized by the statement that "the nearer a norm a writer hovers, the more able is he to vary his feelings in opposite or even in many directions, and the more significant will be his variations." The norm which Winters espouses is iambic; for him it represents a useable tradition of civilized thought and feeling. To give it up as the free verse experimenters have done is to limit one's range, to abandon the possibility of really complex or profound statement.

Gerard Manley Hopkins is often considered the first truly modern poet in English, in large part because of his remarkable diction, but also because of his audacious and expressive rhythms. The metrical tradition which Winters considers a necessary basis for precise moral judgment was too tame for Hopkins, and in the two selections presented here he proposes as a norm what, from a traditionalist point of view, must be unprincipled poetic behavior. Carry variation far enough, he says, so that the underlying rhythm can no longer be felt. Contrapuntal effects cease. The "sprung rhythm" which results is remarkable for its flexibility and force, combining as it does the ease of ordinary speech and the intensity of poetry. With considerable variation in the number of unaccented syllables per foot and a stanza which is scanned as a whole, not as a series of individual lines, it is a kind of syncopation syncopated. What it communicates is violent and personal, ecstasy or risk, not, in any case, the measured understanding which Winters demands.

The budding modernity of Hopkins is apparent in the kinds of precedent he invokes. Whereas Winters finds sanction in a high literary tradition, Hopkins finally turns elsewhere to justify his violent procedures, to common speech, music, and nursery rhymes. In Bertolt Brecht this awareness of a world beyond literature becomes a dominant pressure. Brecht's clearest influence thus far has been in the theatre where his urgency has brought about radical changes in the relation between actor and audience. In the essay on free verse reprinted here he takes precise account of the conditions in which he found himself at work as a poet and of the effects of those conditions on his work. As he relates his experiments in free verse to its gestural qualities, to his political sense, to jazz and the change in the "acoustical universe," Brecht suggests how broad areas of experience apparently remote from art may enter into an artist's minute technical concerns.

HUGH KENNER

From *The Art of Poetry*

RHYTHM AND SOUND

The words of verse move in *rhythm,* which may be anything from

| ti TUM | ti TUM | ti TUM | ti TUM |
| I NE | ver SAW | a PUR | ple COW |

to the most intricate arrangement of stresses:

> When, when, and whenever death closes our eyelids,
> Moving naked over Acheron
> Upon the one raft, victor and conquered together,
> Marius and Jugurtha together,
>   one tangle of shadows. . . .

(You will sometimes hear writing like this referred to as "free verse." This term survives from forty years ago, when new elaborate rhythms were puzzling ears long trained to a rocking-horse beat. It is easier now to see that verse is never "free" if it has any life at all.)

It is a common mistake to suppose that "normal" verse moves, as nearly as the poet can manage, with mechanical regularity:

How SWEET| the MOON-| light SLEEPS| up-ON| this BANK|
Here will we sit, and let the sounds of music
Creep in our ears; soft stillness and the night
Become the touches of sweet harmony.

—*William Shakespeare*

One wouldn't *speak* the first line the way it has been printed above. There is no reason to speak it so, simply because it occurs in a passage of verse.

How sweet the moonlight sleeps upon this bank!

Probably "the" and "up" are the only really unobtrusive syllables.

How   sweet
(the)   m o o n l i g h t s l e e p s
(up)ón   thís bánk!

"Bank" gets a decided emphasis (accent); "light" gets rather a prolongation than an accent; "sleeps" may be said to get some of both. The usual systems for classifying English rhythms tend to assume that only accent need be taken into account. For limited purposes of classification it is sometimes useful to say that Shakespeare's verse "normally" has ten syllables per line, the alternate ones stressed, but you would search through the plays a long time to find a line that really went like that.

Rhythm doesn't by its mere presence make interesting verse. It is when the poet puts it to intelligent *use* that torpid words leap.

In its simplest use, rhythm binds into its pattern and renders unmistakable the varying degrees of stress which the words require to make the sense perfectly plain. When the guards make for the ghost of Hamlet's father with pikes, Horatio might say,

"Wait a minute, we shouldn't treat it like that. We're making a mistake to threaten such a majestic figure with common weapons. We can't hurt it any more than we can hurt the air. Our violence is empty and stupid; petty malice, and useless besides."

Shakespeare makes him say,

We do it wrong, being so majestical,
To offer it the show of violence;

> For it is, as the air, invulnerable,
> And our vain blows malicious mockery.

Verse enables him to compress this speech to twenty-seven words with perfect clarity, and to convey besides in the ordered march of syllables a good deal of ceremonious respect that has leaked out of our prose paraphrase. Each group of words ("You do it wrong," "as the air," and so on) is marked off by one rhythmic device or another, and the structure of the single complex sentence is perfectly clear at one hearing.

Shakespeare was writing for a theater audience and had to be clear at one hearing, however complex his meaning. That is one reason his verse technique developed so rapidly.

To start grasping the sense of a passage of verse, READ IT ALOUD AND TRUST THE RHYTHM. If on repeated trials the rhythm gives no support, there is probably something wrong, either with the verse or with your reading.

Bernard Shaw's theater prose is also perfectly clear at one hearing, but he has far less complex material to convey with each speech, and gets infinitely less onto a page than does Shakespeare. In particular, the *feelings* Shaw's highly accomplished prose can convey are of diagrammatic simplicity.

Not only does verse get more onto a page; there are some kinds of meaning that can't be communicated at all unless they are communicated as *rapidly* as only verse can manage. The elements of the "moonlight" speech on page 189 would convey no charge if they were spread out through a paragraph. (Try it.)

You have to bring the wires close together to get a spark.

You have to juxtapose images to get more than a bare meaning. When you do this, rhythm keeps the sense from clotting.

This account omits the pleasure that rhythm gives in its own right. But this pleasure is never at its highest unless rhythm cooperates with the sense of the words.

METER

Rhythm is inescapable. The most casual everyday speech falls into phrases / with ascertainable rhythms.

Meter (from the Greek word for *measure*) denotes the intelligent control of rhythm. It does not occur by accident. The rhythms of speech, even highly deliberate speech, are largely accidental. A good prose writer is aware of various rhythmic devices he can use / to group / or enforce / his meanings. / He will not use them conspicuously, / because part of the decorum of modern prose / is its pretense of being casual speech / with the false starts left out. / Prose approaches verse as the rhythms inherent in all manifestations of language are put to more and more deliberate *use*. When we are in the presence of verse it is no longer sufficient to say that intelligent use is being made of rhythmic patterns that crop up here and there. Verse is *built* out of rhythmic units. It is not necessarily true to say that the rhythms of verse are more regular (i.e., more repetitious) than those of prose. They may not even draw attention to their presence, though they generally do. The essential truth is that they *function* continually, not spasmodically.

The Greek grammarians noted that lines of verse are built out of rhythmic units, and gave names to a number of possible kinds of units or "feet." There is no poem that knowledge of these names will help you to understand or appreciate. The value of making their acquaintance is to sharpen your perception. When you know of the metrical phenomenon called a "spondee" you are more likely to be aware of its presence and function in the poem you are reading.

Many lines of verse reveal themselves to have been built mainly out of two-syllable units:

That time / of year / thou mayst / in me / behold

Obviously either the first syllable or the second of a pair may be the more prominent; or both may assert themselves. The easiest kind of prominence to recognize is imparted by *accent*. Anyone can tell that the word "double" or the phrase "beat it" is accented on the first syllable, the word "afraid" or the phrase "be gone" on the second. A foot like "double" (′ ˘) is called a *trochee,* or trochaic foot. A foot like "afraid" (˘ ′) is called an *iamb,* or iambic foot. The iamb is probably the commonest rhythmic unit in English verse.

Note that the amount of difference between the accented and unaccented syllables may vary. The word "pilgrim" is trochaic, but the contrast between the two syllables is much less marked than in "double." In the same way, the word "except" is iambic, but less markedly so than "afraid." If you don't hear these distinctions, you are not pronouncing the words clearly.

There are probably no words with two adjoining equally accented syllables, though a word like "upend" comes pretty close. A better example is a phrase like "gold cup" or "dry rot." such a foot ($''$) is called a *spondee,* or spondaic foot.

One is normally concerned with the rhythms of lines, not words.

> A mighty maze, but not without a plan

is an iambic line. By this we mean, not that it is composed of iambic words ("mighty" is not an iambic word) but that one feels a prevailingly iambic rhythm governing the line, even though printing it in a way that draws attention to this fact will falsify the normal way of reading it:

> A MIGHT | y MAZE | but NOT | with OUT | a PLAN.

If one is interested in reading the line rather than forcing it into a pattern, one begins

> a | mighty | maze,

and pauses more markedly after "maze" than at any other point in the line. Good poets constantly play the speech rhythm against the formal pattern in this way. To be fully aware of such effects one must be able to recognize what the underlying pattern is. This is the main use of being aware of metrical types.

(Even experienced readers cannot always feel sure of the governing rhythm of single lines, but normally one has a passage of some length to inspect.)

> Ever through the burning distance

is a trochaic line:

> EV er | THROUGH the | BURN ing | DIS tance

It is worth noticing that the presence of the metrical pattern tends to affect the accents words normally have. If you change "through" in the preceding example to "in," you have, as far as normal speech is concerned, replaced an accented syllable by an unobtrusive one:

> EV er | in the | BURN ing | DIS tance

But if the reader has caught the governing rhythm of the passage, he will tend to give "in" the accent suggested by the surrounding pattern.

Spondaic lines of any length are not found; but one may come upon two or three spondaic feet in succession:

SO, SO | BREAK OFF | this LAST | la MENT | ing KISS
WHICH SUCKS | TWO SOULS | and VA | pors BOTH | a WAY

It could also be argued that these are iambic lines in which the accents in the opening feet approach equivalence; but that seems to point to a less effective way of reading them.

One also discovers lines of verse built out of three-syllable units. When the accent is on the first syllable, (′ ˘ ˘) the foot is called a *dactyl*, or *dactylic foot*, as in "pottery." When the accent is on the last syllable, (˘ ˘ ′) the foot is called an *anapest*, or *anapestic foot*, as in "intervene." There are all sorts of fine shadings: "undermine," for instance, has a *secondary accent* on the first syllable, partly deriving from our awareness of the normal accenting of "under."

> Christopher Robin goes hoppity hoppity

is a dactylic line, a type rare except for comic effects. For other purposes the last foot is normally brought to a more abrupt halt:

> Just for a handful of silver he left us,
> Just for a riband to stick in his coat.

An example of an anapestic line is:

> Where the blue of the night meets the gold of the day . . .

> *Mnemonic*
> Trochee trips from long to short;
> From long to long in solemn sort
> Slow Spondee stalks; strong foot! yea ill able
> Ever to come up with Dactyl's trisyllable.
> Iambics march from short to long;
> With a leap and a bound the swift Anapests throng.
> —Samuel Taylor Coleridge in
> *Metrical Feet: Lesson for a Boy*

It cannot be too much emphasized that the main use of knowing these elements is to help you listen for the underlying rhythms of the verse you happen to be reading. You will never meet a pure case of any of them. For that matter, you will never encounter a round face, though the term is helpful; and if the idea of a circle had never been defined for you, you might not be clearly aware of how a round face differs from a long one, even though the existence of some sort of difference is evident to the eye. The term "iambic foot" has the same sort of status as the term "round face."

In the anapestic example given above, "blue" and "gold" are more prominent than the other accented words, "night" and "day"; "meets" is accented in speech but subdued by the meter; and "where," the key word of the line, is slighted by the official metrical pattern. With a sufficiently elaborate system of marks and names it is possible to affix labels to most of the things that happen in lines of verse, and construct uninteresting models of them, but the usefulness of this procedure is not evident.

Listen to the way the verse moves.

"Rhythm is form cut into time."

—*Ezra Pound*

SONG AND SONORITY

Though rhythm and sound are among the most powerful and exact means of definition the poet has at his disposal, they are too often used and relished for their own sake. This misuse is a recurring temptation to English poets for a number of ascertainable reasons. For instance, the fact that in its period of greatest life so much English verse was written to be declaimed from a stage hasn't been wholly fortunate. Inferior seventeenth-century dramatists discovered ways of counterfeiting verse aimed at the ear alone, and their example was imitated.

Some kinds of poetry are like chocolates, in individual instances pleasant and harmless, but as a staple diet destructive to the senses, the digestion, and the appetite.

To approach this point from another direction: good writing aims at setting something before the reader's mind by means of language. If the reader is moved or enlightened, it will be the thing presented that moves or enlightens him, not the mechanics of presentation. Less good writing sets out directly to impress the reader, and ultimately impresses only the reader who doesn't really believe that words have meanings and that structures of words preserve meanings. Such readers got that way by a long period of never paying strict attention to the meaning of anything; and when they like a piece of verse, they are probably responding more to the sound than to anything else.

> Silent music, either other
> Sweetly gracing.
>
> Lovely forms do flow
> From concent divinely framed;
> Heaven is music, and thy beauty's
> Birth is heav'nly.
>
> These dull notes we sing
> Discords need for helps to grace them;
> Only beauty purely loving
> Knows no discord;
>
> But still moves delight,
> Like clear springs renew'd by flowing,
> Ever perfect, ever in them-
> selves eternal.

It wasn't until the eighteenth century that a poem became something to look at in a book. The art which began with Homer began with a reciter's speaking voice. There are poems intended to be sung that are almost as old as Homer. Although Dante's and Chaucer's narrative poems and a great many Renaissance lyrics and sonnets were intended for circulation in manuscript, the continuous tradition that relates verse to the speaking or singing voice is unbroken from 800 years before Christ until 1800 years after. Print, for such verse, is purely a means of preservation, like the printed score of a Mozart opera.

Many of the most familiar attributes of lyric verse arose from its long history of conjunction with music. Regular and sometimes intricate stanza forms, for instance, repeated several times, were originally a means of fitting a long poem to a short tune.

Songs written for concert performance show off the musician's skill and the singer's voice. The words to the pieces in the average concert artist's repertoire are of little importance. The much more intricate art of making intelligible to the ear a set of words of some interest flourished in England from the fifteenth to the seventeenth centuries, before music was delivered at public concerts. You will find words and music to some eighty songs from the most prolific quarter-century of this period in An Elizabethan Song Book (ed. Noah Greenberg, W. H. Auden and Chester Kallman, 1956). And a half-hour spent listening to the Deller Consort recording of *Tavern Songs* (Vanguard BG-561) or some of the other Deller recordings (*The Three Ravens; The Cries of London; The Wraggle Taggle Gypsies; The Holly and the Ivy*) will convince you of the artistry of even unpretentious popular song of the same period. English culture in those centuries—Henry VIII to Charles II—was steeped in music. The number of rounds on the Deller *Tavern Songs* record is suggestive. After a round has gotten fairly under way it is fully intelligible only to the singers: from which one gathers that a highly sophisticated vocal art was not only listened to but practiced by a very large number of people. The rounds would not have been written down, printed, and preserved if they had interested only a few dozen people in the entire country.

Every small town in the United States today contains passably expert ballplayers. A similar diffusion of musical *expertise* lifted many anonymous song writers of Shakespeare's generation to a high standard of performance. The essentially solitary poets of the eighteenth, nineteenth, and twentieth centuries, writing for a book-reading audience, have occasionally reached a comparable level of lyric proficiency by hard study and long practice. Even so, since they are not writing for music, they write a different *kind* of verse.

MARK VAN DOREN

They Flee from Me

I

They flee from me that sometime did me seek,
With naked foot stalking *with*in my chamber.
Once have I seen them gentle, tame, and meek,
That now are wild, and do not *once* remember
That sometime they *have* put themselves in danger   5
To take bread at my hand; and now they range,
Busily seeking *in* continual change.

Thanked be fortune it hath been otherwise,
Twenty times better; but once *e*special,
In thin array, after a pleasant guise,   10
When her loose gown *did from her shoulders fall*
And she me caught in her arms long and small,
And therewith*al* so sweetly did me kiss
And softly said, Dear heart, how like you this?

It was no dream, *for* I lay broad *a*waking.   15
But all is turned *now,* through my gentleness,
Into a *bitter* fashion of forsaking;
And I have leave to go, of her goodness,
And she also to use newfangleness.
But since that I *unkindly so* am served,   20
How like you this? what hath she *now* deserved?

II

They flee from me that sometime did me seek,
With naked foot stalking in my chamber.
I have seen them gentle, tame, and meek,
That now are wild, and do not remember
That some time they put themselves in danger   5
To take bread at my hand; and now they range,
Busily seeking with a continual change.

Thanked be fortune, it hath been otherwise
Twenty times better; but once, in speciall,
In thin array, after a pleasant guise,   10
When her loose gown from her shoulders. did fall,
And she me caught in her arms long and small.
Therewith all sweetly did me kiss,
And softly said, Dear heart, how like you this?

It was no dream; I lay broad waking.   15
But all is turned, through my gentleness,
Into a strange fashion of forsaking;
And I have leave to go of her goodness,
And she also to use newfangleness.
But since that I so kindly am served,   20
I fain would know what she hath deserved.

—Sir Thomas Wyatt

An accident of history has made this poem even more interesting than it would otherwise be. It would be interesting in any case, but we may learn a great deal from the fact that it exists in two forms. In the form first given here it was famous for three and a half centuries; it is still more famous in its second form, unknown until a few decades ago. The second form is Wyatt's own, and therefore the first in fact; but the other was the first to be printed, and the only one that could be read until the author's manuscript was studied. The person responsible for I was Richard Tottell, an anthologist who in 1557 published a celebrated *Miscellany,* and who "improved" this poem before he put it in print. He seems to have believed that Wyatt was ignorant of versification. The poem was intended to be in iambic pentameter; so Tottell made sure that the intention was carried out—to his ear, anyway.

The ear of Tottell was not satisfied by an apparent shortage of syllables in lines 2, 3, 4, 5, 13, 15, 17, and 21. The shortage was real by the metronome, for by count there is a syllable missing in each of those lines. Tottell's additions to cure the malady are italicized in the present text. They supply what was never here, and ruin the rhythm Wyatt achieved. Wyatt knew what he was doing when he wrote, for instance:

> With naked foot stalking in my chamber.

The missing syllable between "foot" and "stalking" causes the line to *stalk,* as the pronoun "I" at the beginning of the next line, naked of any sound before it, assumes the importance it has for him who uses it. The experience of the poem is not only personal, it is unique; and it is communicated to us with a bewildered sense of strangeness—it could not be, yet it is. So the "I" here needs to be naked, for the same reason that "once" in line 4 would be gratuitous. *"And* do not remember"—we are forced then to accent the "and," as if we understood: *"And,* mind you!" The speaker is very serious, and so prolongs certain syllables in his speech, for emphasis and to make us comprehend not merely his meaning but the uniqueness of it, and possibly the enormity. Tottell's "have" in line 5 prevents us from hearing the italics in "some" which Wyatt surely heard. *"Some* time—oh, not now, but I tell you it was true *then."*

When Tottell came to line 7, the last in its stanza, he found Wyatt in what he thought was the opposite error: he had put in an extra syllable. Wyatt had done this so that we might have a sudden sense of coming and going, hither and yon, on the part of those who do not come to him any more. The stanza as he wrote it ran away as they had run, in a light chaos of syllables and feet. So in line 9, though there was nothing wrong with the number of sounds, Tottell appears to have thought that "especial" was smoother than "in speciall" set off with commas. But Wyatt had wanted emphasis there, not smoothness; he was about to describe the remarkable thing that happens, or happened, in this stanza. What happened was that a lady came, in a thin loose gown, and the gown fell from her shoulders as she caught him and kissed him. Wyatt's eleventh line keeps the gown on as long as it can, then lets it fall abruptly, even awkwardly, in the words "from her shoulders did fall." Tottell, all for smoothness, transfers the "did" to its place in the natural word order; and the fall becomes ordinary. "Therewith," writes Wyatt at the beginning of line 13, "all sweetly did me kiss"—that is to say, very sweetly, or completely so. But Tottell returns to the normal range by writing "And therewithal."

Line 15 suffers as much as any line in the poem from the blacksmith's hand that hammered it out longer. "It was no dream," insists Wyatt, though you may think so; I tell you, and you must believe it, "I *lay broad wak*ing." Each of the italicized syllables demands to be heard, even though in this case there will be only eight syllables in the entire line. Tottell makes it ten, and goes on in line 16 to supply an unnecessary "now" before "through," which for Wyatt had been "thorough"—an older form, more suitable in the environment of "my gentleness," and more effective because no syllable intrudes between it and "turned." The change of "strange" to "bitter" in the next line was of a more radical sort, since it altered the meaning. But Tottell, eager to get in his tenth syllable, may not have thought it mattered; or may not have thought the meaning *was* changed. Wyatt could have thought "bitter," but he wrote "strange"—a term of understatement, introducing irony. The irony in line 20 was stronger still. Of course Wyatt meant "unkindly," as Tottell blunderingly makes clear. But he wrote "kindely," a word of three syllables which made the line complete even for such as Tottell. It was not smoothly complete, however, so the improver said "unkindly so," making sure that we should miss the mockery in Wyatt's little syllable "*e*." Something like the same thing was done to the last line, which Wyatt must have meant to be heard slowly, as if it were spoken with a drawl, the pronoun "she" coming in of course for special emphasis. Tottell's bright question at the beginning of the line is much too bright; and there is that nonsensical "now" for which nothing but a metrical excuse can be offered.

Wyatt's meter was perfect as it stood. The time of each line was right, however many syllables had been suppressed. When a syllable was missing, another one, or several others, pronounced themselves slowly enough to make up the difference. Tottell might have heard this as we do, and admired the result. But Tottell did not know how important verse is to poetry. Verse is not the same thing as poetry, but it makes poetry become the thing it is—the spoken, the individual thing which someone wants to say and have understood in its own terms and no others. Even with Tottell's tampering the poem is distinguished, and for a long time was thought so by those who did not know what had been done to it. It is now more beautiful because it is more itself. It has its own voice, in which it tells a tale that is true only of him who speaks, and of his lady.

What would the tale be if anybody else told it? If we did, for instance? Two lovers have become free of each other, and one of them confesses how it happened. "Through my gentleness," he says, "I let it happen. I do not know precisely how, but there it is. We are both free now to go where we please. I am free, I know, because something that used to be true for me is not true any more. When I was bound to my lady I had strange dreams. Or were they dreams? At any rate, my chamber was visited and inhabited by—what were they, girls? Dreams of girls? Animals, padding on their naked feet? Cats? Leopards? People? I am too confused to say, now that my mind is clear. I wish it were not so clear. I knew what they were then, even if I could not have named them. I did not need to name them. They were the signs of my bondage—and, by a paradox of love, they were symbols of my wealth, even of my freedom. For though I am said to be free now, I do not feel free. I can go anywhere, but I do not wish to start. I am supposed to be happy, as she tells me she is, but I do not feel happy. Newfangleness—that is all either of us has, and it is a slight thing, well expressed by its absurd name. I know what my reward is, for gently indulging this fashion of infidelity that now is fixed in our society.

My reward is nothing. My lady was curious, and wanted to try the fashion out. Well, then, what is *her* reward? I fain would know. That is all I have to say."

But this is a poor telling, and a wordy one. Wyatt used the fewest possible words, as good poets always do. He used too few, thought Tottell, who sprinkled others in. Yet Tottell could not touch the central mystery of the poem, nor can we in any paraphrase. The mystery of the poem is partly inherent in its subject and partly a creation of Wyatt's words—dark words, delivered with an authority that makes itself heard in every sound the lines make. The lines make their own music—muted by Tottell, but surviving even him—and in the last analysis express themselves.

YVOR WINTERS

From *In Defense of Reason*

Section III: THE SCANSION OF FREE VERSE

I shall begin the description of my system for the scansion of free verse with an account of two poems of my own and of what I endeavored to accomplish in them. The foot which I have used consists of one heavily accented syllable, an unlimited number of unaccented syllables, and an unlimited number of syllables of secondary accent. This resembles the accentual meter of Hopkins, except that Hopkins employed rhyme. He appears to have had the secondary accent, or subordinate and extra-metrical "foot," in mind, when he spoke of "hangers" and "outrides."

Accents, as I have already pointed out, cannot be placed in a definite number of arbitrary categories; language is fluid, and a syllable is accented in a certain way only in relation to the rest of the foot. The secondary accent is discernible as a type if the poet makes it so. A dozen types of accent are possible in theory, but in practice no more than two can be kept distinct in the mind; in fact it is not always easy to keep two.

Ambiguity of accent will be more common in such verse as I am describing than in the older verse, but up to a certain point this is not a defect, this kind of ambiguity being one of the chief beauties

of Milton's verse, for example. The poet must be permitted to use
his judgment in dubious instances, and the critic must do his best
to perceive the reason for any decision. Quantity will obviously
complicate this type of foot more than it will the foot of the more
familiar meters.

I shall mark and discuss two poems of my own, and shall then
proceed to specimens of free verse from some of the chief poets of
the Experimental generation, upon whose work my own ear for
this medium was trained. Since a line which is complete metrically
may for the sake of emphasis be printed as two lines, I shall place a
cross-bar (/) at the end of each complete line. I shall number the
lines which are so marked, for ease in reference. Lines which are
incomplete metrically, but which are independent and not parts of
complete lines, will likewise be marked and numbered, and these
lines will also be marked with an asterisk (*). I shall mark each
primary stress with double points (″) and each secondary stress
with a single point (′).

"Quod Tegit Omnia"

1	Earth dărkens and is bĕaded/
2	wĭth a swéat of bŭshes ańd/
3	the bĕar comes fórth:
	the mĭnd stored wíth/
4	magnĭficénce proceĕds inío/
5	the mỹsterý of Tĭme, nów/
6	cĕrtain óf its chŏice of/
7	păssion but úncĕrtain óf the/
8	pássion's eńd.

	Whĕn/
9	Pláto tĕmporízes on the năture/
10	of the plŭmage óf the sóul, the/
11	wĭnd hums ín the fĕathers ás/
12	acróss a cŏrd impĕccable ín/
13	taŭtness but of nŏ mind:/
14	Tĭme,
	the síne-pŏndere, móst/
15	ímpertŭrbable of ĕlemeńts,/
16	assŭmes its ówn propórtions/
17	sĭlentlý, of its ówn prŏperties—/
18	an ĕxcelleńce at which óne

	sĭghs/
19	Advĕnturer in
	lĭving făct, the póet/
20	mŏunts intó the spr̆ing/
21	upón his tŏngue the tăste of/
22	aĭr becóming b̆ody: ĭs/
23	Embĕdded in thĭs cr̆ystallíne/
24	precĭpitáte of Tĭme./

There are no incomplete lines in the preceding poem, though a few lines are broken in two for the sake of emphasis.

The next poem is more difficult. I shall mark it as if it contained two feet to the line, and as if most of the lines were printed in two parts. The imperfect lines (unassimilable half-lines) are marked with a single asterisk (*). Unbroken lines are marked with a double asterisk (**).

The Bitter Moon

1	Dry snŏw runs búrning
	on the gr̆ound like fíre—/
2	the quíck of H̆ell spin ón
	the wĭnd. Should Í beli̇̆eve/
3	in thĭs your bódy, táke it
	at its w̆ŏrd? I háve belíeved/
4	in nóthing. Eărth burns wíth a
	shádow thát has h̆eld my/
5	flésh; the ĕye is a shádow
	that cons̆umes the mínd/
6	* Scréam into ăir! The vóices/
7	** Of the deăd stíll v̆ibrate—/
8	théy will fĭnd them, thréading
	ăll the păst with twínging/
9	** w̆ires alíve like h̆air in cóld./
10	* Thése are the nĕrves/
11	** of dĕath. Í am its brăin./

12	** Yóu are the w̆ay, the ŏath/
13	I táke. I hóld to thĭs—
	I bĕnt and thwárted by a w̆ill/
14	** to lĭve amóng the lĭving déad/
15	** insteăd of the dead lĭving; Í/
16	* becóme a vóice to sŏund for./

17   ** Can you féel through Spáce,/
18   ** imágine beyond Tíme?
                                              The/
19   snów alíve with móonlight
                lícks aboút my ánkles./
20   ** Can you fíñd this eñd?/

This poem is marked, as I have said, as if it contained two feet to the line. It is possible, however, to regard the poem as having a one-foot line, in which case the lines marked with the single asterisk and those unmarked are regular, and those marked with the double asterisk are irregular. The two-foot hypothesis involves the smaller number of irregular lines, and it would eliminate for this poem a difficulty in the matter of theory; to wit the question of whether a one-foot line is a practical possibility. Consider, for example, the possibility of a poem in iambic lines of one foot each. The poem will be, if unrhymed, equal to an indefinite progression of iambic prose. But in reply, one may object that except for iambic pentameter, and except for occasional imitations of classical verse, no unrhymed verse has ever been successful in English in the past, and that Herrick, at any rate, composed one excellent poem in lines each of one iambic foot ("Thus I / Pass by / To Die," etc.) I believe that this discussion will show that the secondary accent makes possible the use of unrhymed lines of any length, from one foot up to as many as can be managed in any other form of meter whether rhymed or not.

In the poem preceding the last, there was very little difficulty in distinguishing between the primary and secondary accents; the trouble lay in distinguishing between secondary accents and unaccented syllables. But when, as here, it is the two types of stress that are hard to separate, we stand in danger of losing entirely our system of measurement. Now, if the meter is successful, there are in this poem two meters running concurrently and providing a kind of counterpoint: one is the free-verse meter, marked by the heavy beats, and the other is an iambic meter, marked by all the beats, whether heavy or light. The poem cannot be arranged in blank verse, however, for the iambic passages are incomplete, are fragments laid in here and there to provide musical complication and for the sake of their connotative value. If the heavy beats cannot be heard as distinct from the light, then the free verse scheme vanishes and one has left only a fragmentary blank verse, badly arranged.

Mr. William Rose Benét, in the Saturday Review of Literature (New York) for September 6, 1930, objected to the structure of my own free verse, at the same time offering realignments of two passages, which he regarded as superior to my own alignments. A few weeks later, he published a letter from myself, which stated, and for the first time in public, the general principles which I am now discussing. One of his revisions was of the opening lines of the poem which I have just quoted. He heard only the incomplete blank verse and rearranged the passage accordingly, some of the available fragments of blank verse, however, being broken in ways that were to myself inexplicable.

My own free verse was very often balanced on this particular tight-rope. During the period in which I was composing it, I was much interested in the possibility of making the stanza and wherever possible the poem a single rhythmic unit, of which the line was a part not sharply separate. This effect I endeavored to achieve by the use of run-over lines, a device I took over from Dr. Williams, Miss Moore, and Hopkins, and by the extreme use of a continuous iambic undercurrent, so arranged that it could not be written successfully as blank verse and that it would smooth over the gap from one line of free verse to the next.

In the standard meters, the run-over line tends to be awkward because of the heavy rhythmic pause at the end of each line: Milton alone, perhaps, has been highly and uniformly successful in the employment of the device, and he has been so by virtue of the greatest example of the grand manner in literature, a convention so heightened as to enable him to employ this device, which in most poets is destructively violent, as a basis for sensitive modulations of rhetoric. Even in Websterian verse the line-end is too heavily marked for the run-over to be pleasing. But if the *rhythm* can be made to run on rapidly, the meaning can be allowed to do so with impunity: hence the terminations in articles, adjectives, and similar words so common in free verse of this type, and even the frequent terminations in mid-word to be observed in Hopkins and in Miss Moore, this last liberty, of course, being common also

in classical verse, in which, as in much free verse, the line-end
pause is frequently extremely slight. Of the dangers of this type
of free verse I shall have more to say later.

In the poem last quoted, much of the metrical ambiguity arises
from the use of an unusually long foot, which allows quantity an
opportunity somewhat greater than usual to obscure the accent. In
the line, "at its word? I have believed," *word* receives the primary
accent, but *believed,* which receives a secondary accent, is longer
and may seem more heavily accented to the unwary. In the line
"flesh; the eye is a shadow," the heavy accent goes to *eye,* but *flesh,*
because of its position at the beginning of the line and before the
semi-colon, receives more length than it would receive in most
other places, and may seem for the moment to receive the main accent. In most cases, the reader will find that the ambiguity is one
of alternatives; that is, he will naturally place a heavy accent on
one word or on the other, so that the pattern will not be damaged.
Ambiguities of this sort, and within the limits just mentioned, may
be a source of value; they are, as I have said, one of the principle
beauties of Milton's versification. If the ambiguity, in free verse,
however, ceases to be a hesitation between alternatives, and becomes more general, the metrical norm is destroyed.

The poets from whom I learned to write free verse are probably
better subjects than myself for a demonstration of the theory. The
poem quoted below, which is by Dr. Williams, contains two lines
of double length, each of which I have marked with an asterisk:

To Waken an Old Lady

1	Old áge is
2	a flíght of smăll
3	chéeping bĭrds
4	skĭmming
5	bare trēes
6	abóve a snŏw glaze.
7	* Gaĭning and faĭling,
8	théy are bŭffeted
9	by a dărk wind—
10	but whăt?
11	Ón the hársh wĕedstalks
12	the flŏck has résted—
13	the snŏw

14   is cŏvered with bróken
15   seĕd-husks,
16   and the wínd témpered
17   with a shríll
18   *   píping of plénty.

It will be observed that free verse requires a good deal of variation from line to line if the poem is to keep moving, and that as the
one-foot line permits only a limited amount of variation if the foot
is not to be stretched out to the danger-point, the poet must choose
between a very short poem and a good sprinkling of irregular lines.

H. D.'s *Orchard* is one of the principal masterpieces of the free-
verse movement. It employs a one-foot line, with fourteen lines of
double length out of a total of thirty lines:

1   I sáw the first peᷢr
2   As it féll.
3   *   The hŏney-séeking, gŏlden-bánded,
4   The yĕllow swárm
5   Was nót more fleᷢet than Í
6   *   (Spăre us fróm lŏvelinéss!)
7   And I féll prŏstrate,
8   Crẙing
9   *   "Yóu have flãẙed us wíth your blŏssoms;
10   *   Spăre us the beᷢauty
11   Of frŭit-trees!"

12   The hŏney-séeking
13   Păused not;
14   *   The áir thŭndered their sŏng
15   *   And Í alŏne was prŏstrate.

16   O rŏugh-héwn
17   Gód of the ŏrchard
18   *   I bríng yóu an ŏffering;
19   Do yóu alóne unbeᷢautiful
20   Sŏn of the gód
21   *   Spăre us from lŏveliness!

22   These fállen hăzel-nuts
23   *   Stripped lãte of their greᷢen sheaths;
24   *   Grăpes, red-pŭrple,
25   Their bĕrries

26   * Drĭpping with wĭne;
27   * Pómegrănates alréady brŏken
28   And shrúnken fĭgs
29   * And quĭnces untŏuched
30   * I brĭng you as ŏffering.

Some of the details of this poem should be mentioned. Where there is a long foot, the heavily accented syllable usually appears to receive much less weight than in a short foot, the crowd of minor syllables absorbing emphasis from the major syllable. This absorption is sometimes, though not invariably, facilitated by the placing of two long feet in a single line. Line three is an example of this rule; line nine is an exception to it. The position of the accent in these lines is relevant to their respective effects: in line three, the accent is at the beginning of each foot, with the secondary accent and the unaccented syllables following in a rapid flicker, an arrangement which makes for speed; in line nine, the accent falls near the end of the foot, an arrangement which makes for a heavy stop; in both lines the second foot repeats the arrangement of the first foot, except for the very light syllable before the first heavy accent in line three, an arrangement which makes for clarity and emphasis of rhythm.

If the reader will examine again some of the preceding poems, he will find that this device of occasional repetition, either within the line or from line to line, may be used effectively for another purpose: it may provide the poet with a kind of pause, or moment of balance, between different movements, both of them rapid, a pause which is roughly analogous to a pause at the end of a line in the older meters.

Miss Marianne Moore has carried the method of continuity, of unbroken rush, farther than anyone, not even excepting Hopkins. The following lines are from her poem, *A Grave*. Since an extremely long foot is employed, in an extremely long line, I have placed a cross bar at the end of each foot:

1 mén lower nĕts,/ uncónscious óf the făct/ that théy are désecrăting/
   a grăve,/
2 and row quĭckly/ awăy/ the blădes/ of the ŏars/
3 mŏving togéther like the/ fĕet of wáter-spíders/ as íf there wére no
   such thĭng/ as dĕath./

4 The wrínkles progréss/ upón themsélves in a phãlanx,/ beãutifúl/
   únder nétworks of fõam,/
5 and fáde bréathlessly/ whíle the séa rústles/ in and õut of/ the
   séaweed./

Most of the generalizations drawn from the poem by H. D. could
be as well illustrated by examples taken from this passage.

I have spoken of the remarkably continuous movement in Miss
Moore's verse: but Miss Moore is seldom wholly at one with her
meter. There may be, as in this passage, brilliant onomatopoetic
effects, but the breathlessness of the movement is usually in contrast to the minuteness of the details, and this contrast frequently
strengthens the half-ominous, half-ironic quality of the details, at
the same time that it is drawing them rather forcibly into a single
pattern. This is not a defect, at least in the shorter poems: it is a
means of saying something that could have been said in no other
way; and what is said is valuable. But the instrument is highly
specialized and has a very narrow range of effectiveness.

A further danger inherent in the instrument becomes apparent
in Miss Moore's longer poems, such as *Marriage* and *The Octopus.*
These poems are at once satiric and didactic, but the satiric and
didactic forms require of their very nature a coherent rational
frame. The poems have no such frame, but are essentially fragmentary and disconnected. The meter, however, is emphatically
continuous, and creates a kind of temporary illusion of complete
continuity: it is a conventional continuity which never receives its
justification. Despite the brilliance of much of the detail, this un-
supported convention is as disappointing as the Miltonic convention in Thomson; it is a meaningless shell. In the shorter poems,
the stated theme often correlates the details rationally.

Dr. W. C. Williams once remarked to me in a letter that free
verse was to him a means of obtaining widely varying speeds
within a given type of foot. I believe that this describes what we
have seen taking place in the examples of free verse which I have
analyzed. But if the secondary accent becomes negligible for many
lines in sequence, if, in other words, the speed from foot to foot
does not vary widely, the poem becomes one of two things: if the
accentuation is regular, the poem is unrhymed metrical verse of
the old sort; or if the accentuation is irregular, the poem may be
a lose unrhymed doggerel but will probably be prose. Or there may

be an uneven mixture of regularity and of irregularity, which is
the possibility least to be desired.

The opening of Richard Aldington's *Choricos* illustrates the mixture of free and regular verse:

1   The ancient songs
2   Pass deathward mournfully.

3   Cold lips that sing no more, and withered wreaths,
4   Regretful eyes, and drooping breasts and wings—
5   Symbols of ancient songs
6   Mournfully passing
7   Down to the great white surges. . . .

The first four lines comprise three perfect lines of blank verse.

Elsewhere in the same poem, we may find free verse abandoned
for prose, the line-endings serving only as a kind of punctuation:

1   And silently,
2   And with slow feet approaching,
3   And with bowed head and unlit eyes
4   We kneel before thee,
5   And thou, leaning toward us,
6   Caressingly layest upon us
7   Flowers from thy thin cold hands;
8   And, smiling as a chaste woman
9   Knowing love in her heart,
10   Thou sealest our eyes.
11   And the illimitable quietude
12   Comes gently upon us.

The first three lines of this passage might pass for free verse of the
same kind that Mr. Aldington has used elsewhere in the same
poem, but line four, in spite of the fact that it can be given two
major accents, does not continue the movement previously established. Line eight is similarly troublesome, and the remaining
lines are uncertain. The difficulty is not mathematical but rhythmic: the movement of the lines in the context is awkward and
breaks down the context.

This passage raises and answers a rather troublesome question.
It is possible that any passage of prose—even the prose that I am
now writing—might be marked off into more or less discernible feet
of the kind that I have described, each foot having a heavy accent

and one or more or perhaps no light accents, and a varying number of relatively unaccented syllables. These feet could then be written one or two or three to a line. Would the result be free verse? I believe not.

We are supposing in the first place that the writer of prose will instinctively choose syllables that fall naturally into three clearly discernible classes; whereas this classification of syllables in free verse is, in the long run, the result of a deliberate choice, even though the poet may be guided only by ear and not by theory. But let us for the sake of argument neglect this objection.

The accented syllables are necessary to free verse, but more is necessary: the remaining syllables must be disposed in such a way as to establish an harmonious and continuous movement. But can the laws of this harmonious and continuous movement be defined? That is, can one define every possible type of free verse foot and can one then establish all of the combinations possible and rule out all the unsatisfactory combinations? I have never gone into this subject experimentally, but I believe that one can demonstrate rationally that the compilation of such laws is impossible.

The free verse foot is very long, or is likely to be. No two feet composed of different words can ever have exactly the same values either of accent or of quantity. If one will mark off the passage quoted from Mr. Aldington, for example, one will get certain combinations which are unsuccessful; but one cannot say that the duplication of the same series of accent marks in a different group of words will be unsuccessful, because the duplication of accent marks will not mean the duplication of the exact weights and lengths of the original passage. The free verse foot is simply too long and too complicated to be handled in this way. If the reader feels that this proves free verse to be no verse at all, I have two answers: first, that he will have the same difficulty with any other purely accentual verse, from the Anglo-Saxon to Hopkins and with any purely syllabic; secondly, that if the rhythms which I have described can be *perceived* in a fairly large number of poems, and if the failure to establish such rhythms can be perceived in other poems, one has a rhythmic system distinguishable from prose and frequently of poetic intensity, and it matters very little what name it goes by. What is really important is the extent of its usefulness, its effect upon poetic convention.

I do not wish to claim that the poets of whom I write in this essay had my system of scansion in mind when writing their poems. Probably none of them had it. What I wish to claim is this: that the really good free verse of the movement can be scanned in this way, and that the nature of our language and the difficulties of abandoning the old forms led inevitably to this system, though frequently by way of a good deal of uncertain experimenting.

Mr. Aldington's *Choricos* is an attempt to combine certain traditional meters, English and classical, and a little biblical prose, in a single poem, just as Hugo, for example, employed different meters in a single poem, but this procedure, whether employed by Hugo or by Richard Aldington, is inevitably too loose to be satisfactory. Other poets have quite deliberately employed simple prose rhythms. Sometimes the prose is very good, as in *One City Only,* by Alice Corbin, or as in a few poems by Mina Loy. But it is not verse, and it is not often a satisfactory medium for poetic writing.

The masters of free verse of the Experimental Generation are William Carlos Williams, Ezra Pound, Marianne Moore, Wallace Stevens, H. D., and perhaps Mina Loy in a few poems, though the movement of Mina Loy's verse is usually so simplified, so denuded of secondary accent, as to be indistinguishable from prose. Mr. Eliot never got beyond Websterian verse, a bastard variety, though in *Gerontion,* he handled it with great skill—with far greater skill than Webster usually expends upon it. Mr. T. Sturge Moore, at the very beginning of the twentieth century, published a very brilliant and very curious specimen of experimental meter, in *The Rout of the Amazons,* which, like the neo-Websterian verse of Mr. Eliot and of others, employs blank verse as its norm, but departs farther from the norm than the neo-Websterian poets have been able to depart, and, unlike the neo-Websterian verse, never seems to approach prose, but rather approaches a firm and controlled free verse as its extreme limit.

Free verse has been all but abandoned by the next generation: a few good specimens are to be found in minor poems by Glenway Wescott, Grant Code, and the late Kathleen Tankersley Young; but Messrs. Wescott and Code have written their best poems in other forms, and so have all of their ablest contemporaries.

A major objection to free verse as it has been written by H. D.,

Dr. Williams, and perhaps others, and the objection can be raised against much of Hopkins as well, is this: that it tends to a rapid run-over line, so that the poem, or in the case of a fairly long poem, the stanza or paragraph, is likely to be the most important rhythmic unit, the lines being secondary. Hopkins was aware of this tendency in his poems, but apparently not of its danger. In his own preface to his poems, he writes: ". . . it is natural . . . for the lines to be *rove over,* that is, for the scanning of each line immediately to take up that of the one before, so that if the first has one or more syllables at its end the other must have as many the less at its beginning; and in fact the scanning runs on without break from the beginning, say, of a stanza to the end and all the stanza is one long strain, though written in lines asunder." The result is a kind of breathless rush, which may very well be exciting, but which tends to exclude or to falsify all save a certain kind of feeling, by enforcing what I have called, in my essay on Poetic Convention, a convention of heightened intensity.

Hopkins meets the difficulty by excluding from his poetry nearly all feeling that is not ecstatic; Dr. Williams meets it by allowing and utilizing a great deal of language that is largely conventional. But if a poem is written wholly in conventional language, it becomes, when the convention is of this type, merely melodramatic and violent, and, when the convention is of some other type, weak in some other and corresponding manner. Dr. Williams has thrown away much good material thus; so has H. D. done; and so have others.

The extremely abnormal convention is seldom necessary, I believe, to the expression of powerful feeling. Shakespeare can be just as mad in a sonnet as can Hopkins, and he can be at the same time a great many other things which Hopkins cannot be. He has a more limber medium and is able to deal with more complex feelings. I mean by this, that if no one quality receives extreme emphasis, many diverse qualities may be controlled simultaneously, but that if one single quality (the ecstasy of the thirteenth century lyric, *Alisoun,* for example) does receive extreme emphasis, it crowds other qualities out of the poem. The meter, the entire tone, of *Alisoun,* render impossible the overtone of grief which would have been present had Hardy dealt with the same material, and which would have given the poem greater scope, greater universality. One may state it as a general law, moral as well as metrical, that an increase in complexity commonly results in a decrease in emphasis: extreme emphasis, with the resultant limitation of scope, is a form of unbalance. Sexual experience is over-emphasized in the works of D. H. Lawrence, because Lawrence understood so little else—and consequently understood sexual experience so ill. In a very few poems, notably in the sonnet *To R. B.,* Hopkins avoids his usual tone in a considerable measure, by reverting toward standard meter. His rhymes and his consequent independence of the secondary accent enable him to do this, but a similar reversion is impossible in free verse, a medium in which the reversion would simply result in a break-down of form. It is difficult to achieve in free verse the freedom of movement and the range of material offered one by the older forms.

A few poems appear to indicate that a greater variety of feeling is possible in free verse, however, than one might be led to suspect by the poems thus far quoted. One of the best is *The Snow Man,* by Wallace Stevens:

1   * Ońe must háve a mínd of wínter
2   To regárd the fröst and the bŏughs
3   Of the píne-trees crústed with snow;

4   And háve been cŏld a lŏng tíme
5   * Tó behŏld the júnipers shăgged with íce,
6   The sprúces rŏugh in the dístant glítter

7   Óf the Jánuáry sŭn; and nŏt to thínk
8   Of ány míserý in the sŏund of the wínd,
9   In the sŏund of a féw léaves,

10   * Whích is the sŏund of the lánd
11   Fúll of the săme wínd

12   Thát is blŏwing ín the săme báre plăce
13   For the lĭstenér, who lístens in the snów,
14   And, nŏthing himsĕlf, behŏlds
15   * Nŏthing thát is nót thére and the nŏthing that ís.

The norm is of three beats, and there are four irregular lines, the first and third having two beats each, the second and fourth having four. Each line in this poem ends on a very heavy pause, provides, that is, a long moment of balance before the next movement begins.

The manner in which the secondary accents are disposed in the
fifth, sixth, and seventh lines, in order to level and accelerate the
line, is remarkably fine, as is also the manner in which the beat
becomes slow and heavy in the next few lines and the way in
which the two movements are resolved at the close. There is complete repose between the lines, great speed and great slowness
within the line, and all in a very short poem. Dr. Williams has got
comparable effects here and there. The following poem by Dr.
Williams is called *The Widow's Lament in Springtime*:

1	Sórrow ís my ŏwn ўard
2	Whére the nĕw grăss
3	Flămes as ít has flămed
4	óften befŏre, but nŏt
5	wíth the cŏld fĭre
6	that clŏses róund me thĭs yéar.
7	Thírty-fíve yĕars
8	I lĭved with mý hŭsband.
9	The plŭm-tree is whíte todáy
10	with mässes of flŏwers.
11	Măsses of flŏwers
12	lóad the chĕrry brănches
13	and cŏlor sóme bŭshes
14	ўellow ánd sŏme réd,
15	but the gríef in my heárt
16	is strŏnger than theў;
17	for thŏugh they wére my jŏy
18	fŏrmerlý, todáy I nŏtice thém
19	and tŭrn awáy forgétting.
20	Todáy my són tŏld me
21	* Thát in the meädow
22	at the ĕdge of the heávy wóods
23	in the dĭstance, he săw
24	treĕs of whíte flŏwers.
25	I feĕl that Í would lĭke
26	* to gŏ there
27	and făll into those flŏwers
28	* and sĭnk into the mărsh neár them.

The slow heavy movement of this poem of two-foot lines is accen-
tuated by the periodic swift lines (four, six, nine, thirteen and
fourteen, seventeen and eighteen and nineteen, twenty-two, along

with a few more or less intermediate lines, like one, ten, eleven, twelve, and twenty-eight) out of which the slow lines fall with greater emphasis. A poem of much greater length which displays a remarkable range of feeling is Mr. T. Sturge Moore's play (or, to be more exact, Eclogue) entitled *The Rout of the Amazons*. Mr. Pound's *Cantos* offer a slow and deliberative movement, but are as bound to it as is H. D. to her ecstasy.

There are at least two additional objections which I should mention in connection with the tyranny of free-verse movements, objections perhaps inclusive or causative of those already made; namely, that two of the principles of variation—substitution and immeasurably variable degrees of accent—which are open to the poet employing the old meters, are not open to the poet employing free verse, for, as regards substitution, there is no normal foot from which to depart, and, as regards accent, there is no foot to indicate which syllables are to be considered accented, but the accented syllable must identify itself in relation to the entire line, the result being that accents are of fairly fixed degrees, and certain ranges of possible accent are necessarily represented by gaps. In free verse the only norm, so far as the structure of the foot is concerned, is perpetual variation, and the only principle governing the selection of any foot is a feeling of rhythmical continuity; and on the other hand the norm of the line, a certain number of accents of recognizably constant intensity, and in spite of the presence of the relatively variable secondary accents, inevitably results in the species of inflexibility which we have seen equally in the fast meters of Williams and in the slow meters of Pound.

The free-verse poet, however, achieves effects roughly comparable to those of substitution in the old meters in two ways: first by the use of lines of irregular length, a device which he employs much more commonly than does the poet of the old meters and with an effect quite foreign to the effect of too few or of extra feet in the old meters; and, secondly, since the norm is perpetual variation, by the approximate repetition of a foot or of a series of feet. It is a question whether such effects can be employed with a subtlety equal to that of fine substitution. Personally I am convinced that they cannot be; for in traditional verse, each variation, no matter how slight, is exactly perceptible and as a result can be given exact meaning as an act of moral perception. Exactness of language is always a great advantage, and the deficiencies of free verse in this respect will be more evident after an examination of some of the traditional meters.

SECTION IV: EXPERIMENTAL AND TRADITIONAL METERS

In describing the consequences of the swifter forms of free verse and of the meters of Hopkins, I have indicated a general principle which accounts for a definite and often-regretted tendency in the history of English meter—the tendency of successive generations of poets to level their meters more and more toward the iambic, that is, toward the normal meter of the language, and at the same time to simplify their rhyme schemes, to depart, at least, from those schemes, which, like that of *Alisoun,* contribute to a swift and lilting music or to some other highly specialized effect. Without assuming the truth of any theories of evolution, of progress, or of continuous development in poetry, we may recognize the facts that within limited historical patterns, early poetry is simple and later poetry is likely to be relatively complex, these two adjectives being understood as relating to the content of the poetry, the moral consciousness of the art; that, as the complex poetry deadens, or, the commoner phenomenon, as the critical sensibility to it deadens and the fashion begins to change, there are likely to be new outbreaks of emphatic and relatively simple, but nevertheless fresh, feeling, which eventually may reinvigorate the older tradition.

How, then, can one reconcile in theory this tendency to increasing complexity of feeling with the tendency to increasing simplicity of means? The answer, I believe, is fairly simple. The nearer a norm a writer hovers, the more able is he to vary his feelings in opposite or even in many directions, and the more significant will be his variations. I have observed elsewhere that variations of any kind are more important in proportion as they are habitually less pronounced: a man who speaks habitually at the top of his voice cannot raise his voice, but a man who speaks quietly commands attention by means of a minute inflection. So elaborately and emphatically joyous a poem as *Alisoun,* for example, can be only and exclusively joyous; but Hardy, in the more level and calmer song, *During Wind and Rain,* can define a joy fully as profound, indeed more profound, at the same time that he is dealing primarily with a

tragic theme. To extend the comparison to free verse, H. D.'s
Orchard is purely ecstatic; it is as limited in its theme as is *Alisoun,*
and as specialized in its meter. But Dr. Williams' poem, *The
Widow's Lament,* is at once simpler and calmer in meter and more
profound in feeling. The difference between these two poems, of
course, is due wholly to a difference in temperament, and not to
the passage of centuries. That a specimen of free verse can be
found displaying a complexity and a profundity comparable to
those of such poems as Hardy's *During Wind and Rain* and
Bridges' *Love not too much,* I do not believe; nor do I believe that
such a poem can ever be composed. For reasons that will become
increasingly clear as this discussion progresses, I believe that the
nature of free verse is a permanent obstacle to such a composition.

It is worth noting that the songs of Shakespeare are, for the most
part, the most varied and brilliant exhibitions of minutely skillful
writing which we possess, as well as the most song-like of songs.
They are likewise nearly as frail, nearly as minor, as any wholly
successful poetry could be. The sonnets, on the other hand, remain,
I suppose, our standard of the greatest possible poetry; they are
written in the normal line of our poetry and in the simplest form
of the sonnet.

The lilting movement of the sixteenth century lyrical meters,
of Sidney, of *England's Helicon,* disappears from the work of the
great masters of the seventeenth century. Even Herrick suggests
the old feeling ever so slightly, though quite deliberately—his line
has a stony solidity utterly foreign to the lyrics of fifty years earlier.
Donne employs at times movements which suggest the earlier
movements, as, for example, in the songs, *Sweetest love I do not
go,* and *Go and catch a falling star,* but his bony step is wholly
different from the light pausing and shifting of Sidney; it is a
grimly serious parody. George Herbert's *Church Monuments,* perhaps the most polished and urbane poem of the Metaphysical
School and one of the half dozen most profound, is written in an
iambic pentameter line so carefully modulated, and with its rhymes
so carefully concealed at different and unexpected points in the
syntax, that the poem suggests something of the quiet plainness
of excellent prose without losing the organization and variety of
verse.

Crashaw, in his most beautiful devotional poetry, employs cadences and imagery suggestive of earlier love poetry and drinking songs. Thus, in his paraphrase of the *Twenty-third Psalm,* he writes:

> When my wayward breath is flying,
> He calls home my soul from dying.

This passage corresponds closely to a passage in a translation made by Crashaw from an Italian love song, a fact which might lead one to suspect that he sought deliberately for relationships between disparate modes of experience and that the correspondences—and there are many of them—in his other poems are not accidental:

> When my dying
> Life is flying,
> Those sweet airs, that often slew me
> Shall revive me,
> Or reprieve me,
> And to many deaths renew me.

The reader should observe that there is here not only a resemblance between the first couplet of the translated stanza and the couplet of the psalm, but that the traditional image of physical love, as it appears in the translated stanza, serves as a basis for the image of salvation in the psalm; something similar occurs at the climax of the famous poem to Saint Theresa; similar also is the use, in his various references to the Virgin, of imagery borrowed from Petrarchan love-poetry; similar also is his application of Petrarchan wit to sacred subjects, as if he were, like some celestial tumbler, displaying his finest training and ingenuity for the greater glory, and out of the purest love, of God—in fact, it is in Crashaw that the relationship between the Petrarchan conceit and the Metaphysical conceit is perhaps most obvious. The paraphrase of the psalm, which is the more complex and profound of the two poems just mentioned, is written in couplets and exhibits very few feminine rhymes. The sudden shift into the feminine rhyme in this particular couplet gives an unexpected and swiftly dissipated feeling of an earlier, more emphatic, and more naïve lyricism.

In the following couplet, likewise from the paraphrase of the psalm, there is both in the meter and in the imagery a strong suggestion of the poetry of conviviality:

> How my head in ointment swims!
> How my cup o'erlooks her brims!

The head, of course, is not swimming with drink, and the cup is the cup of bliss, but the instant of delirium is deliberately sought and impeccably fixed. The meter contributes to this effect in two ways: through the approximate coincidence of length and accent, with the resultant swift and simplified movement, and through the almost exact metrical similarity of the two lines. The spiritualization, if one may employ such a term, of the convivial image is partly, of course, the work of the context, but it is also, in a large measure, the work of the startling word *o'erlooks,* which takes the place of the commoner and purely physical *o'erflows:* the word not only implies animation, but suggests a trembling balance. The last couplet of the same poem recalls the earlier love-lyrics in a similar manner:

> And thence my ripe soul will I breath
> Warm into the Arms of Death.

One can find many other passages in Crashaw's devotional verse to illustrate this practice. Crashaw does not, in passages like these, quote or borrow from earlier poetry; he does not ordinarily even suggest a particular passage or line from an earlier poet. Rather, by fleeting nuances of language, he suggests an anterior mode of poetic expression and hence of experience, and in a context which is new to it. More commonly than not, he suggests in this manner not what is most striking in an earlier body of poetry but what is most commonplace: an earlier poetic convention becomes the material of his perception, and contributes, along with other, apparently disparate, and non-literary material, the material of an extremely complex poetic structure. It is in ways such as this that Crashaw is traditional; he is experimental in the ways in which he pushes metaphor beyond the bounds of custom and frequently even of reason. Crashaw is noted for his experiments; the large amount of poetry in which the traditional predominates and the experimental is under full control is too seldom appreciated.

This illusion of simplicity, this retreat toward the norm, of which I have been speaking, can, however, be achieved only by those writers who have mastered the more emphatic and athletic exercises; it is inconceivable that a poet insensitive to the fresh and

skillful enthusiasm of Sidney should achieve the subdued complexity of Crashaw, Jonson, or Herrick. The beauty of the later
masters resides in a good measure in what they suggest and refrain
from doing, not in that of which they are ignorant or incapable.
Within the pattern of free verse, this kind of suggestion is impossible: to depart from a given movement is to abandon it; the absence of a metrical frame accounting for the agreement or variation of every syllable, heavy or light, and allowing immeasurable
variation of accent, makes exact and subtle variation and suggestion impossible. Similarly, there is no manner in which the rhythms
of a poem in free verse, such as H. D.'s *Orchard,* could be utilized
or suggested in a poem in accentual-syllabic meter, for the two
systems are unrelated and mutually destructive. In so far, however,
as the difficulties of maintaining rhythm in new and structurally
unsatisfactory patterns, may have forced poets and their readers
to strain the attention upon certain fine shades of accent and quantity, it is possible that the free-verse poets may have eventually a
beneficial effect upon poets writing in accentual-syllabic verse; in
so far as free verse has encouraged careless substitution in the older
meter, has encouraged an approximation of the movement of
accentual-syllabic verse to that of purely accentual, its effect has
quite perceptibly been undesirable. Eliot, Tate, and MacLeish
exemplify the latter influence.

GERARD MANLEY HOPKINS

Letter to R. W. Dixon

111 Mount Street,
Grosvenor Square, W.
Oct. 5 1878

Very Reverend and Dear Sir,

A visit to Great Yarmouth and pressure of work have kept me
from answering before yr. very kind letter, and my reply will now
not be written at once but as I shall find leisure.

I hope, to begin with, you have quite recovered from the effects
of your accident. I escaped from such a one with very little hurt

not long ago in Wales, but I witnessed a terrible and fatal coach-accident years ago in the Vale of Maentwrog.

I have forgotten not only what I said about 'Fr. Prout' but even that I ever read him. I always understood that he was a very amusing writer. I do remember that I was a very conceited boy.

I have quite lost sight of Mr. Lobb; I do not even know whether he is alive or dead. The truth is I had no love for my schooldays and wished to banish the remembrance of them, even, I am ashamed to say, to the degree of neglecting some people who had been very kind to me. Of Oxford on the other hand I was very fond. I became a Catholic there. But I have not visited it, except once for three quarters of an hour, since I took my degree. We have a church and house there now.

Oct. 6—The other day Dr. Bridges told me he had in vain tried to get yr. volumes of poems, for want of knowing the publisher. I promised I wd. enquire of you. Was it not Smith and Elder?

I quite agree with what you write about Milton. His verse as one reads it seems something necessary and eternal (so to me does Purcell's music). As for 'proper hue' *now* it wd. be priggish, but I suppose Milton means *own hue* and they talk of *proper colours* in heraldry; not but what there is a Puritan touch about the line even so. However the word must once have had a different feeling. The Welsh have borrowed it for *pretty;* they talk of birds singing 'properly' and a little Welsh boy to whom I shewed the flowers in a green house exclaimed 'They *are* proper!'—Milton seems now coming to be studied better, and Masson is writing or has written his life at prodigious length. There was an interesting review by Matthew Arnold in one of the Quarterlies of 'a French critic on Milton'—Scherer I think. The same M. Arnold says Milton and Campbell are our two greatest masters of *style*. Milton's art is incomparable, not only in English literature but, I shd. think, almost in any; equal, if not more than equal, to the finest of Greek or Roman. And considering that this is shewn especially in his verse, his rhythm and metrical system, it is amazing that so great a writer as Newman should have fallen into the blunder of comparing the first chorus of the *Agonistes* with the opening of *Thalaba* as instancing the gain in smoothness and correctness of versification made since Milton's time—Milton having been not only ahead of his own time as well as all aftertimes in verse-structure but these particular choruses being his own highwater mark. It is as if you were to compare the Panathenaic frieze and a teaboard and decide in the teaboard's favour.

I have paid a good deal of attention to Milton's versification and collected his later rhythms: I did it when I had to lecture on rhetoric some years since. I found his most advanced effects in the *Paradise Regained* and, lyrically, in the *Agonistes*. I have often thought of writing on them, indeed on rhythm in general; I think the subject is little understood.

You ask, do I write verse myself. What I had written I burnt before I became a Jesuit and resolved to write no more, as not belonging to my profession, unless it were by the wish of my superiors; so for seven years I wrote nothing but two or three little presentation pieces which occasion called for. But when in the winter of '75 the Deutschland was wrecked in the mouth of the Thames and five Franciscan nuns, exiles from Germany by the Falck Laws, aboard of her were drowned I was affected by the account and happening to say so to my rector he said that he wished someone would write a poem on the subject. On this hint I set to work and, though my hand was out at first, produced one. I had long had haunting my ear the echo of a new rhythm which now I realised on paper. To speak shortly, it consist in scanning by accents or stresses alone, without any account of the number of syllables, so that a foot may be one strong syllable or it may be many light and one strong. I do not say the idea is altogether new; there are hints of it in music, in nursery rhymes and popular jingles, in the poets themselves, and, since then, I have seen it talked about as a thing possible in critics. Here are instances—'*Díng, dóng, béll*; Pússy's ín the wéll; *Whó pút* her ín? Líttle Jóhnny Thín. *Whó púlled* her óut? Líttle Johnny Stóut.' For if each line has three stresses or three feet it follows that some of the feet are of one syllable only. So too '*Óne, twó,* Búckle my shóe' *passim*. In Campbell you have 'Ánd their fléet alóng the *déep próudly* shóne' —'Ít was tén of Ápril *mórn by* the chíme' etc; in Shakespere 'Whý shd. *thís* désert bé?' corrected wrongly by the editors; in Moore a little melody I cannot quote; etc. But no one has professedly used it and made it the principle throughout, that I know of. Nevertheless to me it appears, I own, to be a better and more natural principle than the ordinary system, much more flexible, and capable of

much greater effects. However I had to mark the stresses in blue
chalk, and this and my rhymes carried on from one line into another and certain chimes suggested by the Welsh poetry I had been
reading (what they call *cynghanedd*) and a great many more odd-
nesses could not but dismay an editor's eye, so that when I offered
it to our magazine the *Month,* though at first they accepted it,
after a time they withdrew and dared not print it. After writing
this I held myself free to compose, but cannot find it in my conscience to spend time upon it; so I have done little and shall do
less. But I wrote a shorter piece on the Eurydice, also in 'sprung
rhythm', as I call it, but simpler, shorter, and without marks, and
offered the *Month* that too, but they did not like it either. Also I
have written some sonnets and a few other little things; some in
sprung rhythm, with various other experiments—as 'outriding feet',
that is parts of which do not count in the scanning (such as you
find in Shakespere's plays, but as a licence, whereas mine are rather
calculated effects); others in the ordinary scanning *counterpointed*
(this is counterpoint: 'Hóme to his móther's hóuse *prívate* re-
túrned' and '*Bút to vánquish* by wísdom héllish wíles' etc); others,
one or two, in common uncounterpointed rhythm. But even the
impulse to write is wanting, for I have no thought of publishing.

I should add that Milton is the great standard in the use of
counterpoint. In *Paradise Lost* and *Regained,* in the last more
freely, it being an advance in his art, he employs counterpoint more
or less everywhere, markedly now and then; but the choruses of
Samson Agonistes are in my judgment counterpointed throughout;
that is, each line (or nearly so) has two different coexisting scan-
sions. But when you reach that point the secondary or 'mounted
rhythm', which is necessarily a sprung rhythm, overpowers the
original or conventional one and then this becomes superfluous
and may be got rid of; by taking that last step you reach simple
sprung rhythm. Milton must have known this but had reasons for
not taking it.

I read Arnold's *Essays in Criticism* at Oxford and got Maurice de
Guérin's Journal in consequence, admired it, but for some reason
or other never got far in it. I should be glad to read it now if I had
time. But I have no time for more pressing interests. I hear con-
fessions, preach, and so forth; when these are done I have still a

good deal of time to myself, but I find I can do very little with
it. . . .

Believe me, dear Sir, very sincerely yours

Gerard Hopkins.

Oct. 10

Author's Preface to Poems, 1876-1889

The poems in this book are written some in Running Rhythm,
the common rhythm in English use, some in Sprung Rhythm, and
some in a mixture of the two. And those in the common rhythm
are some counterpointed, some not.

Common English rhythm, called Running Rhythm above, is
measured by feet of either two or three syllables and (putting aside
the imperfect feet at the beginning and end of lines and also some
unusual measures, in which feet seem to be paired together and
double or composite feet to arise) never more or less.

Every foot has one principal stress or accent, and this or the
syllable it falls on may be called the Stress of the foot and the other
part, the one or two unaccented syllables, the Slack. Feet (and the
rhythms made out of them) in which the stress comes first are
called Falling Feet and Falling Rrythms, feet and rhythm in which
the slack comes first are called Rising Feet and Rhythms, and if
the stress is between two slacks there will be Rocking Feet and
Rhythms. These distinctions are real and true to nature; but for
purposes of scanning it is a great convenience to follow the example of music and take the stress always first, as the accent or the
chief accent always comes first in a musical bar. If this is done there
will be in common English verse only two possible feet—the so-
called accentual Trochee and Dactyl, and correspondingly only two
possible uniform rhythms, the so-called Trochaic and Dactylic.
But they may be mixed and then what the Greeks called a Logaoedic Rhythm arises. These are the facts and according to these the
scanning of ordinary regularly-written English verse is very simple
indeed and to bring in other principles is here unnecessary.

But because verse written strictly in these feet and by these
principles will become same and tame the poets have brought in
licences and departures from rule to give variety, and especially

when the natural rhythm is rising, as in the common ten-syllable or five-foot verse, rhymed or blank. These irregularities are chiefly Reversed Feet and Reversed or Counterpoint Rhythm, which two things are two steps or degrees of licence in the same kind. By a reversed foot I mean the putting the stress where, to judge by the rest of the measure, the slack should be and the slack where the stress, and this is done freely at the beginning of a line and, in the course of a line, after a pause; only scarcely ever in the second foot or place and never in the last, unless when the poet designs some extraordinary effect; for these places are characteristic and sensitive and cannot well be touched. But the reversal of the first foot and of some middle foot after a strong pause is a thing so natural that our poets have generally done it, from Chaucer down, without remark and it commonly passes unnoticed and cannot be said to amount to a formal change of rhythm, but rather is that irregularity which all natural growth and motion shews. If however the reversal is repeated in two feet running, especially so as to include the sensitive second foot, it must be due either to great want of ear or else is a calculated effect, the superinducing or *mounting* of a new rhythm upon the old; and since the new or mounted rhythm is actually heard and at the same time the mind naturally supplies the natural or standard foregoing rhythm, for we do not forget what the rhythm is that by rights we should be hearing, two rhythms are in some manner running at once and we have something answerable to counterpoint in music, which is two or more strains of tune going on together, and this is Counterpoint Rhythm. Of this kind of verse Milton is the great master and the choruses of *Samson Agonistes* are written throughout in it—but with the disadvantage that he does not let the reader clearly know what the ground-rhythm is meant to be and so they have struck most readers as merely irregular. And in fact if you counterpoint throughout, since one only of the counter rhythms is actually heard, the other is really destroyed or cannot come to exist, and what is written is one rhythm only and probably Sprung Rhythm, of which I now speak.

Sprung Rhythm, as used in this book, is measured by feet of from one to four syllables, regularly, and for particular effects any number of weak or slack syllables may be used. It has one stress, which falls on the only syllable, if there is only one, or, if there are

more, then scanning as above, on the first, and so gives rise to four
sorts of feet, a monosyllable and the so-called accentual Trochee,
Dactyl, and the First Paeon. And there will be four corresponding
natural rhythms; but nominally the feet are mixed and any one
may follow any other. And hence Sprung Rhythm differs from
Running Rhythm in having or being only one nominal rhythm, a
mixed or 'logaoedic' one, instead of three, but on the other hand
in having twice the flexibility of foot, so that any two stresses may
either follow one another running or be divided by one, two, or
three slack syllables. But strict Sprung Rhythm cannot be counterpointed. In Sprung Rhythm, as in logaoedic rhythm generally, the
feet are assumed to be equally long or strong and their seeming inequality is made up by pause or stressing.

Remark also that it is natural in Sprung Rhythm for the lines to
be *rove over,* that is for the scanning of each line immediately to
take up that of the one before, so that if the first has one or more
syllables at its end the other must have so many the less at its beginning; and in fact the scanning runs on without break from the
beginning, say, of a stanza to the end and all the stanza is one long
strain, though written in lines asunder.

Two licences are natural to Sprung Rhythm. The one is rests,
as in music; but of this an example is scarcely to be found in this
book, unless in the *Echos,* second line. The other is *hangers* or
outrides, that is one, two, or three slack syllables added to a foot
and not counting in the nominal scanning. They are so called
because they seem to hang below the line or ride forward or backward from it in another dimension than the line itself, according
to a principle needless to explain here. These outriding half feet
or hangers are marked by a loop underneath them, and plenty of
them will be found.

The other marks are easily understood, namely accents, where
the reader might be in doubt which syllable should have the stress;
slurs, that is loops *over* syllables, to tie them together into the time
of one; little loops at the end of a line to shew that the rhyme goes
on to the first letter of the next line; what in music are called
pauses ⌒, to shew that the syllable should be dwelt on; and twirls
⁓, to mark reversed or counterpointed rhythm.

Note on the nature and history of Sprung Rhythm—Sprung
Rhythm is the most natural of things. For (1) it is the rhythm of

common speech and of written prose, when rhythm is perceived in them. (2) It is the rhythm of all but the most monotonously regular music, so that in the words of choruses and refrains and in songs written closely to music it arises. (3) It is found in nursery rhymes, weather saws, and so on; because, however these may have been once made in running rhythm, the terminations having dropped off by the change of language, the stresses come together and so the rhythm is sprung. (4) It arises in common verse when reversed or counterpointed, for the same reason.

But nevertheless in spite of all this and though Greek and Latin lyric verse, which is well known, and the old English verse seen in 'Pierce Ploughman' are in sprung rhythm, it has in fact ceased to be used since the Elizabethan age, Greene being the last writer who can be said to have recognized it. For perhaps there was not, down to our days, a single, even short, poem in English in which sprung rhythm is employed—not for single effects or in fixed places —but as the governing principle of the scansion. I say this because the contrary has been asserted: if it is otherwise the poem should be cited.

Some of the sonnets in this book are in five-foot, some in six-foot or Alexandrine lines.

Nos. 13 and 22 are Curtal-Sonnets, that is they are constructed in proportions resembling those of the sonnet proper, namely, 6+4 instead of 8+6, with however a halfline tailpiece (so that the equation is rather $\frac{12}{2} + \frac{9}{2} = \frac{21}{2} = 10\frac{1}{2}$).

BERTOLT BRECHT

On Unrhymed Lyrics in Irregular Rhythms

I have been asked from time to time, whenever I published unrhymed lyrics, how I came to designate such verse as *lyric*. The last time this happened was in connection with my *Deutsche Satiren* (German Satires). The question is justified, because even when lyrics abandon rhyme they generally have at least a fixed rhythm. Many of my recent lyric pieces show neither rhyme nor regularly fixed rhythm. The reason

I call them *lyric* is that, although they do not have a regular rhythm, they do have *rhythm*—shifting, syncopated, gestural.

My first book of poems contained for the most part only songs and ballads, and the verse forms are comparatively regular. Most of them were supposed to be sung, and in the simplest fashion— I myself was the composer. Only one poem was unrhymed, and its rhythm was regular. On the other hand, nearly all the rhymed poems had irregular rhythms. In the *Ballade vom toten Soldaten* (Ballad of the Dead Soldier) there are in 19 stanzas nine different rhythmical arrangements of the second line:

1.	v v —v v —v —	*Keinen Ausblick auf Frieden bot*
2.	v — v v —v —	*Drum tat es dem Kaiser leid*
3.	v v v— — —	*Und der Soldat schlief schon*
4.	v —v —v v—	*Zum Gottesacker hinaus*
5.	v v — v — v — —	*Oder was von ihm noch da war*
6.	v — v — v —	*Die Nacht war blau und schön*
14.	v — v v — v v —	*Die Ratzen im Feld pfeifen wüst*
15.	v v — v —v —	*Warren alle Weiber de*
18.	— v —v —	*Dass inn keiner sah*

After this, in connection with a play, *Im Dickicht der Städte,* I was occupied with the elevated prose of Arthur Rimbaud (in his *Season in Hell*). In connection with another play, *Leben Eduards des Zweiten von England* (The Life of Edward the Second of England), I had to concern myself with the problem of the iambic. I had noted how much more powerful the actors' delivery was when they spoke the hard-to-read, rough verse of the old Schlegel-Tieck translation of Shakespeare instead of the new, smooth Rothe translation. How much more strongly the conflict of ideas in the great soliloquies was brought out there. How much richer the verse architecture was! The problem was simple. I required elevated language, but I was repelled by the oily smoothness of the customary iambic pentameter. I needed rhythm, but not the customary clatter. I proceeded in the following way. Instead of writing:

Seit sie das Trommeln rührten überm Sumpf
Und um mich Ross und Katapult versank
Ist mir verrückt mein Kopf. Ob alle schon
Ertrunken sind und aus und nur mehr Lärm hängt
Leer und verspätet zwischen Erd und Himmel? Ich
Sollt nicht so laufen.

I wrote:

> *Seit diese Trommeln waren, der Sumpf, ersäufend*
> *Katapult und Pferde, ist wohl verrückt*
> *Meiner Mutter Sohn Kopf. Keuch nicht! Ob alle*
> *Schon ertrunken sind und aus und nur mehr Lärm ist*
> *Hängend noch zwischen Erd und Himmel. Ich will auch nicht*
> *Mehr rennen.*

This conveyed the panting of the runner, and the contradictory emotions of the speaker were better revealed in the syncopations. My political knowledge at that time was shamefully small. Nevertheless, I was aware of great inconsistencies in human society, and I did not think it my task to use forms which would neutralize all the disharmonies and confusions I strongly felt. I caught these disharmonies and confusions in the events of my dramas and the verses of my poems. And this was long before I understood their real nature and their causes. As the texts indicate, I was concerned not only with "swimming against the stream" in respect to form, in protesting against the smoothness and harmony of conventional verse, but in attempting already at that time to show events among human beings as full of contradictions, strife-torn, and violent.

I could proceed even more freely when I wrote operas, *Lehrstücke* (didactic plays), and cantatas for modern musicians. Here I gave up iambic completely and employed fixed but irregular rhythms. They were remarkably well suited to the music, as composers of the most varied tendencies assured me and as I could see for myself.

I subsequently wrote, apart from ballads and songs for the masses which had rhyme and regular or nearly regular rhythm, more and more poems without rhyme and with irregular rhythm. It must be kept in mind that my chief work was for the theater; I was constantly thinking of the spoken word. And I had worked out for myself a definite technique for speaking, whether of prose or verse. I called it *gestural* (*gestisch*).

This meant that the language had to accord entirely with the gesture of the person who was speaking. I will give an example. The sentence in the Bible: "Pluck out thine eye if it offend thee" has at bottom a gesture, one of command, but it is not expressed in a purely gestural way, since "if it offend thee" really has another gesture which is not expressed, namely, giving a reason. Expressed in a purely gestural way the sentence is as follows (and Luther, who studied the speech of the common people, put it this way): "If thine eye offend thee, pluck it out!" One can see at a glance that this formulation is, with regard to gesture, much richer and purer. The first clause contains an hypothesis, and what is peculiar and special about it can be fully expressed in one's intonation. Then comes a short perplexed pause, and only *then* the startling exhortation. Gestural formulation can of course operate within a regular rhythm (as well as in a rhymed poem). An example to show differences:

> *Hast du den Säugling gesehn, der, unbewusst noch der Liebe,*
> *Die ihn wärmet und wiegt, schlafend von Arme zu Arm*
> *Wandert, bis bei der Leidenschaft Ruf der Jüngling erwachet*
> *Und des Bewusstseins Blitz dämmernd die Welt ihm erhellt?*
> SCHILLER: Der philosophische Egoist

and

> *Das aus nichts nichts wird, selbst nicht durch den Willen der*
> *Götter.*
> *Denn so enge beschränket die Furcht die Sterblichen, alle;*
> *Da sie so viel der Erscheinungen sehn, am Himmel, auf Erden,*
> *Deren wirkenden Grund sie nicht zu erfassen vermögen,*
> *Dass sie glauben, durch göttliche Macht sey dies alles entstanden.*
> *Haben wir aber erkannt, dass aus nichts nichts könne hervorgehn,*
> *Werden wir richtiger sehn, wonach wir forschen; woraus denn,*
> *Und wie alles entsteh, auch ohne die Hilfe der Götter.*
> Translation of LUCRETIUS:
De Rerum Natura

The poverty of gestural elements in Schiller's poem and the wealth of such elements in Lucretius' can be easily verified by speaking the verses and noting how often one's own gesture changes.

I began to speak about the problem of gestural formulations because although it is possible for them to occur within regular rhythms, at the same time it seems to me that without gestural formulation *irregular* rhythms are impossible. I recall that two observations of mine were influential in my construction of irregular rhythms. One had to do with those short improvised choruses in workers' demonstrations, the first of which I heard one Christmas Eve. A procession of proletarians marched through the fashionable section of western Berlin and called out *"Wir haben Hunger."* (We are hungry.) The rhythm was as follows:

$$\overline{Wir}\ \overline{ha\text{-}}\ \overline{ben}\ H\breve{u}n\text{-}\ \breve{ger}$$

Later I heard other such choruses in which the text had simply been disciplined and made easy to speak. One went:

$$\overline{Helft}\ \overline{euch}\ s\breve{el}\text{-}\ \breve{ber},\ w\breve{a}hlt\ \overline{Th\ddot{a}l\text{-}}\ \overline{mann}$$

A second experience with the rhythmics of the people was hearing the cry of a Berlin street peddler who was selling radio librettos in front of the Kaufhaus des Westens. His rhythmical arrangement was as follows:

$$\overline{Text\text{-}}\ b\breve{u}ch\ f\ddot{u}r\ d\breve{i}\breve{e}\ \overline{O\text{-}}\ \overline{per}\ F\breve{ra}\text{-}\ \overline{tel\text{-}}\ l\breve{a}\ w\breve{e}l\breve{che}$$
$$h\breve{eu}\text{-}\ t\breve{e}\ \breve{A}\text{-}\ b\breve{en}d\ \breve{im}\ \overline{Rund\text{-}}\ \overline{funk}\ g\breve{e}\text{-}\ \overline{h\ddot{o}rt}\ \overline{wird}$$

The man constantly changed the intonation and volume, but he kept the rhythm steady.

Anyone can study the technique used by newspaper sellers in working out the rhythms of their cries.

Irregular rhythmical arrangement is, however, also employed in written matter, where a certain impressiveness is desired. Two examples of many:

> *Du sollst nur Ma-*
> *no- li rau- chen*

and (with rhyme):

> *Al- len an- de- ren zu- vor*
> *der Sa-*
> *rot- ti- mohr*

These experiences affected my development of irregular rhythms.

What do these irregular rhythms look like? I shall take an example from the *Deutsche Satiren,* the last two stanzas of *Die Jugend und das Dritte Reich* (Youth and the Third Reich):

> *Ja, wenn die Kinder Kinder blieben, dann*
> *Könnte man ihnen immer Märchen erzählen*

> *Da sie aber älter werden*
> *Kann man es nicht.*

How is this to be read? First let us write in the underlying regular rhythm:

```
 — v — v — v —   v  —  v —  v  — v
Ja wenn die Kin- der Kin- der blie- ben, dann
  — v —  v — v  — v—v  — v — v — v—v
Könn- te man ih- nen im- mer Mär- chen er- zäh- len
  —v—v— v — v —
Da sie a- ber äl- ter wer- den
  — v —v—v —
Kann man es nicht.
```

The missing feet must be taken care of either by a lengthening of the preceding foot or by pauses. Division into verses is helpful. The end of a line always indicates a caesura. I chose this stanza because if the second verse is made into two verses, divided thus:

> *Könnte man ihnen immer*
> *Märchen erzählen*

it becomes even easier to read, so that the principle can be studied in a borderline case. One sees the effect of division on the sound of the poem and the way it makes its point if the last stanza—

> *Wenn das Regime händereibend von der Jungend spricht*
> *Gleicht es einem Mann, der*
> *Die beschneite Halde betrachtend, sich die Hände reibt und sagt:*
> *Wie werde ich es im Sommer kühl haben mit*
> *So viel Schnee—*

is divided differently, thus, say:

> *Wenn das Regime händereibend von der Jungend spricht*
> *Gleicht es einem Mann*
> *Der, die beschneite Halde betrachtend, sich die Hände reibt und*
>   *sagt:*
> *Wie werde ich es im Sommer kühl haben*
> *Mit so viel Schnee.*

Actually, it can also be read rhythmically when written thus. Yet the *qualitative* difference is immediately obvious. It must be admitted that on the whole this free manner of handling the verse is a great temptation to formlessness: rhythmical excellence is guaranteed even less than by rhythmic regularity. (Then again, the careful counting out of metrical feet has no rhythm at all.) The proof of the pudding is in the eating.

It must be further admitted that the reading of irregular rhythms at first offers several difficulties. I do not think, however, that this says anything against them. The ear is undoubtedly going through a physiological transformation. Our acoustical environment has changed tremendously. There was a scene in an American movie in which Fred Astaire did a tap dance to the noises of an engine room; the tap rhythm showed the startling similarity between the new noises and jazz. Jazz meant a broad influx of popular musical elements into recent music, no matter what was later made of it in our commercial world. The relationship of jazz to the emancipation of the Negro is well known.

The very wholesome campaign against formalism has made it possible to be *productive* in the futher development of forms in art. It proved that an absolutely decisive condition for the development of forms is the further development of social content. Any formal innovation which does not subordinate itself to this development of content, which does not take its function from the development of content, remains completely barren.

The *Deutsche Satiren* were written for the German Freedom Station. It was a matter of sending out isolated sentences to a distant, artificially dispersed audience. The sentences had to be put into the most concise form, and interruptions (from jamming) had to make little difference. Rhyme did not seem to me suitable since it easily gives a poem an air of being shut in; rather than going into the ears, it easily passes lightly, as it were, over them. Regular rhythms with their even cadence are likewise not easy enough to catch on to at once, and they lead to circumlocutions: many common expressions do not fit into them. It was necessary to have the tone of direct, actual conversation. It seemed to me that unrhymed lyrics in irregular rhythm were suited to the purpose.

Translated by BEATRICE GOTTLIEB

Form

With the last
group of selections in Part Two the subject shifts from style to form:
from the details to the larger element which shapes poems, the principle which runs through the details and determines their place and
function within the whole. These essays provide three conceptions of
form, form as "voice," as "impurity," and as "symbolic action." Each is
helpful in alerting the reader to what is going on in poems; each has its
own implications for critical judgment.

T. S. Eliot's "The Three Voices of Poetry" offers "voice" as a determining principle. As we confront a poem, Eliot directs us to ask to
whom the poet is speaking. Is he talking to himself or to nobody, is he
addressing an audience, or is he creating a dramatic character speaking
in verse? Eliot distinguishes clearly among these possibilities; he insists,
however, that in really good poems more than one voice is active, and
in so doing he assumes a critical position which effectively answers certain charges which readers often level against poets. Eliot argues that
troublesome obscurity may well be the unavoidable result of a private
intention, that a poem written in wholly private language is not yet a
poem, that although a poet may ordinarily employ a very public tone,
there may be moments when he wishes not to be heard but to be overheard.

Robert Penn Warren's preference for "impurity" is evidence of a
typically modern mind sensitive to its own inner conflicts and aware of
the difficulty of communication in a world of conflicting values. In requiring the poet somehow to adjust his wordless impulse to the demands of language, Eliot allows for a certain variety of elements in
poetry, some combination of public and private. Variety of another
kind is, for Warren, poetry's central organizing or informing principle,
not the mere display of differing elements or the adaptation of one element to another, but their resistance to one another, their dramatic

235

*interplay. A good poem, he says, expresses its original impulse; but it
includes elements inimical to that impulse, for the poet, encountering
resistances during the creative process, preserves them in the poem.
The poem, then, is conflictual, a kind of dramatic action rather than a
statement; Warren likens the poet to the saint who "proves" his vision
by stepping willingly into the flames.*

*For Kenneth Burke too the poem is an "action," but Burke's ap-
proach, more interpretive than judgmental, allows far wider application
of the term. In order to discover what is going on in a work of art,
Burke is willing to use insights provided by any relevant discipline.
For him "form" is best understood as the functioning of form—every
motif, we might say, expresses a motive. Drawing upon the perspectives of the psychologist, the economist, the rhetorician, and the an-
thropologist, and analogizing among the insights they provide, he suggests some of the richness of what may be happening in poems.*

T. S. ELIOT

The Three Voices of Poetry

The first voice
is the voice of the poet talking to himself—or to nobody. The second is the voice of the poet addressing an audience, whether large
or small. The third is the voice of the poet when he attempts to
create a dramatic character speaking in verse; when he is saying,
not what he would say in his own person, but only what he can say
within the limits of one imaginary character addressing another
imaginary character. The distinction between the first and the second voice, between the poet speaking to himself and the poet
speaking to other people, points to the problem of poetic communication; the distinction between the poet addressing other people
in either his own voice or an assumed voice, and the poet inventing
speech in which imaginary characters address each other, points
to the problem of the difference between dramatic, quasi-dramatic,
and non-dramatic verse.

I wish to anticipate a question that some of you may well raise.
Cannot a poem be written for the ear, or for the eye, of one person
alone? You may say simply, "Isn't love poetry at times a form

of communication between one person and one other, with no thought of a further audience?"

There are at least two people who might have disagreed with me on this point: Mr. and Mrs. Robert Browning. In the poem "One Word More," written as an epilogue to *Men and Women,* and addressed to Mrs. Browning, the husband makes a striking value judgment:

> Rafael made a century of sonnets,
> Made and wrote them in a certain volume,
> Dinted with the silver-pointed pencil
> Else he only used to draw Madonnas:
> These, the world might view—but one, the volume.
> Who that one, you ask? Your heart instructs you . . .
>
> You and I would rather read that volume . . .
> Would we not? than wonder at Madonnas . . .
>
> Dante once prepared to paint an angel:
> Whom to please? You whisper 'Beatrice' . . .
> You and I would rather see that angel,
> Painted by the tenderness of Dante,
> Would we not?—than read a fresh Inferno.

I agree that one *Inferno,* even by Dante, is enough; and perhaps we need not too much regret the fact that Rafael did not multiply his Madonnas: but I can only say that I feel no curiosity whatever about Rafael's sonnets or Dante's angel. If Rafael wrote, or Dante painted, for the eyes of one person alone, let their privacy be respected. We know that Mr. and Mrs. Browning liked to write poems to each other, because they published them, and some of them are good poems. We know that Rossetti thought that he was writing his "House of Life" sonnets for one person, and that he was only persuaded by his friends to disinter them. Now, I do not deny that a poem may be addressed to one person: there is a well-known form, not always amatory in content, called The Epistle. We shall never have conclusive evidence: for the testimony of poets as to what they thought they were doing when they wrote a poem, cannot be taken altogether at its face value. But my opinion is, that a good love poem, though it may be addressed to one person, is always meant to be overheard by other people. Surely, the proper language of love—that is, of communication to the beloved and to no one else—is prose.

Having dismissed as an illusion the voice of the poet talking to one person only, I think that the best way for me to try to make my three voices audible, is to trace the genesis of the distinction in my own mind. The writer to whose mind the distinction is most likely to occur is probably the writer like myself, who has spent a good many years in writing poetry, before attempting to write for the stage at all. It may be, as I have read, that there is a dramatic element in much of my early work. It may be that from the beginning I aspired unconsciously to the theatre—or, unfriendly critics might say, to Shaftesbury Avenue and Broadway. I have, however, gradually come to the conclusion that in writing verse for the stage both the process and the outcome are very different from what they are in writing verse to be read or recited. Twenty years ago I was commissioned to write a pageant play to be called *The Rock*. The invitation to write the words for this spectacle—the occasion of which was an appeal for funds for church-building in new housing areas—came at a moment when I seemed to myself to have exhausted my meager poetic gifts, and to have nothing more to say. To be, at such a moment, commissioned to write something which, good or bad, must be delivered by a certain date, may have the effect that vigorous cranking sometimes has upon a motor car when the battery is run down. The task was clearly laid out: I had only to write the words of prose dialogue for scenes of the usual historical pageant pattern, for which I had been given a scenario. I had also to provide a number of choral passages in verse, the content of which was left to my own devices: except for the reasonable stipulation that all the choruses were expected to have some relevance to the purpose of the pageant, and that each chorus was to occupy a precise number of minutes of stage time. But in carrying out this second part of my task, there was nothing to call my attention to the third, or dramatic voice: it was the second voice, that of myself addressing—indeed haranguing—an audience, that was most distinctly audible. Apart from the obvious fact that writing to order is not the same thing as writing to please oneself, I learned only that verse to be spoken by a choir should be different from verse to be spoken by one person; and that the more voices you have in your choir, the simpler and more direct the vocabulary, the syntax, and the content of your lines must be. This chorus of *The Rock* was not a dramatic voice; though many lines were distributed, the personages were unindividuated. Its members were speaking *for me*, not uttering words that really represented any supposed character of their own.

The chorus in *Murder in the Cathedral* does, I think, represent some advance in dramatic development: that is to say, I set myself the task of writing lines, not for an anonymous chorus, but for a chorus of women of Canterbury—one might almost say, charwomen of Canterbury. I had to make some effort to identify myself with these women, instead of merely identifying them with myself. But as for the dialogue of the play, the plot had the drawback (from the point of view of my own dramatic education) of presenting only one dominant character; and what dramatic conflict there is takes place within the mind of that character. The third, or dramatic voice, did not make itself audible to me until I first attacked the problem of presenting two (or more) characters, in some sort of conflict, misunderstanding, or attempt to understand each other, characters with each of whom I had to try to identify myself while writing the words for him or her to speak. You may remember that Mrs. Cluppins, in the trial of the case of Bardell *v.* Pickwick, testified that "the voices was very loud, sir, and forced themselves upon my ear." "Well, Mrs. Cluppins," said Sergeant Buzfuz, "you were not listening, but you heard the voices." It was in 1938, then, that the third voice began to force itself upon my ear.

At this point I can fancy the reader murmuring: "I'm sure he has said all this before." I will assist memory by supplying the reference. In a lecture on "Poetry and Drama," delivered exactly three years ago and subsequently published, I said:

> In writing other verse (*i.e.* non-dramatic verse) I think that one is writing, so to speak, in terms of one's own voice: the way it sounds when you read it to yourself is the test. For it is yourself speaking. The question of communication, of what the reader will get from it, is not paramount. . . .

There is some confusion of pronouns in this passage, but I think that the meaning is clear; so clear, as to be a glimpse of the obvious. At that stage, I noted only the difference between speaking for oneself, and speaking for an imaginary character; and I passed on to other considerations about the nature of poetic drama. I was beginning to be aware of the difference between the first and the third voice, but gave no attention to the second voice, of which I shall say more presently. I am now trying to penetrate a little further into the problem. So, before going on to consider the other voices, I want to pursue for a few moments the complexities of the third voice.

In a verse play, you will probably have to find words for several characters differing widely from each other in background, temperament, education, and intelligence. You cannot afford to identify one of these characters with yourself, and give him (or her) all the "poetry" to speak. The poetry (I mean, the language at those dramatic moments when it reaches intensity) must be as widely distributed as characterization permits; and each of your characters, when he has words to speak which are poetry and not merely verse, must be given lines appropriate to himself. When the poetry comes, the personage on the stage must not give the impression of being merely a mouthpiece for the author. Hence the author is limited by the kind of poetry, and the degree of intensity in its kind, which can be plausibly attributed to each character in his play. And these lines of poetry must also justify themselves by their development of the situation in which they are spoken. Even if a burst of magnificent poetry is suitable enough for the character to which it is assigned, it must also convince us that it is necessary to the action; that it is helping to extract the utmost emotional intensity out of the situation. The poet writing for the theater may, as I have found, make two mistakes: that of assigning to a personage lines of poetry not suitable to be spoken by that personage, and that of assigning lines which, however suitable to the personage, yet fail to forward the action of the play. There are, in some of the minor Elizabethan dramatists, passages of magnificent poetry which are in both respects out of place— fine enough to preserve the play for ever as literature, but yet so inappropriate as to prevent the play from being a dramatic masterpiece. The best-known instances occur in Marlowe's *Tamburlaine*.

How have the very great dramatic poets—Sophocles, or Shakespeare, or Racine—dealt with this difficulty? This is, of course, a problem which concerns all imaginative fiction—novels and prose plays—in which the characters may be said to live. I can't see, myself, any way to make a character live except to have a profound sympathy with that character. Ideally, a dramatist, who has usually far fewer characters to manipulate than a novelist, and who has only two hours or so of life to allow them, should sympathize profoundly with all of his characters: but that is a counsel of perfection, because the plot of a play with even a very small cast may require the presence of one or more characters in whose reality, apart from their contribution to the action, we are uninterested. I wonder, however, whether it is possible to make completely real a wholly villainous character—one toward whom neither the author nor anyone else can feel anything but antipathy. We need an admixture of *weakness* with either heroic virtue or satanic villainy, to make character plausible. Iago frightens me more than Richard III; I am not sure that Parolles, in *All's Well That Ends Well,* does not disturb me more than Iago. (And I am quite sure that Rosamund Vincy, in *Middlemarch,* frightens me far more than Goneril or Regan.) It seems to me that what happens, when an author creates a vital character, is a sort of give-and-take. The author may put into that character, besides its other attributes, some trait of his own, some strength or weakness, some tendency to violence or to indecision, some eccentricity even, that he has found in himself. Something perhaps never realized in his own life, something of which those who know him best may be unaware, something not restricted in transmission to characters of the same temperament, the same age, and, least of all, of the same sex. Some bit of himself that the author gives to a character may be the germ from which the life of that character starts. On the other hand, a character which succeeds in interesting its author may elicit from the author latent potentialities of his own being. I believe that the author imparts something of himself to his characters, but I also believe that he is influenced by the characters he creates. It would be only too easy to lose oneself in a maze of speculation about the process by which an imaginary character can become as real for us as people we have known. I have penetrated into this maze so far only to indicate the difficulties, the limitations, the fascination, for a poet who is used to writing poetry in his own person, of the problem of making imaginary personages talk poetry. And the difference, the abyss, between writing for the first and for the third voice.

The peculiarity of my third voice, the voice of poetic drama, is brought out in another way by comparing it with the voice of the poet in non-dramatic poetry which has a dramatic element in it—and conspicuously in the dramatic monologue. Browning, in an uncritical moment, addressed himself as "Robert Browning, you writer of plays." How many of us have read a play by Browning more than once; and, if we have read it more than once, was our motive the expectation of enjoyment? What personage, in a play by Browning, remains living in our mind? On the other hand, who can forget Fra Lippo Lippi, or Andrea del Sarto, or Bishop Blougram, or the other bishop who ordered his tomb? It would seem without further examination, from Browning's mastery of the dramatic monologue, and his very moderate achievement in the drama, that the two forms must be essentially different. Is there, perhaps, another voice which I have failed to hear, the voice of the dramatic poet whose dramatic gifts are best exercised outside of the theater? And certainly, if any poetry, not of the stage, deserves to be characterized as "dramatic," it is Browning's.

In a play, as I have said, an author must have divided loyalties; he must sympathize with characters who may be in no way sympathetic to each other. And he must allocate the "poetry" as widely as the limitations of each imaginary character permit. This necessity to divide the poetry implies some variation of the style of the poetry according to the character to whom it is given. The fact that a number of characters in a play have claims upon the author, for their allotment of poetic speech, compels him to try to extract the poetry from the character, rather than impose his poetry upon it. Now, in the dramatic monologue we have no such check. The author is just as likely to identify the character with himself, as himself with the character: for the check is missing that will prevent him from doing so—and that check is the necessity for identifying himself with some other character replying to the first. What we normally hear, in fact, in the dramatic monologue, is the voice of the poet, who has put on the costume and make-up either of some historical character, or of one out of fiction. His personage must be identified to us—as an individual, or at least as a type—before he begins to speak. If, as frequently with Browning, the poet is speaking in the role of an historical personage, like Lippo Lippi, or in the role of a known character of fiction, like Caliban, he has taken possession of that character. And the difference is most evident in his "Caliban upon Setebos." In *The Tempest,* it is Caliban who speaks; in "Caliban upon Setebos," it is Browning's voice that we hear, Browning talking aloud through Caliban. It was Browning's greatest disciple, Mr. Ezra Pound, who adopted the term "persona" to indicate the several historical characters through whom he spoke: and the term is just.

I risk the generalization also, which may indeed be far too sweeping, that dramatic monologue cannot create a character. For character is created and made real only in an action, a communication between imaginary people. It is not irrelevant that when the dramatic monologue is not put into the mouth of some character already known to the reader—from history or from fiction—we are likely to ask the question "Who was the original?" About Bishop Blougram people have always been impelled to ask, how far was this intended to be a portrait of Cardinal Manning, or of some other ecclesiastic? The poet, speaking, as Browning does, in his own voice, cannot bring a character to life: he can only mimic a character otherwise known to us. And does not the point of mimicry lie in the recognition of the person mimicked, and in the incompleteness of the illusion? We have to be aware that the mimic and the person mimicked are different people: if we are actually deceived, mimicry becomes impersonation. When we listen to a play by Shakespeare, we listen not to Shakespeare but to his characters; when we read a dramatic monologue by Browning, we cannot suppose that we are listening to any other voice than that of Browning himself.

In the dramatic monologue, then, it is surely the second voice, the voice of the poet talking to other people, that is dominant. The mere fact that he is assuming a role, that he is speaking through a mask, implies the presence of an audience: why should a man put on fancy dress and a mask only to talk to himself? The second voice is, in fact, the voice most often and most clearly heard in poetry that is not of the theater: in all poetry, certainly, that has a conscious social purpose—poetry intended to amuse or to instruct, poetry that tells a story, poetry that preaches or points a moral, or satire which is a form of preaching. For what is the point of a story without an audience, or of a sermon without a congregation? The voice of the poet addressing other people is the dominant voice of epic, though not the only voice. In Homer, for instance, there is heard also, from time to time, the dramatic voice: there are moments when we hear, not Homer telling us what a hero said, but the voice of the hero himself. *The Divine Comedy* is not in the exact sense an epic, but here also we hear men and women speaking to us. And we have no reason to suppose that Milton's sympathy with Satan was so exclusive as to seal him of the Devil's Party. But the epic is essentially a tale told to an audience, while drama is essentially an action exhibited to an audience.

Now, what about the poetry of the first voice—that which is not primarily an attempt to communicate with anyone at all?

I must make the point that this poetry is not necessarily what we call loosely "lyric poetry." The term "lyric" itself is unsatisfactory. We think first of verse intended to be sung—from the songs of Campion and Shakespeare and Burns, to the arias of W. S. Gilbert, or the words of the latest "musical number." But we apply it also to poetry that was never intended for a musical setting, or which we dissociate from its music: we speak of the "lyric verse" of the metaphysical poets, of Vaughan and Marvell as well as Donne and Herbert. The very definition of "lyric," in the Oxford Dictionary, indicates that the word cannot be satisfactorily defined:

> Lyric: Now the name for short poems, usually divided into stanzas or strophes, and directly expressing the poet's own thoughts and sentiments.

How short does a poem have to be, to be called a "lyric"? The emphasis on brevity, and the suggestion of division into stanzas, seem residual from the association of the voice with music. But there is no necessary relation between brevity and the expression of the poet's own thoughts and feelings. "Come unto these yellow sands" or "Hark! hark! the lark" are lyrics—are they not?—but what sense is there in saying that they express directly the poet's own thoughts and sentiments? *London, The Vanity of Human Wishes,* and *The Deserted Village* are all poems which appear to express the poet's own thoughts and sentiments, but do we ever think of such poems as "lyrical"? They are certainly not short. Between them, all the poems I have mentioned seem to fail to qualify as lyrics, just as Mr. Daddy Longlegs and Mr. Floppy Fly failed to qualify as courtiers:

> One never more can go to court,
> Because his legs have grown too short;
> The other cannot sing a song,
> Because his legs have grown too long!

It is obviously the lyric in the sense of a poem "directly express-ing the poet's own thoughts and sentiments," not in the quite un-related sense of a short poem intended to be set to music, that is relevant to my first voice—the voice of the poet talking to himself —or to nobody. It is in this sense that the German poet Gottfried Benn, in a very interesting lecture entitled *Probleme der Lyrik*, thinks of lyric as the poetry of the first voice: he includes, I feel sure, such poems as Rilke's Duinese Elegies and Valéry's *La Jeune Parque*. Where he speaks of "lyric poetry," then, I should prefer to say "meditative verse."

What, asks Herr Benn in this lecture, does the writer of such a poem, "addressed to no one," start with? There is first, he says, an inert embryo or "creative germ" (*ein dumpfer schöpferischer Keim*) and, on the other hand, the Language, the resources of the words at the poet's command. He has something germinating in him for which he must find words; but he cannot know what words he wants until he has found the words; he cannot identify this embryo until it has been transformed into an arrangement of the right words in the right order. When you have the words for it, the "thing" for which the words had to be found has dis-appeared, replaced by a poem. What you start from is nothing so definite as an emotion, in any ordinary sense; it is still more cer-tainly not an idea; it is—to adapt two lines of Beddoes to a different meaning—a

> bodiless childful of life in the gloom
> Crying with frog voice, "what shall I be?"

I agree with Gottfried Benn, and I would go a little further. In a poem which is neither didactic nor narrative, and not animated by any other social purpose, the poet may be concerned solely with expressing in verse—using all his resources of words, with their history, their connotations, their music—this obscure impulse. He does not know what he has to say until he has said it, and in the effort to say it he is not concerned with making other people understand anything. He is not concerned, at this stage, with other people at all: only with finding the right words or, anyhow, the least wrong words. He is not concerned whether anybody else will ever listen to them or not, or whether anybody else will ever understand them if he does. He is oppressed by a burden which he must bring to birth in order to obtain relief. Or, to change the figure of speech, he is haunted by a demon, a demon against which he feels powerless, because in its first manifestation it has no face, no name, nothing; and the words, the poem he makes, are a kind of form of exorcism of this demon. In other words again, he is going to all that trouble, not in order to communicate with anyone, but to gain relief from acute discomfort; and when the words are finally arranged in the right way—or in what he comes to accept as the best arrangement he can find—he may experience a moment of exhaustion, of appeasement, of absolution, and of something very near annihilation, which is in itself indescribable. And then he can say to the poem: "Go away! Find a place for yourself in a book—and don't expect *me* to take any further interest in you."

I don't believe that the relation of a poem to its origins is capable of being more clearly traced. You can read the essays of Paul Valéry, who studied the workings of his own mind in the composition of a poem more perseveringly than any other poet has done. But if, either on the basis of what poets try to tell you, or by biographical research, with or without the tools of the psychologist, you attempt to explain a poem, you will probably be getting further and further away from the poem without arriving at any other destination. The attempt to explain the poem by tracing it back to its origins will distract attention from the poem, to direct it on to something else which, in the form in which it can be apprehended by the critic and his readers, has no relation to the poem and throws no light upon it. I should not like you to think that I am trying to make the writing of a poem more of a mystery than it is. What I am maintaining is, that the first effort of the poet should be to achieve clarity for himself, to assure himself that the poem is the right outcome of the process that has taken place. The most bungling form of obscurity is that of the poet who has not been able to express himself *to* himself; the shoddiest form is found when the poet is trying to persuade himself that he has something to say when he hasn't.

So far I have been speaking, for the sake of simplicity, of the three voices as if they were mutually exclusive: as if the poet, in any particular poem, was speaking *either* to himself or to others, and as if neither of the first two voices was audible in good dramatic verse. And this indeed is the conclusion to which Herr Benn's argument appears to lead him: he speaks as if the poetry of the first voice—which he considers, moreover, to be on the whole a development of our own age—was a totally different kind of poetry from that of the poet addressing an audience. But for me the voices are most often found together—the first and second, I mean—in non-dramatic poetry; and together with the third in dramatic poetry too. Even though, as I have maintained, the author of a poem may have written it primarily without thought of an audience, he will also want to know what the poem which has satisfied *him* will have to say to other people. There are, first of all, those few friends to whose criticism he may wish to submit it before considering it completed. They can be very helpful, in suggesting a word or a phrase which the author has not been able to find for himself; though their greatest service perhaps is to say simply "this passage won't do"—thus confirming a suspicion which the author has been suppressing from his own consciousness. But I am not thinking primarily of the few judicious friends whose opinion the author prizes, but of the larger and unknown audience—people to whom the author's name means only his poem which they have read. The final handing over, so to speak, of the poem to an unknown audience, for what that audience will make of it, seems to me the consummation of the process begun in solitude and without thought of the audience, the long process of gestation of the poem, because it marks the final separation of the poem from the author. Let the author, at this point, rest in peace.

So much for the poem which is primarily a poem of the first voice. I think that in every poem, from the private meditation to the epic or the drama, there is more than one voice to be heard. If the author never spoke to himself, the result would not be poetry, though it might be magnificent rhetoric; and part of our enjoyment of great poetry is the enjoyment of *overhearing* words

which are not addressed to us. But if the poem were exclusively
for the author, it would be a poem in a private and unknown
language; and a poem which was a poem only for the author would
not be a poem at all. And in poetic drama, I am inclined to believe that all three voices are audible. First, the voice of each character—an individual voice different from that of any other character: so that of each utterance we can say, that it could only have
come from that character. There may be from time to time, and
perhaps when we least notice it, the voices of the author and the
character in unison, saying something appropriate to the character,
but something which the author could say for himself also, though
the words may not have quite the same meaning for both. That
may be a very different thing from the ventriloquism which makes
the character only a mouthpiece for the author's ideas or sentiments.

> To-morrow and to-morrow and to-morrow . . .

Is not the perpetual shock and surprise of these hackneyed lines
evidence that Shakespeare and Macbeth are uttering the words in
unison, though perhaps with somewhat different meaning? And
finally there are the lines, in plays by one of the supreme poetic
dramatists, in which we hear a more impersonal voice still than
that of either the character or the author.

> Ripeness is all

or

> Simply the thing I am
> Shall make me live.

And now I should like to return for a moment to Gottfried Benn
and his unknown, dark *psychic material*—we might say, the octopus or angel with which the poet struggles. I suggest that between
the three kinds of poetry to which my three voices correspond
there is a certain difference of process. In the poem in which the
first voice, that of the poet talking to himself, dominates, the
"psychic material" tends to create its own form—the eventual form
will be to a greater or less degree the form for that one poem and
for no other. It is misleading, of course, to speak of the material
as creating or imposing its own form: what happens is a simultaneous development of form and material; for the form affects the

material at every stage; and perhaps all the material does is to repeat "not that! not that!" in the face of each unsuccessful attempt at formal organization; and finally the material is identified with its form. But in poetry of the second and in that of the third voice, the form is already to some extent given. However much it may be *trans*formed before the poem is finished, it can be represented from the start by an outline or scenario. If I choose to tell a story, I must have some notion of the plot of the story I propose to tell; if I undertake satire, moralizing, or invective, there is already something given which I can recognize and which exists for others as well as myself. And if I set out to write a play, I start by an act of choice: I settle upon a particular emotional situation, out of which characters and a plot will emerge, and I can make a plain prose outline of the play in advance—however much that outline may be altered before the play is finished, by the way in which the characters develop. It is likely, of course, that it is in the beginning the pressure of some rude unknown *psychic material* that directs the poet to tell that particular story, to develop that particular situation. And on the other hand, the frame, once chosen, within which the author has elected to work, may itself evoke other psychic material; and then, lines of poetry may come into being, not from the original impulse, but from a secondary stimulation of the unconscious mind. All that matters is, that in the end the voices should be heard in harmony; and, as I have said, I doubt whether in any real poem only one voice is audible.

The reader may well, by now, have been asking himself what I have been up to in all these speculations. Have I been toiling to weave a labored web of useless ingenuity? Well, I have been trying to talk, not to myself—as you may have been tempted to think —but to the reader of poetry. I should like to think that it might interest the reader of poetry to test my assertions in his own reading. Can you distinguish these voices in the poetry you read, or hear recited, or hear in the theater? If you complain that a poet is obscure, and apparently ignoring you, the reader, or that he is speaking only to a limited circle of initiates from which you are excluded—remember that what he may have been trying to do, was to put something into words which could not be said in any other way, and therefore in a language which may be worth the trouble of learning. If you complain that a poet is too rhetorical,

and that he addresses you as if you were a public meeting, try to
listen for the moments when he is not speaking to you, but merely
allowing himself to be overheard: he may be a Dryden, a Pope, or
a Byron. And if you have to listen to a verse play, take it first at
its face value, as entertainment, for each character speaking for
himself with whatever degree of reality his author has been able
to endow him. Perhaps, if it is a great play, and you do not try
too hard to hear them, you may discern the other voices too. For
the work of a great poetic dramatist, like Shakespeare, constitutes a
world. Each character speaks for himself, but no other poet could
have found those words for him to speak. If you seek for Shakespeare, you will find him only in the characters he created; for the
one thing in common between the characters is that no one but
Shakespeare could have created any of them. The world of a great
poetic dramatist is a world in which the creator is everywhere present, and everywhere hidden.

ROBERT PENN WARREN

Pure and Impure Poetry

Critics are rarely faithful to
their labels and their special strategies. Usually the critic will confess that no one strategy—the psychological, the moralistic, the for-
malistic, the historical—or combination of strategies, will quite
work the defeat of the poem. For the poem is like the monstrous
Orillo in Boiardo's *Orlando Innamorato*. When the sword lops off
any member of the monster, that member is immediately rejoined
to the body, and the monster is as formidable as ever. But the poem
is even more formidable than the monster, for Orillo's adversary
finally gained a victory by an astonishing feat of dexterity: he
slashed off both the monster's arms and quick as a wink seized
them and flung them into the river. The critic who vaingloriously
trusts his method to account for the poem, to exhaust the poem, is
trying to emulate this dexterity: he thinks that he, too, can win by
throwing the lopped-off arms into the river. But he is doomed to
failure. Neither fire nor water will suffice to prevent the rejoining
of the mutilated members to the monstrous torso. There is only one

way to conquer the monster: you must eat it, bones, blood, skin, pelt, and gristle. And even then the monster is not dead, for it lives in you, is assimilated into you, and you are different, and somewhat monstrous yourself, for having eaten it.

So the monster will always win, and the critic knows this. He does not want to win. He knows that he must always play stooge to the monster. All he wants to do is to give the monster a chance to exhibit again its miraculous power.

With this fable, I shall begin by observing that poetry wants to be pure. And it always succeeds in this ambition. In so far as we have poetry at all, it is always pure poetry; that is, it is not non-poetry. The poetry of Shakespeare, the poetry of Pope, the poetry of Herrick, is pure, in so far as it is poetry at all. We call the poetry "higher" or "lower," we say, "more powerful" or "less powerful" about it, and we are, no doubt, quite right in doing so. The souls that form the great rose of Paradise are seated in banks and tiers of ascending blessedness, but they are all saved, they are all perfectly happy; they are all "pure," for they have all been purged of mortal taint. This is not to say, however, that if we get poetry from one source, such a single source, say Shakespeare, should suffice us in as much as we can always appeal to it, or that, since all poetry is equally pure, we engage in a superfluous labor in trying to explore or create new sources of poetry. No, for we can remember that every soul in the great rose is precious in the eyes of God. No soul is the substitute for another.

Poetry wants to be pure, but poems do not. At least, most of them do not want to be too pure. The poems want to give us poetry, which is pure, and the elements of a poem, in so far as it is a good poem, will work together toward that end, but many of the elements, taken in themselves, may actually seem to contradict that end, or be neutral toward the achieving of that end. Are we then to conclude that, because neutral or recalcitrant elements appear in poems, even in poems called great, these elements are simply an index to human frailty, that in a perfect world there would be no dross in poems which would, then, be perfectly pure? No, it does not seem to be merely the fault of our world, for the poems include, deliberately, more of the so-called dross than would appear necessary. They are not even as pure as they might be in this imperfect world. They mar themselves with cacophonies, jagged rhythms,

ugly words and ugly thoughts, colloquialisms, clichés, sterile technical terms, head work and argument, self-contradictions, clever-
nesses, irony, realism—all things which call us back to the world
of prose and imperfection.

Sometimes a poet will reflect on this state of affairs, and grieve.
He will decide that he, at least, will try to make one poem as pure
as possible. So he writes:

> Now sleeps the crimson petal, now the white;
> Nor waves the cypress in the palace walk;
> Nor winks the gold fin in the porphyry font:
> The firefly wakens: waken thou with me.

We know the famous garden. We know how all nature conspires
here to express the purity of the moment: how the milk-white pea-
cock glimmers like a ghost, and how like a ghost the unnamed
"she" glimmers on to her tryst; how each lies "all Danaé to the
stars," as the beloved's heart lies open to the lover; and how, in
the end, the lily folds up her sweetness, "and slips into the bosom
of the lake," as the lovers are lost in the sweet dissolution of love.

And we know another poet and another garden. Or perhaps it
is the same garden, after all:

> I arise from dreams of thee
> In the first sweet sleep of night,
> When the winds are breathing low
> And the stars are shining bright.
> I arise from dreams of thee,
> And a spirit in my feet
> Hath led me—who knows how?
> To thy chamber window, Sweet!

We remember how, again, all nature conspires, how the wandering
airs "faint," how the Champak's odors "pine," how the nightingale's
complaint "dies upon her heart," as the lover will die upon the
beloved's heart. Nature here strains out of nature, it wants to be
called by another name, it wants to spiritualize itself by calling
itself another name. How does the lover get to the chamber window? He refuses to say how, in his semi-somnambulistic daze, he
got there. He blames, he says, "a spirit in my feet," and hastens to
disavow any knowledge of how that spirit operates. In any case,
he arrives at the chamber window. Subsequent events and the

lover's reaction toward them are somewhat hazy. We only know that the lover, who faints and fails at the opening of the last stanza, and who asks to be lifted from the grass by a more enterprising beloved, is in a condition of delectable passivity, in which distinctions blur out in the "purity" of the moment.

Let us turn to another garden: the place, Verona; the time, a summer night, with full moon. The lover speaks:

> But soft! what light through yonder window breaks?
> It is the east . . .

But we know the rest, and know that this garden, in which nature for the moment conspires again with the lover, is the most famous of them all, for the scene is justly admired for its purity of effect, for giving us the very essence of young, untarnished love. Nature conspires beneficently here, but we may chance to remember that beyond the garden wall strolls Mercutio, who can celebrate Queen Mab, but who is always aware that nature has other names as well as the names the pure poets and pure lovers put upon her. And we remember that Mercutio, outside the wall, has just said:

> . . . 'twould anger him
> To raise a spirit in his mistress's circle
> Of some strange nature, letting it there stand
> Till she had laid it and conjured it down.

Mercutio has made a joke, a bawdy joke. That is bad enough, but worse, he has made his joke witty and, worst of all, intellectually complicated in its form. Realism, wit, intellectual complication—these are the enemies of the garden purity.

But the poet has not only let us see Mercutio outside the garden wall. Within the garden itself, when the lover invokes nature, when he spiritualizes and innocently trusts her, and says,

> Lady, by yonder blessed moon I swear,

the lady herself replies,

> O, swear not by the moon, the inconstant moon,
> That monthly changes in her circled orb.

The lady distrusts "pure" poems, nature spiritualized into forgetfulness. She has, as it were, a rigorous taste in metaphor, too; she brings a logical criticism to bear on the metaphor which is too easy; the metaphor must prove itself to her, must be willing to subject itself to scrutiny beyond the moment's enthusiasm. She injects the impurity of an intellectual style into the lover's pure poem.

And we must not forget the voice of the nurse, who calls from within, a voice which, we discover, is the voice of expediency, of half-measures, of the view that circumstances alter cases—the voice of prose and imperfection.

It is time to ask ourselves if the celebrated poetry of this scene, which as poetry is pure, exists despite the impurities of the total composition, if the effect would be more purely poetic were the nurse and Mercutio absent and the lady a more sympathetic critic of pure poems. I do not think so. The effect might even be more vulnerable poetically if the impurities were purged away. Mercutio, the lady, and the nurse are critics of the lover, who believes in pure poems, but perhaps they are necessary. Perhaps the lover can only be accepted in their context. The poet seems to say: "I know the worst that can be said on this subject, and I am giving fair warning. Read at your own risk." So the poetry arises from a recalcitrant and contradictory context; and finally involves that context.

Let us return to one of the other gardens, in which there is no Mercutio or nurse, and in which the lady is more sympathetic. Let us mar its purity by installing Mercutio in the shrubbery, from which the poet was so careful to banish him. You can hear his comment when the lover says:

> And a spirit in my feet
> Hath led me—who knows how?
> To thy chamber window, Sweet!

And we can guess what the wicked tongue would have to say in response to the last stanza.

It may be that the poet should have made his peace early with Mercutio, and have appealed to his better nature. For Mercutio seems to be glad to cooperate with a poet. But he must be invited; otherwise, he is apt to show a streak of merry vindictiveness about the finished product. Poems are vulnerable enough at best. Bright reason mocks them like sun from a wintry sky. They are easily left naked to laughter when leaves fall in the garden and the cold winds come. Therefore, they need all the friends they can get, and Mercutio, who is an ally of reason and who himself is given to mocking laughter, is a good friend for a poem to have.

On what terms does a poet make his peace with Mercutio? There are about as many sets of terms as there are good poets. I know that I have loaded the answer with the word *good* here, that I have implied a scale of excellence based, in part at least, on degree of complication. I shall return to this question. For the moment, however, let us examine a poem whose apparent innocence and simple lyric cry should earn it a place in any anthology of "pure poetry."

> Western wind, when wilt thou blow
>   That the small rain down can rain?
> Christ, that my love were in my arms
>   And I in my bed again!

The lover, grieving for the absent beloved, cries out for relief. Several kinds of relief are involved in the appeal to the wind. First there is the relief that would be had from the sympathetic manifestation of nature. The lover, in his perturbation of spirit, invokes the perturbations of nature. He exclaims,

> Western wind, when wilt thou blow

and Lear exclaims,

> Blow, winds, and crack your cheeks! rage! blow!

Second, there is the relief that would be had by the fulfillment of grief—the frost of grief, the drouth of grief broken, the full anguish expressed, then the violence allayed in the peace of tears. Third, there is the relief that would be had in the excitement and fulfillment of love itself. There seems to be a contrast between the first two types of relief and the third type; speaking loosely, we may say that the first two types are romantic and general, the third type realistic and specific. So much for the first two lines.

In the last two lines, the lover cries out for the specific solace of his case: reunion with his beloved. But there is a difference between the two lines. The first is general, and romantic. The phrase "in my arms" does not seem to mean exactly what it says. True, it has a literal meaning, if we can look close at the words, but it is hard to look close because of the romantic aura—the spiritualized

mist about them.[1] But with the last line the perfectly literal meaning suddenly comes into sharp focus. The mist is rifted and we can
look straight at the words, which, we discover with a slight shock
of surprise, do mean exactly what they say. The last line is realistic
and specific. It is not even content to say,

> And I in bed again!

It is, rather, more scrupulously specific, and says,

> And I in *my* bed again![2]

All of this does not go to say that the realistic elements here are
to be taken as cancelling, or negating, the romantic elements.
There is no ironical leer. The poem is not a celebration of carnality.
It is a faithful lover who speaks. He is faithful to the absent beloved, and he is also faithful to the full experience of love. That is,
he does not abstract one aspect of the experience and call it the
whole experience. He does not strain nature out of nature; he does
not over-spiritualize nature. This nameless poet would never have
said, in the happier days of his love, that he had been led to his
Sweet's chamber window by "a spirit in my feet"; and he certainly
would not have added the coy disavowal, "who knows how?" But
because the nameless poet refused to over-spiritualize nature, we
can accept the spirituality of the poem.

Another poem gives us another problem.

> Ah, what avails the sceptered race,
>   Ah, what the form divine!
> What every virtue, every grace!
>   Rose Aylmer, all were thine.

[1] It may be objected here that I am reading the phrase "in my arms" as a
twentieth-century reader. I confess the fact. Certainly, several centuries have
passed since the composition of the little poem, and those centuries have
thickened the romantic mist about the words, but it is scarcely to be believed
that the sixteenth century was the clear, literal Eden dawn of poetry when
words walked without the fig leaf.

[2] In connection with the word *my* in this line, we may also feel that it
helps to set over the comfort and satisfaction there specified against the bad
weather of the first two lines. We may also glance at the word *small* in the
second line. It is the scrupulous word, the word that, realistically, makes us
believe in the rain. But, too, it is broader in its function. The storm which
the lover invokes will not rend the firmament, it will not end the world; it
will simply bring down the "small" rain, a credible rain.

> Rose Aylmer, whom those wakeful eyes
> May weep, but never see,
> A night of memories and of sighs
> I consecrate to thee.

This is another poem about lost love: a "soft" subject. Now to one kind of poet the soft subject presents a sore temptation. Because it is soft in its natural state, he is inclined to feel that to get at its poetic essence he must make it softer still, that he must insist on its softness, that he must render it as "pure" as possible. At first glance, it may seem that Landor is trying to do just that. What he says seems to be emphatic, unqualified, and open. Not every power, grace, and virtue could avail to preserve his love. That statement insists on the pathetic contrast. And in the next stanza, wakefulness and tearfulness are mentioned quite unashamedly, along with memories and sighs. It is all blurted out, as pure as possible.

But only in the paraphrase is it "blurted." The actual quality of the first stanza is hard, not soft. It is a chiseled stanza, in which formality is insisted upon. We may observe the balance of the first and second lines; the balance of the first half with the second half of the third line, which recapitulates the structure of the first two lines; the balance of the two parts of the last line, though here the balance is merely a rhythmical and not a sense balance as in the preceding instances; the binders of discreet alliteration, repetition, and assonance. The stanza is built up, as it were, of units which are firmly defined and sharply separated, phrase by phrase, line by line. We have the formal control of the soft subject, ritual and not surrender.

But in the second stanza the rigor of this formality is somewhat abated, as the more general, speculative emphasis (why cannot pomp, virtue, and grace avail?) gives way to the personal emphasis, as though the repetition of the beloved's name had, momentarily, released the flood of feeling. The first line of the second stanza spills over into the second; the "wakeful eyes" as subject find their verb in the next line, "weep," and the *wake-weep* alliteration, along with the rest after *weep,* points up the disintegration of the line, just as it emphasizes the situation. Then with the phrase "but never see" falling away from the long thrust of the rhetorical structure to the pause after *weep,* the poem seems to go completely soft, the frame is broken. But, even as the poet insists on "memories and

sighs" in the last two lines he restores the balance. Notice the
understatement of "A night." It says: "I know that life is a fairly
complicated affair, and that I am committed to it and to its complications. I intend to stand by my commitment, as a man of integrity, that is, to live despite the grief. Since life is complicated,
I cannot, if I am to live, spare too much time for indulging grief.
I can give *a* night, but not all nights." The lover, like the hero of
Frost's poem "Stopping by Woods on a Winter Evening," tears
himself from the temptation of staring into the treacherous, delicious blackness, for he, too, has "promises to keep." Or he resembles
the Homeric heroes who, after the perilous passage is made, after
their energy has saved their lives, and after they have beached their
craft and eaten their meal, can then set aside an hour before sleep
to mourn the comrades lost by the way—the heroes who, as Aldous
Huxley says, understand realistically a whole truth as contrasted
with a half-truth.

Is this a denial of the depth and sincerity of the grief? The soft
reader, who wants the poem pure, may be inclined to say so. But
let us look at the last line to see what it gives us in answer to this
question. The answer seems to lie in the word *consecrate*. The
meter thrusts this word at us; we observe that two of the three
metrical accents in the line fall on syllables of this word forcing it
beyond its prose emphasis. The word is important and the importance is justified, for the word tells us that the single night is not
merely a lapse into weakness, a trivial event to be forgotten when
the weakness is overcome. It is, rather, an event of the most extreme and focal importance, an event formally dedicated, "set apart
for sacred uses," an event by which other events are to be measured. So the word *consecrate* formalizes, philosophizes, ritualizes
the grief; it specifies what style in the first stanza has implied.

But here is another poem of grief, grief at the death of a child:

> There was such speed in her little body,
> And such lightness in her footfall,
> It is no wonder that her brown study
> Astonishes us all.
>
> Her wars were bruited in our high window.
> We looked among orchard trees and beyond
> Where she took arms against her shadow,
> Or harried unto the pond

> The lazy geese, like a snow cloud
> Dripping their snow on the green grass,
> Tricking and stopping, sleepy and proud,
> Who cried in goose, Alas,
>
> For the tireless heart within the little
> Lady with rod that made them rise
> From their noon apple dreams, and scuttle
> Goose-fashion under the skies!
>
> But now go the bells, and we are ready;
> In one house we are sternly stopped
> To say we are vexed at her brown study,
> Lying so primly propped.

Another soft subject, softer, if anything, than the subject of "Rose Aylmer," and it presents the same problem. But the problem is solved in a different way.

The first stanza is based on two time-honored clichés: first, "Heaven, won't that child ever be still, she is driving me distracted"; and second, "She was such an active, healthy-looking child, would you've ever thought she would just up and die?" In fact, the whole poem develops these clichés, and exploits, in a backhand fashion, the ironies implicit in their inter-relation. And in this connection, we may note that the fact of the clichés, rather than more original or profound observations, at the root of the poem is important; there is in the poem the contrast between the staleness of the clichés and the shock of the reality. Further, we may note that the second cliché is an answer, savagely ironical in itself, to the first: the child you wished would be still *is* still, despite all that activity which your adult occupations deplored.

But such a savage irony is not the game here. It is too desperate, too naked, in a word, too pure. And ultimately, it is, in a sense, a meaningless irony if left in its pure state, because it depends on a mechanical, accidental contrast in nature, void of moral content. The poem is concerned with modifications and modulations of this brute, basic irony, modulations and modifications contingent upon an attitude taken toward it by a responsible human being, the speaker of the poem. The savagery is masked, or ameliorated.

In this connection, we may observe, first, the phrase "brown study." It is not the "frosted flower," the "marmoreal immobility," or any one of a thousand such phrases which would aim for the pure effect. It is merely the brown study which astonishes—a phrase which denies, as it were, the finality of the situation, underplays the pathos, and merely reminds one of those moments of childish pensiveness into which the grown-up cannot penetrate. And the phrase itself is a cliché—the common now echoed in the uncommon.

Next, we may observe that stanzas two, three, and four simply document, with a busy yet wavering rhythm (one sentence runs through the three stanzas), the tireless naughtiness which was once the cause of rebuke, the naughtiness which disturbed the mature goings-on in the room with the "high window." But the naughtiness has been transmuted, by events just transpired, into a kind of fanciful story-book dream-world in which geese are whiter than nature, and the grass greener, in which geese speak in goose language, saying "Alas," and have apple dreams. It is a drowsy, delicious world, in which the geese are bigger than life, and more important. It is an unreal (now unreal because lost), stylized world. Notice how the phrase "the little lady with rod" works: the detached, grown-up primness of "little lady"; the formal, stiff effect gained by the omission of the article before *rod;* the slightly unnatural use of the word *rod* itself, which sets some distance between use and the scene (perhaps with the hint of the fairy story, a magic wand, or a magic rod—not a common, every-day stick). But the stanzas tie back into the premises of the poem in other ways. The little girl, in her naughtiness, warred against her shadow. Is it crowding matters too hard to surmise that the shadow here achieves a sort of covert symbolic significance? The little girl lost her war against her "shadow," which was always with her. Certainly the phrase "tireless heart" has some rich connotations. And the geese which say "Alas!" conspire with the family to deplore the excessive activity of the child. (They do not conspire to express the present grief, only the past vexation—an inversion of the method of the pastoral elegy, or of the method of the first two garden poems.)

The business of the three stanzas, then, may be said to be twofold. First, they make us believe more fully in the child and therefore in the fact of the grief itself. They "prove" the grief, and they show the deliciousness of the lost world which will never look the same from the high window. Second, and contrariwise, they "transcend" the grief, or at least give a hint of a means for transcending the immediate anguish: the lost world is, in one sense, redeemed out of time, it enters the pages of the picture book where geese speak, where the untrue is true, where the fleeting is fixed. What was had cannot, after all, be lost. (By way of comparison—a comparison which, because extreme, may be helpful—I cite the transcendence in *A La Recherche du Temps Perdu*.) The three stanzas, then, to state it in another way, have validated the first stanza and have prepared for the last.

The three stanzas have made it possible for us to say, when the bell tolls, "we are ready." Some kind of terms, perhaps not the best terms possible but some kind, have been made with the savage underlying irony. But the terms arrived at do not prevent the occasion from being a "stern" one. The transcendence is not absolute, and in the end is possible only because of an exercise of will and self-control. Because we control ourselves, we can say "vexed" and not some big word. And the word itself picks up the first of the domestic clichés on which the poem is based—the outburst of impatience at the naughty child who, by dying, has performed her most serious piece of naughtiness. But now the word comes to us charged with the burden of the poem, and further, as re-echoed here by the phrase "brown study," charged by the sentence in which it occurs: we are gathered formally, ritualistically, sternly together to say the word *vexed*.[3] *Vexed* becomes the ritualistic, the summarizing word.

I have used the words *pure* and *impure* often in the foregoing

---

[3] It might be profitable, in contrast with this poem, to analyze "After the Burial," by James Russell Lowell, a poem which is identical in situation. But in Lowell's poem the savagery of the irony is unqualified. In fact, the whole poem insists, quite literally, that qualification is impossible: the scheme of the poem is to set up the brute fact of death against possible consolations. It insists on "tears," the "thin-worn locket," the "anguish of deathless hair," "the smallness of the child's grave," the "little shoe in the corner." It is a poem which, we might say, does not progress, but ends where it begins, resting in the savage irony from which it stems; or we might say that it is a poem without any "insides," for the hero of the poem is not attempting to do anything about the problem which confronts him—it is a poem without issue, without conflict, a poem of unconditional surrender. In other words, it tries to be a pure poem, pure grief, absolutely inconsolable. It is a strident poem, and strident in its rhythms. The fact that we know this poem to be an expression of a bereavement historically real makes it an embarrassing poem, as well. It is a naked poem.

pages, and I confess that I have used them rather loosely. But perhaps it has been evident that I have meant something like this: the pure poem tries to be pure by excluding, more or less rigidly, certain elements which might qualify or contradict its original impulse. In other words the pure poems want to be, and desperately, all of a piece. It has also been evident, no doubt, that the kinds of impurity which are admitted or excluded by the various little anthology pieces which have been analyzed, are different in the different poems. This is only to be expected, for there is not one doctrine of "pure poetry"—not one definition of what constitutes impurity in poems—but many. And not all of the doctrines are recent. When, for example, one cites Poe as the father of *the* doctrine of pure poetry, one is in error; Poe simply fathered *a* particular doctrine of pure poetry. One can find other doctrines of purity long antedating Poe. When Sir Philip Sidney, for example, legislated against tragi-comedy, he was repeating a current doctrine of purity. When Ben Jonson told William Drummond that Donne, for not keeping of accent, deserved hanging, he was defending another kind of purity, and when Dryden spoke to save the ear of the fair sex from metaphysical perplexities in amorous poems, he was defending another kind of purity, just as he was defending another when he defined the nature of the heroic drama. The eighteenth century had a doctrine of pure poetry, which may be summed up under the word *sublimity,* but which involved two corollary doctrines, one concerning diction and the other concerning imagery. But at the same time that this century, by means of these corollary doctrines, was tidying up and purifying, as Mr. Monk and Mr. Henn have indicated, the doctrine derived from Longinus, it was admitting into the drama certain impurities which the theorists of the heroic drama would not have admitted.[4]

But when we think of the modern doctrine of pure poetry, we usually think of Poe, as critic and poet, perhaps of Shelley, of the Symbolists, of the Abbé Brémond, perhaps of Pater, and certainly of George Moore and the Imagists. We know Poe's position: the long poem is "a flat contradiction in terms," because intense excitement, which is essential in poetry, cannot be long maintained; the moral sense and the intellect function more satisfactorily in

----

[4] Samuel Holt Monk, *The Sublime: a Study of Critical Theories in XVIII-Century England,* and T. R. Henn, *Longinus and English Criticism.*

prose than in poetry, and, in fact, "Truth" and the "Passions," which are for Poe associated with intellect and the moral sense, may actually be inimical to poetry; vagueness, suggestiveness, are central virtues, for poetry has for "its object an *indefinite* instead of a *definite* pleasure"; poetry is not supposed to undergo close inspection, only a cursory glance, for it, "above all things, is a beautiful painting whose tints, to minute inspection, are confusion worse confounded, but start out boldly to the cursory glance of the connoisseur"; poetry aspires toward music, since it is concerned with "indefinite sensations, to which music is an *essential,* since the comprehension of sweet sound is our more indefinite conception"; melancholy is the most poetical effect and enters into all the higher manifestations of beauty. We know, too, the Abbé Brémond's mystical interpretation, and the preface to George Moore's anthology, and the Imagist manifesto.

But these views are not identical. Shelley, for instance, delights in the imprecision praised and practiced by Poe, but he has an enormous appetite for "Truth" and the "Passions," which are, except for purposes of contrast, excluded by Poe. The Imagist manifesto, while excluding ideas, endorses precision rather than vagueness in rendering the image, and admits diction and objects which would have seemed impure to Poe and to many poets of the nineteenth century, and does not take much stock in the importance of verbal music. George Moore emphasizes the objective aspect of his pure poetry, which he describes as "something which the poet creates outside his own personality," and this is opposed to the subjective emphasis in Poe and Shelley; but he shares with both an emphasis on verbal music, and with the former a distaste for ideas.

But more recently, the notion of poetic purity has emerged in other contexts, contexts which sometimes obscure the connection of the new theories with the older theories. For instance Max Eastman has a theory. "Pure poetry," he says in *The Literary Mind,* "is the pure effort to heighten consciousness." Mr. Eastman, we discover elsewhere in his book, would ban idea from poetry, but his motive is different from, say, the motive of Poe, and the difference is important: Poe would kick out the ideas because the ideas hurt the poetry, and Mr. Eastman would kick out the ideas because the poetry hurts the ideas. Only the scientist, he tells us, is entitled to have ideas on any subject, and the rest of the citizenry must wait to be told what attitude to take toward the ideas which they are not permitted to have except at second-hand. Literary truth, he says, is truth which is "uncertain or comparatively unimportant." But he assigns the poet a function—to heighten consciousness. But in the light of this context we would have to rewrite his original definition: pure poetry is the pure effort to heighten consciousness, but the consciousness which is heightened must not have any connection with ideas, must involve no attitude toward any ideas.

Furthermore, to assist the poet in fulfilling the assigned function, Mr. Eastman gives him a somewhat sketchy doctrine of "pure" poetic diction. For instance, the word *bloated* is not admissible into a poem because it is, as he testifies, "sacred to the memory of dead fish," and the word *tangy* is, though he knows not exactly how, "intrinsically poetic." The notion of a vocabulary which is intrinsically poetic seems, with Mr. Eastman, to mean a vocabulary which indicates agreeable or beautiful objects. So we might rewrite the original definition to read: pure poetry is the pure effort to heighten consciousness, but the consciousness which is heightened must be a consciousness exclusively of agreeable or beautiful objects—certainly not a consciousness of any ideas.

In a recent book, *The Idiom of Poetry*, Frederick Pottle has discussed the question of pure poetry. He distinguishes another type of pure poetry in addition to the types already mentioned. He calls it the "Elliptical," and would include in it symbolist and metaphysical poetry (old and new) and some work by poets such as Collins, Blake, and Browning. He observes—without any pejorative implication, for he is a critical relativist and scarcely permits himself the luxury of evaluative judgments—that the contemporary product differs from older examples of the elliptical type in that "the modern poet goes much farther in employing private experiences or ideas than would formerly have been thought legitimate." To the common reader, he says, "the prime characteristic of this kind of poetry is not the nature of its imagery but its obscurity: its urgent suggestion that you add something to the poem without telling you what that something is." This omitted "something" he interprets as the prose "frame," to use his word, the statement of the occasion, the logical or narrative transitions, the generalized application derived from the poem, etc. In other words, this type of pure poetry contends that "the effect would be more powerful if we could somehow manage to feel the images fully and accurately without having the effect diluted by any words put in to give us a 'meaning'—that is, if we could expel all the talk *about* the imaginative realization and have the pure realization itself."[5]

For the moment I shall pass the question of the accuracy of Mr. Pottle's description of the impulse of Elliptical Poetry and present the question which ultimately concerns him. How pure does poetry need to be in practice? That is the question which Mr. Pottle ask. He answers by saying that a great degree of impurity *may* be admitted, and cites our famous didactic poems, *The Faerie Queene, The Essay on Man, The Vanity of Human Wishes, The Excursion.* That is the only answer which the relativist, and nominalist, can give. Then he turns to what he calls the hardest question in the theory of poetry: what kind of prosaism is acceptable and what is not? His answer, which he advances very modestly, is this:

> . . . the element of prose is innocent and even salutary when it appears as—take your choice of three metaphors—a background on which the images are projected, or a frame in which they are shown, or a thread on which they are strung. In short, when it serves a *structural* purpose. Prose in a poem seems offensive to me when . . . the prosaisms are sharp, obvious, individual, and ranked coordinately with the images.

At first glance this looks plausible, and the critic has used the sanctified word *structural.* But at second glance we may begin to wonder what the sanctified word means to the critic. It means something rather mechanical—background, frame, thread. The

---

[5] F. W. Bateson, in *English Poetry and the English Language,* discusses the impulse in contemporary poetry. Tennyson, he points out in connection with "The Sailor Boy," dilutes his poetry by telling a story as well as writing a poem, and "a shorter poem would have spoilt his story." The claims of prose conquer the claims of poetry. Of the Victorians in general: "The dramatic and narrative framework of their poems, by circumventing the disconcerting plunges into *medias res* which are the essence of poetry, brings it down to a level of prose. The reader knows where he is; it serves the purpose of introduction and note." Such introduction and notes in the body of the poem itself are exactly what Mr. Pottle says is missing in Elliptical Poetry. Mr. Bateson agrees with Poe in accepting intensity as the criterion of the poetic effect, and in accepting the corollary that a poem should be short. But he, contradicting Poe, seems to admire precise and complicated incidental effects.

structure is a showcase, say a jeweler's showcase, in which the little
jewels of poetry are exhibited, the images. The showcase shouldn't
be ornamental itself ("sharp, obvious, individual," Mr. Pottle says),
for it would then distract us from the jewels; it should be chastely
designed, and the jewels should repose on black velvet and not on
flowered chintz. But Mr. Pottle doesn't ask what the relation
among the bright jewels should be. Apparently, not only does the
showcase bear no relation to the jewels, but the jewels bear no
relation to each other. Each one is a shining little focus of heightened consciousness, or pure realization, existing for itself alone. Or
perhaps he should desire that they be arranged in some mechanical
pattern, such a pattern, perhaps, as would make it easier for the
eye to travel from one little jewel to the next when the time comes
to move on. Structure becomes here simply a device of salesman-
ship, a well arranged showcase.

It is all mechanical. And this means that Mr. Pottle, after all,
is himself an exponent of pure poetry. He locates the poetry simply
in the images, the nodes of "pure realization." This means that
what he calls the "element of prose" includes definition of situation,
movement of narrative, logical transition, factual description, generalization, ideas. Such things, for him, do not participate in the
poetic effect of the poem; in fact, they work against the poetic
effect, and so, though necessary as a frame, should be kept from
being "sharp, obvious, individual."[6]

I have referred to *The Idiom of Poetry*, first, because it is such
an admirable and provocative book, sane, lucid, generous-spirited,
and second, because, to my mind, it illustrates the insidiousness

---

[6] Several other difficulties concerning Mr. Pottle's statement may suggest
themselves. First, since he seems to infer that the poetic essence resides in
the image, what view would he take of meter and rhythm? His statement,
strictly construed, would mean that these factors do not participate in the
poetic effect, but are simply part of the frame. Second, what view of dramatic poetry is implied? It seems again that a strict interpretation would
mean that the story and the images bear no essential relation to each other,
that the story is simply part of the frame. That is, the story, characters,
rhythms, and ideas are on one level and the images, in which the poetry
inheres, are on another. But Miss Spurgeon, Mr. Knight, and other critics
have given us some reason for holding that the images do bear some relation
to the business of the other items. In fact, all of the items, as M. Maritain
has said, "feelings, ideas, representations, are for the artist merely materials
and means, still symbols." That is, they are all elements in a single expressive
structure.

with which a doctrine of pure poetry can penetrate into the theory of a critic who is suspicious of such a doctrine. Furthermore, I have felt that Mr. Pottle's analysis might help me to define the common denominator of the various doctrines of pure poetry.

That common denominator seems to be the belief that poetry is an essence that is to be located at some particular place in a poem, or in some particular element. The exponent of pure poetry persuades himself that he has determined the particular something in which the poetry inheres, and then proceeds to decree that poems shall be composed, as nearly as possible, of that element and of nothing else. If we add up the things excluded by various critics and practitioners, we get a list about like this:

1. ideas, truths, generalizations, "meaning"
2. precise, complicated, "intellectual" images
3. unbeautiful, disagreeable, or neutral materials
4. situation, narrative, logical transition
5. realistic details, exact descriptions, realism in general
6. shifts in tone or mood
7. irony
8. metrical variation, dramatic adaptations of rhythm, cacophony, etc.
9. meter itself
10. subjective and personal elements

No one theory of pure poetry excludes all of these items, and, as a matter of fact, the items listed are not on the same level of importance. Nor do the items always bear the same interpretation. For example, if one item seems to be central to discussions of pure poetry, it is the first: "ideas," it is said, "are not involved in the poetic effect, and may even be inimical to it." But this view can be interpreted in a variety of ways. If it is interpreted as simply meaning that the paraphrase of a poem is not equivalent to the poem, that the poetic gist is not to be defined as the statement embodied in the poem with the sugar-coating as bait, then the view can be held by opponents as well as exponents of any theory of pure poetry. We might scale down from this interpretation to the other extreme interpretation that the poem should merely give the sharp image in isolation. But there are many complicated and confused variations possible between the two extremes. There is, for exam-

ple, the interpretation that "ideas," though they are not involved
in the poetic effect, must appear in poems to provide, as Mr. Pottle's prosaisms do, a kind of frame, or thread, for the poetry—a
spine to support the poetic flesh or a Christmas tree on which the
baubles of poetry are hung.[7] T. S. Eliot has said something of this
sort:

> The chief use of the "meaning" of a poem, in the ordinary sense,
> may be (for here again I am speaking of some kinds of poetry and
> not all) to satisfy one habit of the reader, to keep his mind diverted
> and quiet, while the poem does its work upon him: much as the
> imaginary burglar is always provided with a bit of nice meat for the
> house-dog.

Here, it would seem, Mr. Eliot has simply inverted the old sugar-
coated pill theory: the idea becomes the sugar-coating and the
"poetry" becomes the medicine. This seems to say that the idea in
a poem does not participate in the poetic effect, and seems to commit Mr. Eliot to a theory of pure poetry. But to do justice to the
quotation, we should first observe that the parenthesis indicates
that the writer is referring to some sort of provisional and superficial distinction and not to a fundamental one, and second observe
that the passage is out of its context. In the context, Mr. Eliot goes
on to say that some poets "become impatient of this 'meaning'
[explicit statement of ideas in logical order] which seems superfluous, and perceive possibilities of intensity through its elimination." This may mean either of two things. It may mean that ideas
do not participate in the poetic effect, or it may mean, though they
do participate in the poetic effect, they need not appear in the
poem in an explicit and argued form. And this second reading
would scarcely be a doctrine of pure poetry at all, for it would involve poetic casuistry and not poetic principle.

We might, however, illustrate the second interpretation by
glancing at Marvell's "Horatian Ode" on Cromwell. Marvell does
not give us narrative; he does not give us an account of the issues
behind the Civil War; he does not state the two competing ideas

[7] Such an interpretation seems to find a parallel in E. M. Forster's treatment of plot in fiction. Plot in his theory becomes a mere spine and does not
really participate, except in a narrow, formal sense, in the fictional effect. By
his inversion of the Aristotelian principle, the plot becomes merely a necessary evil.

which are dramatized in the poem, the idea of "sanction" and the idea of "efficiency."' But the effect of the poem does involve these two factors; the special reserved, scarcely resolved, irony, which is realized in the historical situation, is an irony derived from un-stated materials and ideas. It is, to use Mr. Pottle's term again, a pure poem in so far as it is elliptical in method, but it is anything but a pure poem if by purity we mean the exclusion of idea from participation in the poetic effect. And Mr. Eliot's own practice implies that he believes that ideas do participate in the poetic ef-fect. Otherwise, why did he put the clues to his ideas in the notes at the end of the *Waste Land* after so carefully excluding any ex-plicit statement of them from the body of the poem? If he is re-garding those ideas as mere bait—the "bit of nice meat for the house-dog"—he has put the ideas in a peculiar place, in the back of the book—like giving the dog the meat on the way out of the house with the swag or giving the mouse the cheese after he is in the trap. All this would lead one to the speculation that Marvell and Mr. Eliot have purged away statement of ideas from their poems, not because they wanted the ideas to participate less in the poetry, but because they wanted them to participate more fully, intensely, and immediately. This impulse, then, would account for the character-istic type of image, types in which precision, complication, and complicated intellectual relation to the theme are exploited; in other words, they are trying—whatever may be their final success—to carry the movement of mind to the center of the process. On these grounds they are the exact opposite of poets who, presumably on grounds of purity, exclude the movement of mind from the center of the poetic process—from the internal structure of the poem—but pay their respect to it as a kind of footnote, or gloss, or application coming at the end. Marvell and Eliot, by their cutting away of frame, are trying to emphasize the participation of ideas in the poetic process. Then Elliptical Poetry is not, as Mr. Pottle says it is, a pure poetry at all if we regard intention; the elliptical poet is elliptical for purposes of inclusion, not exclusion.

But waiving the question of Elliptical Poetry, no one of the other theories does—or could—exclude all the items on the list above. And that fact may instruct us. If all of these items were ex-cluded, we might not have any poem at all. For instance, we know how some critics have pointed out that even in the strictest imagist poetry idea creeps in—when the image leaves its natural habitat and enters a poem it begins to "mean" something. The attempt to read ideas out of the poetic party violates the unity of our being and the unity of our experience. "For this reason," as Santayana puts it, "philosophy, when a poet is not mindless, enters inevitably into his poetry, since it has entered into his life; or rather, the detail of things and the detail of ideas pass equally into his verse, when both alike lie in the path that has led him to his ideal. To object to theory in poetry would be like objecting to words there; for words, too, are symbols without the sensuous character of the things they stand for; and yet it is only by the net of new connections which words throw over things, in recalling them, that poetry arises at all. Poetry is an attenuation, a rehandling, an echo of crude experience; it is itself a theoretic vision of things at arm's length." Does this not lead us to the conclusion that poetry does not inhere in any particular element but depends upon the set of relationships, the structure, which we call the poem?

Then the question arises: what elements cannot be used in such a structure? I should answer that nothing that is available in human experience is to be legislated out of poetry. This does not mean that anything can be used in *any* poem, or that some materials or elements may not prove more recalcitrant than others, or that it might not be easy to have too much of some things. But it does mean that, granted certain contexts, any sort of material, a chemical formula for instance, might appear functionally in a poem. It also may mean that, other things being equal, the greatness of a poet depends upon the extent of the area of experience which he can master poetically.

Can we make any generalizations about the nature of the poetic structure? First, it involves resistances, at various levels. There is the tension between the rhythm of the poem and the rhythm of speech (a tension which is very low at the extreme of free verse and at the extreme of verse such as that of "ulalume," which verges toward a walloping doggerel); between the formality of the rhythm and the informality of the language; between the particular and the general, the concrete and the abstract; between the elements of even the simplest metaphor; between the beautiful and the ugly; between ideas (as in Marvell's poem); between the elements involved in irony (as in "Bells for John Whiteside's Daughter" or

"Rose Aylmer"); between prosisms and poeticisms (as in "Western Wind"). This list is not intended to be exhaustive; it is intended to be merely suggestive. But it may be taken to imply that the poet is like the jujitsu expert; he wins by utilizing the resistance of his opponent—the materials of the poem. In other words, a poem, to be good, must earn itself. It is a motion toward a point of rest, but if it is not a resisted motion, it is motion of no consequence. For example, a poem which depends upon stock materials and stock responses is simply a toboggan slide, or a fall through space. And the good poem must, in some way, involve the resistances; it must carry something of the context of its own creation; it must come to terms with Mercutio. This is another way of saying that a good poem involves the participation of the reader; it must, as Coleridge puts it, make the reader into "an active creative being." Perhaps we can see this most readily in the case of tragedy: the definition of good or evil is not a "given"' in tragedy, it is something to be earned in the process, and even the tragic villain must be "loved." We must kill him, as Brutus killed Caesar, not as butchers but as sacrificers. And all of this adds up to the fact that the structure is a dramatic structure, a movement through action toward rest, through complication toward simplicity of effect.

In the foregoing discussion, I have deliberately omitted reference to another type of pure poetry, a type which, in the context of the present war, may well become dominant. Perhaps the most sensible description of this type can be found in any essay by Herbert Muller:

> If it is not the primary business of the poet to be eloquent about these matters [faith and ideals], it still does not follow that he has more dignity or wisdom than those who are, or that he should have more sophistication. At any rate the fact is that almost all poets of the past did freely make large, simple statements, and not in their prosy or lax moments.

Mr. Muller then goes on to illustrate by quoting three famous, large, simple statements:

> *In la sua voluntade e nostra pace*

and

> We are such stuff
> As dreams are made on; and our little lives

> Are rounded with a sleep.

and

> The mind is its own place, and in itself
> Can make a heaven of hell, a hell of heaven.

Mr. Muller is here attacking the critical emphasis on ironic tension in poetry. His attack really involves two lines of argument. First, the poet is not wiser than the stateman, philosopher, or saint, people who are eloquent about faith and ideals and who say what they mean, without benefit of irony. This Platonic (or pseudo-Platonic) line of argument is, I think, off the point in the present context. Second, the poets of the past have made large, simple affirmations which have said what they meant. This line of argument is very much on the point.

Poets *have* tried very hard, for thousands of years, to say what they mean. But they have not only tried to say what they mean, they have tried to prove what they mean. The saint proves his vision by stepping cheerfully into the fires. The poet, somewhat less spectacularly, proves his vision by submitting it to the fires of irony —to the drama of his structure—in the hope that the fires will refine it. In other words, the poet wishes to indicate that his vision has been earned, that it can survive reference to the complexities and contradictions of experience. And irony is one such device of reference.

In this connection let us look at the first of Mr. Muller's exhibits. The famous line occurs in Canto III of the *Paradiso*. It is spoken by Piccarda Donati, in answer to Dante's question as to why she does not desire to rise higher than her present sphere, the sphere of the moon. But it expresses, in unequivocal terms, a central theme of the *Commedia,* as of Christian experience. On the one hand, it may be a pious truism, fit for sampler work, and on the other hand, it way be a burning conviction, tested and earned. Dante, in his poem, sets out to show how it has been earned and tested. One set of ironic tensions, for instance, which centers about this theme concerns the opposition between the notion of human justice and the notion of divine justice. The story of Paolo and Francesca is so warm, appealing, and pathetic in its human terms and their punishment so savage and unrelenting, so incommensurable, it seems, with the fault, that Dante, torn by the conflict, falls down as a dead body falls. Or Farinata, the enemy of Dante's house, is presented by the poet in terms of his human grandeur, which now, in Hell, is transmuted into a superhuman grandeur,

com' avesse l'inferno in gran dispitto.

Ulysses remains a hero, a hero who should draw special applause from Dante, who defined the temporal end of man as the conquest of knowledge. But Ulysses is damned, as the great Brutus is damned, who hangs from the jaws of the fiend in the lowest pit of traitors. So divine justice is set over against human pathos, human dignity, human grandeur, human intellect, human justice. And we recall how Virgil, more than once, reminds Dante that he must not apply human standards to the sights he sees. It is this long conflict, which appears in many forms, this ironic tension, which finally gives body to the simple eloquence of the line in question; the statement is meaningful, not for what it says, but for what has gone before. It is earned. It has been earned by the entire poem.

I do not want to misrepresent Mr. Muller. He does follow his quotations by the sentence: "If they are properly qualified in the work as a whole, they may still be taken straight, they *are* [he italicizes the word] taken so in recollection as in their immediate impact." But can this line be taken so in recollection, and was it taken so in its "immediate impact"? And if one does take it so, is he not violating, very definitely, the poet's meaning, for the poet means the *poem,* he doesn't mean the line.

It would be interesting to try to develop the contexts of the other passages which Mr. Muller quotes. But in any case, he was simply trying, in his essay, to guard against what he considered to be, rightly or wrongly, a too narrow description of poetry; he was not trying to legislate all poetry into the type of simple eloquence, the unqualified statement of "faith and ideas." But we have already witnessed certain, probably preliminary, attempts to legislate literature into becoming a simple, unqualified, "pure" statement of faith and ideal. We have seen the writers of the 1920's called the "irresponsibles.'" We have seen writers such as Proust, Eliot, Dreiser, and Faulkner, called writers of the "death drive." Why are these writers condemned? Because they have tried, within the limits of their gifts, to remain faithful to the complexities of the problems with which they were dealing, because they refused to take the easy statement as solution, because they tried to define the context in which, and the terms by which, faith and ideals could be earned. But this method will scarcely satisfy the mind which is hot for certainties; to that mind it will seem merely an index to lukewarmness, indecision, disunity, treason. The new theory of purity would purge out all complexities and all ironies and all self-criticism. And this theory will forget that the hand-me-down faith, the hand-me-down ideals, no matter what the professed content, is in the end not only meaningless but vicious. It is vicious because, as parody, it is the enemy of all faith.

KENNETH BURKE

From *The Philosophy of Literary Form*

Situations and Strategies

Let us suppose that I ask you: "What did the man say?" And that you answer: "He said 'yes.'" You still do not know what the man said. You would not know unless you knew more about the situation, and about the remarks that preceded his answer.

Critical and imaginative works are answers to questions posed by the situation in which they arose. They are not merely answers, they are *strategic* answers, *stylized* answers. For there is a difference in style or strategy, if one says "yes" in tonalities that imply "thank God" or in tonalities that imply "alas!" So I should propose an initial working distinction between "strategies" and "situations," whereby we think of poetry (I here use the term to include any work of critical or imaginative cast) as the adopting of various strategies for the encompassing of situations. These strategies size up the situations, name their structure and outstanding ingredients, and name them in a way that contains an attitude towards them.

This point of view does not, by any means vow us to personal or historical subjectivism. The situations are real; the strategies for handling them have public content; and in so far as situations overlap from individual to individual, or from one historical period to another, the strategies possess universal relevance.

Situations do overlap, if only because men now have the same neural and muscular structure as men who have left their records from past ages. We and they are in much the same biological situation. Furthermore, even the concrete details of social texture have a great measure of overlap. And the nature of the human mind itself, with the function of abstraction rooted in the nature of language, also provides us with "levels of generalization" (to employ Korzybski's term) by which situations greatly different in their particularities may be felt to belong in the same class (to have a common substance or essence).

Consider a proverb, for instance. Think of the endless variety of situations, distinct in their particularities, which this proverb may "size up," or attitudinally name. To examine one of my favorites: "Whether the pitcher strikes the stone, or the stone the pitcher, it's bad for the pitcher." Think of some primitive society in which an incipient philosopher, in disfavor with the priests, attempted to criticize their lore. They are powerful, he is by comparison weak. And they control all the channels of power. Hence, whether they attack him or he attacks them, he is the loser. And he could quite adequately size up this situation by saying, "Whether the pitcher strikes the stone, or the stone the pitcher, it's bad for the pitcher." Or Aristophanes could well have used it, in describing his motivation when, under the threats of political dictatorship, he gave up the lampooning of political figures and used the harmless Socrates as his goat instead. Socrates was propounding new values—and Aristophanes, by aligning himself with conservative values, against the materially powerless dialectician, could himself take on the rôle of the stone in the stone-pitcher ratio. Or the proverb could be employed to name the predicament of a man in Hitler's Germany who might come forward with an argument, however well reasoned, against Hitler. Or a local clerk would find the proverb apt, if he would make public sport of his boss. These situations are all distinct in their particularities; each occurs in a totally different texture of history; yet all are classifiable together under the generalizing head of the same proverb.

Might we think of poetry as complex variants and recombinations of such material as we find in proverbs? There are situations typical and recurrent enough for men to feel the need of having a

name for them. In sophisticated work, this naming is done with
great complexity. Think of how much modern psychology, for instance, might be placed as a highly alembicated way of *seeing
through to the end* the formulation now become proverbial: "The
wish is father to the thought." Or think of how much in the Hegelian dialectic might be summed up, as an over-all title, in the
idealist Coleridge's favorite proverb, "Extremes meet." And in all
work, as in proverbs, the naming is done "strategically" or "stylistically," in modes that embody attitudes, of resignation, solace,
vengeance, expectancy, etc.

Magic and Religion

In addition to the leads or cues, for the analysis of poetic strategy, that we get from proverbs, with their strongly realistic element, we may get leads from magic and religion.

Magic, verbal coercion, establishment or management by decree,
says, in effect: " 'Let there be'—and there was." And men share in
the magical resources of some power by speaking "in the name of"
that power. As Ogden and Richards remind us in *The Meaning
of Meaning,* modern Biblical scholarship has disclosed that we
should interpret in this wise the formula, "taking the name of the
Lord in vain." The formula referred to the offense of conjuring for
malign purposes by uttering one's magical decrees "in the name of"
the Lord.

The device, in attenuated and alembicated variants, is not so
dead, or even so impotent, as one might at first suppose. Today, for
instance, we are facing problems that arise from an attempt to fit
private enterprise with the requirements of the citizenry as a
whole. Think of the difference in magic if you confront this situation in the *strategic name of* "planned economy" or, employing a
different strategy, *in the name of* "regimentation."

The magical decree is implicit in all language; for the mere act
of naming an object or situation decrees that it is to be singled out
as such-and-such rather than as something-other. Hence, I think
that an attempt to *eliminate* magic, in this sense, would involve
us in the elimination of vocabulary itself as a way of sizing up
reality. Rather, what we may need is *correct* magic, magic whose
decrees about the naming of real situations is the closest possible
approximation to the situation named (with the greater accuracy

of approximation being supplied by the "collective revelation" of testing and discussion).

If magic says, *"Let there be* such and such," religion says, *"Please do* such and such." The decree of magic, the petition of prayer. Freud has discussed the "optative as indicative" in dreams (where "would that it were" is stylistically rephrased: "it is"—as when the dreamer, desiring to be rid of a certain person, dreams that this person is departing). Neo-positivism has done much in revealing the secret commands and exhortations in words—as Edward M. Maisel, in *An Anatomy of Literature,* reveals in a quotation from Carnap, noting how the apparent historical creed: "There is only one race of superior men, say the race of Hottentots, and this race alone is worthy of ruling other races. Members of these other races are inferior," should be analytically translated as: "Members of the race of Hottentots! Unite and battle to dominate the other races!" The "facts" of the historical assertion here are but a strategy of inducement (apparently describing the *scene* for the action of a drama, they are themselves a dramatic *act prodding to a further dramatic act*).

It is difficult to keep the magical *decree* and the religious *petition* totally distinct. Though the distinction between the *coercive command* and the *conducive request* is clear enough in its extremes, there are many borderline cases. Ordinarily, we find three ingredients interwoven in a given utterance: the spell and the counter-spell, the curse; the prayer and the prayer-in-reverse, oath, indictment, invective; the dream, and the dream gone sour, nightmare.

So, taking this ingredient as common to all verbal action, we might make the following three subdivisions for the analysis of an act in poetry:

Dream (the unconscious or subconscious factors in a poem—the factor slighted by the Aristotelians, though by no means left unconsidered, as John Crowe Ransom's chapters on "The Cathartic Principle" and "The Mimetic Principle" in *The World's Body* make apparent),

Prayer (the communicative functions of a poem, which leads us into the many considerations of form, since the poet's inducements can lead us to participate in his poem only in so far as his

work has a public, or communicative, structure—the factor
slighted by the various expressionistic doctrines, the Art for
Art's Sake school stressing the work solely as the poet's exter-
nalizing of himself, or naming of his own peculiar number),
Chart (the realistic sizing-up of situations that is sometimes explicit, sometimes implicit, in poetic strategies—the factor that
Richards and the psychoanalysts have slighted).

It may annoy some persons that I take the realistic chart to
possess "magical" ingredients. That is, if you size up a situation in
the name of regimentation you *decree* it a different essence than if
you sized it up in the name of planned economy. The choice here
is not a choice between magic and no magic, but a choice between
magics that vary in their degree of approximation to the truth. In
both these magics, for instance, there is usually an assumption (or
implied *fiat*) to the effect that increased industrial production is
itself a good. But when we recall that every increase in the *consumption* of natural resources could with equal relevance be characterized as a corresponding increase in the *destruction* of natural
resources, we can glimpse the opportunity for a totally different
magic here, that would size up the situation by a different quality
of namings. And when I read recently of an estimate that more
soil had been lost through erosion in the last twenty years than in
all the rest of human history, I began to ask whether either the
"regimentation" magic or the "planned economy" magic is a close
enough approximate for the naming of the situation in which we
now are. The "regimentation" magic is on its face by far the worse,
since its implicit demand, "Let us have no collective control over
production," calls for as much wastage as is possible in an ailing
property structure. But this wastage is, ironically, curtailed mainly
by the maladjustments of the very property structure that the "regimentation" magic would perpetuate. The "planned economy"
magic is much superior, but only when corrected by a criticism of
"new needs." It is a menace when combined, as it usually is, with
a doctrine that increased industrial output is synonymous with
"progress." The irony is that a readjusted property structure would
make possible greater wastage (or "consumption") than our present ailing one. Hence, the magic that made greater production
possible would be the worst of calamities unless corrected by an-

other magic decreeing that many of our present kinds of industrial output are culturally sinister.

The ideal magic is that in which our assertions (or verbal decrees) as to the nature of the situation come closest to a correct gauging of that situation as it actually is. Any *approximate* chart is a "decree." Only a *completely accurate* chart would dissolve magic, by making the structure of names identical with the structure named. This latter is the kind of chart that Spinoza, in his doctrine of the "adequate idea," selected as the goal of philosophy, uniting free will and determinism, since the "So be it" is identical with the "It must be so" and the "It is so." A completely adequate chart would, of course, be possible only to an infinite, omniscient mind.

"It is (morally or technically) wrong" is a stylized variant of "Don't do it." However, to note this translation of a command into the idiom of realism must not be taken as identical with a "debunking" of the verbal assertion. For a command may be a good command, involving a strategy that is quite accurate for encompassing the situation. Science simultaneously admits and conceals the element of *fiat* in a calculus by Latinistic stylization, as when it explicitly states the commands basic to a calculus but couches these in terms of "postulates" (*postulatum*: command, demand), a kind of "*provisory* command," in keeping with the customary trend towards *attenuation* in scientific stylizations. It replaces "big commands" with a whole lot of "little commands" that fall across one another on the bias, quite as modern poetry has replaced the "big spell" with a lot of "little spells," each work pulling us in a different direction and these directions tending to cancel off one another, as with the conflicting interests of a parliament.

Symbolic Action

We might sum all this up by saying that poetry, or any verbal act, is to be considered as "symbolic action." But though I must use this term, I object strenuously to having the general perspective labeled as "symbolism." I recognize that people like to label, that labeling *comforts* them by *getting things placed*. But I object to "symbolism" as a label, because it suggests too close a link with a particular school of poetry, the Symbolist Movement, and usually implies the unreality of the world in which we live, as though nothing could be what it is, but must always be something else (as though a house could never be a house, but must be, let us say, the concealed surrogate for a woman, or as though the woman one marries could never be the woman one marries, but must be a surrogate for one's mother, etc.).

Still, there is a difference, and a radical difference, between building a house and writing a poem about building a house—and a poem about having children by marriage is not the same thing as having children by marriage. There are *practical* acts, and there are symbolic acts (nor is the distinction, clear enough in its extremes, to be dropped simply because there is a borderline area wherein many practical acts take on a symbolic ingredient, as one may buy a certain commodity not merely to use it, but also because its possession testifies to his enrollment in a certain stratum of society).

The symbolic act is the *dancing of an attitude* (a point that Richards has brought out, though I should want to revise his position to the extent of noting that in Richards' doctrines the attitude is pictured as too sparse in realistic content). In this attitudinizing of the poem, the whole body may finally become involved, in ways suggested by the doctrines of behaviorism. The correlation between mind and body here is neatly conveyed in two remarks by Hazlitt, concerning Coleridge:

> I observed that he continually crossed me on the way by shifting from one side of the foot-path to the other. This struck me as an odd movement; but I did not at that time connect it with any instability of purpose or involuntary change of principle, as I have done since. . . .
>
> There is a *chaunt* in the recitation both of Coleridge and Wordsworth, which acts as a spell upon the hearer, and disarms the judgment. Perhaps they have deceived themselves by making habitual use of this ambiguous accompaniment. Coleridge's manner is more full, animated, and varied; Wordsworth's more equable, sustained, and internal. The one might be termed more *dramatic,* the other more *lyrical.* Coleridge has told me that he himself liked to compose in walking over uneven ground, or breaking through the straggling branches of a copse-wood; whereas Wordsworth always wrote (if he could) walking up and down a straight gravel-walk, or in some spot where the continuity of his verse met with no collateral interruption.[1]

[1] The quotations are lifted from Lawrence Hanson's excellent study, *The Life of S. T. Coleridge.*

We might also cite from a letter of Hopkins, mentioned by R. P. Blackmur in *The Kenyon Review* (Winter, 1939):

> As there is something of the "old Adam" in all but the holiest men and in them at least enough to make them understand it in others, so there is an old Adam of barbarism, boyishness, wildness, rawness, rankness, the disreputable, the unrefined in the refined and educated. It is that that I meant by tykishness (a tyke is a stray sly unowned dog).

Do we not glimpse the labyrinthine mind of Coleridge, the *puzzle* in its pace, "danced" in the act of walking—and do we not glimpse behind the agitated rhythm of Hopkins' verse, the conflict between the priest and the "tyke," with the jerkiness of his lines "symbolically enacting" the mental conflict? So we today seem to immunize ourselves to the arhythmic quality of both traffic and accountancy by a distrust of the lullaby and the rocking cradle as formative stylistic equipment for our children.

The accumulating lore on the nature of "psychogenic illness" has revealed that something so "practical" as a bodily ailment may be a "symbolic" act on the part of the body which, in this materialization, *dances* a corresponding state of mind, reordering the glandular and neural behavior of the organism in obedience to mind-body correspondences, quite as the formal dancer reorders his externally observable gesturing to match his attitudes. Thus, I know of a man who, going to a dentist, was proud of the calmness with which he took his punishment. But after the session was ended, the dentist said to him: "I observe that you are very much afraid of me. For I have noted that, when patients are frightened, their saliva becomes thicker, more sticky. And yours was exceptionally so." Which would indicate that, while the man in the dentist's chair was "dancing an attitude of calmness" on the public level, as a social façade, on the purely bodily or biological level his salivary glands were "dancing his true attitude." For he *was* apprehensive of pain, and his glandular secretions "said so." Similarly I have read that there is an especially high incidence of stomach ulcers among taxi drivers—an occupational illness that would not seem to be accounted for merely by poor and irregular meals, since these are equally the lot of workers at other kinds of jobs. Do we not see, rather, a bodily response to the intensely arhythmic quality of the work itself, the irritation in the continual jagginess of traffic, all puzzle and no pace, and only the timing of the cylinders performing with regularity, as if all the *ritual* of the occupational act had been drained off, into the *routine* of the motor's explosions and revolutions?

In such ways, the whole body is involved in an enactment. And we might make up a hypothetical illustration of this sort: imagine a poet who, on perfectly rational grounds rejecting the political and social authority of the powers that be, wrote poems enacting this attitude of rejection. This position we might call his symbolic act on the abstract level. On the personal, or intimate level, he might embody the same attitude in a vindictive style (as so much of modern work, proud of its emancipation from prayer, has got this emancipation dubiously, by simply substituting prayer-in-reverse, the oath). And on the biological level, this same attitude might be enacted in the imagery of excretion, as with the scene of vomiting with which Farrell ends the second volume of his Studs Lonigan trilogy.

Sir Richard Paget's theory of gesture speech gives us inklings of the way in which such enactment might involve even the selection of words themselves on a basis of tonality. According to Paget's theory, language arose in this wise: If a man is firmly gripping something, the muscles of his tongue and throat adopt a position in conformity with the muscles with which he performs the act of gripping. He does not merely grip with his hands; he "grips all over." Thus, in conformity with the act of gripping, he would simultaneously grip with his mouth, by closing his lips firmly. If, now, he uttered a sound with his lips in this position, the only sound he could utter would be *m*. *M* therefore is the sound you get when you "give voice" to the posture of gripping. Hence, *m* would be the proper tonality corresponding to the act of gripping, as in contact words like "maul," "mix," "mammae," and "slam." The relation between sound and sense here would not be an onomatopoetic one, as with a word like "sizzle," but it would rather be like that between the visual designs on a sound track and the auditory vibrations that arise when the instrument has "given voice" to these designs (except that, in the case of human speech, the designs would be those of the tongue and throat, plastic rather than graphic).

The great resistance to Paget's theory doubtless arises in large part from the conservatism of philological specialists. They have an investment in other theories—and only the most pliant among them are likely to see around the corner of their received ideas (Paget cites remarks by Jespersen that hit about the edges of his theory). But some of the resistance, I think, also arises from an error in Paget's strategy of presentation. He offers his theory as a *philological* one, whereas it should be offered as a contribution to *poetics.* Philology, because of its involvement in historicism, really deals with *the ways in which, if Paget's theory were 100 per cent correct, such linguistic mimesis as he is discussing would become obscured by historical accretions.*

Let us suppose, for instance, that *f* is an excellent linguistic gesture for the *p* sound prolonged, and the lips take the posture of *p* in the act of spitting—hence, the *p* is preserved in the word itself, in "spittle" and "puke," and in words of re*p*ulsion and re*p*ugnance. The close phonetic relation between *p* and *f* is observed in the German exclamation of repugnance, "*pfui.*" Mencken, in *The American Language,* cites two synthetic words by Winchell that perfectly exemplify this faugh-*f*: "phfft" and "foofff." These are "nonsense syllables" Winchell has invented to convey, by tonality alone, the idea that is denoted in our word "*p*est." Here, since the inventor has complete freedom, there are no historical accidents of language to complicate his mimesis, so he can symbolically spit long and hard.

Imagine, however, a new movement arising in history—and, as is so often the case with new movements, imagine that it is named by the enemy (as "liberalism" was named by the Jesuits, to convey connotations of "licentiousness," in contrast with "*servile,*" to convey connotations of "loyal"). If we hypothetically grant the existence of a faugh-*f,* we should discover that the enemy danced the attitude towards this new movement with perfect accuracy in naming the new movement "phfftism" or "foofffism." However, as so often happens in history, the advocates of "foofffism" accepted the term, and set out to "live it down" (as with "liberalism"—and also "nihilism," which was named by the enemy, but in the late nineteenth century recruited nihilistic *heroes*). And let us finally imagine, as so often happens in history, that the new movement, beginning in great disrepute, finally triumphs and becomes the norm. Though the attitude towards the name is now changed, the name itself may be retained, and so we may find earnest fellows saying, "I hereby solemnly swear allegiance to the flag of fofffism."

Now, philology would deal with these historical developments whereby the originally accurate mimesis became *obscured*—and it is in this sense that, to my way of thinking, Paget's theory should be presented as a contribution not to philology, but to poetics. The greatest attempt at a *poetics* of sound is Dante's *De Vulgari Eloquio*, which is equally concerned with a *rational selection* of a poetic language, its systematic isolation from a common speech that had developed by the hazards of historical accretion. And Paget's theory should, I contend, be viewed as a corresponding enterprise, except that now, given the change of reference from Dante's day to ours, the theory is grounded on a *biological* or *naturalistic* base.

A possible way whereby these theories might be empirically tested is this: We should begin by asking whether our system of phonetic recording might be inaccurate. Might there, for instance, be at least *two* sounds of *f*, whereas both were recorded in writing as the same sound (as in French three different sounds of *e* are explicitly indicated, whereas the English ways of recording *e* do not indicate such differences)? Why, in the light of such evidence, should we assume that there is but one *f* simply because our mode of recording this sound indicates but one? Might there, let us say, be a faugh-*f* and a flower-*f* (with the second trying to bring out the smoothness of *f*, as were one to recite sympathetically Coleridge's line, "Flowers are lovely, love is flowerlike," and the other trying to stress its expulsive quality, as when I once heard a reactionary orator, spewing forth a spray of spittle, fulminate against "fiery, frenzied fanatics")? I do not know how accurate the electric recordings of a sound-track are, or how close a microscopic analysis of them could be: but if these recordings are accurate enough, and if microscopic analysis can be refined to the point of discriminating very minute differences in the design of the sound-track, one could select flower-passages and faugh-passages, have them recited by a skilled actor (without telling him of the theory), take an electric recording of his recitation, and then examine the sound-track for *quantitative* evidence (in the design of the sound-track) of a distinction in *f* not indicated by our present conventions of writing. We might perhaps more accurately use *two* symbols, thus: *f′* and *f″. It should be noted, however, that such a difference would not be absolute and constant.* That is, one might pronounce a word like "of" differently if it appeared expressively in a "flower" context than if it appeared in a "faugh" context. Which would again take us out of philology into poetics.

Similarly, inasmuch as *b* is midway between mammal *m* and the repulsion *p,* we might expect it to have an *m*-like sound on some occasions and a *p*-like sound on others. Thus, in the lines

> O blasphemy! to mingle fiendish deeds
> With blessedness!

we could expect "*b*lasphemy" to approximate "*p*lasphemy," and "*b*lessedness" to be more like "*m*lessedness," and explosive possibilities of *b* being purposely coached in the first case and tempered in the second. (Incidentally, no words are more like home to an idealist philosopher than "subject" and "object"—and we are told that when Coleridge had fallen into one of his famous monologues, he pronounced them "sumject" and "omject.")

Our gradual change of emphasis from the spoken to the documentary (with many symbols of mathematics and logic having no tonal associations whatsoever, being hardly other than designs) has made increasingly for a purely ocular style—so that children now are sometimes even trained to read wholly by eye. And there are indeed many essayistic styles that profit greatly if one can master the art of reading them without hearing them at all. For they are as arthythmic as traffic itself, and can even give one a palpitation of the heart if he still reads with an encumbrance of auditory imagery, and so accommodates his bodily responses to their total tonal aimlessness. But whatever may be the value of such styles, for bookkeeping purposes, they have wandered far afield from the gesturing of heard poetic speech. Paradoxically, their greatest accuracy, from the standpoint of mimesis, is in their *very absence* of such, for by this absence they conform with our sedentary trend from the bodily to the abstract (our secular variant of the spiritual). It is the style of men and women whose occupations have become dissociated from the bodily level, and whose expression accordingly does not arise from a physical act as the rhythms of a Negro work song arise from the rhythms of Negroes at work.

In any event, as regards the correlation between mind and body, we may note for future application in this essay, that the poet will naturally tend to write about that which most deeply engrosses him—and nothing more deeply engrosses a man than his *burdens,* including those of a physical nature, such as disease. We win by capitalizing on our debts, by turning our liabilities into assets, by using our burdens as a basis of insight. And so the poet may come to have a "vested interest" in his handicaps; these handicaps may become an integral part of his method; and in so far as his style grows out of a disease, his loyalty to it may reinforce the disease. It is a matter that Thomas Mann has often been concerned with. And it bears again upon the subject of "symbolic action," with the poet's burdens symbolic of his style, and his style symbolic of his burdens. I think we should not be far wrong if, seeking the area where states of mind are best available to empirical observation, we sought for correlations between styles and physical disease (particularly since there is no discomfiture, however mental in origin, that does not have its physiological correlates). So we might look for "dropsical" styles (Chesterton), "asthmatic" (Proust), "phthisic" (Mann), "apoplectic" (Flaubert), "blind" (Milton), etc. The one great objection to such a nosological mode of classification is that it leads to a Max Nordau mode of equating genius with degeneracy. This is not the case, however, if one properly discounts his terminology, reminding himself that the true locus of assertion is not in the *disease,* but in the *structural powers* by which the poet encompasses it. The disease, seen from this point of view, is hardly more than the *caricature* of the man, the oversimplification of his act—hence, most easily observable because it is an oversimplification. This oversimplifying indicator is deceptive unless its obviousness as a caricature is discounted.

Another Word for "Symbolic"

I respect the resistance to the notion of "symbolic action," since this resistance is based upon a healthy distrust of the irrational (the only question being whether we are rational enough in merely trying to outlaw the irrational by magical decree, and whether we might be more rational in confronting it). Respecting the resistance, I want to offer some considerations that may ease the pain. One of the most "rational" of words today is our word *statistical,* as applied for instance to the thorough rationality of an actuarial table. So I want to see whether we might be justified in borrowing this word for our purposes, in considering at least some aspects of "symbolic action." I propose to offer reasons why we might equate the word *symbolic* with the word *statistical*.

Mr. Q writes a novel. He has a score to settle with the world, and he settles it on paper, symbolically. Let us suppose that his novel is about a deserving individual in conflict with an undeserving society. He writes the work from the standpoint of his unique engrossments. However, as Malcolm Cowley has pointed out, there is a whole *class* of such novels. And if we take them all together, in the lump "statistically," they become about as unique as various objects all going downstream together in a flood. They are "all doing the same"—they become but different individuations of a common paradigm. As so considered, they become "symbolic" of something—they become "representative" of a social trend.

Or consider the matter from another angle. One puts his arms on the table. This is a unique, real act—and one is perfectly conscious of what he is doing. There is, to be sure, a lot that he doesn't know: he is not conscious, for instance, of the infinite muscular and nervous adjustments that accompany the act. But he is perfectly conscious of the overall event: he knows what he is doing. Yet I have heard a portrait-painter exclaim at such a moment, when a man placed his arm on the table: "There—just like that—that's your characteristic posture." Thus, for this painter, the act had become "symbolic," "representative" of the man's character. There was a kind of informal fact-gathering that had been going on, as the painter had observed this man—and his exclamation was a kind of informally statistical conclusion.

But let's make one more try at taking the fearsomeness out of the word "symbolic." John Crowe Ransom, in *The World's Body*, makes some praiseworthy attempts to reaffirm a realistic basis for poetry; as part of his tactics, he would present even the lyric poem as the enactment of a dramatic rôle. The poet is "play-acting"—and so we must not consider his work as merely a symbolization of his private problems. Well and good. But let us suppose that a writer has piled up a considerable body of work; and upon inspecting the lot, we find that there has been great selectivity in his adoption of dramatic rôles. We find that his rôles have not been like "repertory acting," but like "type casting." This "statistical" view of his work, in disclosing a *trend*, puts us upon the track of the ways in which his selection of rôle is a "symbolic act." He is like a man with a tic, who spasmodically blinks his eyes when certain subjects are mentioned. If you kept a list of these subjects, noting what was said each time he spasmodically blinked his eyes, you would find what the tic was "symbolic" of.

Now, the work of every writer contains a set of implicit equations. He uses "associational clusters." And you may, by examining his work, find "what goes with what" in these clusters—what kinds of acts and images and personalities and situations go with his notions of heroism, villainy, consolation, despair, etc. And though he be perfectly conscious of the act of writing, conscious of selecting a certain kind of imagery to reinforce a certain kind of mood, etc., he cannot possibly be conscious of the interrelationships among all these equations. Afterwards, by inspecting his work "statistically," we or he may disclose by objective citation the structure of motivation operating here. There is no need to "supply" motives. The interrelationships themselves *are* his motives. For they are his *situation;* and *situation* is but another word for *motives*. The motivation out of which he writes is synonymous with the structural way in which he puts events and values together when he writes; and however consciously he may go about such work, there is a kind of generalization about these interrelations that he could not have been conscious of, since the generalization could be made by the kind of inspection that is possible only *after the completion* of the work.

At present I am attempting such a "symbolic" analysis of Coleridge's writings. His highly complex mind makes the job of charting difficult. The associational interweavings are so manifold as to present quite a problem in bookkeeping. Thus, even if my method were hypothetically granted to be correct, it is as though one invented a machine for recovering the exact course each person had taken on passing through Times Square. Even if one's machine were completely trustworthy, he would have difficulty in trying to present, on a design, the different paths taken. The lines would merge into a blot.

However, there are two advantages about the case of Coleridge that make the job worth trying. In the first place, there is the fact that he left so full a record, and that he employed the same imagery in his poems, literary criticism, political and religious tracts, letters, lectures, and introspective jottings. Thus we have objective bridges for getting from one area to another; these images "pontificate" among his various interests, and so provide us with a maximum opportunity to work out a psychology by objective citation, by "scissor work." If you want to say that this equals that, you have the imagery, explicitly shared by this and that in common, to substantiate the claim. In fact, a psychology of poetry, so conceived, is about as near to the use of objective, empirical evidence as even the physical sciences. For though there must be purely theoretical grounds for selecting some interrelationships rather than others as more significant, the interrelationships themselves can be shown *by citation* to be there.

The second advantage in the case of Coleridge is that, along with his highly complex mind (perhaps one of the most complex that has left us a full record) you have an easily observable *simplification*. I refer to the burden of his drug addiction. Criticism is usually up against a problem of this sort: The critic tries to explain a complexity in terms of a simplicity, and when he is finished, his opponent need but answer: "But you have explained a complexity in terms of a simplicity, and a simplicity is precisely what a complexity is *not*. So you have explained something in terms of what it isn't." Explanation entails simplification; and any simplification is open to the charge of "oversimplification." So we have tried to explain human beings in terms of mechanistic psychology, adults in terms of child psychology, sophisticates in terms of primitive psychology, and the normal in terms of abnormal psychology— with the opponent's categorical refutation of the effort implicit in the nature of the effort itself. In the case of Coleridge's enslavement to his drug, however, you get an observable simplification, a burden the manifestations of which can be trailed through his work—yet at the same time you have him left in all his complexity, and so may observe the complex ways in which this burden becomes interwoven with his many other concerns.

To note the matter of symbolic action, however, is by no means to involve oneself in a purely subjectivist position. There are respects in which the clusters (or "what goes with what") are private, and respects in which they are public. Thus, I think we can,

by analysis of the "clusters" in Coleridge's work, find ingredients
in the figure of the Albatross slain in "The Ancient Mariner"
that are peculiar to Coleridge (i.e., the figure is "doing something
for Coleridge" that it is not doing for anyone else); yet the introduction of the Albatross, as victim of a crime to motivate the sense
of guilt in the poem, was suggested by Wordsworth. And as Lowes
has shown amply, "The Ancient Mariner" also drew upon legends
as public as those of the Wandering Jew and the fratricide of Cain.
There are many points at which we, as readers, "cut in"—otherwise
the poem would not affect us, would not communicate. But to
grasp the full nature of the symbolic enactment going on in the
poem, we must study the interrelationships disclosable by a study
of Coleridge's mind itself. If a critic prefers to so restrict the rules
of critical analysis that these private elements are excluded, that is
his right. I see no formal or categorical objection to criticism so conceived. But if his interest happens to be in the structure of the
poetic act, he will use everything that is available—and would even
consider it a kind of vandalism to exclude certain material that
Coleridge has left, basing such exclusion upon some conventions as
to the ideal of criticism. The main ideal of criticism, as I conceive
it, is to use all that is there to use. And merely because some ancient
author has left us scant biographical material, I do not see why we
should confine our study of a modern author, who has left us rich
biographical material, to the same coördinates as we should apply
in studying the work of the ancient author. If there is any slogan
that should reign among critical precepts, it is that "circumstances
alter occasions."

However, I shall try to show, later in this essay, that the perspective which I employ can quite naturally include observations as to
the structure of a poem, even considered in isolation, and regardless
of the poem's bearing upon symbolic action peculiar to the poet.

Maybe we could clarify the relation between the public act and
the private act in this way: Suppose that we began by analyzing
the structure of "The Ancient Mariner" as though we did not
know one single detail about the author, and had not one single
other line written by this author. We would note such events as the
peripety in the fourth part, where the water snakes become transubstantiated (removed from the category of the loathsome into
the category of the beautiful and blessed). We would note that the

Mariner suffered his punishments under the aegis of the Sun, and that his cure was effected under the aegis of the Moon. We would have some "equations" to work on, as the Sun is "like God's own head," and the "loon," whose cure began when "the moving Moon went up the sky," was laved by a curative rain that, in ending the state of drought, filled "silly buckets"; and when the Mariner entered the Pilot's boat the Pilot's boy, "who now doth crazy go," called him the Devil. We may also see inklings of a "problem of marriage," in the setting of the poem, and in the closing explicit statement as to a preference for church over marriage.

If we had other poems, we could trail down these equations farther. For instance, we would find the "guilt, Sun at noon, problem of marriage" equations recurring. If we had the letters and introspective jottings, we could by imagistic bridging disclose the part that Coleridge's struggles with his drug played in the "loon, Moon, silly, crazy" equations (as Coleridge in despair speaks of his addiction as idiocy, talks of going to an asylum to be cured, and also employs the snake image with reference to the addiction). Now, if we had the one poem alone, we could note something like a dramatized "problem of metaphysical evil" (much like the basis of *Moby Dick*). Given other poems, we could make this more precise. Given biographical reference, we could also show the part played by his drug addiction and his marital difficulties in giving this general problem explicit content for Coleridge.

This would not vow us to the assertion that "you cannot understand 'The Ancient Mariner' unless you know of Coleridge's drug addiction and marriage problems." You can give a perfectly accurate account of its structure on the basis of the one poem alone. But in studying the full nature of a symbolic act you are entitled, if the material is available, to disclose also the things that the act is doing for the poet and no one else. Such private goads stimulate the artist, yet we may respond to imagery of guilt from totally different private goads of our own. We do not have to be drug addicts to respond to the guilt of a drug addict. The addiction is private, the guilt public. It is in such ways that the private and public areas of a symbolic act at once overlap and diverge. The recording has omitted some of these private ingredients, quite as it has omitted the exact personal way in which Coleridge recited the poem. If we happened to have liked Coleridge's "chaunt," this necessary omis-

sion from the stage directions for its recital is a loss; otherwise, it
is a gain.

Other Words for "Symbolic"

It may have been noted that, while equating "symbolic" with
"statistical," I also brought in another word: "representative." "Statistical" analysis discloses the ways in which a "symbolic" act is
"representative," as Lady Macbeth's washing of her hands after the
crime is "representative" of guilt. This moves us into the matter of
synecdoche, the figure of speech wherein the part is used for the
whole, the whole for the part, the container for the thing contained, the cause for the effect, the effect for the cause, etc. Simplest example: "twenty noses" for "twenty men."

The more I examine both the structure of poetry and the structure of human relations outside of poetry, the more I become
convinced that this is the "basic" figure of speech, and that it
occurs in many modes besides that of the formal trope. I feel it to
be no mere accident of language that we use the same word for
sensory, artistic, and political representation. A tree, for instance, is
an infinity of events—and among these our senses abstract certain
recordings which "represent" the tree. Nor is there any "illusion"
here. In so far as we see correctly, and do not mistake something
else for a tree, our perceptions *do really* represent the tree. Stress
upon synecdochic representation is thus seen to be a necessary ingredient of a truly realistic philosophy (as against a naturalistic
one, that would tend to consider our sensory representations as
"illusory"). As to artistic representation, the term needs no further
comment: the colors and forms in the painting of a tree *represent*
the tree. In theories of politics prevailing at different periods in
history, there have been quarrels as to the precise vessel of authority that is to be considered "representative" of the society as a whole
(chief, nobles, monarch, churchmen, parliamentary delegates, poet,
leader, the majority, the average, the propertied, or the property-
less, etc.) but all agree in assuming that there is *some* part representative of the whole,[2] hence fit to stand for it.

[2] Periods of social crisis occur when an authoritative class, whose purpose
and ideals had been generally considered as *representative* of the total society's purposes and ideals, becomes considered as *antagonistic*. Their class
character, once felt to be a *culminating* part of the whole, is now felt to be
a *divisive* part of the whole.

A "fetish," usually thought of as belonging in a totally different category, is thus seen likewise to be an aspect of the synecdochic function, as when the beloved's shoe is proxy for the beloved. The "scapegoat" becomes another kind of "representative," in serving as the symbolic vessel of certain burdens, which are ritualistically delegated to it. And as regards our speculations upon the nature of "clusters" or "equations," would it not follow that if there are, let us say, seven ingredients composing a cluster, any one of them could be treated as "representing" the rest? It is in this way that such an image as a "house" in a poem can become a "house plus," as it does proxy for the other ingredients that cluster about it (e.g., for the beloved that lives in the house, and is thus "identified" with it). Usually, several of these other ingredients will appear surrounding the one temporarily featured.

Our introduction of the word "identified" suggests also the importance of the *name* as an important aspect of synecdoche (the name as fetishistic representative of the named, as a very revealing part of the same cluster). Thus, such protagonists as "He," or "Man," or "The Poet," or Kafka's "K——" indicate by their very labeling a "problem of identity." And you will often find a change of identity, signalized by a change of name (the "Saul—Paul" reversal, or Coleridge's shift of epithets for his water snakes; Hitler speaks of his early period as a time when he and his group were "nameless," and he proclaims with exulting the later period when they "had names"). Such identification by name has a variant in change of clothes, or a change of surroundings in general, a change of "environmental clothes."[3] Such investing by environment may sometimes enlist the very heavens, as with the change of identity in "The Ancient Mariner" as we move from suffering under the aegis of the Sun to release under the aegis of the Moon. In Aeschylus we have an equally thorough variant, when guilt is transformed into charity (i.e., the Erinyes are renamed the Eumenides).

[3] The thought suggests a possible interpretation of nudism as a symbolic divesting (unclothing) of guilt, a symbolic purification arrived at thus: (1) There has been the hiding of the shameful, hence the clothing of the pudenda as the "essence" of guilt: (2) the covering, as synecdochic representative of the covered, has come to participate in the same set of equations, taking on the same quality or essence, literally "by contagion"; (3) hence, by removing the clothes, one may at the same time ritualistically remove the shame of which the clothes are "representative." The resultant identity is a *social* one, in that the nudists form a colony, but of strongly naturalistic cast.

The synecdochic function may also be revealed in the form of a poem, from the purely technical angle. If event 2, for instance, follows from event 1 and leads into event 3, each of these events may synecdochically represent the others (the interwovenness often being revealed objectively in such processes as "foreshadow-ing"). If the Albatross is put there to be killed, it could be said to "participate in the crime" in the sense that the savage, after a suc-cessful hunt, thanks the quarry for its coöperation in the enterprise. In being placed there as a "motivation" of the Mariner's guilt, its function as something-to-be-murdered is synonymous with its func-tion as incitement-to-murder (recall that among the functions of synecdoche is the substitution of cause for effect and effect for cause). And since "the very deep did rot" as a result of this murder, the Albatross should be expected also to contain, implicitly, by foreshadowing, the substance of the water snakes that grew in this rot. This may explain why the Mariner, who was to kill the Alba-tross, fed it "biscuit worms" (in a later version this fatal incipience was obscured: "It ate the things it ne'er had eat"). In totemic thought, as in the communion service, consubstantiality is got by the eating of food in common. "Tell me what you eat, and I'll tell you what you are." And in the "what you are" there is implicit the "what you will be." Thus, the Albatross names simultaneously its identity, its fate, and the outcome of that fate, in eating a food that is of the same substance as that fate and its outcome. The relation between the slain Albatross and the "thousand thousand slimy things" that grew out of its destruction may be disclosed by some lines from *Remorse*, where another variant of the metaphysical bat-tle between good and evil (and behind it, the battle between the benign and malign effects of opium) is being fought. Ordonio, the villain, speaks:

> Say, I had laid a body in the sun!
> Well! in a month there swarms forth from the corse
> A thousand, nay, ten thousand sentient beings
> In place of that one man.—Say, I had killed him!
> Yet who shall tell me, that each one and all
> Of these ten thousand lives is not as happy,
> As that one life, which being push'd aside,
> Made room for these unnumbered—

Valdez interrupts: "O mere madness!" (we should also note that the epithet "happy" is also applied by the Mariner to the water snakes, as he impulsively sees them in their transubstantiated identity, their evil origin transcended into goodness).

To sum up, as illustration of the way in which these various terms could, for our purposes, all be brought together as aspects of synecdoche: A house lived in by a woman loved, would be "representative" of the woman who was "identified" with it (i.e., it would be in the same "associational cluster" or "set of equations"). As such, it could be a "fetishistic surrogate" for the woman. It could serve as "scapegoat" in that some forbidden impulse of the lover could be enacted vicariously in a "symbolic act" towards the house (as were she virginal, and were he impulsively to break the window in its door). The equations could be disclosed by a "statistical" analysis of the correlations within the imagery, establishing by objective citation "what goes with what." And formally, as foreshadowing in a poem, the breaking of a window at the opening of the poem might *implicitly* contain a scene of rape to be enacted later in the poem.

This last point might go far to explain the increasing proportion of *fragmentary* poems to be noted since the beginning of the nineteenth century. This we should attribute to an increased emphasis upon lyrical associationism, and a decreased emphasis upon rationally extricated dramatic plot (as most clearly revealed in the elaborate *intrigues* that are usually the basis of plot structure in the plays of Shakespeare). We could make the distinction clear in this way: Imagine an author who had laid out a five-act drama of the rational, intricate, intrigue sort—a situation that was wound up at the start, and was to be unwound, step by step, through the five successive acts. Imagine that this plot was scheduled, in Act V, to culminate in a scene of battle. Dramatic consistency would require the playwright to "foreshadow" this battle. Hence, in Act III, he might give us this battle incipiently, or implicitly, in a vigorous battle of words between the antagonists. But since there was much business still to be transacted, in unwinding the plot to its conclusion, he would treat Act III as a mere foreshadowing of Act V, and would proceed with his composition until the promises emergent in Act III had been fulfilled in Act V.

On the other hand, imagine a "lyric" plot that had reduced the intrigue business to a minimum. When the poet had completed Act III, his job would be ended, and despite his intention to write a work in five acts, he might very well feel a loss of inclination to continue into Acts IV and V. For the act of foreshadowing, in Act III, would already *implicitly contain* the culmination of the promises. The battle of words would itself be the *symbolic equivalent* of the mortal combat scheduled for Act V. Hence, it would *serve as surrogate* for the *quality* with which he had intended to end Act V, whereat the poet would have no good reason to continue further. He would "lose interest"—and precisely because the quality of Act V had been "telescoped" into the quality of Act III that foreshadowed it (and in foreshadowing it, was of the same substance or essence). Act III would be a kind of ejaculation too soon, with the purpose of the composition forthwith dwindling.

In *The World's Body*, John Crowe Ransom treats associationism as *dramatic,* citing Shakespeare as an example, in contrast with Donne. That is: Donne continues *one* conceit throughout a poem, whereas Shakespeare leaps about from one image to another, using each to deliver a quick blow and then shifting to fresh images, with none maintained over a long duration, or rationally exploited. It is a very acute and suggestive distinction—though I should want to interpret it differently. Shakespeare, I should say, had the rational intrigue, or business of his plot, as the basis of his consistency. This *permitted* him great shiftiness of imagery, as he tried to convey the quality of the action by views from various angles. Also, I will agree that, in a plot of this sort, the attempt to carry one conceit throughout would be more of an encumbrance than a help. Since the plot itself provided the groundwork of consistency, the explicit riding of one image would attain the effect by excess, which would be tiresome.

Later lyricists (of the non-Donne sort) adopted the Shakespearean associationism while dropping its proper corrective: a plot of pronounced intrigue, or business. But I should want to place Donne in this pattern as follows: His exploitation of *one* metaphor throughout an entire poetic unit was the *equivalent,* in the lyric, for the *plottiness* of drama. It pledged the poet to much *rational business* in the unwinding of the poem's situation.

Thus, I should want to place Shakespeare, Donne, and the romantic lyric with relation to one another as follows: Shakespeare uses rational intrigue with associationism; Donne's lyric compensates for the loss of rational intrigue by using an equivalent, the business of exploiting one metaphor; the romantic lyric uses Shakespeare's associationism without either Shakespears's or Donne's tactics of rational counterweighting. It is "free." However, we should also note that there usually is, even in the free associational procedure, some underlying "key" image that recurs in varying exploitations. Caroline Spurgeon's *Shakespeare's Imagery* has disclosed this practice as an important factor making for consistency of effect in the plays of Shakespeare. And Lane Cooper has done similar work on "The Ancient Mariner," showing the many overt and covert variants of the fixing, magnetic eye that prevail throughout the poem. The surprising thing about Lane Cooper's study, however, is that the critic seems to have been "disillusioned" by his own discovery. He tells of it in the accents of "indictment," where he could with more justice have employed the accents of admiration.

Equations Illustrated in Golden Boy

An especially convenient work to use as illustration of "cluster" or "equations" is Clifford Odets' *Golden Boy,* since it is formed about two opposed principles symbolized as an opposition between "violin" and "prizefight." The total dramatic agon is broken down, by analytic dissociation, into "violin" as the *symbol* of the protagonist and "prizefight" as the *symbol* of the antagonist, with the two symbols competing in an over-all coöperative act, as teams competitively work together to make a game. Here the equations are especially easy to observe, as you find, by statistically charting the course of the plot, that prizefight equals competition, cult of money, leaving home, getting the girl, while violin equals coöperative social unity, disdain of money, staying home, not needing the girl. Obviously, "prizefight" and "violin" don't mean that for all of us. But that is the way the clusters line up, within the conditions of the drama.

I do not wish, at this time, to attempt an exhaustive analysis of the interrelationships peculiar to Odets. I shall simply indicate the kind of "leads" I think one should follow, if he wanted to complete such a chart by "statistical" or "symbolic" analysis. At one point,

Moody says: "Monica, if I had fifty bucks I'd buy myself a big juicy coffin—what?—so throw me in jail." Surely, such an unusual adjective for "coffin" would justify watching. Nothing may come of it; but it is worth noting as a "cue," a hunch that puts us vaguely on the track of something, and that may or may not materialize. Particularly in view of the fact that previously, when the boy's father had presented him with the violin, another character present had remarked: "It looks like a coffin for a baby."[4] Another character makes a speech that proceeds from talk of bad world conditions, to talk of spring, to talk of war, to: "Where's Joe? Did you give him the fiddle yet?" As a "first approximation," this sequence might indicate either that these various subjects "equal" one another, all being consistently part of the same cluster, or that some are compensatory to the others.

When we recall the prizefight-violin opposition, however, we get indications for a "closer approximation" here, as prizefight is in the war cluster by consistency, whereas violin is in the opposing cluster. So, at this point, the hunches begin to take form as follows: That the violin, in its relations to home (it was presented to the boy by his father, against whom his plans to be a fighter are a treachery, and Joe says: "You don't know what it means to sit around here and watch the months go ticking by! Do you think that's a life for a boy of my age? Tomorrow's my birthday! I change my life!"—a *vita nuova* in opposition to the father's ideals)—this violin is "tied up with" death to babies, quite as it is tied up with the continuity of life from pre-adolescence, a period of unity with sexual partner omitted.

Were we to trail down these interrelationships of the playwright's "psychic economy" further, we might, for statistical assistance, borrow help from his other plays. The antagonism between violin and prizefight, for instance, has a common agonistic ground in the fate of the boy's hand, which is broken in the prizefight, thus also ruining him as a violinist. We might then examine Odet's Nazi play for cues, since the theme of the crushed hand also figures there.

---

[4] When someone gives a gift, one may well ask himself what the gift "represents." What is going from the giver to the receiver? What relationship between them is being identified? Or we might put it this way: If the gift were to be accompanied by a verbal compliment, what compliment would be most appropriate?

As for violin, much of the action in *Paradise Lost* takes place to the playing of music off stage. The correspondence between this music and other contents might be got by looking for some common quality of action or speech that runs through all the events on the stage concurrent with the playing off stage (including entrances or exits of characters, a kind of break that often supplies significant cues). Ideally, however, this relation would require us to dig out an explicit "pontification" in Odets that justified us, by objective "scissor-work," as against subjective interpretation, in treating the piano music of *Paradise Lost* as the equivalent of the violin in *Golden Boy*. (As, for instance, were a character to refer to a piano as a "key-fiddle" or to a violin as a "portable piano," or to speak of "fiddling around with the piano.") I leave this analysis unfinished, since I am not now attempting to make an exhaustive analysis of Odets, but simply to illustrate the rules of thumb by which it might proceed.

The "symbolism" of a word consists in the fact that no one quite uses the word in its mere dictionary sense. And the overtones of a usage are revealed "by the company it keeps" in the utterances of a given speaker or writer. Odets' "prizefight" is not Joe Louis's. If you tracked down all interrelations as revealed by the cluster in which a word has active membership, you would dissolve symbolism into an infinity of particulars. The "symbolic" attribute is like the title of a chapter; the particulars are like the details that fill out a chapter. The title is a kind of "first approximation"; the detailed filling-out a kind of "closer approximation."

Levels of Symbolic Action

The various levels of symbolic action that we might look for, in the analysis of poem as enactment, might be categorized as follows:

(1) The bodily or biological level. Kinaesthetic imagery. Symbolic acts of gripping, repelling, eating, excreting, sleeping, waking (insomnia), even and uneven rhythms (pace and puzzle, as tentative thought corresponds somewhat to the arhythmic movements of an experimenter's animal in an unfamiliar maze, while assertive thought corresponds to the thoroughly coördinated movements of an animal that has learned the workings of the maze, and proceeds to freedom without hesitancy).

We may also include sensory imagery here, with natural objects or events treated as replicas of corresponding mental states. Thus, no matter how concrete and realistic the details of a book, they may be found, when taken in the lump, to "symbolize" some over-all quality of experience, as growth, decay, drought, fixity, ice, desiccation, stability, etc. (Contrast the medieval liking for the architectural metaphor, or for the stable tree in familistic descent, with the "America on wheels" emphasis in *The Grapes of Wrath*.)

Note that, by employing such a "level of abstraction," we might properly group works as different in their concrete details as "The Ancient Mariner," *The Waste Land*, the Dos Passos trilogy, and *The Grapes of Wrath*. It should be noted, however, that such a procedure is critically truncated if it stops at the inclusion of various works in a common *genus*. It must proceed to the discussion of the *differentiae*. For it would be absurd, on noting the imagery of drought common to Eliot's poem and Steinbeck's novel, to conclude: "*The Grapes of Wrath* is just *The Waste Land* over again."[5]

(2) The personal, intimate, familiar, familistic level. Relationships to father, mother, doctor, nurse, friends, etc. In the mention of the "family tree" above, we see how the sensory imagery may overlap upon this level. The levels are, in fact, but conveniences of discourse, for analytic purposes, and the actual event in a work of art usually contains an intermingling of them all. And since both a father and a state may be "authorities," we see how readily this personal level merges into a third,

(3) The abstract level. Here we move into the concern with the part played by *insignia* in poetic action, their use by the poet as ways of enrolling himself in a band. Sometimes this kind of symbolic act is explicit, as with "proletarian" school today, where the choice of a certain kind of hero is in itself a kind of "literary vote," a statement of one's "stand."

Sometimes this *"Bundschuh"* ingredient in art is but *implicit*, as with Pope's stylistic ways of enrolling himself with a new propertied class eager for "correctness." His neat couplet served stylistically to get everything "placed" for them; his poetry was perhaps the most sensitive "Book of Etiquette" ever written. It was a

[5] Kinaesthetic imagery is probably more active, sensory imagery ("impressions") more passive. At least, the latter has gained stress under modern sedentary conditions, and its percentage is greatly decreased in work songs and songs for people on the march.

kind of "landscape gardening of the mind"—and in Edgar Johnson's *One Mighty Torrent* we get an almost startling picture of the change in symbolic enrollment that took place as we turned from this deft way of sitting on the lid to the romantic's blowing off the lid—as we turn from landscape gardening of the mind, to an imagery of crags, chasms, volcanoes, earthquakes, cataracts, dizzying vistas, upheavals, and cataclysms.[6]

Here we get a symbolic proclaiming and formation of identity—while again, it is worthy of note, that the romantic movement tended greatly to conceive of man's identity in nonsocial, purely naturalistic terms, specializing in such objective imagery as would most directly correspond in quality with subjective states. It was "neoprimitive" in its notions of rôle, or identity, as against the strong emphasis upon the labels of social status in Pope.

The *formation* of rôle, however, involves, in its working out, a *transformation* of rôle. Even if one would symbolically form a rôle by becoming "most thoroughly and efficiently himself," he must slough off ingredients that are irrelevant to this purpose (ingredients that are "impure," if only in the chemical sense). So we watch, in the structural analysis of the symbolic act, not only the matter of "what equals what," but also the matter of "from what to what." And we detect, under various guises, the abandonment of an old self, in symbolic suicide, parricide, or prolicide.

Psychologists, particularly Otto Rank, have characterized this manifestation of art as the result of a "death wish." But I should contend that this interpretation is not "dialectical" enough. Look closer at poetic examples of the "death wish," and you will see that the symbolic slaying of an old self is complemented by the

[6] Think of Joseph and Josephine, a married couple, engaged in a caricatured quarrel. Josephine, in anger, seizes a plate and sends it smashing to the floor. This may sober Joseph. He may say, "Come now. This is going too far. Let's try to contain ourselves and talk the matter over." In this he would speak with the voice of Pope and Pope's etiquette. Or Joseph might respond quite differently, by "transcending" the old rules, as he seized a dozen plates, muttering, "So that's what we're in for! Plate smashing! Very well—here's going you a lot better!" whereat he splintered the whole dozen, and did a very thorough job of it. Joseph here would speak with the voice of romanticism. He would change the rules, and burn out temptation by efficient excess of it. He would start himself and Josephine on an uncompromising journey "to the end of the line," as Josephine's rejoinder was to smash more efficiently still, and he in his repartee again outbid her, and so on, progressively.

emergence of a new self. In fact, even though every action and person in the plot led downwards, we should find an assertion of identity in the constructive act of the poem itself. I should want to treat even suicide in real life as but the act of rebirth reduced to its simplest and most restricted form (its least complex idiom of expression).

But however one may feel about that point, the act of will in poetic organization justifies our claim that a *symbolic* suicide (on the page) is an *assertion*, the *building* of a rôle and not merely the abandonment of oneself to the disintegration of all rôles. True, the rôle that is so built may, by social tests, not be a very wholesome one—and in much contemporary art, introducing into the act of poetic construction itself an aesthetic of disintegration unmatched by an aesthetic of reintegration, we come close, even in the poem, to a "pure" suicide. Rather, we come *closer* than in most art of the past; but there is still an appreciable margin of difference, inherent in the act of composition itself. Implicit in poetic organization *per se* there is the assertion of an identity. . . .

Part Three

THE FUNCTION OF POETRY

Poetry and Reality

This act which arises from a source deep in the psyche of the poet, which makes complex use of the resources of language—what is its bearing on reality? A human creation, imaginary, fictive, not "real"—what does the poem do for inhabitants of the "real" world? The question is one expression of the more general problem of art and life, of their relation to each other; it is vividly put by Pedro Salinas in a short passage from Reality and the Poet in Spanish Poetry. *Poems, he says, are "luminous shadows" created when the poet places himself before the radiant "light of life." But what is this light which shadows give?*

Some answers have already been proposed or implied in the essays we have examined. Herbert Read, for example, held that poetry materializes our deepest instinctual life; A. C. Bradley, that it satisfies the imagination while promising some ultimate satisfaction; Philip Wheelwright, that it provides a non-scientific kind of knowledge. But when such suggestions appeared, the writer's attention was focused on other matters. In Part Three theorists address themselves directly to the function of poetry.

PEDRO SALINAS

From *Reality and the Poet in Spanish Poetry*

I propose to discuss, in these lectures, the attitude of the poet toward reality throughout Spanish poetry. I must add at once that I am using the word reality in a general and comprehensive sense: by it I mean all that lives outside of the poet, the material world which surrounds him,

things, society, beings, all of life from a blade of grass to a moral
doctrine elaborated over centuries. Reality, the life of the world
that surrounds and limits us, that gives to the individual the measure, at once tragic and magnificent, of his own solitude and of his
creative possibilities. Perhaps I should say too, to avoid confusion,
that I am not referring to the so-called Spanish realism, although
some of the inferences to be drawn from my opinions may apply to
it. No, what I intend to consider here is a problem which I think
should be the first to be examined in connection with every poet:
the relation between his poetic world and the real world, the contact between external reality and his own inner, spiritual reality.

The poet is born into a world that is already made, amid a reality
that is given to him and that forces itself upon him. If each poet
were given the world in a plastic state, he would mold it in his own
way and we could not even be sure that summer would come after
spring. But fortunately the world is already made. And yet at the
same time constantly to be made. The poet has as his object the
creation of a new reality within the old reality. How will these two
worlds come together, meet, how can they agree? On the one hand
a magnificent world, the material world, imperial with the majesty
of sun and mountain, with the delicacy of the shell or the dragon-
fly, imperial external reality. And on the other, a small spark, full
of mystery and longing, flickering in a human mind that wants to
use that outer reality only as a point of departure, as a springboard
to the other reality within him. For me, poetry is nothing but the
aggregate of relations between this psychological reality, strange
and abnormal, the poetic soul, so exceptional and clairvoyant, and
external reality, usual and ordinary, the reality of the outside world.
And so, for me, the first thing that characterizes a poet is his way
of perceiving reality, of according his own with that outer reality,
in short, his attitude toward the world, which from his birth, surrounds him.

Reality is indispensable to the poet, but it alone is not enough.
The real is a raw state. The world is a possibility, but it is incomplete and perfectible. Keats in a letter, in speaking of the beauty
of a morning which tempts one to idle it away, writes: "The morning was right." And Guillén says: "The world is well made." What
does this mean? Simply that reality must be revised, confirmed,
approved by the poet. And he confirms or re-creates it by means of

a word, by merely putting it into words. It is the poet's gift to name realities fully, to draw them out of that enormous mass of the anonymous. The poet who first sang the rose, in christening it, in naming it, gave it a new distinct life. Language itself is poetry. And the poet is therefore the one who uses languages best, who utilizes most completely its power of giving life to the anonymous, of giving a reality distinct and poetic to indistinct, crude reality. It is an error to say that the poet does not live in reality: he lives in it more than anyone else, more than the banker or doctor. It hurts him more, for he is peculiarly sensitive to it. The poet reacts to reality pretty much as the human organism reacts to air: man breathes in air, without which he cannot live, and so does the poet reality. Here then are two existing real things: lungs and air. How do they behave? The poet absorbs reality but in absorbing it reacts against it; and just as the air is breathed out after undergoing a chemical change in the lungs, reality is also returned to the world, transformed, in one way or another, by a poetic operation.

Poetry always operates on reality. The poet places himself before reality like a human body before light, in order to create something else, a shadow. The shadow is the result of the interposition of the body between light and some other substance. The poet adds shadows to the world, bright and luminous shadows, like new lights. All poetry operates on one reality for the sake of creating another. It cannot operate on a vacuum. So that the way a poet places himself, interposes himself between the radiant light of life and life itself will determine his peculiar way of being, his quality, that is, the form, the personality of his shadow. Nothing is complete without its shadow. Ever since the beginning of time poets have been creating realities of utmost purity, marvelous reflections, just as a tree in early spring covers a white wall with immaterial leaves of new springs taken from the real spring. Those who do not love shadows should never open a book of poetry. Things abound for those who prefer their concrete, raw substance. Let them eat, drink, embrace, touch. But when the enjoyment derived from embracing and touching material things is ended, another remains: the possession of a higher reality, raised to its ultimate impalpable category, shadows, the pure and luminous forms of the spirit.

Let us see now how some poets stand before the light called reality and then we shall know to what shadows they give eternal life. For that is the ultimate miracle of poetry: that matter dies, perishes, while the shadows remain and endure forever. That is why I intend to study Spanish poetry by observing the poetic attitude that our poets have taken toward reality.

Poetry as Knowledge

With Wheelwright, Allen Tate questions the
notion that poetry's value as truth is incidental or negligible. But
Tate's argument takes a different route. Whereas Wheelwright proposes a language for communicating experiences which do not lend
themselves to the language of science, Tate examines various efforts to
separate the pleasures of poetry from its truth and finds them wanting.
If the subject and the language of poetry are one—here he echoes
Bradley's unity of "form" and "substance"—if its meaning is inseparable from its words, its pleasure is not to be divorced from its truth.
Tate says that the knowledge which poetry gives is "complete" and
that this completeness is "not of the experimental order, but of the experienced order," "of the mythical order." But he refuses to subject this
completeness to a conclusive definition. It is for him, finally, a problem
"to be preserved."

Without dispelling the mystery on which Tate insists, Archibald
MacLeish offers a useable definition of poetic knowledge and a reasonable explanation of the means whereby it is communicated. Most contemporary theory finds that either symbol or metaphor is the poet's central instrument. MacLeish insists upon something more fundamental
and fundamental to both: coupled images. When the poet sets dis-
similar elements of experience side by side, when he couples images, he
stirs us, says MacLeish, to glimpse the unity which underlies all things.
Our perception of this "universal analogy" makes sense of our experience, and makes sense directly—not by translation, not in other
terms, but in the very terms of that experience. In thus tracing the
meaning of poetry to an all-encompassing relation, MacLeish develops
Bradley's suggestion that poetry promises some ultimate perfection.
And he illuminates Tate's assertion, cryptic but deliberate, that the
knowledge which poetry provides is "complete."

ALLEN TATE

Literature as Knowledge

Comment and Comparison

Matthew Arnold's war on the Philistines was fought, as everybody knows; but nobody thinks that it was won. Arnold conducted it in what he considered to be the scientific spirit. The Philistines had a passion for "acting and instituting," but they did not know "what we ought to act and to institute." This sort of knowledge must be founded upon "the scientific passion for knowing." But it must not stop there. Culture, which is the study of perfection and the constant effort to achieve it, is superior to the scientific spirit because it includes and passes beyond it. Arnold was, in short, looking for a principle of unity, but it must be a unity of experience. There was before him the accumulating body of the inert, descriptive facts of science, and something had to be done about it.

Yet if it is true, as T. S. Eliot said many years ago, that were Arnold to come back he would have his work to do over again, he would at any rate have to do it very differently. His program, culture added to science and perhaps correcting it, has been our program for nearly a century, and it has not worked. For the facts of science are not inert facts waiting for the poet, as emblematic guardian of culture, to bring to life in the nicely cooperative enterprise of scientist and poet which the nineteenth century puts its faith in. In this view the poet is merely the scientist who achieves completeness. "It is a result of no little culture," Arnold says, "to attain to a clear perception that science and religion are two wholly different things." Religion had yielded to the "fact" of science, but poetry on a positive scientific base could take over the work of religion, and its future was "immense." The "fact" had undermined religion, but it could support poetry.

Although Arnold betrayed not a little uneasiness about this easy solution, it was his way of putting literature upon an equal footing with science. If Arnold failed, can we hope to succeed? Whether literature and science considered philosophically, as Coleridge would phrase it, are the same thing, or different but equal, or the one subordinate to the other, has become a private question. It does not concern the public at large. While Arnold's poet was extending the hand of fellowship to the scientist, the scientist did not return the greeting; for never for an instant did he see himself as the inert and useful partner in an enterprise of which he would not be permitted to define the entire scope. He was not, alas, confined to the inertia of fact; his procedure was dynamic all along; and it was animated by the confident spirit of positivism which has since captured the modern world.

Had he been what Arnold thought he was, how conveniently the partnership would have worked! For what was Arnold's scientist doing? He was giving us exact observation and description of the external world. The poet could give us that, and he could add to it exact observation and description of man's inner life, a realm that the positivist would never be so bold as to invade. But the poet's advantage was actually twofold. Not only did he have this inner field of experience denied to the scientist, he had a resource which was his peculiar and hereditary right—figurative language and the power of rhetoric.

If the inert fact alone could not move us, poetic diction could make it moving by heightening it; for poetry is "thought and art in one." This is an injustice to Arnold; he was a great critic of ideas, of currents of ideas, of the situation of the writer in his time; and from this point of view his theory of poetry is of secondary importance. But since I am now interested in the failure, ours as well as his, to understand the relation of poetry and science, it has been necessary to put his poetic theory in terms that will bring out its defects. On one side it is an eighteenth-century view of poetic language as the rhetorical vehicle of ideas; and it is connected with Arnold's famous definition of religion as "morality touched with emotion." Poetry is descriptive science or experience at that level, touched with emotion.

If Arnold had taste, he had very simple analytical powers, and we are never quite convinced by his fine quotations from the poets. Why is this so? Because he admires good things for bad reasons; or because at any rate his reasons invariably beg the question. In the famous passage on Dryden and Pope in "The Study of Poetry," these poets are not poetic because they are not *poetic*. (Arnold himself is responsible for the italics.) And he looks to us for immediate assent to a distinction between a "prose" classic and a "poetic" classic that has not been actually made. He cites his "touchstones" for the purpose of moving us, and the nice discrimination of feeling which awareness of the touchstones induces will permit us to judge other passages of verse in terms of feeling. The "high seriousness" is partly the elevated tone, a tone which is a quality of the poet's feeling about his subject: it is the poet's business to communicate it to the reader.

This attitude, this tone, centers in emotion. But its relation to what it is about, whether it is external to the subject or inherent in it, Arnold refuses to make clear. The high seriousness may be said to reflect the subject, which must have Aristotelian magnitude and completeness. Arnold had a shrewd sense of the disproportions of tone and subject which he developed into a principle in the Preface to the 1853 edition of his poems. He was suppressing the very fine "Empedocles on Aetna" because, he said, it has no action; it is all passive suffering; and passive suffering is not a proper subject for poetry. (A view that has been revived in our time by the late W. B. Yeats.) Action, then, is the subject of the greatest poetry. This conviction is so strong—who will question its rightness, *as far as it goes?*—that he actually puts into quotation marks words which are not quoted from anybody at all but which represent for him the consensus of the ancients on the importance of action: " 'All depends upon the subject; choose a fitting action, penetrate yourself with the feeling of its situations; this done, everything else will follow.' " But will everything else follow? Does a great style follow? To a gift for action Shakespeare "added a special one of his own; a gift, namely, of happy, abundant, and ingenious expression. . . ." I think we should attend closely here to the words "added" and "ingenious," for they reveal Arnold's view of the function of language. And suppose you have lyric poetry which may be, like Arnold's own fine lyrics, more meditative than dramatic, and more concerned with the futility of action than with action itself? It has never, I believe, been pointed out that the Preface of 1853 cuts all the props from under lyric poetry. The lyric at its best is "dramatic," but there is no evidence that Arnold thought it so; for the lyric, though it may be a moment of action, lacks magnitude and completeness; it may be the beginning, or the middle, or the end, but never all three. What, then, is the subject of the lyric? Is it all feeling, nothing but feeling? It is feeling about "ideas," not actions; and the feeling communicates "power and joy."

This gross summary of Arnold's poetics omits all the sensitive discriminations that he felt in reading the poets; it omits all but the framework of his thought. Yet the framework alone must concern us on this occasion. Arnold is still the great critical influence in the universities, and it is perhaps not an exaggeration of his influence to say that debased Arnold is the main stream of popular appreciation of poetry. It would be fairer to say that Arnold the critic was superior to his critical theory; yet at the distance of three generations we may look back upon his lack of a critical dialectic—he even had a certain contempt for it in other critics—as a calamity for that culture which it was his great desire to strengthen and pass on.

His critical theory was elementary, and if you compare him with Coleridge a generation earlier, he represents a loss. His position is nearer to the neo-classicism of Lessing, whom he praises in *Culture and Anarchy* for humanizing knowledge, a leveling-off of distinctions of which Lessing as a matter of fact was not guilty. He shares with Lessing the belief—but not its dialectical basis—that the language of poetry is of secondary importance to the subject, that it is less difficult than the medium of painting, and that, given the action, all else follows.

This remnant of neo-classicism in Arnold has been ably discerned by Mr. Cleanth Brooks in *Modern Poetry and the Tradition*. I go into it here not to deny that action is necessary to the long poem; for Arnold's view contains a fundamental truth. But it is not the whole truth; asserted in his terms, it may not be a truth at all. The important question goes further. It is: What is the relation of language to the "subject," to the dramatic and narrative subject as action, or to the lyrical subject as "idea"? The question may be pushed even further: Is it possible finally to distinguish the language from the subject? Are not subject and language one?

For Arnold the subject is what we commonly call the prose subject; that is to say, as much of the poetic subject as we can put into ordinary prose. The poet takes it up at the level at which the scientist—or Arnold's simulacrum of him—takes it: the level of observation and description. The poet now puts it into language that will bring the inert facts to life and move us. The language is strictly what Mr. Richards calls the "vehicle"—it does not embody the subject; it conveys it and remains external to it.

For what are action and subject? The positivists have their own notion of these terms; and their language of physical determinism suits that notion better than the poet's. The poet's language is useless.

II

Is it not easy to see how such a poetics gives the case for poetry away to the scientist? Not to Arnold's straw scientist, who politely kept to his descriptive place and left to literature man's evaluation of his experience; but to the scientist as he is: a remarkably ingenious and dynamic fellow whose simple fanaticism brooks no compromise with his special projects. Whatever these on occasion may be, he demands an exact one-to-one relevance of language to the objects and the events to which it refers. In this relevance lies the "meaning" of all terms and propositions in so far as they are used for the purpose of giving us valid knowledge. It is, of course, knowledge for action; and apart from this specific purpose, the problem of meaning is not even a real problem.

"Meaning has been replaced by a concept of "operational validity"; that is to say, the "true" meaning of a term is not its definition, it is the number of statements containing it which can be referred to empirically observed events. Along with meaning and definition, universals also disappear; and with universals, cognition. A proposition does not represent an act of knowing by a knower—that is, a mind; it is, in a chemical metaphor, the expression of an interaction among certain elements of a "situation."

This advanced position in the philosophy of science has been set forth in the new *International Encyclopedia of Unified Science,* which is being published serially at the University of Chicago. Of great interest from the point of view of literary criticism are the brilliant studies of "semiosis," or the functioning of language as "signs." Mr. Charles W. Morris' "Foundations for the Theory of Signs,"[1] is a model of exact exposition in a field of enormous complication. This field is popularly known as "semantics," but seman-

[1] *International Encyclopedia of Unified Science,* Vol. I, No. 2 (Chicago, 1938).

tics in any exact sense is only one "dimension" of semiosis. In this brief glance at the aesthetic and critical implications of Mr. Morris' writings, his theory as a whole cannot be set forth.

Semiosis is the actual functioning of language in three dimensions, which are located and described by means of the science of "semiotic." Semiotic, then, is the study of semiosis. The three dimensions in which all language, verbal, or mathematical, functions are: (1) the semantical, (2) the syntactical, and (3) the pragmatical; and the respective studies in these dimensions are semantics, syntactics, and pragmatics. It must be borne in mind that in semiosis the three dimensions are never separate; in semiotic they are distinguished abstractly for study. Semiotic looks towards the formation of rules which will govern the use of all language (signs), and it lays claim to an ultimate unification of all "knowledge."

That need not concern us here. Let us take a simple declarative sentence: "This county has an annual rainfall of fifty-one inches." From the semantical point of view the sentence designates certain conditions, or a situation: it is the "sign-vehicle" for that designation. If upon investigation we find that the situation actually exists, then it has not only been designated; it has also been *denoted*. From the syntactical point of view we are not concerned with what the sign-vehicle points to; for syntactics deals with the formal structure of the sentence, the relations of the words. From the pragmatical point of view the meaning of the sentence is the effect it has upon somebody who hears it or reads it. If I am about to buy a farm in this county, and learn that "this county has an annual rainfall of fifty-one inches," I may go elsewhere; at the moment I hear the sentence I may light a cigarette, or look the other way, or laugh, or swear. All this behavior would be the functioning of the sign in the pragmatic dimension.

The complex possibilities of semiotic may not be evident in this crude summary. Mr. Morris says: "The sign vehicle itself is simply one object." It is an object that may function in other sign-vehicles; it may be designated, denoted, or reacted to; and the process is infinite. The identification of signs and their relations is equally complex. There are, for example, a characterizing sign, a symbolic sign, an indexical sign, and an iconic sign; and any of these, in certain contexts, may function as any other. I shall return to them presently.

The only philosophic criticism of this system that I have seen is Howard D. Roelofs' article in the symposium on the "New Encyclopedists," published in the *Kenyon Review* (Spring 1939). Mr. Roelofs is concerned with Mr. Morris' rejection of the problem of universals and of cognition. It ought to be plain from my brief exposition of the pragmatic dimension of semiosis that the significant factor is what I *do*, not what I *think* leading to what I do; and that thus the bias of the science of semiotic is pragmatic in the ordinary sense, and even behavioristic. For Mr. Morris says: "A 'concept' [i.e., a universal] may be regarded as a semantical rule determining the use of characterizing signs." Mr. Roelofs' comment is interesting:

> Morris has no trouble with this problem [i.e., the problem of universals]. It is simply a rule of our language that such a term as "man" can be used as often as the conditions stated in its definitions are fulfilled. That makes the term a universal. If we then ask how it happens those conditions are in fact frequently fulfilled, we are informed, "It can only be said the world is such." And those who are tempted by this fact to believe that universals are somehow objective, functioning in nature, are silenced with a threat: to talk as if universals were entities in the world is "to utter pseudo-thing sentences of the quasi-semantical type." . . . the heart of the problem is dismissed with a phrase and a language rule offered as a solution.

The bearing of Mr. Roelofs' criticism will be plainer in a moment. Now Mr. Morris, in discussing the syntactical dimension, says: "Syntactics, as the study of the syntactical relations of signs to one another *in abstraction* from the relations of signs to objects or to interpreters [persons], is the best developed of all the branches of semiotic." Exactly; because syntactics comes out of traditional formal logic and grammar, and because it "deliberately neglects what has here been called the semantical and the pragmatical dimensions of semiosis."

The role of syntactics in the semiotic science remains somewhat obscure; it seems to consist in a number of "transformation rules"— that is, in formulas by which given expressions in words, numbers, or symbols can be changed into equivalent but formally different expressions. What power of the mind there may be which enables us in the first place to form these expressions nowhere appears. (I daresay this statement is of the quasi-semantical type.) But Mr.

Morris tells us how we are to think of the rules of the three dimensions of semiotic:

> Syntactical rules determine the sign relations between sign vehicles; semantical rules correlate sign vehicles with other objects; pragmatical rules state the conditions in the interpreters under which the sign vehicle is a sign. Any rule when actually in use operates as a type of behavior, and in this sense there is a pragmatical component in all rules.

If we imagine with Mr. Roelofs a situation in which semiosis is functioning, we shall see pretty clearly the behavioristic tendency of the science of semiotic; and we shall also see in what sense "there is a pragmatical component in all rules." A simplified process of semiosis, or the actual functioning of signs, is very easy to state. There is first of all the sign, which we get in terms of a sign-vehicle. It looks two ways; first, it points to something, designates something; and, secondly, what is designated elicits a response from persons who are present. The thing pointed to is thus the *designatum;* the response is the *interpretant.* By implication there is an interpreter, a person, a mind; but Mr. Morris is consistently vague about him: he is not a technical factor, he is a superfluous entity, in semiosis. That is to say, not only is he not needed in order to explain the functioning of signs; he would embarrass the explanation. Mr. Roelofs makes this clear, as follows:

> The innocent reader will take the analysis of the use of signs to be the analysis of a cognitive process. The correctness of the analysis as far as it goes conceals the fact that cognition itself has been eliminated. Consider the illustration. A maid enters the room and says to the three persons present, "The doctor called." One person thereupon takes a pen and writes a line in a diary; the second goes to a telephone and makes a call; the third says, "Did he?" According to the analysis offered by Morris, the words uttered by the maid are the sign-vehicle. The actual call of the doctor is the denotatum.[2] The three persons are the interpreters, and their three different actions are the interpretants, the responses of the interpreters to the denotatum via the sign-vehicle. No one is likely to deny these factors are present. It should be noted that the interpretants, to the extent that they are a sequence of physical actions, can be perceived.

[2] *Denotata* are real things: *designata* may be pointed to, but they are not necessarily real. For example, the Phoenix' "spicy nest." The doctor's call is a *designatum* which is also a *denotatum*—it's "real."

It should also be noted that such sequences of action are not cognitions . . . they are "interpretants," but their being such depends
upon the cognitions of the interpreters. These responses are not
themselves knowledge. They do depend upon knowledge, and that
is precisely what Morris leaves out. . . . Morris objects to the term
"meaning." This is not surprising. His analysis leaves out meaning in
the primary sense of meaning. This is not to say that meanings are
"like marbles" [Morris' phrase]. Meanings, indeed, like knowledge
in general, are a unique kind of thing. There is literally nothing
like knowledge except knowledge itself.

I have quoted Mr. Roelofs at length because what he has to say
about the problem of cognition bears directly upon the semiotic
version of the aesthetic problem. He sums up his argument:

The procedure culminates in eliminating not only universals, but
cognition itself. Just as the answer to the problem of universals is
that they do not exist [that is, they are only a semantical rule], the
answer to the problem of knowledge is that there is no such thing.
There are responses, but no cognition; there is a language, but not
knowledge. Knowledge cannot be reduced to exclusively perceptual
terms. Therefore it does not exist. This is not empiricism. *It is positivism.* [Italic mine.]

In this positivist technique for the analysis of language, the interpreting mind, the cognizing intelligence, is lost in the perceptual
account of its external behavior. Mr. Morris says: "In general, from
the point of view of behavior, signs are 'true' in so far as they correctly determine the expectations of the users, and so release more
fully the behavior which is implicitly aroused in the expectation
or interpretation."

In Mr. Morris' aesthetics there is an aesthetic sign. Does it implicitly—or explicitly—arouse expectations in terms of behavior?
Does it correctly determine our expectations? Is the aesthetic sign
"true" in that it is a determinant of our behavior? Mr. Morris is
not unequivocal in his answers to these questions.

III

No—and yes, replies Mr. Morris, in two essays[3] the cunning and
scholastic ingenuity of which make even the beautiful essay on the

[3] "Esthetics and the Theory of Signs," *The Journal of Unified Science,*
VIII, 1-3, pp. 131-150; and "Science, Art, and Technology," *The Kenyon
Review,* I, 4, pp. 409-423.

general theory of signs look amateurish. No, he says, because the aesthetic sign is a special sort of sign: it is *iconic*. It does not correctly determine our behavior. Yes, because it bears the formidable responsibility of showing us what we ought to try to get out of our behavior. The function of the aesthetic sign is nothing less than the "vivid presentation" of *values*, a presentation that is not only vivid, but *immediate*—without mediation—for direct apprehension. The iconic sign, in other words, designates without denoting; or if it does denote anything its *denotatum* is already in its own "properties." "In certain kinds of insanity," writes Mr. Morris, "the distinction between the designatum and the denotatum vanishes; the troublesome world of existences is pushed aside, and the frustrated *interests* [italics mine] get what satisfaction they can in the domain of signs. . . ." Likewise *designata* and *denotata* become in aesthetics the same thing; but in this logical shuffle, worthy of a thirteenth-century *doctor subtilis*, the aesthetic sign is never confused "with the object it designates." It is that alone which saves it from the ignominy of insanity.

The difficulties of this theory must already be apparent. First, the difference between insanity and art is the hair's-breadth line, in the interpreter's response to the sign, between substituting the sign for reality and maintaining the distinction between sign and reality. The first question that one must ask, then, is this: With what does the interpreter make this distinction? If the distinction is not inherent in the nature of the sign, does the interpreter not perform an act of cognition? If the distinction is a mere interpretant, a behavioristic response, why do we not respond to a work of art uniformly; and why is that uniform response in every case not insane *unless we are capable of a primary act of knowledge*, of simply knowing the difference?

Secondly, if art is the realm of values—that is, if the peculiar nature of the aesthetic sign is that it shall convey values—the values must be inherent in the aesthetic sign, and must therefore compel in the interpreter the distinction between value and insanity; so that there is no possibility that the interpreter, who is incapable of cognition, will confuse the mere sign with reality. For the nature of the sign must determine the interpretant, or response.

There must therefore be a special "differentia" for the aesthetic sign that distinguishes it from all other signs whatever. "Lyric

poetry," Mr. Morris says, "has a syntax and uses terms which designate things, but the syntax and the terms are so used that what
stand out for the reader are values and evaluations."[4] Does not Mr.
Morris confess his difficulty when he uses the vague metaphorical
expression "stand out" and the even more vague "so used"? Just
what is this use? It is significant that in Mr. Morris' two articles on
aesthetics, in which the word poetry frequently appears, there is no
actual analysis of a passage or even of a line of verse; and not even
a quotation from any poem in any language. He contents himself
with assertions that the future of semiotic in the field of poetry is
immense, and that only the work has to be done.

Now, if the contradiction that I have pointed out in general
terms exists, we may see its origin if we examine further Mr. Morris' idea of the aesthetic sign. It is a special variety of the iconic
sign. To illustrate this it will be sufficient to relate the iconic to
the characterizing sign, and to distinguish the icon from the
symbol.

> A characterizing sign [he says] characterizes that which it can de-
> note. Such a sign may do this by exhibiting in itself the properties
> an object must have to be denoted by it, and in this case the charac-
> terizing sign is an *icon;* if this is not so, the characterizing sign may
> be called a *symbol.* A photograph, a star chart, a model, a chemical
> diagram, are icons, while the word "photographed," the names of
> the stars and of chemical elements are symbols.

The terminology is quite special. Icon is the Greek ($\epsilon\iota\kappa\acute{\omega}\nu$) for
a sculptured figure. Ordinarily a symbol is what Mr. Morris claims
for the icon: it exhibits in itself the qualities it stands for—like
Christ on the Cross; or it represents by convention something other
than itself, like πr^2 for the circumference of a circle. But here the
terms are roughly equivalent, icon to image, symbol to concept;
but only roughly, since in Mr. Morris' list of symbols "photograph"
is not any particular photograph, while the name of a star must be
the name of a particular star. There is a fundamental obscurity,
that we shall have to pass over, in attributing to verbal language
a thoroughly *iconic* property. In the list of icons, there are *a* photograph, *a* star chart, *a* model, *a* chemical diagram—all of them spatial
and perceptual objects; but, while language is always used in a

---

[4] "Foundations for the Theory of Signs," *loc. cit.,* p. 58.

spatial setting, words appear in temporal sequence, and have only the spatial character of their occasion. We cannot *see* the properties of words in the words. We have simply got to know *what* the words convey. The phrase "a star chart" is not a star chart itself. Mr. Morris appears to have found in the term *icon,* at any rate so far as it pertains to aesthetics, merely a convenient evasion of the term *image;* for image would doubtless have held him to the old onto-logical aesthetics.

The essay "Esthetics and the Theory of Signs" deals with the specific problem "of stating the differentia of the esthetic sign." Mr. Morris is constantly reminding us that iconic signs appear in all discourse, and that all discourse is by no means aesthetic dis-course. Yet the special function of the iconic sign makes it possible for us to use it as the aesthetic sign; and that function is stated in a "semantical rule":

> The semantical rule for the use of an iconic sign is that it denotes any object which has the properties (in practice, a selection from the properties) which it itself has. Hence when an interpreter appre-hends an iconic sign-vehicle he apprehends directly what is desig-nated; here mediated and unmediated taking account of certain prop-erties both occur;[5] put in still other terms, every iconic sign has its own sign-vehicle among its denotata.

This is a difficult conception; perhaps it can be illustrated with a few lines of verse:

> That time of year thou mayst in me behold
> When yellow leaves, or none, or few do hang
> Upon those boughs which shake against the cold . . .

According to Mr. Morris, the sign-vehicle here would be the leaves hanging on the boughs. This verbal sign-vehicle has the "proper-ties" of the natural objects which it designates; and that which it denotes is in the designation itself. That is, leaves-bough does not point to a definite situation or condition beyond itself: we get "directly what is designated" because it is of the nature of the iconic sign to contain its own *denotatum.* (I have simplified this analysis by ignoring "That time of year," which I believe would make it impossible to apply Mr. Morris' terms coherently.)

[5] There seems to be evidence in this clause that Mr. Morris is not interested in syntactics.

The treatment of the iconic sign in semiotic is mysterious. If any generalization about it is legitimate, we may surmise that certain terms, which Mr. Morris calls "primary terms," are untranslatable; that is to say, they cannot be handled by any principle of reduction; they have a certain completeness and finality. They denote themselves; certain iconic signs seem to be such terms. They are sign-vehicles for images, and our apprehension of them is direct. For while the iconic sign may denote something beyond itself, its specific character as an iconic sign is that part of what it denotes is the sign itself. "These facts," says Mr. Morris, "taken alone, do not delimit the esthetic sign, for blueprints, photographs, and scientific models are all iconic signs—but seldom works of art." He continues in a passage of great interest:

> If, however, the designatum of an iconic sign be a *value* [italic mine] (and of course not all iconic signs designate values), the situation is changed: there is now not merely the designation of value properties (for such designation takes place even in science), nor merely the functioning of iconic signs (for these as such need not be esthetic signs), but there is the direct apprehension of value properties through the very presence of that which itself has the value it designates.

There are thus three steps in the "delimitation" of the aesthetic sign: First, it is an iconic sign; secondly, it is an iconic sign which designates a value; thirdly, it is an iconic sign which designates a value in the sign itself, so that our "apprehension" of that value is unmediated, that is, *direct*.

The difficulties created by this aesthetic doctrine are slippery and ambiguous. We may, for convenience, see them in two ways. The first set of problems lies in the term "apprehension"; the second, in the term "value."

The primary meaning of apprehension is a grasping or a taking hold of. What does Mr. Morris mean? If it means taking hold of by means of perception, we are asked to see ourselves *perceiving a value*; but a value cannot be an object of perception. If, however, apprehension means a direct, unmediated knowledge of a value, then there is an act of evaluation involved which implies the presence of a knowing mind. For the implied "semantical rule" for the aesthetic sign obviously forbids us to check the value wholly in terms of a situation external to the properties of the sign itself. We have got to *know* the value in itself; and only in an act of cognition can we know it. But if Mr. Morris means by apprehension the response, or mere "interpretant," of semiosis, it is difficult to see how a mere response can be semantically correct unless the sign-vehicle points to a situation outside itself in terms of which the response is relevant. If there is no such situation, is not the interpretant a piece of insanity?

I cannot see how there can be any direct apprehension unless there is an agency to do the apprehending; and the interpretant is not an agent, it is a response. "One additional point may be noted to confirm the sign status of the work of art: The artist often draws attention to the sign-vehicle in such a way as to prevent the interpreter from merely reacting to it as an object and not as a sign. . . ." Mr. Morris' phrases, "in such a way," "so used that," remain painfully evasive. What is that way? Now, if the preventive factor is inherent in the work of art, why did not the birds refrain from trying to eat the grapes in Zeuxis' picture? The citizens of Athens did not mistake the sign-vehicle for an object. Why? Because they *knew* the difference.

Mr. Morris' theory of value will further illuminate his difficulty. It is an "interest" theory of value for which he acknowledges an indebtedness to the pragmatic tradition of Mead and Dewey. Objects, according to this ancient theory, have value in relation to interest. "Values," says Mr. Morris, "are consummatory properties of objects or situations which answer to the consummation of interested acts." If I satisfy my hunger by eating a banana, the banana has value in relation to the specific interest, hunger. Does it follow that we have similar aesthetic interest, which we similarly satisfy? No specific aesthetic interest appears in semiosis. The aesthetic satisfaction proceeds from the frustration of "real" interests, from the blockage of interests as they drive onward to real "consummations." The aesthetic sign is a value that has not been consummated. Art is the expression of what men desire but are not getting.

There are two passages in "Esthetics and the Theory of Signs" which reveal the fundamental ambiguity in Mr. Morris' conception of the aesthetic sign as a "value." We shall be struck, I believe, by the remarkable parallel between Mr. Morris' view of the aesthetic medium and the neo-classical view, which we saw in Matthew Arnold.

> Even though the complexity of the total icon is so very great that no denotatum (other than the esthetic sign vehicle itself) can in actuality be found, the work of art can still be considered a sign—for there can be designation without denotation.

But can the aesthetic sign—and this is the center of the problem—designate an interest "value" if it does not point to an interest? It seems to me that it cannot be a value in any "interest" theory of value whatever. And when the aesthetic sign is so complex that it does not lead to denotation, is not this complexity a semantical failure so great that Mr. Morris actually ought to take it to an institution for the insane?

The traditional prestige of the arts is formidable; so, rather than commit himself to his logic of the aesthetic sign as a designation of a value which cannot be located and which thus cannot be an interest-value, he offers us the ordinary procedure of positivism; that is to say, he shows us how we may reduce the aesthetic sign to a *denotatum* after all.

> Since a statement must say something about something, it must involve signs for locating what is referred to, and such signs are ultimately indexical signs [i.e., "pointing" signs]. An iconic sign in isolation cannot be a statement, and a work of art, conceived as an iconic sign, cannot be true in the semantical sense of the term. Nevertheless, the statement that a work of art is "true" might under analysis turn out to be an elliptical form of syntactical, semantical, or pragmatical statements. Thus semantically it might be intended to affirm that the work in question actually is iconic of the value structure of a certain object or situation. . . .

The work of art is elliptical and iconic; that is, it is an image from which the semantical dimension is omitted, or in which it remains vague. By translating the icon, by expanding it and filling it in with a *denotatum,* we construct a situation external to the work of art: a situation which replaces it. In the usual terms of literary criticism, this situation is the "subject" which exists outside the language of the poem. For the language is merely "iconic of" this ordinary prose subject.

So a neo-classical theory of poetic language not only gave the case for poetry away to the scientist; it has become the foundation of the scientists' theory of poetry. When Mr. Richards remarked, in *Science and Poetry,* that we were now getting on a large scale "genuine knowledge" which would soon reduce poetry to the level of the "pseudo-statement," we could not see how right he was—right from the point of view of neo-classical theory. So long as the scientific procedure was observation, description, and classification, it was not very different from the procedure of common sense and its feeling for the reality of ordinary experience. As late as the first edition (1892) of *The Grammar of Science,* Karl Pearson said: "The aesthetic judgment pronounces for or against the interpretation of the creative imagination according as that interpretation embodies or contradicts the phenomena of life, which we ourselves have observed." But from the point of view of Unified Science, this principle of common-sense observation will no longer serve; it does not go far enough. And so we have a dilemma. Since the langauge of poetry can be shown to be not strictly relevant to objects and situations as these are presented by the positivist techniques, poetry becomes either nonsense or hortatory rhetoric.

The semiotic approach to aesthetics "has the merit of concreteness"; yet we have seen that Mr. Morris never quite gets around to a specific work of art. In "Science, Art, and Technology," he distinguishes three primary forms of discourse and relates them to the three dimensions of semiosis:

1. Scientific discourse: semantical dimension.
2. Aesthetic discourse: syntactical dimension.
3. Technological discourse: pragmatical dimension.

We have seen that the iconic sign is semantically weak; so the aesthetic sign, a variety of iconic sign, must function primarily at the syntactical level; that is, if we look at it "indexically" it "points" first of all to itself. Looking at the aesthetic sign from this point of view, we are forced to see that it wholly lacks cognitive content, and it is subject to the operation of "transformation rules." Does the "concreteness" of the semiotic approach to art consist in this? Again, is the syntactical dimension that in which direct apprehension of the aesthetic sign is possible? Once more it must be said that this direct apprehension seems impossible unless there is an agency of apprehension—a knowing mind; without this we get only an "interpretant," which is conceivable only at the pragmatic level; and if the interpretant is intelligible, it is so in terms of semantical relevance, or of the scientific form of discourse. For Mr. Morris himself confesses: ". . . in so far as the knowledge of value which art gives is the more than the having of value [i.e., is the *knowing* of value] there is no reason to suppose that this knowledge is *other than scientific in character*."

It is significant here that Mr. Morris conceives the character of poetry in the relation of pragmatics and semantics. What is our response to poetry and how do we behave when we read it: what, in a word, does it lead to? There is a certain uneasy piety in the extravagant claim that poetry is the realm of values; and there is no way, I think, to get around the conclusion that, since the values are not attached to reality, they are irresponsible feelings. They are, in fact, rhetoric. And it is also significant that for Mr. Morris the study of rhetoric is a branch of pragmatics; it is even a kind of technological instrument. For, in the essay "Science, Art, and Technology," poetry seems to acquire its main responsibility in the technological function of telling us what we *ought* to want and do. Here again neo-classical didacticism appears in terms of a rigorous instrumentalism.

Does the language of poetry mean what it says, or does it mean the "situation" that we get from it in a process of reduction? Although we have seen Mr. Morris' bias, we have also seen that he has not made up his mind: he would like to have it both ways. The origin of this dilemma is remote. But there is always "the sad ghost of Coleridge beckoning from the shades."

IV

The famous Chapter XIV of *Biographia Literaria* has been the background of the criticism of poetry for more than a hundred years. Its direct influence has been very great; its indirect influence, through Poe upon Baudelaire, and through the French Symbolists down to contemporary English and American poets, has perhaps been even greater. This chapter is the most influential statement on poetry ever formulated by an English critic: its insights, when we have them, are ours, and ours too its contradictions. Yet the remarkable "definition" of poetry, which I shall now quote, is not, as we shall presently see, the chief source of the aesthetic dilemma

that we inherit today. (That source is another passage.) Here is
the definition:

> A poem is that species of composition, which is opposed to works of
> science, by proposing for its *immediate* object pleasure, not truth;
> and from all other species—(having this object in common with it)
> —it is distinguished by proposing to itself such delight from the
> *whole*, as is compatible with a distinct gratification from each com-
> ponent *part*.

Much of the annoyance and misunderstanding caused by this
passage has not been Coleridge's fault; but is rather due to the failure of literary men to observe the accurate use of *species*. For Coleridge is giving us a strict Aristotelian definition of a *species* within
a given *genus*. It is not a qualitative statement, and it does not answer the question: *What* is poetry? The *whatness* of poetry does
not come within the definition; and I believe that nowhere else
does Coleridge offer us an explicit qualitative distinction between
poetry and other "species of composition" which may be "opposed"
to it.

For what is Coleridge saying? (I have never seen a literal reading of the passage by any critic.) There is the generic division:
composition. A poem is a species within the genus; but so is a work
of science. How are the two species distinguished? By their immediate objects. It is curious that Coleridge phrases the passage as if
a poem were a person "proposing" to himself a certain end, pleasure; so for *object* we have got to read *effect*. A poem, then, differs
from a work of science in its immediate effect upon us; and that
immediate effect is pleasure. But other species of composition may
aim at the effect of pleasure. A poem differs from these in the
relation of part to whole: the parts must give us a distinct pleasure,
moment by moment, and they are not to be conceived as subordinate to the whole; they make up the whole.

If there is an objective relation of part to whole, Coleridge does
not say what it is; nor does he distinguish that relation in terms of
any specific poetic work. It is strictly a quantitative analogy taken,
perhaps, from geometry. And the only purpose it serves is this: in
the paragraph following the "definition" he goes on to say that "the
philosophic critics of all ages coincide'" in asserting that beautiful,
isolated lines of distichs are not a poem, and that neither is "an

unsustained composition" of uninteresting parts a *"legitimate poem."* What we have here, then, is a sound but ordinary critical insight; but because it is merely an extension of the pleasure principle implicit in the "definition," we are not prepared by it to distinguish objectively a poem from any other form of expression. The distinction lies in the effect, and it is a psychological effect. In investigating the differentia of poetry—as Mr. Morris would put it—we are eventually led away from the poem into what has been known since Coleridge's time as the psychology of poetry.

The difficulties of this theory Coleridge seems not to have been aware of; yet he illustrates them perfectly. In the second paragraph after the famous definition he writes this remarkable passage:

> The first chapter of Isaiah—(indeed a very large portion of the whole book)—is poetry in the most emphatic sense; yet it would be no less irrational than strange to assert, that pleasure, not truth, was the immediate object of the prophet. In short, whatever specific import we attach to the word, Poetry, there will be found involved in it, as a necessary consequence, that a poem of any length neither can be, nor ought to be, all poetry. Yet if an harmonious whole is to be produced, the remaining parts must be preserved in keeping with the poetry; and this can no otherwise be effected than by such a studied selection and artificial arrangement, as will partake of one, though not a peculiar property of poetry. And this again can be no other than the property of exciting a more continuous and equal attention than the language of prose aims at, whether colloquial or written.

This is probably the most confused statement ever uttered by a great critic, and it has probably done more damage to critical thought than anything else said by any critic. Isaiah is poetry in "the most emphatic sense," although his immediate object (effect) is truth. It will be observed that, whereas in the definition our attention is drawn to a species of composition, a poem, we are here confronted with the personage, Isaiah, who does have the power of proposing an object; and Isaiah's immediate object is truth. But are we to suppose that the effect of the poem and the object of the prophet are to be apprehended in the same way? Is our experience of truth the same as our experience of pleasure? If there is a difference between truth and pleasure, and if an immediate effect of pleasure is the specific "property" of poetry (how a property can be an effect it is difficult to see), how can the first chapter of Isaiah be poetry at all? It cannot be, looked at in these terms; and as a matter of fact Coleridge rather slyly withdraws his compliment to Isaiah when he goes on to say that a "poem of any length neither can be, nor ought to be, all poetry." Isaiah is not all poetry; he is partly truth, or even mostly truth. And the element of truth, while it is strictly speaking insubordinate and unassimilable, can be used by means of an artificial arrangement—meter. There is no doubt that meter does on the whole what Coleridge attributes to it: it demands a "continuous and equal attention." Does he mean to say that the insubordinate element of truth—insubordinate to the immediate effect of pleasure—should be given such conspicuous emphasis? Or does he perhaps mean that the attention will be fixed upon the metrical pattern, so that the nonpoetic element will be less conspicuous?

Coleridge's theory of meter is not quite pertinent here: in the later and more elaborate discussion of meter in *Biographia Literaria* there is the general conclusion that meter is indispensable to poetry. In Chapter XIV, now being examined, he speaks of meter as "an artificial arrangement . . . not a peculiar property of poetry."

There is, then, in Coleridge's poetic theory a persistent dilemma. *He cannot make up his mind whether the specifically poetic element is an objective feature of the poem, or is distinguishable only as a subjective effect.* He cannot, in short, choose between metaphysics and psychology. His general emphasis is psychological, with metaphysical ambiguities.

The distinction between Fancy and Imagination is ultimately a psychological one: he discusses the problem in terms of separate faculties, and the objective poetical properties, presumably resulting from the use of these faculties, are never defined, but are given only occasional illustration. (I have in mind his magnificent analysis of "Venus and Adonis," the value of which lies less perhaps in the critical principles he supposes he is illustrating, than in the perfect taste with which he selects the good passages for admiration.) When Coleridge speaks of the "esemplastic power" of the Imagination, it is always a "faculty" of the mind, not an objective poetic order. When he says that a poem gives us "a more than usual state of emotion with more than usual order," we acknowledge the fact, without being able to discern in the merely comparative degree of the adjective the fundamental difference between the poetic and the philosophic powers which Coleridge frequently asserts, but which he nowhere objectively establishes. The psychological bias of his "system" is perfectly revealed in this summary passage of Chapter XIV:

> My own conclusions on the nature of poetry, in the strictest use of the word, have been in part anticipated in some of the remarks on the Fancy and Imagination in the early part of this work. What is poetry?—is so nearly the same question with, what is a poet?—that the answer to the one is involved in the solution to the other. For it is a distinction resulting from the poetic genius itself, which sustains and modifies the images, thoughts, and emotions of the poet's own mind.

There can be little doubt that Coleridge's failure to get out of the dilemma of Intellect-or-Feeling has been passed on to us as a fatal legacy. If the first object of poetry is an effect, and if that effect is pleasure, does it not necessarily follow that truth and knowledge may be better set forth in some other order altogether? It is true that Coleridge made extravagant claims for a poetic order of truth, and it is upon these claims that Mr. I. A. Richards has based his fine book, *Coleridge on Imagination:* Mr. Richards' own testimony is that the claims were not coherent. The coherent part of Coleridge's theory is the fatal dilemma that I have described. Truth is only the secondary consideration of the poet, and from the point of view of positivism the knowledge, or truth, that poetry gives us is immature and inadequate. What of the primary consideration of the poet—pleasure?

Pleasure is the single qualitative feature of Coleridge's famous definition; but it is not *in* the definition objectively. And with the development of modern psychology it has ceased to be qualitative, even subjectively. It is a *response.* The fate of Coleridge's system, then, has been its gradual extinction in the terminology of experimental psychology. The poetry has been extinguished in the poet. The poetic "effect" is a "response" to a "stimulus"; and in the early works of Mr. Richards we get for the first time the questions, rigorously applied: Is the poetic response relevant to the real world? Is it relevant to action? Poetry has come under the general idea of "operational validity." So we must turn briefly to Mr. Richards.

V

In *Science and Poetry,* Mr. Richards condensed in untechnical language the position that he had set forth in detail earlier, in *The Principles of Literary Criticism.* The positivist side of Mr. Richards' thought at that time is plainly revealed in a passage like this:

> You contrive not to laugh [in church]; but there is no doubt about the activity of the impulses in their restricted form. The much more subtle and elaborate impulses which a poem excites are not different in principle. *They do not show themselves as a rule, they do not come out into the open, largely because they are so complex.* [Italic mine.] When they have adjusted themselves to one another and become organized into a coherent whole, the needs concerned may be satisfied. *In a fully developed man a state of readiness for action will take the place of action when the full appropriate situation for action is not present.*[6] [Mr. Richards' italic.]

The mere state of readiness for action is the poetic experience in terms of value and relevance. The readiness points to the "direct apprehension" of an interest-value in Mr. Morris' sense; but the failure of the action to come off, the lack of the "full appropriate situation for action," indicates the absence of a *denotatum.* We receive the designation of a value without being provided with a situation in which we can act upon it. The remarkable parallel between Mr. Richards' early theories of poetry and the recent theories of Mr. Morris need not detain us. It is enough to point out that Mr. Richards anticipated fifteen years ago everything that Mr. Morris' science of semiotic has to say about the language of poetry.

I have [italicized] a sentence, in the quotation from Mr. Richards, for two reasons: first, the vagueness of the language is significant; secondly, the idea of the coherent whole into which the "impulses" are organized has no experimental basis in terms of impulses. Mr. John Crowe Ransom remarks that Mr. Richards never shows us *how* this ordering act of poetry upon our minds takes place, and then proceeds to discern the reason for Mr. Richards' vague statements about the conduct of poetic stimulation and response:

> Most readers will retort, of course, that in the very large majority of cases the spiritual happenings are the only happenings we have ob-

[6] *Science and Poetry* (New York, 1926), pp. 28-29.

served, and *the neural happenings are simply what the behaviorists would like to observe.* [Italic mine.] At present the mental datum is the fact and the neural datum is the inference.[7]

In throwing out the mental fact Mr. Richards in his early writings preceded Mr. Morris in his rejection of the cognitive powers of the mind. I do not suggest any direct influence from Mr. Richards upon Mr. Morris, although Mr. Morris has acknowledged the work of his predecessor: it is easier to relate these men to a much wider movement. That movement is positivism, and it is more than a strict scientific method.

It is a general attitude towards experience. If it is not, why should Mr. Richards have attempted in his early criticism to represent the total poetic experience and even the structure of poetry in one of the positivist languages—experimental psychology? It was representation by analogy. The experimental basis for such a representation was wholly lacking. Mr. Richards, had we listened hard enough, was saying in *The Principles of Literary Criticism* and *Science and Poetry* that here at last is what poetry would be if we could only reduce it to the same laboratory technique that we use in psychology; and without warning to the unwary reader, whose credulity was already prepared by his own positivist *Zeitgeist,* Mr. Richards went on to state "results" that looked like the results of an experiment; but the experiment had never been made. It had been inferred. The "impulses" that we feel in response to a poem, says Mr. Richards, "do not show themselves as a rule." There is no scientific evidence that they have ever shown themselves to Mr. Richards or to anybody else. Mr. Richards, like a good positivist, was the victim of a deep-seated compulsive analogy, an elusive but all-engrossing assumption that all experience can be reduced to what is actually the very limited frame of reference supplied by a doctrine of correlation, or of the relevance of stimulus to response. This early procedure of Mr. Richards' was not even empiricism, for in empiricism the cognitive intelligence is not eliminated in the pursuit of verifiable facts. Mr. Richards, like Mr. Morris after him, eliminated cognition without demonstrating experimentally the *data* of his behavioristic poetics. So this doctrine was not empiri-

[7] "A Psychologist Looks at Poetry," *The World's Body* (New York, 1938), p. 147. This essay is the most searching I have seen; but it does somewhat less than full justice to Mr. Richards' insights.

cism: it came out of the demi-religion of positivism. The poetry
had been absorbed into a pseudo-scientific jargon, no more "relevant" to poetry than the poetic pseudo-statement was relevant to
the world: the net result was zero from both points of view.

I have put this brief commentary on Mr. Richards' early poetics
in the past tense because it is no longer his poetics. From 1926, the
year of *Science and Poetry,* he has come a long way. It is perhaps
not an extravagant claim to make for Mr. Richards' intellectual
history, that it will probably turn out to be the most instructive,
among critics, of our age. His great intellectual powers, his learning, his devotion to poetry—a devotion somewhat frustrated but as
marked fifteen years ago as now—are qualities of an intellectual
honesty rare in any age. In exactly ten years, from 1926, he arrived,
in *The Philosophy of Rhetoric* (1936), at such a statement as this:

> So far from verbal language being a "compromise for a language of
> intuition"—a thin, but better-than-nothing, substitute for real ex-
> perience—language, well used, is a *completion* and does what the
> intuitions of sensation by themselves cannot do. Words are the
> meeting points at which regions of experience which can never com-
> bine in sensation or intuition, come together. They are the occasion
> and means of that growth which is the mind's endless endeavor to
> order itself. That is why we have language. *It is no mere signalling
> system.* [Italic mine.] It is the instrument of all our distinctively hu-
> man development, of everything in which we go beyond the ani-
> mals. [Pp. 130-131.]

These words should be read and re-read with the greatest care by
critics who still cite the early Richards as the continuing head of a
positivist tradition in criticism. There is, in this passage, first of all,
an implicit repudiation of the leading doctrine of *The Principles
of Literary Criticism.* The early doctrine did look upon poetic language as a "substitute for real experience," if by experience is
meant responses relevant to scientifically ascertained facts and situations: this early doctrine, as I have indicated, anticipated in
psychological terms Mr. Morris' poetic doctrine of designation
without *denotatum,* of value without consummation of value, of
interpretant without an interpreter. Mr. Richards' more familiar
equivalents of the semiotic terms were: pseudo-statement without
referents; poetry as the orderer of our minds, as the valuer, although
the ordering mysteriously operated in fictions irrelevant to the real

world; a response, a behavioristic "readiness for action," without a knowing mind.

Language, says Mr. Richards, "is no mere signalling system." With that sentence the early psychological doctrine is discreetly put away. Is it too much to assume that the adjective "signalling" may indicate the relation of Mr. Richards' present views to the pragmatic bias of Mr. Morris' aesthetics? He speaks of the inadequacy of "sensation" and "intuition," and of the equal inadequacy of "intuitions of sensation." Is not the mere sensation Mr. Morris' interpretant, the intuition of sensation his iconic sign? What is the "completion" which language "well used" can achieve beyond sensation and intuition?

It is doubtless knowledge of a kind that we can discuss only if we assume the action of a knowing mind. Of what is it the completion? In the paragraph following the passage that I have just quoted, Mr. Richards cites Coleridge:

> Are not words parts and germinations of the plant? And what is the law of their growth? In something of this sort I would destroy the old antithesis of Words and Things: elevating, as it were, Words into Things and living things too.

This attribution to the language of poetry of a special kind of "life" goes back to Mr. Richards' *Coleridge on Imagination* (1935), the most ambitious attempt of a modern critic to force into unity the antithesis of language and subject, of pleasure and truth. It is an antithesis which, as we have seen, has harassed critical theory since the time of Coleridge. Mr. Richards' book may be looked upon as an effort to finish Coleridge's own uncompleted struggle with this neo-classical dilemma. This is not the place to describe the entire nature and scope of his effort, or to estimate it. A single chapter of the book, 'The Wind Harp," contains the clearest presentation of the antithesis that I have seen by a modern critic.

There are "two doctrines," he says, which have tended to flourish independently—"And yet, neither is intelligible, apart from Imagination." He continues:

> The two doctrines can be stated as follows:
>
>   1. The mind of the poet at moments . . . gains an insight into reality, reads Nature as a symbol of something behind or within Nature not ordinarily perceived.

2. The mind of the poet creates a Nature into which his own feelings, his aspirations and apprehensions, are projected.

Now the positivist sciences have denied all validity to the first doctrine: as a proposition, in the many forms in which it may be stated, it is strictly meaningless. For the sole effective procedure towards nature is the positivist. The second docrine is the standard poetics of our time: projection of feeling. The confusion and contradiction that we saw in Mr. Morris and in the early Richards came of trying to square a theory of interest-value with a theory of emotional projection which was not firmly based upon positivist knowledge. That contradiction is the clue to the "unintelligibility" of the doctrines if held separately. If you take the first alone, eliminating the second, you eliminate the "mind," and you get pure positivism: in thus eliminating cognition you lose "everything in which we go beyond the animals." If you take the second alone, and eliminate the external world in any of the four meanings[8] that Mr. Richards gives to the phrase, you have a knowing mind without anything that it can know.

Before the development of the positivist procedures towards nature, the pressure of this dilemma was not seriously felt. We have seen in Matthew Arnold (the determined anti-dialectician) the belief that the subject is external to the language—a merely common-sense view inherited from neo-classical theory. The poetic subject was the world of ordinary experience; but as soon as the subject—Nature—became the field of positivism, the language of poetry ceased to represent it; ceased, in fact, to have any validity, or to set forth anything real. (The world of positivism is a world without minds to know the world; and yet Mr. Morris does not hesitate to assert that his Unified Science will save the world. For whom will it be saved?)

What is this Imagination which Mr. Richards says will make the two doctrines intelligible? No doubt it becomes in his hands something different from Coleridge's conception of it: it closely resembles an Hegelian synthesis, which joins the opposites in a new proposition in which their truths, no longer contradictory, are preserved.

[8] *Coleridge on Imagination*, pp. 157-8.

They are [says Mr. Richards of the two doctrines] neither consequences of *a priori* decisions, nor verifiable as the empirical statements of science are verifiable: and all verifiable statements are independent of them. But this does not diminish in the least their interest, or that of the other senses in which they may be true.

With that we are almost ready to leave Mr. Richards, who offers
no final solution of the problem of the unified imagination. "It is
the privilege of poetry," he says finely, "to preserve us from mis-
taking our notions either for things or for ourselves. *Poetry is the
completest mode of utterance.*"9 It is neither the world of verifiable
science nor a projection of ourselves; yet it is *complete*. And because it is complete knowledge we may, I think, claim for it a
unique kind of responsibility, and see in it at times an irresponsi-
bility equally distinct. The order of completeness that it achieves in
the great works of the imagination is not the order of experimental
completeness aimed at by the positivist sciences, whose responsibility is directed towards the verification of limited techniques. The
completeness of science is an abstraction covering an ideal of cooperation among specialized methods. No one can have an experience
of science, or of a single science. For the completeness of *Hamlet*
is not of the experimental order, but of the experienced order: it
is, in short, of the mythical order. And here Mr. Richards can give
us a final insight. Myths, he says,

> . . . are no amusement or diversion to be sought as a relaxation and
> an escape from the hard realities of life. They are these hard reali-
> ties in projection, their symbolic recognition, co-ordination, and ac-
> ceptance. . . . The opposite and discordant qualities in things in
> them acquire a form. . . . Without his mythologies man is only a
> cruel animal without a soul . . . a congeries of possibilities with-
> out order and aim.10

Man, without his mythologies, is an interpretant. Mr. Richards'
books may be seen together as a parable, as a mythical and dramatic
projection, of the failure of the modern mind to understand poetry
on the assumptions underlying the demi-religion of positivism. We
do not need to reject the positive and rational mode of inquiry into
poetry; yet even from Mr. Morris we get the warning lest we sub-

9 *Ibid.*, p. 163.
10 *Ibid.*, pp. 171-172.

stitute the criticism for the poem, and thus commit ourselves to a "learned ignorance." We must return to, we must never leave, the poem itself. Its "interest" value is a cognitive one; it is sufficient that here, in the poem, we get knowledge of a whole object. If rational inquiry is the only mode of criticism, we must yet remember that the way we employ that mode must always powerfully affect our experience of the poem. I have been concerned in this commentary with the compulsive, almost obsessed, application of an all-engrossing principle of pragmatic reduction to a formed realm of our experience, the distinction of which is its complete knowledge, the full body of the experience that it offers us. However we may see the completeness of poetry, it is a problem less to be solved than, in its full import, to be preserved.

ARCHIBALD MacLEISH

Metaphor

If the Chinese poems we have examined [earlier] are true poems—and the test of time would indicate that they are—then we may conclude, I think, that one of the means to meaning in this art is a certain relationship of images: what might be called a coupling of images, though the coupling may include more images than two. One image is established by words which make it sensuous and vivid to the eyes or ears or touch—to any of the senses. Another image is put beside it. And a meaning appears which is neither the meaning of one image nor the meaning of the other nor even the sum of both but a *consequence* of both—a consequence of both in their conjunction, in their relation to each other. There is the blue smoke of war. There are the white bones of men. And there is the heaviness of time in the space between them.

Suppose we press the examination a little further. What is the nature of this meaning which coupled images can contain? Is it emotional only—sadness for that unending war, for all the unending wars, for ourselves in our own time caught between the white bones of our brothers killed forty-two years ago in another country and that enormous mushroom of fiery poisoned smoke on the hori-

zon now? Is that all those images contain? For some, perhaps. And
for some perhaps, it is enough. To feel emotion is at least to feel.
The crime against life, the worst of all crimes, is *not* to feel: And
there was never, perhaps, a civilization in which that crime, the
crime of torpor, of lethargy, of apathy, the snake-like sin of cold-
ness-at-the-heart, was commoner than in our technological civilization in which the emotionless emotions of adolescent boys are mass
produced on television screens to do our feeling for us, and a
woman's longing for her life is twisted, by singing commercials,
into a longing for a new detergent, family size, which will keep her
hands as innocent as though she had never lived. It is the modern
painless death, this commercialized atrophy of the heart. None of
us is safe from it. The intellectual life can become technological
too no matter what its content, and Acedy, you may recall, was
the occupational sin of the medieval clerks. If poetry can call our
numbed emotions to life, its plain human usefulness needs no
further demonstration.

But nevertheless, is it *only* emotion which the coupled images
in a poem capture? Or is the emotion in its turn a means, as the
coupled images are, and is the meaning farther? Do the coupled
images, that is to say, evoke between them feeling, and does the
feeling, in that place between, discover something more than feeling? Bring back to your mind, if you will, that old English song.

> O westron wind when wilt thou blow
> That the small rain down can rain?
> Christ that my love were in my arms
> And I in my bed again.

There is the west wind, the spring wind, and its small rain. There
is a bed and a girl. And there is emotion certainly there between
them, an ache of longing. But is that all? Or is there also, and on
beyond, a recognition of something known, something known before and now, in the space between the bed and the west wind,
realized? Are the bed and the girl and the wind and the rain in
some way caught up together, not in the mind, which cannot
understand these irrelevancies, but in the emotion which can? And
does the emotion itself change in consequence of the images which
create it so that what was at first a passionate longing for that
smooth girl in that warm bed becomes, in the shadow of wind and

rain, bed and girl, a longing which is part of the turning of the earth and the changing of the seasons and the wet Atlantic wind which brings the spring into that island? Has this hollow between the wind and the rain on one side and the bed and the girl on the other filled, not with emotion only, but with something emotion *knows*—something more immediate than knowledge, something tangible and felt, something as tangible as experience itself, felt as immediately as experience? Is it human experience itself, in its livingness as experience, these coupled images and the emotion they evoke, have captured? And was it this that Wordsworth meant when he spoke of truth "carried alive into the heart by passion"?

In part, I should say. But I should not feel, in saying so, that I had answered the question—that I had really explained the power of these coupled images. To carry experience itself alive into the heart is an extraordinary achievement, an achievement neither science nor philosophy has accomplished. But is the possession of experience, even its possession alive, an ultimate conquest? Is it because "O westron wind . . ." enables us to possess a living moment of experience that we have treasured this little four-line poem for hundreds of years as though it had told us a secret? I think not. And certainly Wordsworth did not think so, for what is carried alive into the heart in his saying is, you will remember, "truth." It is *meaning* he means. And it is meaning we must mean also if we are to push our question to conclusions. For there *is* a sense of meaning, an odor of meaning one might almost say, about these coupled images in a poem whenever they work as coupled images. That dead doe under the white rushes in the ancient Chinese poem, and the living girl who lies with her lover in the place beside, seem not only to *be* together but to *mean* together—so much so that one's first impulse is to make them one: dead doe under that bundle of white rushes mistaken for living girl covered by her lover's body—so much so indeed, that Pound, when he translated this poem, was tempted to, and did, introduce a line which is not there: "dead as doe is maidenhead"—with the result that the poem is at once "explained" and destroyed in a single stroke.

But what meaning *can* there be in this collision of images which do not collide—images as logically unrelated as the baily's bell, and the robes in folds, and the sun in the glass window in "The maidens came . . ."? How can the relation of the unrelated be said, in poetry, to *mean* and what kind of meaning is it which only the emotions can understand? This question, obviously, takes me farther than I ought to try to go alone, for it pushes past the gates and doors of the art of poetry to the art itself—to the forbidden place within the art where the Pytho sits above the vapor. What is involved is the *nature* of meaning in poetry. Fortunately however there are witnesses qualified to speak who have spoken. And fortunately also, what they have seen and said has been very much the same. C. Day Lewis sums it up for men of our tongue by saying, in his *Poetic Image,* that if the poets of England were questioned on the ultimates of their art they would all reply, because, in one way or another, they all have, that "poetry's truth comes from the perception of a unity underlying and relating all phenomena." And one of the most French of all French poets, Charles Baudelaire, bore much the same witness in the most unequivocal terms. The poet's imagination, he wrote, is "la plus scientifique des facultés parce que, seule, elle comprend l'analogie universelle"—the most scientific of all faculties because it alone comprehends "the universal analogy."

This comes down to saying, as you see, that it is precisely the relation of the unrelated which *does* mean in poetry: indeed, that the essential meaning of the art *is* that relation . . . and the shadow it can cast . . . or the light. Whether or not one accepts this statement as a definition—and a definition wide enough to include the meaningfulness of all true poems—the fact nevertheless remains that men entitled to an opinion have thought it true. To Wordsworth, for one, "the pleasure which the mind derives from the perception of similitude in dissimilitude . . . is the great spring of the activity of our minds and their chief feeder . . ." and thus a fundamental underpinning of the whole theory of poetry which he was defending in his Preface to *Lyrical Ballads.* But whether one is prepared to go as far as Baudelaire or even as far as Wordsworth the relevance of their doctrines to the meaningfulness of coupled images is obvious. If Baudelaire and Mr. Lewis's English poets are right then images are not coupled in poetry merely to excite emotions. They are not even coupled merely to seize on moments of experience made palpable to the emotions. They are coupled to stir the emotions to comprehend an instant of the *analogie universelle.*

Why the universal analogy? Why should the comprehension of the universal analogy, granted that such an analogy exists, be meaningful? For the obvious reason, of course: because it would *make sense* of experience—and make sense of it, furthermore, in its *own* terms, not in terms of an equation of abstractions on a blackboard or a philosophy of abstractions in a book, in either one of which experience is made to mean by turning it into something else. If the fragments of experience are in truth parts of a whole, and if the relation of the parts to each other and thus to the whole can in truth be *seen, sensed, felt* in the fragments themselves, then there *is* meaning in that seeing, in that sensing, in that feeling—extraordinary meaning.

Even, sometimes, unbearable meaning. There is a poem of Baudelaire's, which Cézanne is said to have had by heart and to have used both as touchstone and lantern, which will show, if you will look at it, just how unbearable the comprehension of the universal analogy can be—the terrible poem called "Une Charogne" (A Carcass, A Carrion) in which death and sexuality are coupled in the incongruous congruity of panting lasciviousness and heaving putrescence. When you read it—if you read it—ask yourself if you think it was written merely to shock. And ask yourself too whether you think you will remember it only because it is horrible.

> Rappelez-vous l'objet que nous vîmes, mon âme,
>   Ce beau matin d'été si doux:
> Au détour d'un sentier une charogne infâme
>   Sur un lit semé de cailloux,
>
> Les jambes en l'air, comme une femme lubrique,
>   Brûlante et suant les poisons,
> Ouvrait d'une façon nonchalante et cynique
>   Son ventre plein d'exhalaisons.
>
> Le soleil rayonnait sur cette pourriture,
>   Comme afin de la cuire à point,
> Et de rendre au centuple à la grande Nature
>   Tout ce qu'ensemble elle avait joint.
>
> Et le ciel regardait la carcasse superbe
>   Comme une fleur s'épanouir;
> — La puanteur était si forte, que sur l'herbe
>   Vous crûtes vous évanouir; —

Les mouches bourdonnaient sur ce ventre putride
    D'où sortaient de noirs bataillons
De larves, qui coulaient comme un épais liquide
    Le long de ces vivants haillons.

Tout cela descendait, montait comme une vague,
    Ou s'élançait en pétillant;
On eut dit que le corps, enflé d'un souffle vague,
    Vivait en se multipliant.

Et ce monde rendait une étrange musique,
    Comme l'eau courante et le vent,
Ou le grain qu'un vanneur d'un mouvement rythmique
    Agite et tourne dans son van.

Les formes s'effaçaient et n'étaient plus qu'un rêve,
    Un ébauche lente à venir,
Sur la toile oubliée, et que l'artiste achève
    Seulement par le souvenir.

Derrière les rochers une chienne inquiète
    Nous regardait d'un oeil fâché,
Epiant le moment de reprendre au squelette
    Le morceau qu'elle avait lâché.

— Et pourtant vous serez semblable à cette ordure,
    A cette horrible infection,
Etoile de mes yeux, soleil de ma nature,
    Vous, mon ange et ma passion!

Oui! telle vous serez, ô la reine des grâces,
    Après les derniers sacrements,
Quand vous irez, sous l'herbe et les floraisons grasses,
    Moisir parmi les ossements.

Alors, ô ma beauté, dites à la vermine
    Qui vous mangera de baisers
Que j'ai gardé la forme et l'essence divine
    Des mes amours décomposés!

There are aspects of experience from which, quite naturally and quite understandably, we turn away our eyes—aspects which, unwillingly seen, we eradicate from our memories. But poetry does not turn away from them, because it cannot turn away from them: because to turn away from them would be to betray the *analogie universelle*. It is this the censors never understand. To the censors, and those who impose censorship on their fellow citizens, Baudelaire did not *have* to write "Une Charogne." He could perfectly well have gone on about that "Beau matin d'été si doux" with which he began the poem. Neither censors nor the churches which promote censorship nor the readers of poems who find this image or that "too terrible" will ever understand the little sentence Emily Dickinson wrote to Colonel Higginson: "Candor is the only wile." If they did they would excommunicate the saint of Amherst and burn her books.

No, to see the universal analogy one must first see the universe and no man can be a reader of poems, to say nothing of being a writer of poems, who cannot, or will not, see that far. And neither can any man be a writer of poems, or a right reader of them, who, when he *has* seen, blinds himself to the congruity of the incongruous because he does not *wish* incongruous things to touch each other—cannot bear the thought that they should touch each other. Most of us keep the bones of the dead out of our minds. Most of us delight in thinking of the bright hair of a lovely girl. But the man who keeps the two so far apart that they can never meet may miss the meaning of his life to say nothing of the meaning of John Donne's "The Relic."

> When my grave is broken up again
> Some second guest to entertain,
>   (For graves have learn'd that womanhead
>   To be to more than one a bed)
>   And he that digs it, spies
> A bracelet of bright hair about the bone,
>   Will he not let'us alone,
> And think that there a loving couple lies,
> Who thought that this device might be some way
> To make their souls, at the last busy day,
> Meet at this grave, and make a little stay?
>
>   If this fall in a time, or land,
>   Where mis-devotion doth command,
>   Then he that digs us up will bring
>   Us to the Bishop and the King,
>   To make us Relics; then
> Thou shalt be a Mary Magdalen, and I

A something else thereby;
All women shall adore us, and some men;
And since at such time, miracles are sought,
I would have that age by this paper taught
What miracles we harmless lovers wrought.

First, we lov'd well and faithfully,
Yet knew not what we lov'd, nor why,
Difference of sex no more we knew
Than our Guardian Angels do;
Coming and going, we
Perchance might kiss, but not between those meals;
Our hands ne'er touch'd the seals
Which nature, injur'd by late law, sets free:
These miracles we did; but now alas,
All measure, and all language, I should pass
Should I tell what a miracle she was.

It would be possible as we all know, because we have all suffered
from it, to read that line "A bracelet of bright hair about the bone"
as a paradox produced characteristically by a poet who, having
been designated *metaphysical* by the professors, had no choice but
to invent paradoxes and other toys. But paradox surprises: it does
not move. And that line *moves*. Why? Because nothing could be
farther from the dead man's bone than the circle of bright hair and
because nothing could be nearer. It is an unexpected conjunction,
yes, but it is not the unexpectedness alone which startles us into
understanding. It is the *rightness* too. The rightness *and* the unexpectedness: the unexpectedness *and* the rightness. We feel a
knowledge which we cannot think—a knowledge which, for its
moment, brings world and death together and gives death a place.
That girl across the street there with her bright gold hair—it is mor-
tality upon that hair which touches us. We knew it but we did not
know it. Now we know.

But if the relation of the unrelated is the ultimate, or, in any
case, the characteristic, meaning of poetry—poetry's "truth," to borrow Day Lewis's umbrella word—why then is not the coupling of
images, which is the relation of the unrelated in practice and in
fact, the characteristic means to meaning? I should have to reply
that I think it is. But in so saying I should find myself at once in a

distinct, and not very distinguished minority of one with the great and dangerous weight of authoritative opinion leaning above me like a cliff: the opinion of the psychologists in letters and the literary men in psychology who have reserved that central place for the symbol, and the opinion of the critics of poetry, headed by the greatest of them all, who holds (I am referring, of course to Ivor Richards) that *"metaphor* is the supreme agent by which disparate and hitherto unconnected things are brought together in poetry." Mine is not a comfortable position to be in even in the relative privacy of a Harvard classroom. In cold public print it demands explanation.

I shall begin by trying to explain why I think the primacy of the coupling of images as means to meaning in poetry can be defended even against the claims of that enormous orbiting sputnik of the modern literary skies: the symbol. But first let me protect my flanks by reminding you that it is symbol *in poetry* I am talking about, not symbol in Jung. In Jung, as I understand it, symbols are not means at all but primordial angels, first things. They cannot be contrived by poets because they are evolved out of racial memory. They cannot be manipulated in art because they are artifacts in their own right; cores of ultimate meaning about which, as about bits of ancient metal dropped into castle wells, crystals of immeasurable meaning have gathered. They are magnets of the soul fallen like meteors out of eternity. In brief, and in Tillich's simple negative, they cannot be invented. This statement I do not question, partly because I cannot and partly because I should like to believe it true. The concept of the immemorial and autonomous symbol stirs me, and at the pitch and elevation of Tillich's thought it seems appropriate and right.

But symbols in poetry are of a very different nature as the simplest example will demonstrate. Take, as nearest thing at hand, the moon. If I say the word "moon," is there a symbol circling overhead? But suppose I repeat the most familiar stanza of that most familiar poem, "The Rime of the Ancient Mariner":

> The moving Moon went up the sky,
> And nowhere did abide;
> Softly she was going up,
> And a star or two beside —

Now is there a symbol in orbit? I don't see it. Nor am I able to see it when I intone these same lines in the most "poetic" surroundings. I say them to myself whenever, on my island in the Antilles, the full moon comes up in her harness of rare stars out of the white rim of night along the horizon and I have never yet seen anything but the beauty of the moon. But now go on a step. Recall if you can the "Rime" as a whole. Put the moon into the "Rime": let it hang there in the poem. What does it do? It changes light does it not?—precisely as it changes light in the actual world when it dissolves the familiar outlines of every day, letting that other world appear. It is when the moon changes the light in the "Rime," changes the world, that those horrible water-snakes become beautiful to the Mariner's eye, and that he blesses them, and that the carrion albatross falls from his neck. It is by the moon, in other words, that he sees—sees beauty even in horror.

> The Moving Moon went up the sky,
> And nowhere did abide;
> Softly she was going up,
> And a star or two beside —
>
> Her beams bemock'd the sultry main,
> Like April hoar-frost spread;
> But where the ship's huge shadow lay,
> The charmèd water burnt alway
> A still and awful red.
>
> Beyond the shadow of the ship,
> I watch'd the water-snakes:
> They moved in tracks of shining white
> And when they rear'd, the elfish light
> Fell off in hoary flakes.
>
> Within the shadow of the ship
> I watch'd their rich attire:
> Blue, glossy green, and velvet black,
> They coil'd and swam; and every track
> Was a flash of golden fire.
>
> O happy living things! no tongue
> Their beauty might declare:

A spring of love gush'd from my heart,
And I bless'd them unaware:
Sure my kind saint took pity on me,
And I bless'd them unaware.

The selfsame moment I could pray;
And from my neck so free
The Albatross fell off, and sank
Like lead into the sea.

Is there a symbol here? Contrast this saving light of the moon with that opposite light of the sun which stands above the mast at noon while the sea rots and the disgusting snakes coil and slide in the decaying calm. Is there a symbol there too? And is it or is it not a symbol made by the poet—by the poem? If you think of sun as sun, you think of light and warmth—of goodness and generation. But if you think of sun *in the poem* you think of thirst and death —the thirst and death of that blazing daytime light in which the snakes are only snakes and the dead men dead.

No, symbols in poetry can be invented and are invented. They are not, of course, invented at will. Mere intent will not produce a symbol even when the intent is in the mind of a poet of the genius of Yeats. "The Second Coming" is a proof of that. There is a sense of symbol at the beginning of that poem—though vague enough so that readers, ignorant (as they should be) of Yeats's "System," take the falconer for Christ. But one has no confidence that Yeats was seeking a symbol here. At the end, however, there can be little question that the rough slouching beast has symbolical ambitions. And yet no symbol is born. One can figure out with the wits and a little reading of *A Vision* what this nightmare creature is, but following him across that magnificent poem is no shadow such as true symbols cast.

Turning and turning in the widening gyre
The falcon cannot hear the falconer;
Things fall apart; the centre cannot hold;
Mere anarchy is loosed upon the world,
The blood-dimmed tide is loosed, and everywhere
The ceremony of innocence is drowned;
The best lack all conviction, while the worst
Are full of passionate intensity.

> Surely some revelation is at hand;
> Surely the Second Coming is at hand.
> The Second Coming! Hardly are those words out
> When a vast image out of *Spiritus Mundi*
> Troubles my sight: somewhere in sands of the desert
> A shape with lion body and the head of a man,
> A gaze blank and pitiless as the sun,
> Is moving its slow thighs, while all about it
> Reel shadows of the indignant desert birds,
> The darkness drops again; but now I know
> That twenty centuries of stony sleep
> Were vexed to nightmare by a rocking cradle,
> And what rough beast, its hour come round at last,
> Slouches towards Bethlehem to be born?

But, exception made for such aborted symbols as this, there can be no question of the power of the art of poetry to invent, even in this thin and difficult air. The question therefore presents itself: what *is* this inventable symbol, known to poetry but not to religion? And to that question the classic answer is still the answer of the poet of the "Rime of the Ancient Mariner" himself, for Coleridge was also, of course, one of the magisterial critics of our tongue. "A symbol," wrote Coleridge, "is characterized by a translucence of the special in the particular, or of the general in the special, or of the universal in the general: above all by the translucence of the eternal through and in the temporal." This is the complete definition, but there is also a more compact statement of Coleridge's which is itself a partial definition and which, being less inclusive, is more useful: a symbol, he says, "partakes of the reality which it renders intelligible."

Now you will notice—and I am returning to the defense of my precarious position—that both this briefer statement and the fuller, define symbol by assuming the existence of two "things" and, further, by postulating a relationship between them. Indeed it is the relationship which *is* the symbol. True, one of the two "things" is described as shining through the other. And the second is described as making intelligible the first. So that one thinks of, *sees*, only one thing: the moon. But the other is there, must be there, or there is no symbol. It is a mistake and a delusion, in other words, to think of symbol in poetry as Yeats sometimes did as one "thing" substituted for another. A symbol no more "stands for" something other than itself than the dead doe "stands for" the excited girl in that Chinese song. A symbol is always what George Whalley has called "a focus of relationship." Unless it is felt as a focus of relationship with both its related parts in play it will not work. It will not indeed exist. Think of any symbol you please. Think of the sign of the cross itself. You can easily imagine a context in which two lines at right angles will mean an illiterate's signature or danger at a railroad crossing. Only when that Other is there behind does this most powerful of all modern symbols become a symbol and *say*.

I am not contending, I need hardly point out—I hope I need hardly point out—that symbols and coupled images are the same thing. They have obvious differences. What I am contending is that their basic *structure* is essentially the same: that it is *relationship* here as elsewhere in poetry which provides the means to meaning. It is true that the relationship here is one of *congruity*: the invisible partner in the relationship must, as Coleridge says, be congruous with the visible if there is to be a symbol, and the visible must "partake of the reality which it renders intelligible": indeed it is precisely because of this congruity that great symbols give that "shock of recognition . . . almost remembrance" of which Keats wrote. It is true also that the relations of coupled images are commonly relationships of *incongruity*. But what is important in both cases is, I submit, the relationship, the *coupling*, and not the way the coupling fits. The "universal analogy" is comprehended in one way by symbol and in another way by coupled images. In a symbol the one "thing" is in front and the other behind. In coupled images they stand there side by side. In a symbol the one "thing" partakes of the nature of the other. In coupled images the two "things" are often as far apart as fleshless bone and bracelet of bright hair. But in both the means to meaning are the same. Both make sense of the world by showing us relationships we had not seen. And unless the relationship is shown, neither has sense to make. That gross beast at the end of "The Second Coming" is not a symbol for that simple reason: the second figure of the intended pair is missing—is not "there."

Which brings me to my second, and equally vulnerable front. Here authoritative opinion is not so much opposed as merely averted. When Ivor Richards says that metaphor is "the supreme agent by which disparate and hitherto unconnected things are brought together in poetry" he is not denying the power of images in conjunction—a power to which he is as sensitive as any man alive. He is merely saying that this power is inferior to the power of metaphor—a subordinate instance—an implicit *kind* of metaphor, to which metaphor itself must be "supreme." I am therefore not only outnumbered but ignored before I even begin to argue. And yet I cannot bring myself to submit. The considerations which apply in the case of symbol seem to me to apply with equal or even greater force in the case of metaphor. For what gives a metaphor its power is not, as some writers seem to imply, a mysterious virtue inherent in the name. What gives a metaphor its power is precisely the coupling of the images of which all metaphors are composed.

But here again, as in the case of symbol, I must repeat that it is metaphor *in poetry* I am discussing. For metaphors, of course, exist outside of poetry. They are common animals found in every use of words, including—particularly including—ordinary conversation. The difference is that in ordinary conversation, and in most kinds of prose, metaphors are only half alive, and tend, like grey cats at night, to disappear into the verbiage. They become clichés. Indeed a surprising number of the most depressing clichés in the language are precisely half-dead metaphors. They have ceased to express a relationship. Which means, since a metaphor *is* a relationship, that they have ceased to express. We say that a ship plows the sea but all we communicate is a ship moving. There is no plow. No plowshare. Nothing but a ship. And eventually even the ship vanishes into its verb.

In poetry, on the other hand—in a good poem—a metaphor is always a relationship: "the application," as Aristotle puts it in the *Poetics*, "of an alien name by transference either from genus to species, or from species to species, or by analogy, that is, proportion." Or, to use the language of a modern dictionary, a metaphor is a figure of speech characterized by the transference of a name or descriptive term to some object to which it is not properly applicable. A carrying-over, in other words, of a name, applicable to one object, to another object to which it is not applicable: an "alien name": a name which becomes "alien" in the process of transference. There are always, that is to say, two objects, two "things," in any live metaphor, any metaphor live enough to be used in a good poem. Let me take an example from that mine of live metaphors, Andrew Marvell's "To His Coy Mistress":

> My vegetable love should grow
> Vaster than empires, and more slow . . .

Here the two "things" are a vegetable—my students were drawn toward a cabbage implacably but imperceptibly bloating itself on the fat soil of a garden bed—and love: in the context of the poem, eager, instant, breathless desiring love. And the name of the first— "alien" indeed—has been transferred to the second. An incongruous pair have been married but they are still a pair and the incongruity is only the more noticeable, like that of a small husband and a large wife, because they are now to be treated as one. Indeed the whole force of the metaphor, and this is a metaphor of memorable force, lies precisely in the fact that although the two are one they are still two. And this is so not only of Marvell's metaphor but of all live metaphors. What else does that famous saying of Aristotle's mean: that "a good metaphor implies the intuitive perception of the similarity in dissimilars"?

But how then, if there are always two "things," two objects, in a live metaphor, and if this dissimilarity as well as their similarity remains visible—how does the power of metaphor differ from the power of the coupling of images? The "alien name," the marriage, does of course affect the relation of the partners to each other. They lie, not side by side in the oakenshaw; but roped together by a borrowed word. But because they are closer linked do they move us more deeply and so enable us more immediately or more profoundly to perceive that similarity in dissimilars which Aristotle and Baudelaire and all the English poets agree to be the key to "meaning" in poetry?

Questions like these can only be carried to poems for there is no other judge to judge. I should like to submit this particular question to the famous poem of Marvell I have just cited.

> Had we but world enough, and time,
> This coyness, lady, were no crime.
> We would sit down, and think which way
> To walk, and pass our long love's day.

Thou by the Indian Ganges' side
Should'st rubies find: I by the tide
Of Humber would complain. I would
Love you ten years before the Flood,
And you should, if you please, refuse
Till the conversion of the Jews.
My vegetable love should grow
Vaster than empires, and more slow,
An hundred years should go to praise
Thine eyes, and on thy forehead gaze:
Two hundred to adore each breast:
But thirty thousand to the rest;
An age at least to every part,
And the last age should show your heart.
For, lady, you deserve this state,
Nor would I love at lower rate.

But at my back I always hear
Time's wingèd chariot hurrying near:
And yonder all before us lie
Deserts of vast eternity.
Thy beauty shall no more be found;
Nor, in thy marble vault, shall sound
My echoing song: then worms shall try
That long-preserved virginity.
And your quaint honour turn to dust,
And into ashes all my lust.
The grave's a fine and private place,
But none, I think, do there embrace.

Now, therefore, while the youthful hue
Sits on thy skin like morning dew,
And while thy willing soul transpires
At every pore with instant fires,
Now let us sport us while we may;
And now, like amorous birds of prey,
Rather at once our Time devour,
Than languish in his slow-chapt power.
Let us roll all our strength and all
Our sweetness up into one ball,
And tear our pleasures with rough strife
Thorough the iron gates of life.
Thus, though we cannot make our sun
Stand still, yet we will make him run.

On its face this poem is, of course, a speech in three parts, or an epistle in three pleadings, or a one-sided conversation in three *reprises,* having for end and aim to persuade a young lady upon whose skin there still sits "the youthful hue" to a certain course of conduct. An invitation, you might say, to the oldest waltz. As a piece of persuasion, it is not particularly elegant. The argument comes down to this: if we had all the time in the world, or all the world in time, we could spend both adoring and being adored, but since we haven't, let's get on with it. Logical enough, candid enough, brutal enough—so brutal that one of my students (and it did his feelings credit) once stopped right there—but scarcely a poem worth reading after adolescence. Sex—the preconceptions of certain of our younger contemporaries among the novelists to the contrary notwithstanding—is interesting but not as interesting as all that. It is not, except momentarily, an end in itself.

But Marvell's poem *is* interesting—has been continuously interesting for more than three hundred years—is indeed far more than interesting. And why? Because it is obviously *not* the simple exercise in amorous rhetoric it appears to be. But why is it more? Again for an obvious reason: because it is constructed of a series of vivid figures which will not let it lie inert in the inanity of its apparent theme. But how can they prevent it from lying so? Because, like all such figures, they are two-legged creatures, and because they stand, in this poem, with one leg in the little amorous game and with the other in tragic life. Because the *time* they know, and the time the poem, through them, comes to know, is not the little hour of delay between the lover's wanting and the lover's having, but the little length of life itself with deserts of vast eternity beyond it. Because the *desire* they know is not the lover's instant urgency of desiring but the urgency of that wingèd chariot "I always hear"—which *we* too always hear when we are brave enough to listen. Because the *coyness* they know is not the coyness of that girl's refusal for *now,* for a moment, but of life's ultimate refusal forever—which is not coy.

We have a cliché we use too often when we discuss the reading of poems. We talk about "levels." We say, at this level it means this; at a second level something quite different; at a third . . . at a fourth. . . . It is a word which saves time perhaps and may even mean something as a shorthand sign but as a metaphor it is deceptive. It implies that a poem is like an apartment house: you climb from one story to the next and each floor is separate and distinct: the rooms—the arrangement of the rooms—are identical but everything else is different . . . the furniture . . . the view. One does not read a poem in this way. One does not read one's self from one floor up to the next until finally—I suppose—one emerges from the fire exit on the roof. One never leaves—if you wish to persist in a metaphor from the building trades—one never leaves the first story. And one does not read one's self *up* or *down*. One stands there and reads *through*: through the sounds, but never leaving the sounds, into their references, through the references to the images they make, through the images to their relation to each other, through their relation to each other to the feel of meaning. It is perspective one reads for in a poem, and perspective includes the near things as well as the far and includes them all at the same time and in the same scene.

It is perspective one reads for because meaning in a poem *is* perspective—the perspective which puts everything in place. The universal analogy is never seen but in perspective—in that glimpse.

And it is for this reason that Marvell's poem both is and is not an essay in seduction: because the figures of the poem open *through*. But how do they open through? Some as metaphors: vegetable love, Time's wingèd chariot, Time's slow-chapt power, the iron gates of life. Some as coupled images in which no name is transferred but things remain themselves—remain, in one case, horribly themselves: ". . . then worms shall try/That long preserv'd virginity." Some as neither or both:

> The grave's a fine and private place,
> But none, I think, do there embrace.

Here there is no "alien name" and things remain themselves and what is said is true, grimly true—though that grave is all but turned to dreadful boudoir by the irony of the "fine and private place."

But though this strange enlargement of the seeming cynical poem is accomplished by figures of several kinds of which metaphor is one, all these figures have in common the power of the coupled image. They all compose congruities of incongruousness by placing images side by side: vegetable and love, time and chariot, lover and worm. And it is this mating and matching of what does not mate and match in the habitual mind which gives the poem as a whole its enormous, dark dimension, and leaves its amused and smiling reader staring out through suddenly uncurtained windows at a lonely, cold and unaccustomed sky.

How is this accomplished? By a figure which brings the two impossible halves of the whole scene together:

> Let us roll all our strength and all
> Our sweetness up into one ball,
> And tear our pleasures with rough strife
> Thorough the iron gates of life.
> Thus, though we cannot make our sun
> Stand still, yet we will make him run.

Here on the one side is the amorous play which is the poem's apparent theme: more than the amorous play—the act of love itself: his strength, her sweetness. Here on the other are the iron gates of life: time and death—time which turns lust to ash s and the denial of lust to dust. And suddenly the two are met. We tear our pleasures with rough strife not through the lovely gates of love but through the iron gates of life. We master time and death itself by passion. It is a brief victory: we cannot make our sun stand still. But it is a victory notwithstanding: we can make him run.   ·

True? Is it true that human passion can master time? Well, isn't it?—when time and human passion are brought face to face in the figure of this poem with death before them and the chariot behind? Is not human lust, in *that* perspective, a part of life and death and so not careless lust but tragic love? And is it not conceivable that love can master time? Is it not perhaps in that perspective that the poem "means"?

Poetry as Morality

Yvor Winters is the poet-critic whose preference for a traditional measure we have already considered; his "The Morality of Poetry" establishes theoretical grounds for that preference. According to Winters a poem is ideally discursive, not the presentation of an experience as directly experienced but a statement about the experience. It provides understanding and arouses feelings; it establishes a relation between the two. It is good insofar as the feelings it arouses are appropriate to the understanding it communicates. For Winters the writing of poetry with its self-examination and revision is a moral discipline, a "striving to perfect a moral attitude"; reading poetry improves one's moral attitude and, once acquired, this improvement affects one's actions.

Since Winters is a severe judge of poetry which many critics have been able only to praise, we may be tempted to dismiss him. He does overemphasize the role of reason. But his argument is formidable: that this poetry, by mistakenly attempting to render its subject, abandons rational control over it and fails to evaluate it. Winters' case for moral significance is presented with remarkable explicitness and coherence. Whether they finally accept it or not, this case can exert valuable critical pressure on readers who are actively discovering for themselves the nature and function of poetry.

YVOR WINTERS

The Morality of Poetry

Before attempting to elucidate or to criticize a poetry so difficult and evasive as that of the best moderns, it would appear wise to summarize as clearly as

356

possible those qualities for which one looks in a poem. We may say that a poem in the first place should offer us new perceptions, not only of the exterior universe, but of human experience as well; it should add, in other words, to what we have already seen. This is the elementary function for the reader. The corresponding function for the poet is a sharpening and training of his sensibilities; the very exigencies of the medium as he employs it in the act of perception should force him to the discovery of values which he never would have found without the convening of all the conditions of that particular act, conditions one or more of which will be the necessity of solving some particular difficulty such as the location of a rhyme or the perfection of a cadence without disturbance to the remainder of the poem. The poet who suffers from such difficulties instead of profiting by them is only in a rather rough sense a poet at all.

If, however, the difficulties of versification are a stimulant merely to the *poet,* the reader may argue that he finds them a hindrance to himself and that he prefers some writer of prose who appears to offer him as much with less trouble to all concerned. The answer to such a reader is that the appearance of equal richness in the writer of prose is necessarily deceptive.

For language is a kind of abstraction, even at its most concrete; such a word as "cat," for instance, is generic and not particular. Such a word becomes paricular only in so far as it gets into some kind of experiential complex, which qualifies it and limits it, which gives it, in short, a local habitation as well as a name. Such a complex is the poetic line or other unit, which, in turn, should be a functioning part of the larger complex, or poem. This is, I imagine, what Mallarmé should have had in mind when he demanded that the poetic line be a new word, not found in any dictionary, and partaking of the nature of incantation (that is, having the power to materialize, or perhaps it would be more accurate to say, *being* a new experience.)[1]

[1] Stéphane Mallarmé: *Avant-Dire* du *Traite du Verbe,* par René Ghil. Giraud, 18 Rue Drouot, Paris, 1886. Actually, Mallarmé seems to have had more in mind, though he should have had no more, in my opinion. The margin of difference is the margin in which post-romantic theory has flourished and from which post-romantic poetry has sprung. I quote the entire curious passage:
"Un désir indéniable à l'epoque est de séparer comme en vue d'attribu-

The poem, to be perfect, should likewise be a new word in the
same sense, a word of which the line, as we have defined it, is
merely a syllable. Such a word is, of course, composed of much
more than the sum of its words (as one normally uses the term)
and its syntax. It is composed of an almost fluid complex, if the
adjective and the noun are not too nearly contradictory, of relationships between words (in the normal sense of the term), a relationship involving rational content, cadences, rhymes, juxtapositions,
literary and other connotations, inversions, and so on, almost indefinitely. These relationships, it should be obvious, extend the poet's
vocabulary incalculably. They partake of the fluidity and unpre-

---

tions différentes, le double état de la parole, brut ou immédiate ici, là
essentiel.

"Narrer, enseigner, même décrire, cela va et encore qu'à chacun suffirait
peut-être, pour échanger toute pensée humaine, de prendre ou de mettre dans
la main d'autrui en silence une pièce de monnaie, l'emploi élémentaire du
discours dessert l'universel reportage dont, la Litterature exceptée, participe
tout, entre les genres d'écrits contemporains.

"A quoi bon la merveille de transposer un fait de nature en sa presque
disparition vibratoire selon le jeu de la parole cepedant, si ce n'est pour qu'on
émane, sans la gêne d'un proche ou concret rappel, la notion pure?

"Je dis: une fleur! et, hors de l'oubli où ma voix relègue aucun contour,
en tant que quelque chose d'autre que les calices sus, musicalement se lève,
idée rieuse ou altière, l'absente de tous bouquets.

"Au contraire d'une fonction de numéraire facile et représentatif, comme
le traite d'abord la foule, le parler qui est, après tout, rêve et chant, retrouve
chez le poète, par nécessité constitutive d'un art consacré aux fictions, sa
virtualité.

"Le vers qui de plusieurs vocables refait un mot total, neuf, étranger à la
langue et comme incantatoire, achève cet isolement de la parole: niant, d'un
trait souverain, le hasard demeuré aux termes malgré l'artifice de leur re-
trempe alténée en le sens et la sonorité, et vous cause cette surprise de n'avoir
ouï jamais tel fragment ordinaire d'élocution, en même temps que la rémin-
iscence de l'objet nommé baigne dans une clairvoyante atmosphère."

This is in some respects an admirable summary, and is certainly important
historically. The entire tendency of the passage is to encourage the elimination of the rational from poetry. One should observe the sequence: "narrer,
enseigner, *même* decrire," as if description were more nearly poetic than the
other activities. The word *essentiel,* at the end of the first paragraph is the
crux of the whole passage. The critic says that words have an obvious (that
is, a rational) meaning, and a fringe of feeling, which he chooses to call
essential: if only one kind of content is essential, we are naturally inclined
to try to eliminate the other, and we have in this confusion, which reappears
spontaneously, and without any discernible indebtedness to Mallarmé, in
each successive generation of post-romantic poets, the real basis for post-
romantic obscurantism. The sound idea that a poem is more than its rational
content is thus perverted and distorted.

dictability of experience and so provide a means of treating experience with precision and freedom. If the poet does not wish, as, actually, he seldom does, to reproduce a given experience with approximate exactitude, he can employ the experience as a basis for a new experience that will be just as real, in the sense of being particular, and perhaps more valuable.

Now verse is more valuable than prose in this process for the simple reasons that its rhythms are faster and more highly organized than are those of prose, and so lend themselves to a greater complexity and compression of relationship, and that the intensity of this convention renders possible a greater intensity of other desirable conventions, such as poetic language and devices of rhetoric. The writer of prose must substitute bulk for this kind of intensity; he must define his experience ordinarily by giving all of its past history, the narrative logic leading up to it, whereas the experiential relations given in a good lyric poem, though particular in themselves, are applicable without alteration to a good many past histories. In this sense, the lyric is general as well as particular; in fact, this quality of transferable or generalized experience might be regarded as the defining quality of lyrical poetry.

What I have just said should make plain the difficulty of comprehending a poem exactly and fully; its total intention may be very different from its paraphrasable, or purely logical content. If one take, for example, Mr. Allen Tate's sonnet, *The Subway*, and translate it into good scholarly prose, using nothing but the rational content of the poem as a reference, one will find the author saying that as a result of his ideas and of his metropolitan environment, he is going mad. Now as a matter of fact, the poem says nothing of the sort:

> Dark accurate plunger down the successive knell
> Of arch on arch, where ogives burst a red
> Reverberance of hail upon the dead
> Thunder, like an exploding crucible!
> Harshly articulate, musical steel shell
> Of angry worship, hurled religiously
> Upon your business of humility
> Into the iron forestries of hell!
>
> Till broken in the shift of quieter
> Dense altitudes tangential of your steel,

> I am become geometries—and glut
> Expansions like a blind astronomer
> Dazed, while the worldless heavens bulge and reel
> In the cold revery of an idiot.

The sonnet indicates that the author has faced and defined the possibility of the madness that I have mentioned (a possibility from the consideration of which others as well as himself may have found it impossible to escape) and has arrived at a moral attitude toward it, an attitude which is at once defined and communicated by the poem. This attitude is defined only by the entire poem, not by the logical content alone; it is a matter not only of logical content, but of feeling as well. The feeling is particular and unparaphrasable, but one may indicate the nature of it briefly by saying that it is a feeling of dignity and of self-control in the face of a situation of major difficulty, a difficulty which the poet fully apprehends. This feeling is inseparable from what we call poetic form, or unity, for the creation of a form is nothing more nor less than the act of evaluating and shaping (that is, controlling) a given experience. It should be obvious that any attempt to reduce the rational content of such a poem would tend to confuse or even to eliminate the feeling: the poem consists in the relationship between the two.

To reënforce my point, I shall take the liberty of quoting another poem, this one by Mr. Howard Baker, in which something comparable occurs. The title is *Pont Neuf*:

> Henry the Fourth rides in bronze,
> His shoulders curved and pensive, thrust
> Enormously into electric
> Blazonments of a Christmas trust.

> Children pass him aghast and pleased,
> Reflective of the flickerings
> Of jerky bears and clowns. Alone,
> Astute to all the bickerings

> Of age and death rides Henry the Grand.
> A lean tug shudders in the Seine;
> And Notre Dame is black, a relic
> Of the blood of other men.

> Peace to the other men! And peace
> To the mind that has no century,
> And sees the savage pull the statue down,
> And down the bear and clown.

The spiritual control in a poem, then, is simply a manifestation of the spiritual control within the poet, and, as I have already indicated, it may have been an important means by which the poet arrived at a realization of spiritual control. This conception must not be confused with the conception of the poem as a safety valve, by which feeling is diverted from action, by which the writer escapes from an attitude by pouring it into his work and leaving it behind him. The conception which I am trying to define is a conception of poetry as a technique of contemplation, of comprehension, a technique which does not eliminate the need of philosophy or of religion, but which, rather, completes and enriches them.

One feels, whether rightly or wrongly, a correlation between the control envinced within a poem and the control within the poet behind it. The laxity of the one ordinarily appears to involve laxity in the other. The rather limp versification of Mr. Eliot and of Mr. MacLeish is inseparable from the spiritual limpness that one feels behind the poems, as the fragmentary, ejaculatory, and overexcited quality of a great many of the poems of Hart Crane is inseparable from the intellectual confusion upon which these particular poems seem to rest (for examples, *The Dance, Cape Hatteras,* and *Atlantis*). Crane possessed great energy, but his faculties functioned clearly only within a limited range of experience (*Repose of Rivers, Voyages II, Faustus and Helen II*). Outside of that range he was either numb (*My Grandmother's Love-letters* and *Harbor Dawn*) or unsure of himself and hence uncertain in his detail (as in *The River,* a very powerful poem in spite of its poor construction and its quantities of bad writing) or both (see *Indiana,* probably one of the worst poems in modern literature). Many of the poems of Mr. Eliot and of Mr. MacLeish could be reduced by paraphrase to about the same thing as my paraphrase of Mr. Tate's sonnet; the difference between them and Mr. Tate in this connection is that, as the form of nearly all of their poems is much looser to start with, the process of paraphrasing would constitute a much slighter act of betrayal. And we must not forget that this quality, form, is not something outside the poet, something "æsthetic," and superim-

posed upon his moral content; it is essentially a part, in fact it may
be the decisive part, of the moral content, even though the poet
may be arriving at the final perfection of the condition he is communicating while he communicates it and in a large measure as a
result of the act and technique of communication. For the communication is first of all with himself: it is, as I have said, the last
refinement of contemplation.

I should pause here to remark that many writers have sought to
seize the fluidity of experience by breaking down the limits of
form, but that in so doing, they defeat their own ends. For, as I
have shown, writing, as it approaches the looseness of prose and
departs from the strictness of verse, tends to lose the capacity for
fluid or highly complex relationships between words; language, in
short, reapproaches its original stiffness and generality; and one is
forced to recognize the truth of what appears a paradox, that the
greatest fluidity of statement is possible where the greatest clarity
of form prevails. It is hard to see how the existence of such a work
as Mr. Joyce's latest creation[2] can be anything but precarious, in
spite of its multitudes of incidental felicities; for it departs from the
primary condition of prose—coherent and cumulative logic or narrative—without, since it is, finally, prose, achieving the formal precision of verse. These remarks should not be construed, however, as
an argument against free verse, though, with proper qualification,
they could be brought to bear in such an argument. The free verse
that is really verse—the best, that is, of W. C. Williams, H. D.,
Miss Moore, Wallace Stevens, and Ezra Pound—is, in its peculiar
fashion, the antithesis of free, and the evaluation of this verse is a
difficult problem in itself.

Thus we see that the poet, in striving toward an ideal of poetic
form at which he has arrived through the study of other poets, is
actually striving to perfect a moral attitude toward that range of
experience of which he is aware. Such moral attitudes are contagious from poet to poet, and, within the life of a single poet, from
poem to poem. The presence of Hardy and Arnold, let us say, in so
far as their successful works offer us models and their failures
warnings or unfulfilled suggestions, should make it easier to write
good poetry; they should not only aid us, by providing standards of

[2] Entitled at this writing (1935) *Work in Progress*. (Ultimately published
as *Finnegans Wake*.)

sound feeling, to test the soundness of our own poems, but, since
their range of experience is very wide, they should aid us, as we are
able to enter and share their experience, to grow into regions that
we had not previously mastered or perhaps even discovered. The
discipline of imitation is thus valuable if it leads to understanding
and assimilation. Too often a minor poet or other reader will recognize in such a master the validity of only that part of the master's
experience which corresponds to his own limited range, and will
rule out the poetry to which he is consequently numb as senti-
mental or otherwise imperfect. Inflexibility of critical opinion in
such matters is not particularly conducive to growth.

Random experiment may have a related value: one may hit on
a form (perhaps the rough idea or draft of a form) which induces
some new state or states of mind. I regard as fallacious the notion
that form is determined by a precedent attitude or a precedent subject matter, at least invariably: the form (that is, the general idea
of a certain type of form) *may* precede, and the attitude in any
case, is never definite till the form is achieved.[3] It does not follow
that any attitude resulting from random experiment is intrinsically
desirable; undesirable attitudes, like desirable, are contagious and
may spread widely; it is here that criticism becomes necessary. A
failure, however, to achieve something valuable may offer a valuable suggestion to someone else. The poet who has succeeded once
or twice in mastering difficult and central emotions and in recording his mastery for future reference should find it easier to succeed
again.

I am not endeavoring in the two foregoing paragraphs to establish poetry as a substitute for philosophy or for religion. Religion
is highly desirable if it is really available to the individual; the
study of philosophy is always available and is of incalculable value
as a preliminary and as a check to activities as a poet and as a critic
(that is, as an intelligent reader). I am, then, merely attempting to
define a few of the things which poetry does.

It would perhaps be wise to add another caution: I suffer from

[3] As a single example, consider the manner in which the Petrarchan experimenters in England, most of them feeble poets and the best of them
given to empty and inflated reasoning, worked out the technique of reasoning elaborately in graceful lyrical verse and bequeathed that technique to
the 17th century: the form preceded the matter.

no illusion that any man who can write a good poem has a naturally sweet moral temper or that the man who has written three good poems is a candidate for canonization. Literary history is packed with sickening biographies. But it is worth noting that the poetry of such a man, say, as Rochester (who in this is typical of his age) displays a mastery of an extremely narrow range of experience, and that his moral brutality falls almost wholly in those regions (nearly every region save that of worldly manners, if we except some few poems, notably *Upon Nothing, Absent from Thee,* and, possibly, *A Song of a Young Lady to Her Ancient Lover,* in which last there is a curious blending of the erotic with deep moral feeling) with which his poetry fails to deal or with which it deals badly.

This statement requires elucidation. Rochester frequently writes of his debauchery, and sometimes writes well of it, but in the best poems on the subject, in such poems as *The Maim'd Debauchee* and *Upon Drinking in a Bowl,* he writes, as do his contemporaries in the comedy, as a witty and satirical gentleman: the wit inspired by the material is mastered, and other aspects of the material are ignored. In the worst poems on more or less similar material (for examples, the numerous lampoons upon Charles II and upon Nell Gwyn) we have a grossness of feeling comparable to that of his worst actions. All of this, however, detracts not in the least from the quality of Rochester's best poetry, which is remarkably fine; Rochester seldom extends the standards which he recognizes into fields to which they are inapplicable, and hence he is seldom guilty of false evaluation. In reading him, one is aware that he is a sound and beautiful poet, and that there are greater poets. That is all of which one has a right to be aware.[4]

If a poem, in so far as it is good, represents the comprehension on a moral plane of a given experience, it is only fair to add that some experiences offer very slight difficulties and some very great, and that the poem will be the most valuable, which, granted it achieves formal perfection, represents the most difficult victory. In the great tragic poets, such as Racine or Shakespeare, one feels that a victory has been won over life itself, so much is implicated in the subject matter; that feeling is the source of their power over us,

[4] *The Collected Poems of John Wilmot, Earl of Rochester,* edited by John Hayward. The Nonesuch Press, 16 Great James St., London, W.C. 1926.

whereas a slighter poet will absorb very little of our experience and leave the rest untouched.

This requisite seems to be ignored in a large measure by a good many contemporary poets of more or less mystical tendencies, who avoid the difficult task of mastering the more complex forms of experience by setting up a theoretic escape from them and by then accepting that escape with a good deal of lyrical enthusiasm. Such an escape is offered us, I fear, by Hart Crane, in one of the most extraordinary sections of his volume, *The Bridge,*[5] in the poem called *The Dance,* and such escapes are often employed by Mr. Yeats. In the religious poets of the past, one encounters this vice very seldom; the older religions are fully aware that the heart, to borrow the terms of a poem by Janet Lewis, is untranslatable, whatever may be true of the soul, and that one can escape from the claims of the world only by understanding those claims and by thus accustoming oneself to the thought of eventually putting them by. This necessity is explicitly the subject of one of Sidney's greatest sonnets, *Leave me, O Love, which reachest but to dust,* and of the greatest poem by George Herbert, *Church Monuments;* one can find it elsewhere. The attitude is humane, and does not belittle nor evade the magnitude of the task; it is essentially a tragic attitude.

For this reason, the religious fervor of Gerard Hopkins, of John Donne, or of George Herbert should weaken but little the force of most of their poems for the non-believer, just as the deterministic doctrines, whatever their nature and extent, to be found in Hardy, should not weaken for us those poems which do not deal too pugnaciously with the doctrines, and for the same reason. Though a belief in any form of determinism should, if the belief is pushed to its logical ends, eliminate the belief in, and consequently the functioning of, whatever it is that we call the will, yet there is no trace of any kind of disintegration in Hardy's poetic style, in his sense of form, which we have seen to be, so far as writing is concerned, identical with the will or the ability to control and shape one's experience. The tragic necessity of putting by the claims of the world without the abandonment of self-control, without loss of the ability to go on living, for the present, intelligently and well, is just as definitely the subject of Hardy's poetry as of Herbert's. We have in both poets a common moral territory which is far greater than

[5] *The Bridge,* by Hart Crane, Horace Liveright: N. Y.: 1930.

are the theological regions which they do not share; for, on the one hand, the fundamental concepts of morality are common to intelligent men regardless of theological orientation, except in so far as morality may be simply denied or ignored, and, on the other hand, the Absolute is in its nature inscrutable and offers little material for speculation, except in so far as it is a stimulus to moral speculation. It would be difficult, I think, to find a devotional poem of which most of the implications were not moral and universal. So with Hardy: his determinism was mythic and animistic and tended to dramatize the human struggle, whereas a genuinely rational and coherent determinism would have eliminated the human struggle. He was thrown back upon traditional literary and folk wisdom in working out moral situations, and for these situations his mythology provided a new setting, sometimes magnificent, sometimes melodramatic, but, thanks to its rational incompleteness, not really destructive of a working morality. Like many another man who has been unable to think clearly, he was saved by the inability to think coherently: had he been coherent, he would probably have been about as interesting as Godwin; as it is, his professed beliefs and his working beliefs have only a little in common, and the former damage his work only in a fragmentary way, as when satires of circumstance are dragged into a novel or isolated in a poem to prove a point (and they can prove nothing, of course) and usually to the detriment of coherent feeling and understanding.

Crane's attitude, on the other hand, often suggests a kind of theoretic rejection of all human endeavor in favor of some vaguely apprehended but ecstatically asserted existence of a superior sort. As the exact nature of the superior experience is uncertain, it forms a rather uncertain and infertile source of material for exact poetry; one can write poetry about it only by utilizing in some way more or less metaphorical the realm of experience from which one is trying to escape; but as one *is* endeavoring to escape from this realm, not to master it and understand it, one's feelings about it are certain to be confused, and one's imagery drawn from it is bound to be largely formulary and devoid of meaning. That is, in so far as one endeavors to deal with the Absolute, not as a means of ordering one's moral perception but as the subject itself of perception, one will tend to say nothing, despite the multiplication of words. In *The Dance* there seems to be an effort to apply to each of two mutually

exclusive fields the terms of the other. This is a vice of which
Rochester was not guilty.

Crane's best work, such as *Repose of Rivers* and *Voyages II,*
is not confused, but one feels that the experience is curiously
limited and uncomplicated: it is between the author, isolated from
most human complications, and Eternity. Crane becomes in such
poems a universal symbol of the human mind in a particular situation, a fact which is the source of his power, but of the human
mind in very nearly the simplest form of that situation, a fact
which is the source of his limitation.

Objective proof of this assertion cannot be found in the poems,
any more than proof of the opposite quality can be found in Hardy;
it is in each poet a matter of feeling invading the poetry mainly by
way of the non-paraphrasable content: one feels the fragility of
Crane's finest work, just as one feels the richness of Hardy's. Hardy
is able to utilize, for example, great ranges of literary, historical,
and other connotations in words and cadences; one feels behind
each word the history of the word and the generations of men who
embodied that history; Hardy gets somehow at the wealth of the
race. It should be observed again how the moral discipline is involved in the literary discipline, how it becomes, at times, almost a
matter of living philology. From the greater part of this wealth
Crane appears to be isolated and content to remain isolated. His
isolation, like Hardy's immersion, was in part social and unavoidable, but a clearer mind and a more fixed intention might have
overcome much of the handicap.

I should like to forestall one possible objection to the theory of
poetry which I am trying to elucidate. Poetry, as a moral discipline,
should not be regarded as one more means of escape. That is, moral
responsibility should not be transferred from action to paper in the
face of a particular situation. Poetry, if pursued either by the poet
or by the reader, in the manner which I have suggested, should
offer a means of enriching one's awareness of human experience
and of so rendering greater the possibility of intelligence in the
course of future action; and it should offer likewise a means of in-
ducing certain more or less constant habits of feeling, which should
render greater the possibility of one's acting, in a future situation,
in accordance with the findings of one's improved intelligence. It
should, in other words, increase the intelligence and strengthen the

moral temper; these effects should naturally be carried over into
action, if, through constant discipline, they are made permanent
acquisitions. If the poetic discipline is to have steadiness and direction, it requires an antecedent discipline of ethical thinking and
of at least some ethical feeling, which may be in whole or in part the
gift of religion or of a social tradition, or which may be largely the
result of individual acquisition by way of study. The poetic discipline includes the antecedent discipline and more: it is the rich-
est and most perfect technique of contemplation.

This view of poetry in its general outline is not original, but is
a restatement of ideas that have been current in English criticism
since the time of Sidney, that have appeared again in most of the
famous apologists for poetry since Sidney, especially in Arnold and
in Newman. In summarizing these ideas, I have merely endeavored
to illuminate a few of the most obscure relationships and to dispose
of them in such a way as to prepare the reader for various analyses
of poetic method which I intend, in other essays, to undertake.
Poetic morality and poetic feeling are inseparable; feeling and
technique, or structure, are inseparable. Technique has laws which
govern poetic (and perhaps more general) morality more widely
than is commonly recognized. It is my intention to examine them.

Poetry as Creation

If *Winters gives poetry to the will, Wallace Stevens gives it to the imagination, the human faculty which creates our reality by resisting the pressure of bare fact and endowing fact with meaning. Imagination's aim, says Stevens, is nothing less than happiness, the creation of a world which is satisfyingly ours. When imagination flags, we live in what he calls in one of his poems "an inert savoir"; at its best it turns the world into the only paradise we shall ever know. Since man's highest pursuit is the pursuit of happiness, imagination crowns all other human faculties; poetry, which represents the imagination in language, is of transcendent importance. Poetry moves toward the enunciation of a "supreme fiction" which, Stevens hopes, will take the place of the gods which were once the creators of the world but which have vanished.*

Stevens' poems and essays, taken together, are a single ambitious celebration of imaginative activity. The method of "Two or Three Ideas" is characteristic of both his prose and his poetry; it is an experimental meditation on style which convinces, if it does, by subtle suggestion and the play of analogy rather than direct logical onslaught. It denies to poetry neither the cognitive role which Tate and MacLeish assign nor the moral function of Winters. It affirms poetry as a central creative activity, the source of all intellectual and moral values.

WALLACE STEVENS

Two or Three Ideas

My first proposition is that the style of a poem and the poem itself are one.

One of the better known poems in *Fleurs du Mal* is the one

(XII) entitled "La Vie Antérieure" or "Former Life." It begins with the line

> *J'ai longtemps habité sous de vastes portiques*

or

> A long time I lived beneath tremendous porches.

It continues:

> Which the salt-sea suns tinged with a thousand fires
> And which great columns, upright and majestic,
> At evening, made resemble basalt grottoes.

The poem concerns the life among the images, sounds and colors of those calm, sensual presences.

> At the center of azure, of waves, of brilliances,

and so on. I have chosen this poem to illustrate my first proposition, because it happens to be a poem in which the poem itself is immediately recognizable without reference to the manner in which it is rendered. If the style and the poem are one, one ought to choose, for the purpose of illustration, a poem that illustrates this as, for example, Yeats' *Lake-Isle of Innisfree*. To choose a French poem which has to be translated is to choose an example in which the style is lost in the paraphrase of translation. On the other hand, Baudelaire's poem is useful because it identifies what is meant by the poem itself. The idea of an earlier life is like the idea of a later life, or like the idea of a different life, part of the classic repertory of poetic ideas. It is part of one's inherited store of poetic subjects. Precisely, then, because it is traditional and because we understand its romantic nature and know what to expect from it, we are suddenly and profoundly touched when we hear it declaimed by a voice that says:

> I lived, for long, under huge porticoes.

It is as if we had stepped into a ruin and were startled by a flight of birds that rose as we entered. The familiar experience is made unfamiliar and from that time on, whenever we think of that particular scene, we remember how we held our breath and how the hungry doves of another world rose out of nothingness and whistled away. We stand looking at a remembered habitation. All old dwelling-places are subject to these transmogrifications and the experience of all of us includes a succession of old dwelling-places: abodes of the imagination, ancestral or memories of places that never existed. It is plain that when, in this world of weak feeling and blank thinking, in which we are face to face with the poem every moment of time, we encounter some integration of the poem that pierces and dazzles us, the effect is an effect of style and not of the poem itself or at least not of the poem alone. The effective integration is not a disengaging of the subject. It is a question of the style in which the subject is presented.

Although I have limited myself to an instance of the relation between style and the familiar, one gets the same result in considering the relation between style and its own creations, that is between style and the unfamiliar. What we are really considering here are the creations of modern art and modern literature. If one keeps in mind the fact that most poets who have something to say are content with what they say and that most poets who have little or nothing to say are concerned primarily with the way in which they say it, the importance of this discussion becomes clear. I do not mean to imply that the poets who have something to say are the poets that matter; for obviously if it is true that the style of a poem and the poem itself are one, it follows that, in considering style and its own creations, that is to say, the relation between style and the unfamiliar, it may be, or become, that the poets who have little or nothing to say are, or will be, the poets that matter. Today, painters who have something to say are less admired than painters who seem to have little or nothing to say but who do at least believe that style and the painting are one. The inclination toward arbitrary or schematic constructions in poetry is, from the point of view of style, very strong; and certainly if these constructions were effective it would be true that the style and the poem were one.

In the light of this first idea the prejudice in favor of plain English, for instance, comes to nothing. I have never been able to see why what is called Anglo-Saxon should have the right to higgle and haggle all over the page, contesting the right of other words. If a poem seems to require a hierophantic phrase, the phrase should pass. This is a way of saying that one of the consequences of the

ordination of style is not to limit it, but to enlarge it, not to im-
poverish it, but to enrich and liberate it.

The second idea relates to poetry and the gods, both ancient and
modern, both foreign and domestic. To simplify, I shall speak only
of the ancient and the foreign gods. I do not mean to refer to them
in their religious aspects but as creations of the imagination; and
I suppose that as with all creations of the imagination I have been
thinking of them from the point of view of style, that is to say of
their style. When we think of Jove, while we take him for granted
as the symbol of omnipotence, the ruler of mankind, we do not fear
him. He does have a superhuman size, but at least not so superhuman as to amaze and intimidate us. He has a large head and a
beard and is a relic, a relic that makes a kindly impression on us
and reminds us of stories that we have heard about him. All of the
noble images of all of the gods have been profound and most of
them have been forgotten. To speak of the origin and end of gods
is not a light matter. It is to speak of the origin and end of eras of
human belief. And while it is easy to look back on those that have
disappeared as if they were the playthings of cosmic make-believe,
and on those that made petitions to them and honored them and
received their benefits as legendary innocents, we are bound, nevertheless, to concede that the gods were personae of a peremptory
elevation and glory. It would be wrong to look back to them as if
they had existed in some indigence of the spirit. They were in fact,
as we see them now, the clear giants of a vivid time, who in the
style of their beings made the style of the gods and the gods themselves one.

This brings me to the third idea, which is this: In an age of disbelief, or, what is the same thing, in a time that is largely humanistic, in one sense or another, it is for the poet to supply the satis-
factions of belief, in his measure and in his style. I say in his
measure to indicate that the figures of the philosopher, the artist,
the teacher, the moralist and other figures, including the poet, find
themselves, in such a time, to be figures of an importance greatly
enhanced by the requirements both of the individual and of society; and I say in his style by way of confining the poet to his role
and thereby of intensifying that role. It is this that I want to talk
about today. I want to try to formulate a conception of perfection
in poetry with reference to the present time and the near future

and to speculate on the activities possible to it as it deploys itself throughout the lives of men and women. I think of it as a role of the utmost seriousness. It is, for one thing, a spiritual role. One might stop to draw an ideal portrait of the poet. But that would be parenthetical. In any case, we do not say that the philosopher, the artist or the teacher is to take the place of the gods. Just so, we do not say that the poet is to take the place of the gods.

To see the gods dispelled in mid-air and dissolve like clouds is one of the great human experiences. It is not as if they had gone over the horizon to disappear for a time; nor as if they had been overcome by other gods of greater power and profounder knowledge. It is simply that they came to nothing. Since we have always shared all things with them and have always had a part of their strength and, certainly, all of their knowledge, we shared likewise this experience of annihilation. It was their annihilation, not ours, and yet it left us feeling that in a measure, we, too, had been annihilated. It left us feeling dispossessed and alone in a solitude, like children without parents, in a home that seemed deserted, in which the amical rooms and halls had taken on a look of hardness and emptiness. What was most extraordinary is that they left no momentoes behind, no thrones, no mystic rings, no texts either of the soil or of the soul. It was as if they had never inhabited the earth. There was no crying out for their return. They were not forgotten because they had been a part of the glory of the earth. At the same time, no man ever muttered a petition in his heart for the restoration of those unreal shapes. There was always in every man the increasingly human self, which instead of remaining the observer, the non-participant, the delinquent, became constantly more and more all there was or so it seemed; and whether it was so or merely seemed so still left it for him to resolve life and the world in his own terms.

Thinking about the end of the gods creates singular attitudes in the mind of the thinker. One attitude is that the gods of classical mythology were merely aesthetic projections. They were not the objects of belief. They were expressions of delight. Perhaps delight is too active a word. It is true that they were engaged with the future world and the immortality of the soul. It is true, also, that they were the objects of veneration and therefore of religious dignity and sanctity. But in the blue air of the Mediterranean these white and a little colossal figures had a special propriety, a special felicity. Could they have been created for that propriety, that felicity? Notwithstanding their divinity, they were close to the people among whom they moved. Is it one of the normal activities of humanity, in the solitude of reality and in the unworthy treatment of solitude, to create companions, a little colossal as I have said, who, if not superficially explicative, are, as least, assumed to be full of the secret of things and who in any event bear in themselves even, if they do not always wear it, the peculiar majesty of mankind's sense of worth, neither too much nor too little? To a people of high intelligence, whose gods have benefited by having been accepted and addressed by the superior minds of a superior world, the symbolic paraphernalia of the very great becomes unnecessary and the very great become the very natural. However all that may be, the celestial atmosphere of these deities, their ultimate remote celestial residences are not matters of chance. Their fundamental glory is the fundamental glory of men and women, who being in need of it create it, elevate it, without too much searching of its identity.

The people, not the priests, made the gods. The personages of immortality were something more than the conceptions of priests, although they may have picked up many of the conceits of priests. Who were the priests? Who have always been the high priests of any of the gods? Certainly not those officials or generations of officials who administered rites and observed rituals. The great and true priest of Apollo was he that composed the most moving of Apollo's hymns. The really illustrious archimandrite of Zeus was the one that made the being of Zeus people the whole of Olympus and the Olympian land, just as the only marvelous bishops of heaven have always been those that made it seem like heaven. I said a moment ago that we had not forgotten the gods. What is it that we remember of them? In the case of those masculine do we remember their ethics or is it their port and mien, their size, their color, not to speak of their adventures, that we remember? In the case of those feminine do we remember, as in the case of Diana, their fabulous chastity or their beauty? Do we remember those masculine in any way differently from the way in which we remember Ulysses and other men of supreme interest and excellence? In the case of those feminine do we remember Venus in any way differently from the way in which we remember Penelope and other women of much mark and feeling? In short, while the priests helped to realize the gods, it was the people that spoke of them and to them and heard their replies.

Let us stop now and restate the ideas which we are considering in relation to one another. The first is that the style of a poem and the poem itself are one; the second is that the style of the gods and the gods themselves are one; the third is that in an age of disbelief, when the gods have come to an end, when we think of them as the aesthetic projections of a time that has passed, men turn to a fundamental glory of their own and from that create a style of bearing themselves in reality. They create a new style of a new bearing in a new reality. This third idea, then, may be made to conform to the way in which the other two have been expressed by saying that the style of men and men themselves are one. Now, if the style of a poem and poem itself are one; if the style of the gods and the gods themselves are one; and if the style of men and men themselves are one; and if there is any true relation between these propositions, it might well be the case that the parts of these propositions are interchangeable. Thus, it might be true that the style of a poem and the gods themselves are one; or that the style of the gods and the style of men are one; or that the style of a poem and the style of men are one. As we hear these things said, without having time to think about them, it sounds as if they might be true, at least as if there might be something to them. Most of us are prepared to listen patiently to talk of the identity of the gods and men. But where does the poem come in? And if my answer to that is that I am concerned primarily with the poem and that my purpose this morning is to elevate the poem to the level of one of the major significances of life and to equate it, for the purpose of discussion, with gods and men, I hope it will be clear that it comes in as the central interest, the fresh and foremost object.

If in the minds of men creativeness was the same thing as creation in the natural world, if a spiritual planet matched the sun, or if without any question of a spiritual planet, the light and warmth of spring revitalized all our faculties, as in a measure they do, all the bearings one takes, all the propositions one formulates would be within the scope of that particular domination. The trouble is, however, that men in general do not create in light and

warmth alone. They create in darkness and coldness. They create
when they are hopeless, in the midst of antagonisms, when they are
wrong, when their powers are no longer subject to their control.
They create as the ministers of evil. Here in New England at this
very moment nothing but good seems to be returning; and in that
good, particularly if we ignore the difference between men and the
natural world, how easy it is suddenly to believe in the poem as
one has never believed in it before, suddenly to require of it a
meaning beyond what its words can possibly say, a sound beyond
any giving of the ear, a motion beyond our previous knowledge of
feeling. And, of course, our three ideas have not only to be thought
of as deriving what they have in common from the intricacies of
human nature as distinguished from what the things of the natural
world have in common, derived from strengths like light and
warmth. They have to be thought of with reference to the meaning of style. Style is not something applied. It is something inherent, something that permeates. It is of the nature of that in which
it is found, whether the poem, the manner of a god, the bearing of
a man. It is not a dress. It may be said to be a voice that is inevitable. A man has no choice about his style. When he says I am my
style the truth reminds him that it is his style that is himself. If he
says, as my poem is, so are my gods and so am I, the truth remains
quiet and broods on what he has said. He knows that the gods
of China are always Chinese; that the gods of Greece are always
Greeks and that all gods are created in the images of their creators;
and he sees in these circumstances the operation of a style, a basic
law. He observes the uniform enhancement of all things within
the category of the imagination. He sees, in the struggle between
the perfectible and the imperfectible, how the perfectible prevails,
even though it falls short of perfection.

   It is no doubt true that the creative faculties operate alike on
poems, gods and men up to a point. They are always the same
faculties. One might even say that the things created are always
the same things. In case of a universal artist, all of his productions
are his peculiar own. When we are dealing with racial units of the
creative faculties all of the productions of one unit resemble one
another. We say of a painting that it is Florentine. But we say the
same thing and with equal certainty of a piece of sculpture. There
is no difficulty in arguing about the poems, gods and men of Egypt

or India that they look alike. But if the gods of India disappeared would not the poems of India and the men of India still remain alike. And if there were no poems, a new race of poets would produce poems that would take the place of the gods that had disappeared. What, then, is the nature of poetry in a time of disbelief? The truistic nature of some of the things that I have said shows how the free-will of the poet is limited. They demonstrate that the poetry of the future can never be anything purely eccentric and dissociated. The poetry of the present cannot be purely eccentric and dissociated. Eccentric and dissociated poetry is poetry that tries to exist or is intended to exist separately from the poem, that is to say in a style that is not identical with the poem. It never achieves anything more than a shallow mannerism, like something seen in a glass. Now, a time of disbelief is precisely a time in which the frequency of detached styles is greatest. I am not quite happy about the word detached. By detached, I mean the unsuccessful, the ineffective, the arbitrary, the literary, the non-umbilical, that which in its highest degree would still be words. For the style of the poem and the poem itself to be one there must be a mating and a marriage, not an arid love-song.

Yes: but the gods—now they come into it and make it a delicious subject, as if we were here together wasting our time on something that appears to be whimsical but turns out to be essential. They give to the subject just that degree of effulgence and excess, no more, no less, that the subject requires. Our first proposition, that the style of a poem and the poem itself are one was a definition of perfection in poetry. In the presence of the gods, or of their images, we are in the presence of perfection in created beings. The gods are a definition of perfection in ideal creatures. These remarks expound the second proposition that the style of the gods and the gods themselves are one. The exhilaration of their existence, their freedom from fate, their access to station, their liberty to command fix them in an atmosphere which thrills us as we share it with them. But these are merely attributes. What matters is their manner, their style, which tells us at once that they are as we wished them to be, that they have fulfilled us, that they are us but purified, magnified, in an expansion. It is their style that makes them gods, not merely privileged beings. It is their style most of all that fulfills themselves. If they lost all their privileges, their freedom from fate, their liberty to command, and yet still retained their style, they would still be gods, however destitute. That alone would destroy them, which deprived them of their style. When the time came for them to go, it was a time when their aesthetic had become invalid in the presence not of a greater aesthetic of the same kind, but of a different aesthetic, of which from the point of view of greatness, the difference was that of an intenser humanity. The style of the gods is derived from men. The style of the gods is derived from the style of men.

One has to pierce through the dithyrambic impressions that talk of the gods makes to the reality of what is being said. What is being said must be true and the truth of it must be seen. But the truth about the poet in a time of disbelief is not that he must turn evangelist. After all, he shares the disbelief of his time. He does not turn to Paris or Rome for relief from the monotony of reality. He turns to himself and he denies that reality was ever monotonous except in comparison. He asserts that the source of comparison having been eliminated, reality is returned, as if a shadow had passed and drawn after it and taken away whatever coating had concealed what lay beneath it. Yet the revelation of reality is not a part peculiar to a time of disbelief or, if it is, it is so in a sense singular to that time. Perhaps, the revelation of reality takes on a special meaning, without effort or consciousness on the part of the poet, at such a time. Why should a poem not change in sense when there is a fluctuation of the whole of appearance? Or why should it not change when we realize that the indifferent experience of life is the unique experience, the item of ecstasy which we have been isolating and reserving for another time and place, loftier and more secluded. There is inherent in the words *the revelation of reality* a suggestion that there is a reality of or within or beneath the surface of reality. There are many such realities through which poets constantly pass to and fro, without noticing the imaginary lines that divide one from the other. We were face to face with such a transition at the outset, for Baudelaire's line

A long time I passed beneath an entrance roof

opens like a voice heard in a theatre and a theatre is a reality within a reality. The most provocative of all realities is that reality of which we never lose sight but never see solely as it is. The revela-

tion of that particular reality or of that particular category of realities is like a series of paintings of some natural object affected, as
the appearance of any natural object is affected, by the passage of
time, and the changes that ensue, not least in the painter. That the
revelation of reality has a character or quality peculiar to this time
or that or, what is intended to be the same thing, that it is affected
by states of mind, is elementary. The line from Baudelaire will not
have the same effect on everyone at all times, any more than it will
continue to have the same effect on the same person constantly.
I remember that when a friend of mine in Ireland quoted the line,
a few years ago, in a letter, my feeling about it was that it was a
good instance of the value of knowing people of different educa-
tions. The chances are that my friend in Dublin and I have done
much the same reading. The chances are, also, that we have retained many different things. For instance, this man had chosen
Giorgione as the painter that meant most to him. For my own part,
Giorgione would not have occurred to me. I should like you to be
sure that in speaking of the revelation of reality I am not attempting to forecast the poetry of the future. It would be logical to conclude that, since a time of disbelief is also a time of truth-loving
and since I have emphasized that I recognize that what I am trying
to say is nothing unless it is true and that the truth of it must be
seen, I think that the main characteristic of the poetry of the future
or the near future will be an absence of the poetic. I do not think
that. I cannot see what value it would have if I did, except as a
value to me personally. If there is a logic that controls poetry,
which everything that I have been saying may illustrate, it is not
the narrow logic that exists on the level of prophecy. That there is
a larger logic I have no doubt. But certainly it has to be large
enough to allow for a good many irrelevancies.

One of the irrelevancies is the romantic. It looks like something
completely contemptible in the light of literary intellectualism and
cynicism. The romantic, however, has a way of renewing itself.
It can be said of the romantic, just as it can be said of the imagination, that it can never effectively touch the same thing twice in
the same way. It is partly because the romantic will not be what
has been romantic in the past that it is preposterous to think of
confining poetry hereafter to the revelation of reality. The whole
effort of the imagination is toward the production of the romantic.

When, therefore, the romantic is in abeyance, when it is discred-
ited, it remains true that there is always an unknown romantic and
that the imagination will not be forever denied. There is something
a little romantic about the idea that the style of a poem and the
poem itself are one. It seems to be a much more broadly romantic
thing to say that the style of the gods and the gods themselves are
one. It is completely romantic to say that the style of men and men
themselves are one. To collect and collate these ideas of disparate
things may seem to pass beyond the romantic to the fantastic. I
hope, however, that you will agree that if each one of these ideas is
valid separately, or more or less valid, it is permissible to have
brought them together as a collective source of suppositions. What
is romantic in all of them is the idea of style which I have not defined in any sense uniformly common to all three. A poem is a
restricted creation of the imagination. The gods are the creation of
the imagination at its utmost. Men are a part of reality. The grada-
tions of romance noticeable as the sense of style is used with reference to these three, one by one, are relevant to the difficulties of
the imagination in a truth-loving time. These difficulties exist only
as one foresees them. They may never exist at all. An age in which
the imagination might be expected to become part of time's *re-
jectamenta* may behold it established and protected and enthroned
on one of the few ever-surviving thrones; and, to our surprise, we
may find posted in the portico of its eternal dwelling, on the chief
portal, among the morning's ordinances, three regulations which if
they were once rules of art will then have become rules of conduct.
By that time the one that will matter most is likely to be the last,
that the style of man is man himself, which is about what we have
been saying.

It comes to this that we use the same faculties when we write
poetry that we use when we create gods or when we fix the bearing of men in reality. That this is obvious does not make the statement less. On the contrary, it makes the statement more, because
its obviousness is that of the truth. The three ideas are sources of
perfection. They are of such a nature that they are instances of
aesthetic ideas tantamount to moral ideas, a subject precious in itself but beyond our scope today. For today, they mean that however one time may differ from another, there are always available
to us the faculties of the past, but always vitally new and strong,

as the sources of perfection today and tomorrow. The unity of style and the poem itself is a unity of language and life that exposes both in a supreme sense. Its collation with the unity of style and the gods and the unity of style and men is intended to demonstrate this.

Poetry and Man

Discussion of the function of poetry concludes with a parable. Rainer Maria Rilke found the source of poetry to be the store of remembered experiences which constitute the poet's self, the unique human identity which his song expresses. In "Concerning the Poet" he places that song in the context of mankind and, in a single sweeping figure, proposes a complex relation between art and life, between the poet and other men. Although a curious remoteness seems to dissociate the practical from the aesthetic, they subtly interact. To some extent, Rilke seems to say, the practical efforts of man inspire the poet's song. But practical effort falls short of its aim. What man cannot achieve by effort he is allowed to enjoy in song, the beautiful song which inspires him by reaffirming the attractiveness of the ideal toward which his efforts reach.

RAINER MARIA RILKE

Concerning the Poet

The position of the Poet in the existing world, his "meaning," was once shown to me in a fine similitude. It was on board the large sailing vessel in which we crossed from the island of Philæ to the wide stretching dams. We went up stream at first and the oarsmen had to exert themselves. I had them all facing me, sixteen of them, if I remember rightly, four in each row, two on the right oar and two on the left. Occasionally one caught the eye of one or other, but mostly their eyes saw nothing, their open gaze going out into the air, or their eyes were simply points where the hot vitality of these men lay bare, set in their metallic bodies. But sometimes, looking up quickly, one could catch one of them deep in thought, meditating on the strange disguised phenomenon facing him and on possible situations which might disclose its nature; when noticed, he immediately lost his strenuously thoughtful expression, for a moment all his feelings were in confusion, then, as quickly as he could, he reverted to the watchful gaze of an animal, until the beautiful serious expression became again the usual silly *backshish* face, with its foolish readiness to assume any required humiliating distortion of thanks. This degradation, for which travellers have long been to blame, is generally accompanied by its own penalty, in that the native seldom fails to gaze over and beyond the stranger with a look of deep hatred, lit by a gleam of understanding with the man on the far side of him. I had observed the old man, who was sitting there crouched at the end of the boat, repeatedly. His hands and feet had come into the closest association, and the pole of the rudder moved between them, guided and checked by them. His body, clad in dirty rags, was not worth mentioning, his face, beneath its disreputable turban cloth, was folded in on itself like the parts of a telescope, is extreme flatness seeming to make the eyes ooze moisture. God knows what was in the man, he looked capable of turning one into something repulsive; I should have liked to scrutinize his face, but when I turned round he was as close to me as my own ear, and to attempt to examine him at such short distance seemed too obvious a proceeding. Moreover, the spectacle of the broad river flowing towards us, the beautiful region lying constantly before us, as it were, whilst we penetrated into it, was so worthy of undivided attention and so satisfying in its effect that I ceased to occupy myself with the old man, and instead came to observe with increasing delight the movements of the boys, which, for all their vigor and effort, lost nothing of their ordered rhythm. Their rowing was now so strenuous that those at the end of the great oars rose completely from their seats each time they reached forward and, placing one leg against the seat in front of them, threw themselves back violently, the eight oar blades driving forward in the current below. At the same time they gave voice to a kind of counting in order to keep in time, but so exacting was their work that their voices frequently failed them; often they had simply to suffer such a gap, but at times an unpredictable intervention, felt by all of us in a most peculiar manner, not only helped them rhythmically, but quite perceptibly transformed the powers within them, as it were, so that, being eased, they brought fresh, still untouched sources of strength into play: just as a child, after whetting its appetite in the eating of an apple, will begin to eat afresh, radiant with enjoyment, when it discovers that the side it has been holding is still intact even to the skin.

Now I cannot postpone any longer mention of the man sitting at the front on the right-hand side of the boat. I ended by believing that I could feel in advance when his song was about to begin, but I may have been mistaken. He sang suddenly, at quite irregular intervals, and by no means always when exhaustion increased; on the contrary, his song occurred more than once when all of the rowers were vigorous or even exuberant, but even then it was the right thing; even then it was appropriate. I do not know to what extent the mood of our crew communicated itself to him; they were all behind him, he rarely looked backwards, and was not affected when he did so. What did seem to influence him was the pure movement of his feeling when it met the open distance, in which he was absorbed in a manner half melancholy, half resolute. In him the forward thrust of our vessel and the force opposed to us were continually held in counterpoise—from time to time a surplus accumulated: then he sang. The boat overcame the opposition; but what could not be overcome (was not susceptible of being over-come) he, the magician, transmuted into a series of long floating sounds, detached in space, which each appropriated to himself. While those about him were always occupied with the most im-mediate actuality and the overcoming of it, his voice maintained contact with the farthest distance, linking us with it until we felt its power of attraction.

I do not know how it happened, but suddenly, in this phenome-non, I understood the position of the poet, his place and effect within time, and that one might well dispute his right to every other position but this. This one, though, must be allowed to him.

Translated by G. Craig Houston